JavaScript Application Cookbook

JavaScript Application Cookbook

Jerry Bradenbaugh

O'REILLY®

Beijing · Cambridge · Farnham · Köln · Paris · Sebastopol · Taipei · Tokyo

JavaScript Application Cookbook
by Jerry Bradenbaugh

Copyright © 1999 O'Reilly & Associates, Inc. All rights reserved.
Printed in the United States of America.

Published by O'Reilly & Associates, Inc., 101 Morris Street, Sebastopol, CA 95472.

Editor: Richard Koman

Production Editor: Nicole Arigo

Printing History:

October 1999:   First Edition.

ISBN: 1-56592-577-7
[M]

[4/00]

Table of Contents

Editor's Note

Welcome to *JavaScript Application Cookbook*, the second book in O'Reilly's Cookbook line. This book is different enough from the *Perl Cookbook*, our first offering, that it seems worth explaining. In his foreword to the *Perl Cookbook*, Larry Wall writes that the essence of the book is "not to cook for you (it can't) or even to teach you how to cook (though it helps), but rather to pass on various bits of culture that have been found useful ..."

Perl Cookbook is a compendium of cooking techniques. "Finding the Nth Occurrence of a Match" is roughly equivalent to "How to Brown Butter." "Sorting a Hash" can be thought of as "Peeling Roasted Red Peppers."

JavaScript Application Cookbook, on the other hand, is a pure recipe book. Think of "Shopping Bag: The JavaScript Shopping Cart" as "Mini Scallion Biscuits with Smoked Salmon Spread." Each chapter provides the code and documentation for a useful web application written (mostly) entirely in JavaScript. Prepare each recipe as Jerry has written it or just take key concepts and fold them into your own creations. (Nick Heinle's *Designing with JavaScript* contains smaller recipes that you can drop into a single web page, whereas this book shows you how to write full client-side web applications in JavaScript, the only scripting language that browsers natively understand.)

Given these two different approaches, what's our definition of a Cookbook? A Cookbook isn't content plugged into an inflexible format; it's a book that helps you "cook up code." Expect to see more Cookbooks doing that in a variety of ways.

—Richard Koman, Editor

Preface

Something was missing. Here I was, poring through stacks of JavaScript books and screen after screen of web sites, soaking in as much code and as many concepts as possible. But after picking up some new syntax or a slick technique from the guru de jour, I didn't know what to do with it outside the scope of the example. It was as if I had a kitchen full of ingredients, but no recipes. I had all these cool Java-Script techniques and code snippets, but I wasn't sure how to apply them to solve common web site problems. Sure, some of those books had JavaScript applications, but they weren't relevant to the Web. I mean, a blackjack game is great. So is a spreadsheet app, but I'm not going to put those on a web site any time soon.

So here are some recipes. Not just for checking a browser's identity or doing an image rollover, but full-blown applications that you'll actually want to use on your web site. The applications here are pretty much out of the box. You can copy them into a folder on your web server (or local computer) and run them immediately. The chapters that follow are packed with JavaScript that helps you help users perform common web tasks, such as site searching, collecting survey info, creating image rollovers, viewing online presentations, cyber shopping, and plenty more. Of course, you'll want to modify them to make them work best for you, but they're more or less ready to go. In addition, each application comes with a lengthy explanation so that you can check out what makes each one work.

What You Should Know

This is not a beginner's book. You will not learn JavaScript here. You will learn how to use it. You don't have to be a three-year JavaScript veteran, but if `info.replace(/</g, "&lt;")`, `new Image()`, and `var itemArray = []` seem obscure, make sure you at least have a JavaScript syntax book handy as you work. Try O'Reilly's *JavaScript: The Definitive Guide,* by David Flanagan.

Font Conventions

Italic

>   is used for filenames, directory paths, URLs, and the names of objects, variables, arrays, and other entities.

`Constant Width`

>   is used for HTML tags, code examples, code fragments, functions, and other references to code.

`Constant Width Italic`

>   is used for text that the user enters and for replaceable text.

`Constant Width Bold`

>   is used for text that is displayed on the screen.

Book Structure

For the most part, each chapter follows a similar template with the following four sections.

Execution Requirements

This short section lays out the environment required to run the application. This usually means which versions of Netscape Navigator or Microsoft Internet Explorer are compatible. The section also offers some perspective by discussing any scalability or monitor resolution issues.

Syntax Breakdown

When you're done playing with an application and want to see what's "under the hood," check here. This is where you'll find the code discussion, mostly line-by-line. This is by far the longest section of the chapter, so get comfortable before you tackle these.

JavaScript Techniques

As we make our way through the syntax breakdown, there will be good points to stop and highlight a technique that you can add to your bag of web knowledge.

Potential Extensions

This section suggests ways you can extend each application for even more impressive functionality. Sometimes I make suggestions, sometimes I offer code. And sometimes I just can't help myself and write the code for you—which is included in a code archive that you can download. Either way, this should get the creative juices flowing so you don't get stuck, saying, "Cool, how can I put that on my site?"

About the Code

This book is all about applications. It's no surprise, then, that you are going to see JavaScript code—lots of it. Some applications contain several hundred lines, and most of them are on the pages following the code. In some cases, the code is even repeated so you don't have to always flip back and forth between the discussion and the code.

One of the drawbacks of putting the code in the book, is, well, putting it in the book. There just isn't as much page width to fit all the code as we'd like on one line. The code often wraps onto the next line, and the next. To keep the readability higher, the comments have also been left out, though you'll find plenty of comments in the files themselves. The editing staff has gone to great pains to neatly format the code within the page constraints, but in some cases you might find looking at the files in your text editor easier on your eyes.

Since we expect you to use this code, not just read it, we've made all of the applications available in a zip file that you can download from the O'Reilly web site. Go to *http://www.oreilly.com/catalog/jscook/index.html* and look for the "Download" link. You'll see references to this file in each chapter.

Development and Testing

In no particular order, I've listed the hardware and software used in developing the code for this book. For the most part, everything has been tested for a Windows environment, but Unix and Mac users should encounter few, if any, problems.

Hardware: IBM ThinkPad 55/P75/16M, Compaq Presario/P233/100M, IBM Aptiva C23/P120/128M, DELL OptiPlex/P2-266/128M, Sun SPARC 20

Operating Systems: Win95, WinNT Workstation 4.0, WinNT Server 4.0, Solaris 2.5

Browsers: Netscape Navigator 3.0, 3.04 Gold, 4.0, 4.04, 4.07, 4.08, 4.5; Microsoft Internet Explorer 3.0, 3.02, 4.0, 4.01, 5.00

Resolutions: 640 x 480, 800 x 600, 1024 x 768, 1152 x 900, 1280 x 1024

Of course, not every application was tested under all these conditions. However, I tried to code defensively enough so that the vast majority of user environments would be accommodated.

We'd Like to Hear From You

We have tested and verified all of the information in this book to the best of our ability, but you may find that features have changed (or even that we have made mistakes!). Please let us know about any errors you find, as well as your suggestions for future editions, by writing:

> O'Reilly & Associates, Inc.
> 101 Morris Street
> Sebastopol, CA 95472
> 800-998-9938 (in the United States or Canada)
> 707-829-0515 (international/local)
> 707-829-0104 (fax)

You can also send us messages electronically. To be put on the mailing list or request a catalog, send email to:

> *info@oreilly.com*

To ask technical questions or comment on the book, send email to:

> *bookquestions@oreilly.com*

Acknowledgments

My name is on the cover, but it gives me great pride to credit others in the creation of this book. I'd like to extend heartfelt gratitude to these folks for making this possible.

On the technical side, I'd like to thank Steve Quint and James Chan, Jim Esten, Bill Anderson, Roland Chow, Rodney Myers, Matthew Mastracci, Giorgio Braga, Brock Beauchamp and the others who have let me tap into their massive wealth of JavaScript and other programming experience whenever I got into a bind. And I must pay homage to Patrick Clark, whose code was the inspiration for the online help application. Thanks to Richard Koman, my editor, for keeping an open ear to my ideas and enabling me to put them on paper, and to Tara McGoldrick and Rob Romano for all their behind-the-scenes labors.

On the emotional side, I'd like to sincerely thank my wife, Róndine Bradenbaugh, for putting up with me staring at a PC monitor and typing feverishly, night after night, for months. I'd like to thank my parents for their support and for encouraging me to develop my writing skills.

I'd also like to thank someone else who often gets overlooked—*you*, the reader. It's you who leave your hard-earned cash at the bookstore that makes all of this possible. There are plenty of JavaScript books available. You chose mine. Thanks, big time, for giving me the opportunity to give you your money's worth.

Introduction

This is an unusual book. It's about writing large web applications in JavaScript. That's not what most people think JavaScript is used for. JavaScript is normally (or at least used to be) associated with just adding image rollovers, visitor hit counters, browser detection, and the like.

JavaScript Pros

No one language or technology has the market cornered as the best solution for developing web applications. Each has its pros and cons. Recent advances in JavaScript and other proliferating technologies, such as DHTML, Java, and even Macromedia's Flash, have positioned JavaScript to capitalize on these tools and create relatively powerful web solutions. Here are some other reasons that argue strongly for developing applications in JavaScript.

Easy to Learn, Quick, and Powerful

Since JavaScript is fairly easy to learn, you can begin using it right away. This is perfect for adding some quick functionality to a site. Once you have the basics down, creating full-featured applications isn't much further away.

JavaScript also rates as pretty powerful for a high-level language. You can't do anything at the machine level with it, but it does expose many features of browsers, web pages, and sometimes the system on which the browser is running. JavaScript doesn't have to be compiled like Java™ or C, and the browser doesn't need to load a virtual machine to run the code. Just code it and load it.

JavaScript also works from an object-oriented architecture similar to Java and C++. Features such as constructor functions and prototype-based inheritance add a layer of abstraction to the development schema. This promotes much greater code reusability.

Ubiquity

JavaScript is by far the most popular scripting language on the Web. Not thousands, but millions of web pages around the world contain JavaScript. JavaScript is supported by the most popular web browsers (though we're really talking about JScript in MSIE). Both Netscape and Microsoft seem to be continuously seeking ways to extend the language's functionality. This kind of support means that JavaScript stands a better chance of being supported by the vast majority of browsers used by your web site visitors.

Reducing the Server Load

This was one of the first reasons that web developers adopted JavaScript. It can perform many functions on the client side that used to be handled strictly on the server. One of the best examples of this is form validation. Old-school coders might remember back just a few years when the only way to validate user input of an HTML form was to submit the user information to the web server, then toss that data to a CGI script to make sure the user entered everything correctly.

If the data had no errors, the CGI script processed as normal. If errors were encountered, the script returned a message to the user indicating the problem. While this is one solution, consider the overhead involved. Submitting the form requires another HTTP request from the server. That trip across the Net is also followed by executing the CGI script again. Each time the user makes a mistake in the form, this process repeats. The user has to wait until the error message arrives to learn of the mistake.

Enter JavaScript. Now you can validate the elements of a form *before* the user sends it back to the web server. This reduces the amount of transactions via HTTP and significantly reduces the chance of user error with the form input. JavaScript can also read and write cookies, an operation once performed exclusively by the header-setting power of the web server.

JavaScript Is Growing

When JavaScript 1.1 came out, there was mass hysteria because of the new things called the *Image* object and the *document.images* array that let us create image rollovers. Then JavaScript 1.2 hit the scene. The floodgates were wide open. DHTML support, layers, and a slew of other enhancements bowled over many coders. It was too good to be true.

It hasn't stopped there. JavaScript has since become the design model for EMCA-262, a standardized general-purpose scripting language. At least one company has developed an environment that runs JavaScript from the command line. Macromedia has incorporated custom JavaScript calls in its Flash technology. Allaire's Cold-Fusion has integrated JavaScript into its XML-based technology, Web Distributed Data Exchange (WDDX). JavaScript is getting better and better. More features. More options. More hooks.

Maybe You Have No Choice

Sometimes it's the only way. Suppose your ISP doesn't allow CGI scripts to be executed. Now what are you going to do if you want to add that forms-based email or take advantage of cookie technology? You have to look to client-side solutions. JavaScript is arguably the best one for adding server-side functionality to a "client-side only" web site.

There Are Probably More

I can think of a few more advantages, and you could surely add to the list. The point is: in spite of the advantages of server-side technology, JavaScript applications have their place on the Net.

Basic JavaScript Programming Strategy

Whenever you build an application, JavaScript or not, it is in your best interest to have a strategy. This helps organize your thoughts and code and also speeds the development and debugging process. There are scores of worthy publications that get down to the nitty-gritty of step-by-step application design, and you'll probably want to adopt a strategy that works best for you. So I won't spend too much time here. Keeping the following things in mind, however, before, during, and after you code your way between the `<SCRIPT></SCRIPT>` tags will surely save you some headaches. It's pretty simple: just answer what?, who?, and how?

What Are the Application Features?

First, what is the application going to do? Be as specific as possible. What will the application not offer? Suppose you want to develop an HTML form to send email. Consider these questions.

- How many fields will the form include?
- Will users enter the email address themselves or choose it from a select list?

- Do you want to validate the form input before sending it? If so, what are you going to validate? The message? The email address? Both?

- What happens after the email is sent? Do you want to redirect the user to another page or have nothing happen at all?

This barrage of questions could certainly continue. The good news is that if you take the time to consider such questions, you will have a much better idea of what you want.

Who Is Your Audience?

Identifying who will be using the information is vital for determining the app's capabilities. Make sure you have precise answers to at least the following questions:

- What browsers will people be using? Netscape Navigator? What versions: 2.x, 3.x, 4.x, or higher?

- Is the application going to be used on the Internet, intranet, or locally on individual computers?

- Can you determine the monitor resolution that most users will have?

- What type of connectivity will most users have? 56K modem? ISDN? Fractional T-1? T-3?

Other than the question about browser type, you might think that these questions have nothing to do with JavaScript. "Connectivity . . . who cares? I don't need to configure a router to do this stuff." That's true. You don't need to be Cisco-certified. Let's run through those questions, one by one, though, and see why they are important to you.

The browser issue is arguably the most pressing. In general, the more recent the browser, the more recent the version of JavaScript you can use. For example, if your audience is confined to NN 2.x and MSIE 3.x (though I can't think why this would be the case), you can automatically rule out image rollovers. The versions of JavaScript and JScript in both browsers don't support the *Image* or *document. images* objects.*

Since most people have upgraded to at least the 4.x version of these browsers, image rollovers are acceptable. But now you have to reckon with dueling object models. That means you have to make your applications cross-browser compatible or write separate applications for each version (which can be a lesson in futility).

Where will the application reside? The Internet, an intranet, or maybe on someone's PC converted into a kiosk? The answer to this question will in turn provide

---

* Some MSIE 3.x browsers for the Mac do support image rollovers.

many more clues to what you can get away with. For example, if the application will run on the Internet, you can rest assured that just about any type of browser imaginable will hit your site and use (or at least try to use) the app. If the application is restricted to an intranet or a local machine, chances are some kind of browser standard is in place. At the time of this writing, I'm doing consulting work for a firm that is one big Microsoft shop. If my intranet code chokes in Navigator, I don't care; users must have MSIE.

Monitor resolution is another major issue. If you've included a table 900 pixels wide on your page, and users only have an 800 × 600 resolution, they're going to miss out on some of your hard work. Can you count on a fixed resolution for all visitors? If this is for the Internet, your answer is no. If the audience is on an intranet, you might be in luck. Some corporations standardize PC hardware, software, browsers, monitors, and even resolutions.

Connectivity issues also have an effect. Suppose you've whipped up a mind-blowing image rollover sequence that would give Steven Spielberg's movie animations a run for their money (if so, maybe you and I should . . . umm . . . *collaborate*). Pretty cool, but users with 56K modems could probably go out and see a movie before your code loads all those images. Most users understand that the Net can get bogged down with heavy traffic, but after a minute or so, most will move on to other sites. Take the bandwidth issue into consideration.

How Can You Get Around the Obstacles?

Juggling all of these issues may sound pretty cut and dried, but it's actually not that simple. You might have no way to accommodate all browser versions, monitor resolutions, or connectivity specs. Now what? How do you keep everybody happy and still wow them with your 500K image rollover extravaganza?

Consider one or more of the approaches I've proposed below. Read them all so you can make a better-informed decision.

Try the cross-browser approach

This egalitarian method of "the greatest good for the greatest number" cross-browser coding is probably the most common and arguably the best approach. By the greatest good for the greatest number, I mean that most users probably have MSIE 4.x and NN 4.x. You can scoop up a large web-surfing population if you implement significant browser detection and code your application so that it capitalizes on the common features of the 4.x generation while it accommodates their differences.

Elegantly degrade or change performance

This makes a nice corollary to the cross-browser strategy. For example, if your image rollover script is loaded into an unsupporting browser such as MSIE 3.x, you're bound to get nasty JavaScript errors. Use browser detection to disable the rollovers for these browsers. By the same token, you might want to load different pages according to monitor resolution.

Aim low

This approach assumes that everyone has NN 2.0 browsers, 640 × 480 screen resolutions, 14.4K modems, and a Pentium 33 MHz. The bad new is that you won't be able to use anything but JavaScript 1.0. No rollovers, no layers, no regular expressions, and no external technologies (be thankful you can use frames). The good news is: the masses will be able to use your application. Actually, recent changes in JavaScript may make even that untrue. I'm admittedly aiming really low, but it's not uncommon to shoot for, say, NN 3.x and MSIE 3.x. Obsolescence has its advantages.

Aim high

If your users don't have MSIE 5.0, assume they're technological nitwits and not worthy of seeing your application, let alone using it. Now you can code away, accessing the MSIE document object model, event model, data binding, and so on. Of course, that sharply drops the size of your viewing audience and can have long-term effects on your ego.

Offer multiple versions of the same app

If you're a glutton for punishment, you can write multiple versions of the application, say for example, one for NN, the other for MSIE. This method is definitely for those into monotony, but there is at least one twist that can pay off. Let's go back to the connectivity issue. Since it's often impossible to determine what type of bandwidth users have, allow them to choose. A couple of links from the homepage will enable users with T-1 connections to load your image rollover spectacular, or users with modems to view the benign version.

JavaScript Approaches in These Applications

Those are the basics. You'll see that I incorporated a couple of these strategies in the applications in this book. I should also mention the JavaScript approaches, or coding conventions. That'll give you a better idea of where I'm coming from, and whether the approaches will work for you.

The first thing I did when considering an application was to decide whether your (and my) web site visitors might have any use for it. Each application solves one or more basic problems. Searching, emailing, online help, setting personal preferences, testing or gathering information, creating image rollovers, and so on are fairly common features that web surfers like. If a potential application didn't pass the justification test, I didn't spend any time on it.

The next thing I did was to decide whether JavaScript could pull off the functionality I wanted. This was pretty easy. If the answer was yes, then I went for it. If not, it was into the JavaScript landfill.

Once I singled out an application, it was off to the text editor. Here are some of the conventions I used for the codes.

Reuse as Much Code as Possible

This is where JavaScript source files come into play. That is, these applications make use of the JavaScript source files loaded in using the following syntax:

```
<SCRIPT LANGUAGE="JavaScript1.1" SRC="someJSFile.js"></SCRIPT>
```

someJSFile.js contains code that can be used by multiple scripts—any one that uses the above syntax. Many of the applications throughout the book use JavaScript source files. This just makes sense. Why reinvent the wheel? You can also use JavaScript source files to hide code from the rest of the application. You might find it useful to keep a very large JavaScript array in a source file. Using JavaScript source files are definitely worthwhile, so Chapter 6, *Implementing JavaScript Source Files*, is devoted to it.

Some of the applications contain code that is simply cut and pasted from one place to another. This code could easily qualify as a candidate for a source file. I did it this way so you don't have to spend so much time reading: *"See the code in the library file three chapters back . . ."* This way, the code stays in front of you until you understand it, and cuts down on the page flipping. After you get the apps comfortably running on your site, consider creating a JavaScript source file.

Isolate the JavaScript

Keep as much within a single set of <SCRIPT></SCRIPT> tags as possible between the <HEAD></HEAD> tags.

Declare Global Variables and Arrays near the Top

Even if they are originally set to an empty string or undefined, declaring global variables and arrays at the top of the script is a good way to manage your variables, especially when they are used throughout the script. That way, you don't have to sift through a bunch of code to change a variable value. You know it'll be somewhere near the top.

Declare Constructor Functions
After the Global Variables

I generally include functions that create user-defined objects at the top. This is simply because most of my objects are created early in the life of the script.

Define Functions from Top to Bottom
in "Chronological" Order

In other words, I try to define functions according to the order in which they will be called in the application. The first function defined in the script is called first, second is called second, and so forth. At times, this can be difficult or even impossible to enforce. This approach, however, at least improves the organization and the chances that adjacent functions will be called in succession.

Each Function Performs a Single Operation

I try to limit each function to performing one distinct operation, such as validating user input, setting or getting cookie info, automating a slideshow, showing or hiding layers, etc. That's a great theory, but it can be tough to apply in every case. In fact, I make several flagrant violations in Chapter 5, *ImageMachine*. The functions perform one basic operation, but wind up dozens of lines in length.

Use as Many Local Variables as Possible

I do this to conserve memory. Since local JavaScript variables die after a function finishes executing, the memory they occupy is returned to the system. If a variable doesn't need to last for the life of the application, I make it local instead of global.

Moving On

This should give you a general picture of how to go about building your JavaScript applications, and how I built mine. Now let's get to the fun stuff.

1

The Client-Side Search Engine

Every site could use a search engine, but why force your server to deal with all those queries? The Client-Side Search Engine allows users to search through your pages completely on the client side. Rather than sending queries to a database or application server, each user downloads the "database" within the requested web pages. This makeshift database is simply a JavaScript array. Each record is kept in one element of the array.

This approach has some significant benefits, chiefly reducing the server's workload and improving response time. As good as that sounds, keep in mind that this application is restricted by the limitations of the user's resources, especially processor speed and available memory. Nonetheless, it can be a great utility for your web site. You can find the code for this application in the *ch01* folder of the zip file. Figure 1-1 shows the opening interface.

This application comes equipped with two Boolean search methods: AND and OR. You can search by document title and description, or by document URL. User functionality is pretty straightforward. It's as easy as entering the terms you want to match, then pressing Enter. Here's the search option breakdown:

- Entering terms separated by spaces returns all records containing *any* of the terms you included (Boolean OR).

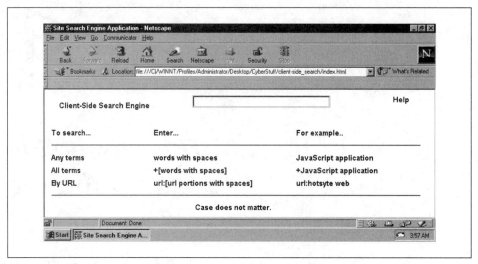

Figure 1-1. The opening interface

- Placing a plus sign (+) before your string of query term(s) matches only those records containing *all* of the terms you enter (Boolean AND).

- Entering `url:` before a full or partial URL returns those records that match any of the terms in the URL you enter.

 Don't forget your zip file! As noted in the preface, all the code used in this book is available in a zip file on the O'Reilly site. To grab the zip, go to *http://www.oreilly.com/catalog/jscook/index.html*.

Figure 1-2 shows the results page of a simple search. Notice this particular query uses the default (no prefixes) search method and *javascript* as the search term. Each search generates on the fly a results page that displays the fruits of the most recent search, followed by a link back to the help page for quick reference.

It's also nice to be able to search by URL. Figure 1-3 shows a site search using the *url:* prefix to instruct the engine to search URLs only. In this case the string *html* is passed, so the engine returns all documents with *html* in the URL. The document description is still displayed, but the URL comes first. The URL search method is restricted to single-match qualification, just like the default method. That shouldn't be a problem, though. Not many people will be eager to perform complex search algorithms on your URLs.

This application can limit the number of results displayed per page and create buttons to view successive or previous pages so that users aren't buried with mile-long displays of record matches. The number displayed per page is completely up to you, though the default is 10.

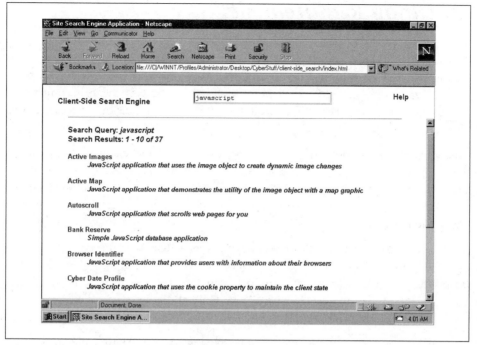

Figure 1-2. A typical search results page

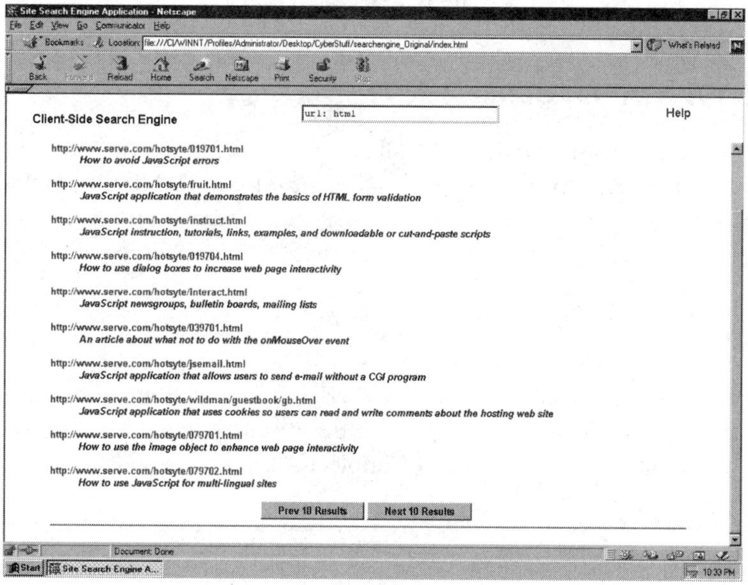

Figure 1-3. Results page based on searching record URLs

Execution Requirements

The version of the application discussed here requires a browser that supports JavaScript 1.1. That's good news for people using Netscape Navigator 3 and 4 and Microsoft Internet Explorer 4 and 5, and bad news for IE 3 users. If you're intent on backwards compatibility, don't fret. I'll show you how you can accommodate IE 3 users (at the price of functionality) in the "Potential Extensions" section of this chapter.

All client-side applications depend on the resources of the client machine, a fact that's especially true here. It's a safe bet the client will have the resources to run the code, but if you pass the client a huge database (more than about 6,000 or 7,000 records), your performance will begin to degrade, and you'll eventually choke the machine.

I had no problem using a database of slightly fewer than 10,000 records in MSIE 4 and Navigator 4. Incidentally, the JavaScript source file holding the records was larger than 1 MB. I had anywhere between 24 and 128 MB of RAM on the machine. I tried the same setup with NN 3.0 Gold and got a stack overflow error— just too many records in the array.

On the low end, the JavaScript 1.0 version viewed with MSIE 3.02 on an IBM ThinkPad didn't allow more than 215 records. Don't let that low number scare you. The laptop was so outdated you could hear the rat on the exercise wheel powering the CPU. Most users will likely have a better capacity.

The Syntax Breakdown

This application consists of three HTML files (*index.html*, *nav.html*, and *main. html*) and a JavaScript source file (*records.js*). The three HTML files include a tiny frameset, a header page where you enter the search terms, and a default page in the display frame with the "how-to" instructions.

nav.html

The brains of the application lie in the header file named *nav.html*. In fact, the only other place you'll see JavaScript is in the results pages manufactured on the fly. Let's have a glimpse at the code. Example 1-1 leads the way.

Example 1-1. Source Code for nav.html

```
1 <HTML>
2 <HEAD>
3 <TITLE>Search Nav Page</TITLE>
4
```

Example 1-1. Source Code for nav.html (continued)

```
 5 <SCRIPT LANGUAGE="JavaScript1.1" SRC="records.js"></SCRIPT>
 6 <SCRIPT LANGUAGE="JavaScript1.1">
 7 <!--
 8
 9 var SEARCHANY  = 1;
10 var SEARCHALL  = 2;
11 var SEARCHURL  = 4;
12 var searchType = "";
13 var showMatches    = 10;
14 var currentMatch  = 0;
15 var copyArray     = new Array();
16 var docObj  = parent.frames[1].document;
17
18 function validate(entry) {
19   if (entry.charAt(0) == "+") {
20     entry = entry.substring(1,entry.length);
21     searchType = SEARCHALL;
22   }
23   else if (entry.substring(0,4) == "url:") {
24     entry = entry.substring(5,entry.length);
25     searchType = SEARCHURL;
26   }
27   else { searchType = SEARCHANY; }
28   while (entry.charAt(0) == " ") {
29     entry = entry.substring(1,entry.length);
30     document.forms[0].query.value = entry;
31   }
32   while (entry.charAt(entry.length - 1) == " ") {
33     entry = entry.substring(0,entry.length - 1);
34     document.forms[0].query.value = entry;
35   }
36   if (entry.length < 3) {
37     alert("You cannot search strings that small. Elaborate a little.");
38     document.forms[0].query.focus();
39     return;
40   }
41   convertString(entry);
42 }
43
44 function convertString(reentry) {
45   var searchArray = reentry.split(" ");
46   if (searchType == (SEARCHALL)) { requireAll(searchArray); }
47   else { allowAny(searchArray); }
48 }
49
50 function allowAny(t) {
51   var findings = new Array(0);
52   for (i = 0; i < profiles.length; i++) {
53     var compareElement  = profiles[i].toUpperCase();
54     if(searchType == SEARCHANY) {
55       var refineElement = compareElement.substring(0,
56         compareElement.indexOf('|HTTP'));
```

Example 1-1. Source Code for nav.html (continued)

```
57        }
58      else {
59        var refineElement =
60          compareElement.substring(compareElement.indexOf('|HTTP'),
61          compareElement.length);
62      }
63      for (j = 0; j < t.length; j++) {
64        .var compareString = t[j].toUpperCase();
65        if (refineElement.indexOf(compareString) != -1) {
66          findings[findings.length] = profiles[i];
67          break;
68          }
69        }
70      }
71    verifyManage(findings);
72    }
73
74  function requireAll(t) {
75    var findings = new Array();
76    for (i = 0; i < profiles.length; i++) {
77      var allConfirmation = true;
78      var allString      = profiles[i].toUpperCase();
79      var refineAllString = allString.substring(0,
80        allString.indexOf('|HTTP'));
81      for (j = 0; j < t.length; j++) {
82        var allElement = t[j].toUpperCase();
83        if (refineAllString.indexOf(allElement) == -1) {
84          allConfirmation = false;
85          continue;
86          }
87        }
88      if (allConfirmation) {
89        findings[findings.length] = profiles[i];
90        }
91      }
92    verifyManage(findings);
93    }
94
95  function verifyManage(resultSet) {
96    if (resultSet.length == 0) { noMatch(); }
97    else {
98      copyArray = resultSet.sort();
99      formatResults(copyArray, currentMatch, showMatches);
100       }
101   }
102
103 function noMatch() {
104   docObj.open();
105   docObj.writeln('<HTML><HEAD><TITLE>Search Results</TITLE></HEAD>' +
106     '<BODY BGCOLOR=WHITE TEXT=BLACK>' +
107     '<TABLE WIDTH=90% BORDER=0 ALIGN=CENTER><TR><TD VALIGN=TOP>' +
108 '<FONT FACE=Arial><B><DL>' +
```

Example 1-1. Source Code for nav.html (continued)

```
109     '<HR NOSHADE WIDTH=100%>"' + document.forms[0].query.value +
110     '" returned no results.<HR NOSHADE WIDTH=100%>' +
111     '</TD></TR></TABLE></BODY></HTML>');
112   docObj.close();
113   document.forms[0].query.select();
114   }
115
116 function formatResults(results, reference, offset) {
117   var currentRecord = (results.length < reference + offset ?
118     results.length : reference + offset);
119   docObj.open();
120   docObj.writeln('<HTML><HEAD><TITLE>Search Results</TITLE>\n</HEAD>' +
121     '<BODY BGCOLOR=WHITE TEXT=BLACK>' +
122     '<TABLE WIDTH=90% BORDER=0 ALIGN=CENTER CELLPADDING=3><TR><TD>' +
123     '<HR NOSHADE WIDTH=100%></TD></TR><TR><TD VALIGN=TOP>' +
124     '<FONT FACE=Arial><B>Search Query: <I>' +
125     parent.frames[0].document.forms[0].query.value + '</I><BR>\n' +
126     'Search Results: <I>' + (reference + 1) + ' - ' +
127     currentRecord + ' of ' + results.length + '</I><BR><BR></FONT>' +
128     '<FONT FACE=Arial SIZE=-1><B>' +
129     '\n\n<!-- Begin result set //-->\n\n\t<DL>');
130   if (searchType == SEARCHURL) {
131     for (var i = reference; i < currentRecord; i++) {
132       var divide = results[i].split('|');
133       docObj.writeln('\t<DT>' + '<A HREF="' + divide[2] + '">' +
134         divide[2] + '</A>\t<DD><I>' + divide[1] + '</I><P>\n\n');
135     }
136   }
137   else {
138     for (var i = reference; i < currentRecord; i++) {
139       var divide = results[i].split('|');
140       docObj.writeln('\n\n\t<DT>' + '<A HREF="' + divide[2] + '>' +
141         divide[0] + '</A>' + '\t<DD>' + '<I>' + divide[1] + '</I><P>');
142     }
143   }
144   docObj.writeln('\n\t</DL>\n\n<!-- End result set //-->\n\n');
145   prevNextResults(results.length, reference, offset);
146   docObj.writeln('<HR NOSHADE WIDTH=100%>' +
147     '</TD>\n</TR>\n</TABLE>\n</BODY>\n</HTML>');
148   docObj.close();
149   document.forms[0].query.select();
150   }
151
152 function prevNextResults(ceiling, reference, offset) {
153   docObj.writeln('<CENTER><FORM>');
154   if(reference > 0) {
155     docObj.writeln('<INPUT TYPE=BUTTON VALUE="Prev ' + offset +
156     ' Results" ' +
157 'onClick="parent.frames[0].formatResults(parent.frames[0].copyArray, ' +
158       (reference - offset) + ', ' + offset + ')">');
159   }
160   if(reference >= 0 && reference + offset < ceiling) {
```

Example 1-1. Source Code for nav.html (continued)

```
161     var trueTop = ((ceiling - (offset + reference) < offset) ?
162       ceiling - (reference + offset) : offset);
163     var howMany = (trueTop > 1 ? "s" : "");
164     docObj.writeln('<INPUT TYPE=BUTTON VALUE="Next ' + trueTop +
165       ' Result' + howMany + '" ' +
166  'onClick="parent.frames[0].formatResults(parent.frames[0].copyArray, ' +
167       (reference + offset) + ', ' + offset + ')">');
168     }
169   docObj.writeln('</CENTER>');
170   }
171
172 //-->
173 </SCRIPT>
174 </HEAD>
175 <BODY BGCOLOR="WHITE">
176 <TABLE WIDTH="95%" BORDER="0" ALIGN="CENTER">
177 <TR>
178   <TD VALIGN=MIDDLE>
179   <FONT FACE="Arial">
180   <B>Client-Side Search Engine</B>
181   </TD>
182
183   <TD VALIGN=ABSMIDDLE>
184   <FORM NAME="search"
185     onsubmit="validate(document.forms[0].query.value); return false;">
186   <INPUT TYPE=TEXT NAME="query" SIZE="33">
187   <INPUT TYPE=HIDDEN NAME="standin" VALUE="">
188   </FORM>
189   </TD>
190
191   <TD VALIGN=ABSMIDDLE>
192   <FONT FACE="Arial">
193   <B><A HREF="main.html" TARGET="main">Help</A></B>
194   </TD>
195 </TR>
196 </TABLE>
197 </BODY>
198 </HTML>
```

That's a lot of code. The easiest way to understand what's going on here is simply to start at the top, and work down. Fortunately, the code was written to proceed from function to function in more or less the same order.

We'll examine this in the following order:

- The *records.js* source file
- The global variables
- The functions
- The HTML

records.js

The first item worth examining is the JavaScript source file *records.js.* You'll find it in the `<SCRIPT>` tag at line 5.

It contains a fairly lengthy array of elements called *profiles.* The contents of this file have been omitted from this book, as they would have to be scrunched together. So after you've extracted the files in the zip file, start up your text editor and open *ch01/records.js.* Behold: it's your database. Each element is a three-part string. Here's one example:

```
"http://www.serve.com/hotsyte|HotSyte-The JavaScript Resource|The " +
    "HotSyte home page featuring links, tutorials, free scripts, and more"
```

Record parts are separated by the pipe character (|). These characters will come in handy when matching database records are printed to the screen. The second record part is the document title (it has nothing to do with **TITLE** tags); the third is the document description; and the first is the document's URL.

By the way, there's no law against using character(s) other than "|" to separate your record parts. Just be sure it's something the user isn't likely to enter as part of a query string (perhaps &^ or ~[%). Keep the backslash character (\) out of the mix. JavaScript will interpret that as an escape character and give you funky search results or choke the app altogether.

Why is all this material included in a JavaScript source file? Two reasons: modularity and cleanliness. If your site has more than a few hundred web pages, you'll probably want to have a server-side program generate the code containing all the records. It's a bit more organized to have this generated in a JavaScript source file.

You can also use this database in other search applications simply by including *records.js* in your code. In addition, I'd hate to have all that code copied into an HTML file and displayed as source code.

The Global Variables

Lines 9 through 16 of Example 1-1 declare and initialize the global variables.

```
var SEARCHANY    = 1;
var SEARCHALL    = 2;
var SEARCHURL    = 4;
var searchType   = '';
var showMatches  = 10;
var currentMatch = 0;
var copyArray    = new Array();
var docObj       = parent.frames[1].document;
```

JavaScript Technique:
Using Delimited Strings to Contain Multiple Records

This application relies on searching pieces of information, much like a database. To emulate searching a database, JavaScript can parse (search) an array with similarly formatted data.

It might seem like common sense to set each array element equal to one piece of data (such as a URL or the title of a web page). That works, but you're setting yourself up for potential grief.

You can significantly reduce the number of global array elements if you concatenate multiple substrings with a known delimiter (such as |) into one array element. When you parse each array element, JavaScript's `split()` method of the *String* object can create an array of each of the elements. In other words, why have a global array such as:

```
var records = new Array("The Good", "The Bad",
   "and The JavaScript Programmer"),
```

when you can have a local array inside the function? For example:

```
var records = "The Good|TheBad|and The JavaScript Programmer".
   split('|');
```

Now you're probably thinking, "Six of one and a half dozen of the other. What's the difference?" The difference is that the first version declares three global elements that take up memory until you get rid of them. The second declares only one global element. The three elements created with `split('|')` at search time are temporary because they are created locally.

With the latter, JavaScript disposes of the *records* variable after the search function runs. That frees memory. Plus that's less coding for you. For myself, I'll take the second option. We'll hit this concept again when we take a look at the code that does the parsing.

The following list explains the variable functions:

SEARCHANY

   Indicates to search using any of the entered terms.

SEARCHALL

   Indicates to search using all of the entered terms.

SEARCHURL

   Indicates to search the URL only (using any of the entered terms).

searchType

   Indicates the type of search (set to *SEARCHANY*, *SEARCHALL*, or *SEARCHURL*).

showMatches

Determines the number of records to display per results page.

currentMatch

Determines which record will first be printed on the current results page.

copyArray

Copy of the temporary array of matches used to display the next or previous set of results.

docObj

Variable referring to the document object of the second frame. This isn't critical to the application, but it helps manage your code because you'll need to access the object (`parent.frames[1].document`) many times when you print the search results. *docObj* refers to that object, reducing the amount of code and serving as a centralized point for making changes.

The Functions

Next, let's look at the major functions:

validate()

When the user hits the Enter button, the `validate()` function at line 18 determines what the user wants to search and how to search it. Recall the three options:

- Search the document title and description, requiring only one term to match.

- Search the document title and description, requiring all of the terms to match.

- Search the document URL or path, requiring only one of the terms to match.

`validate()` determines what and how to search by evaluating the first few characters of the string it receives. How is the search method set? Using the *searchType* variable. If the user wants all terms to be included, then *searchType* is set to *SEARCHALL*. If the user wants to search the title and description, `validate()` sets *searchType* to *SEARCHALL* (that's the default, by the way). If the user wants to search the URL, *searchType* is set to *SEARCHURL*. Here's how it happens:

Line 19 shows the `charAt()` method of the *String* object looking for the + sign as the first character. If found, the search method is set to option 2 (the Boolean AND method).

```
if (entry.charAt(0) == "+") {
 entry = entry.substring(1,entry.length);
 searchType = SEARCHALL;
 }
```

Line 23 shows the **substring()** method of the *String* object looking for "url:". If the string is found, *searchType* is set accordingly.

```
if (entry.substring(0,4) == "url:") {
  entry = entry.substring(5,entry.length);
  searchType = SEARCHURL;
  }
```

What about the **substring()** methods in lines 20 and 24? Well, after **validate()** knows what and how to search, those character indicators (+ and **url:**) are no longer needed. Therefore, **validate()** removes the required number of characters from the front of the string and moves on.

If neither + nor **url:** is found at the front of the string, **validate()** sets variable *searchType* to *SEARCHANY*, and does a little cleanup before calling **convertString()**. The *while* statements at lines 28 and 32 trim excess white space from the beginning and end of the string.

After discovering the user preference and trimming excess whitespace, **validate()** has to make sure that there is something left to use in a search. Line 36 verifies that the query string has at least three characters. Searching fewer might not produce useful results, but you can change this to your liking:

```
if (entry.length < 3) {
  alert("You cannot search strings that small. Elaborate a little.");
  document.forms[0].query.focus();
  return;
  }
```

If all goes well to this point, **validate()** makes the call to **convertString()**, passing a clean copy of the query string (**entry**).

convertString()

convertString() performs two related operations: it splits the string into array elements, and calls the appropriate search function. The **split()** method of the *String* object divides the user-entered string by whitespace and puts the outcome into the array *searchArray*. This happens at line 45 as shown below:

```
var searchArray = reentry.split(" ");
```

For example, if the user enters the string "client-side JavaScript development" in the search field, *searchArray* will contain the values **client-side**, **JavaScript**, and **development** for elements 0, 1, and 2, respectively. With that taken care of, **convertString()** calls the appropriate search function according to the value of *searchType*. You can see this in lines 46 and 47:

```
if (searchType == (SEARCHALL)) { requireAll(searchArray); }
else { allowAny(searchArray); }
```

As you can see, one of two functions is called. Both behave similarly, but they have their differences. Here's a look at both functions: `allowAny()` and `requireAll()`.

allowAny()

As the name implies, this function gets called from the bench when the application has only a one-match minimum. Here's what you'll see in lines 50-68:

```
function allowAny(t) {
  var findings = new Array(0);
  for (i = 0; i < profiles.length; i++) {
    var compareElement  = profiles[i].toUpperCase();
    if(searchType == SEARCHANY) {
      var refineElement  =
        compareElement.substring(0,compareElement.indexOf('|HTTP'));
      }
    else {
      var refineElement =
        compareElement.substring(compareElement.indexOf('|HTTP'),
        compareElement.length);
      }
    for (j = 0; j < t.length; j++) {
      var compareString = t[j].toUpperCase();
      if (refineElement.indexOf(compareString) != -1) {
        findings[findings.length] = profiles[i];
        break;
        }
```

The guts behind both search functions is comparing strings with nested *for* loops. See the "JavaScript Technique: Nested for Loops" sidebar for more information. The *for* loops go to work at lines 52 and 63. The first *for* loop has the task of iterating through each of the *profiles* array elements (from the source file). For each *profiles* element, the second *for* loop iterates through each of the query terms passed to it from `convertString()`.

To ensure that users don't miss matching records because they use uppercase or lowercase letters, lines 53 and 64 declare local variables *compareElement* and *compareString*, respectively, and then initialize each to an uppercase version of the record and query term. Now it doesn't matter if users search for "JavaScript," "javascript," or even "jAvasCRIpt."

`allowAny()` still needs to determine whether to search by document title and description or by URL. So local variable *refineElement*, the substring that will be compared to each of the query terms, is set according to the value of *searchType* at line 55 or 59. If *searchType* equals *SEARCHANY*, *refineElement* is set to the substring containing the record's document title and description. Otherwise *searchType* must be *SEARCHURL*, so *refineElement* is set to the substring containing the document URL.

Remember the | symbols? That's how JavaScript can distinguish the different record parts. So the `substring()` method returns a string starting from 0 and ending at the character before the first instance of "|HTTP", or returns a string starting at the first instance of "|HTTP" until the end of the element. Now we have what we're about to compare with what the user entered. Check it out at line 65:

```
if (refineElement.indexOf(compareString) != -1) {
    findings[findings.length] = profiles[i];
    break;
}
```

If *compareString* is found within *refineElement*, we have a match (it's about time). That original record (not the URL-truncated version we searched) is added to the *findings* array at line 66. We can use *findings.length* as an indexer to continually assign elements.

Once we've found a match, there is certainly no reason to compare the record with other query strings. Line 67 contains the break statement that stops the *for* loop comparison for the current record. This isn't strictly necessary, but it reduces excess processing.

After iterating through all records and search terms, `allowAny()` passes any matching records in the *findings* array to function `verifyManage()` at lines 95 through 101. If the search was successful, function `formatResults()` gets the call to print the results. Otherwise, function `noMatch()` will let the user know that the search was unsuccessful. Functions `formatResults()` and `noMatch()` are discussed later in the chapter. Let's finish examining the remaining search methods with `requireAll()`.

requireAll()

Put a + in front of your search terms, and `requireAll()` gets the call. This function is nearly identical to `allowAny()`, except that all terms the user enters must match the search. With `allowAny()`, records were added to the result set as soon as one term matched. In this function, we have to wait until all terms have been compared to each record before deciding to add anything to the result set. Line 74 starts things off:

```
function requireAll(t) {
    var findings = new Array();
    for (i = 0; i < profiles.length; i++) {
        var allConfirmation = true;
        var allString      = profiles[i].toUpperCase();
        var refineAllString = allString.substring(0,
            allString.indexOf('|HTTP'));
        for (j = 0; j < t.length; j++) {
            var allElement = t[j].toUpperCase();
            if (refineAllString.indexOf(allElement) == -1) {
```

```
          allConfirmation = false;
          continue;
          }
       }
    if (allConfirmation) {
       findings[findings.length] = profiles[i];
       }
    }
  verifyManage(findings);
  }
```

At first glance, things seem much as they were with **allowAny()**. The nested *for* loops, the uppercase conversion, and the confirmation variable—they're all there. Things change, however, at lines 79–80:

```
var refineAllString = allString.substring(0,allString.indexOf('|HTTP'));
```

Notice that variable *searchType* was not checked to determine which part of the record to keep for searching as it was in **allowAny()** at line 50. There's no need. **requireAll()** gets called only if *searchType* equals *SEARCHALL* (see line 46). URL searching doesn't include the Boolean AND method, so it's a known fact that the document title and description will be compared.

Function **requireAll()** is a little tougher to please. Since all the terms a user enters must be found in the compared string, so the searching logic will be more restrictive than it is in **allowAny()**. See lines 83 through 86:

```
if (refineAllString.indexOf(allElement) == -1) {
  allConfirmation = false;
  continue;
  }
```

It will be far easier to reject a record the first time it doesn't match a term than it will be to compare the number of terms with the number of matches. Therefore, the first time a record does not contain a match, the **continue** statement tells JavaScript to forget about it and move to the next record.

If all terms have been compared to a record and local variable *allConfirmation* is still true, we have a match. *allConfirmation* becomes false the moment a record fails to match its first term. The current record is then added to the temporary *findings* array at line 89. This condition is harder to achieve, but the search results will likely be more specific.

Once all records have been evaluated this way, *findings* is passed to **verifyManage()** to check for worthy results. If there are any matches at all, **formatResults()** gets the call. Otherwise, **verifyManage()** calls **noMatch()** to bring the bad news to the user.

JavaScript Technique: Nested for Loops

Both the searching functions `allowAny()` and `requireAll()` use nested *for* loops. This is a handy technique to iterate multidimensional arrays as opposed to single-dimension arrays. (JavaScript arrays are technically one-dimensional. However, JavaScript can emulate multidimensional arrays as described here.) Consider this five-element, single-dimension array:

```
var numbers = ("one", "two", "three", "four", "five");
```

If you want to compare a string to each of these, you simply run a *for* (or *while*) loop, comparing each array element to the string as you go. Like this:

```
for (var i = 0; i < numbers.length; i++) {
    if (myString == numbers[i]) { alert("That's the number");
    break;
    }
```

Not too demanding, so let's up the ante. Multidimensional arrays are, well, arrays of arrays. For example:

```
var numbers = new Array(
new Array("one", "two", "three", "four", "five"),
new Array("uno", "dos", "tres", "cuatro", "cinco"),
new Array("won", "too", "tree", "for", "fife")
);
```

A single *for* loop won't cut it. We'll need more fire power. The first *numbers* array is a single-dimension array (1 × 5). The new version is a multidimensional array (3 × 5). Going through all 15 elements (3 × 5) means we'll need an extra loop:

```
for (var i = 0; i < numbers.length; i++) {          // 1...
    for (var j = 0; j < numbers[i].length; j++) {   // and 2.
      if (myString == numbers[i][j]) {
        alert("Finally found it.");
        break;
        }
      }
    }
```

That's the two-dimensional answer to getting a shot at each element. Let's take it a notch further. What if we build a color palette in a table of all 216 web-safe colors—one in each cell? Nested *for* loops to the rescue. This time, however, we'll only use a single-dimension array.

Using hexadecimal numbers, web-safe colors come in six-digit groups—two digits for each color component—such as FFFFF, 336699, and 99AACC. The two-digit pairs that make up all web-safe colors are: 33, 66, 99, AA, CC, and FF. Let's spark up an array:

```
var hexPairs = new Array("33","66","99","AA","CC","FF");
```

—continued—

"There's only one array and one dimension. I want my money back."

Don't run to the bookstore yet. There are three dimensions, but we'll use the same array for each dimension. Here's how:

```
var str = '';

// Strike up a table
document.writeln('<H2>Web Safe Colors</H2>' +
  '<TABLE BORDER=1 CELLSPACING=0>');
for (var i = 0; i < hexPairs.length; i++) {
  // Create a row
  document.writeln('<TR>');
  for (var j = 0; j < hexPairs.length; j++) {
    for (var k = 0; k < hexPairs.length; k++) {
      // Create a string of data cells for the row with whitespace in each
      // Notice each background color is made with three hexPairs elements
      str += '<TD BGCOLOR="' + hexPairs[i]  + hexPairs[j] + hexPairs[k] +
      '">   </TD>';
      }
    // Write the row of data cells and reset str
    document.writeln(str);
    str ='';
    }
  // End the row
  document.writeln('</TR>');
  }
// End the table
document.writeln('</TABLE>');
```

Drop this code in a web document (it's in the zip file, at *\Ch01\websafe.html*), and you'll get a 6 × 36 table with all 216 (that's 6 × 6 × 6) web-safe colors. Three *for* loops and three dimensions. Of course, you could modify the palette table in plenty of ways, but this just shows you how nested *for* loops can solve your coding woes.

verifyManage()

As you've probably realized, this function determines whether the user's search produced any record matches and calls one of two printout functions pending the result. It all starts at line 95:

```
function verifyManage(resultSet) {
if (resultSet.length == 0) {
   noMatch();
    return;
    }
  copyArray = resultSet.sort();
  formatResults(copyArray, currentMatch, showMatches);
  }
```

Both `allowAny()` and `requireAll()` call `verifyManage()` after running the respective course and pass the *findings* array as an argument. Line 96 shows that `verifyManage()` calls function `noMatch()` if array *resultSet* (a copy of *findings*) contains nothing.

If *resultSet* contains at least one matched record, however, global variable *copyArray* is set to the lexically sorted version of all the elements in *resultSet*. Sorting is not necessary, but it's a great way to add order to your result set, and you don't have to worry about the order in which you add records to the *profiles* array. You can keep adding them on the end, knowing that they'll be sorted if a match occurs.

So why should we make an extra copy of a bunch of records we already have? Remember that *findings* is a local, and thus temporary, array. Once a search has been performed (that is, the application executes one of the search functions), *findings* dies, and its allocated memory is freed for further use. That's a good thing. There's no reason to hold onto memory we could possibly use elsewhere, but we still need access to those records.

Since the application displays, say, 10 records per page, users potentially see only a subset of the matching results. Variable *copyArray* is global, so sorting the temporary result set and assigning that to *copyArray* keeps all matching records intact. Users can now view the results 10, 15, or however many at a time. This global variable will keep the matching results until the user submits a new query.

The last thing `verifyManage()` does is call `formatResults()`, passing an index number (*currentMatch*), indicating which record to begin with and how many records to display per page (*showMatches*). Both *currentMatch* and *showMatches* are global variables. They don't die after functions execute. We need them for the life of the application.

noMatch()

`noMatch()` does what it implies. If your query produces no matches, this function is the bearer of the bad news. It is rather short and sweet, though it still generates a custom results (or lack of results) page, stating that the query term(s) the user entered didn't produce at least one match. Here it is starting at line 103:

```
function noMatch() {
  docObj.open();
  docObj.writeln('<HTML><HEAD><TITLE>Search Results</TITLE></HEAD>' +
    '<BODY BGCOLOR=WHITE TEXT=BLACK>' +
    '<TABLE WIDTH=90% BORDER=0 ALIGN=CENTER><TR><TD VALIGN=TOP>' +
    '<FONT FACE=Arial><B><DL>' +
    '<HR NOSHADE WIDTH=100%"' + document.forms[0].query.value +
    '" returned no results.<HR NOSHADE WIDTH=100%>' +
    '</TD></TR></TABLE></BODY></HTML>');
```

```
    docObj.close();
    document.forms[0].query.select();
    }
```

formatResults()

This function's job is to neatly display the matching records for the user. Not terribly difficult, but this function does cover a lot of ground. Here are the ingredients for a successful results display:

- An HTML head, title, and body

- The document title, description, and URL of each matching record with a link to the URL of the each matching record

- "Previous" and "Next" buttons to view earlier or later records, if applicable

The HTML head and title

The HTML head and title are straightforward. Lines 116 through 129 print the head, title, and the beginning of the body contents. Take a look:

```
function formatResults(results, reference, offset) {
  var currentRecord = (results.length < reference + offset ?
    results.length : reference + offset);
  docObj.open();
  docObj.writeln('<HTML><HEAD><TITLE>Search Results</TITLE>\n</HEAD>' +
    '<BODY BGCOLOR=WHITE TEXT=BLACK>' +
    '<TABLE WIDTH=90% BORDER=0 ALIGN=CENTER CELLPADDING=3><TR><TD>' +
    '<HR NOSHADE WIDTH=100%></TD></TR><TR><TD VALIGN=TOP>' +
    '<FONT FACE=Arial><B>Search Query: <I>' +
    parent.frames[0].document.forms[0].query.value + '</I><BR>\n' +
    'Search Results: <I>' + (reference + 1) + ' - ' + currentRecord +
    ' of ' + results.length + '</I><BR><BR></FONT>' +
    '<FONT FACE=Arial SIZE=-1><B>' +
    '\n\n<!- Begin result set //-->\n\n\t<DL>');
```

Before printing the heading and title, let's find out which record we're going to start with. We know the first record to print starts at **results[reference]**. And we should display *offset* records unless *reference + offset* is greater than the total number of records. To find out, the ternary operator is used to determine which is larger. Variable *currentRecord* is set to that number at line 117. We'll use that value shortly.

Now, **formatResults()** prints your run-of-the-Internet HTML heading and title. The body starts with a centered table and a horizontal rule. The application easily gives the user a reminder of the search query (line 125), which came from the form field value:

```
parent.frames[0].document.forms[0].query.value
```

Things get more involved at line 126, however. This marks the beginning of the result set. The line of printed text on the page displays the current subset of matching records and the total number of matches, for instance:

```
Search Results:  1 - 10 of 38
```

We'll need three numbers to pull this off—the first record of the subset to display, the number of records to display, and the length of *copyArray*, where the matching records are stored. Let's take a look at this in terms of steps. Remember, this is not the logic used to display the records. This logic lets the user know *how many* records and with *which* record to start. Here is how things happen:

1. Assign the number of the current record to variable *reference*, then print it.

2. Add another number called *offset*, which is how many records to display per page (in this case, 10).

3. If the sum of *reference* + *offset* is greater than the total number of matches, print the total number of matches. Otherwise, print the sum of *reference* + *offset*. (This value has already been determined and is reflected in *currentRecord*).

4. Print the total number of matches.

Steps 1 and 2 seem simple enough. Recall the code in **verifyManage()**, particularly line 99:

```
formatResult(copyArray, currentMatch, showMatches);
```

The local variable *results* is a copy of *copyArray*. The variable *reference* is set to *currentMatch*, so the sum of *reference* + *offset* is the sum of *currentMatch* + *showResults*. In the first few lines of this code (13 and 14 to be exact), *showMatches* was set to 10, and *currentMatch* was set to 0. Therefore, *reference* starts as 0, and *reference* + *offset* equals 10. Step 1 is taken care of as soon as *reference* is printed. The math we just did takes care of step 2.

In step 3, we use the ternary operator (at lines 117–118) to decide whether the sum of *reference* + *offset* is greater than the total number of matches. In other words, will adding *offset* more records to *reference* yield a number higher than the total number of records? If *reference* is 20, and there are 38 total records, adding 10 to *reference* gives us 30. The display would look like this:

```
Search Results: 20 - 30 of 38
```

If *reference* is 30, however, and there are 38 total records, adding 10 to *reference* gives us 40. The display would look like this:

```
Search Results: 30 - 40 of 38
```

Can't happen. The search engine cannot display records 39 and 40 if it only found 38. This then indicates that the end of the records has been reached. So the total number of records will be displayed instead of the sum of *reference* + *offset*. That brings us to step 4, and the end of the process:

Search Results: 30 - 38 of 38

Function `formatResults()` is sprinkled with special characters such as \n and \t. \n represents a newline character, which is equivalent to pressing Enter on your keyboard while writing code in your text editor. \t is equivalent to pressing the Tab key. All that these characters do in this case is make the HTML of the search results look neater if you view the source code. I included them here to show you how they look. Keep in mind that they are not necessary and don't affect your applications. If you think they clutter your code, don't use them. I use them sparingly in the rest of the book.

Displaying document titles, descriptions, and linked URLs

Now that the subset of records has been indicated, it's time to print that subset to the page. Enter lines 130 through 143:

```
if (searchType == SEARCHURL) {
   for (var i = reference; i < currentRecord; i++) {
      var divide = results[i].split('|');
      docObj.writeln('\t<DT>' + '<A HREF="' + divide[2] + '">' +
         divide[2] + '</A>' + '\t<DD>' + '<I>' + divide[1] + '</I><P>\n\n');
      }
   }
else {
   for (var i = reference; i < currentRecord; i++) {
      var divide = results[i].split('|');
      docObj.writeln('\n\n\t<DT>' + '<A HREF="' + divide[2] + '">' +
         divide[0] + '</A>' + '\t<DD>' + '<I>' + divide[1] + '</I><P>');
      }
   }
```

Lines 131 and 138 show both *for* loops, which perform the same operation with *currentRecord*, except that the order of the printed items is different. Variable *searchType* comes up again. If it equals *SEARCHURL*, the URL will be displayed as the link text. Otherwise, *searchType* equals *SEARCHANY* or *SEARCHALL*. In either case the document title will be displayed as the link text.

The type of search has been determined, but how do you neatly display the records? We need only loop through the record subset, and split the record parts accordingly by title, description and URL, placing them however we so desire along the way. Here is the *for* loop used in either case (URL search or not):

```
for (var i = reference; i < lastRecord; i++) {
```

Now for the record parts. Think back to the *records.js* file. Each element of *profiles* is a string that identifies the record | separating its parts. And that is how we'll pull them apart:

```
var divide = results[i].split('|');
```

For each element, local variable *divide* is set to an array of elements also separated by |. The first element (`divide[0]`) is the URL, the second element (`divide[1]`) is the document title, and the third (`divide[2]`) is the document description. Each of these elements is printed to the page with accompanying HTML to suit (I chose <DL>, <DT>, and <DD> tags). If the user searched by URL, the URL would be shown as the link text. Otherwise, the document title becomes the link text.

Adding "Previous" and "Next" buttons

The only thing left to do is add buttons so that the user can view the previous or next subset(s) of records. This actually happens in function **prevNextResults()**, which we'll discuss shortly, but here are the last few lines of **formatResults()**:

```
docObj.writeln('\n\t</DL>\n\n<!- End result set //-->\n\n');
prevNextResults(results.length, reference, offset);
docObj.writeln('<HR NOSHADE WIDTH=100%>' +
  '</TD>\n</TR>\n</TABLE>\n</BODY>\n</HTML>');
docObj.close();
}
```

This part of the function calls **prevNextResults()**, adds some final HTML, then sets the focus to the query string text field.

prevNextResults()

If you've made it this far without screaming, this function shouldn't be that much of a stretch. **prevNextResults()** is as follows, starting with line 152.

```
function prevNextResults(ceiling, reference, offset) {
  docObj.writeln('<CENTER><FORM>');
  if(reference > 0) {
    docObj.writeln('<INPUT TYPE=BUTTON VALUE="Prev ' + offset +
      ' Results" onClick="' +
      parent.frames[0].formatResults(parent.frames[0].copyArray, ' +
      (reference - offset) + ', ' + offset + ')">');
  }
  if(reference >= 0 && reference + offset < ceiling) {
    var trueTop = ((ceiling - (offset + reference) < offset) ?
      ceiling - (reference + offset) : offset);
    var howMany = (trueTop > 1 ? "s" : "");
    docObj.writeln('<INPUT TYPE=BUTTON VALUE="Next ' + trueTop +
      ' Result' + howMany + '" onClick="' +
      parent.frames[0].formatResults(parent.frames[0].copyArray, ' +
```

```
            (reference + offset) + ', ' + offset + ')">');
        }
    docObj.writeln('</CENTER>');
    }
```

This function prints a centered HTML form at the bottom of the results page with one or two buttons. Figure 1-3 shows a results page with both a "Prev" and a "Next" button. There are three possible combinations of buttons:

- A "Next" button only—for the first results page displayed. There aren't any previous records.

- A "Prev" button and a "Next" button—for those results pages that are between the first and last results pages. There are records before and after those currently displayed.

- A "Prev" button only—for the last results page. There are no more records ahead.

Three combinations. Two buttons. That means this application must know when to print or not print a button. The following list describes the circumstances under which each combination will occur.

"Next" Button Only

Where should we include a Next button? Answer: every results page except the last. In other words, whenever the last record (*reference* + *offset*) of the results page is less than the total number of records.

Now, where do we exclude the "Prev" button? Answer: on the first results page. In other words, when *reference* equals 0 (which we got from *currentMatch*).

"Prev" and the "Next" Buttons

When should both be displayed? Given that a "Next" button should be included on every results page except the last, and a "Prev" button should be included on every results page except the first, we'll need a "Prev" button as long as *reference* is greater than 0, and a "Next" button if *reference* + *offset* is less than the total number of records.

"Prev" Button Only

Knowing when to include a "Prev" button, under what circumstances should we exclude the "Next" button? Answer: when the last results page is displayed. In other words, when *reference* + *offset* is greater than or equal to the total number of matching records.

Things might still be a little sketchy, but at least we know when to include which button(s), and the *if* statements in lines 154 and 160 do just that. These statements include one or both the "Prev" and "Next" buttons depending on the current subset and how many results remain.

JavaScript Technique: Go Easy on document.write()

Take another look at `formatResults()`. You'll see that HTML written to the page with a call to `document.write()` or `document.writeln()`. The string passed to these methods is generally long and spans multiple lines concatenated by +. While you may argue that the code would be more readable with a call to `document.writeln()` on each line, there is a reason for doing otherwise. Here's what I mean. The few lines of `formatResults()` are as follows:

```
function formatResults(results, reference, offset) {
    docObj.open();
    docObj.writeln('<HTML>\n<HEAD>\n<TITLE>Search Results</TITLE>\n
      </HEAD>' +
    '<BODY BGCOLOR=WHITE TEXT=BLACK>' +
    '<TABLE WIDTH=90% BORDER=0 ALIGN=CENTER CELLPADDING=3><TR><TD>' +
    '<HR NOSHADE WIDTH=100%></TD></TR><TR><TD VALIGN=TOP>' +
    '<FONT FACE=Arial><B>Search Query: <I>' +
    parent.frames[0].document.forms[0].query.value + '</I><BR>\n' +
    'Search Results: <I>' + (reference + 1) + ' - ' +
    (reference + offset > results.length ? results.length :
      reference + offset) +
    ' of ' + results.length + '</I><BR><BR></FONT>' +
    '<FONT FACE=Arial SIZE=-1><B>' +
    '\n\n<!- Begin result set //-->\n\n\t<DL>');
```

There is only one method call to write the text to the page. Not too attractive. One alternative would be to line things up neatly with a method call on each line:

```
function formatResults(results, reference, offset) {
    docObj.open();
    docObj.writeln('<HTML><HEAD><TITLE>Search Results</TITLE>\n</HEAD>');
    docObj.writeln('<BODY BGCOLOR=WHITE TEXT=BLACK>');
    docObj.writeln('<TABLE WIDTH=90% BORDER=0 ALIGN=CENTER ' +
      'CELLPADDING=3><TR><TD>');
    docObj.writeln('<HR NOSHADE WIDTH=100%></TD></TR><TR><TD VALIGN=TOP');
    docObj.writeln('<FONT FACE=Arial><B>' + 'Search Query: <I>' +
      parent.frames[0].document.forms[0].query.value + '</I><BR>\n');
    docObj.writeln('Search Results: <I>' + (reference + 1) + ' - ' );
    docObj.writeln( (reference + offset > results.length ?
      results.length : reference + offset) +
      ' of ' + results.length + '</I><BR><BR></FONT>' +
      '<FONT FACE=Arial SIZE=-1><B>');
    docObj.writeln('\n\n<!- Begin result set //-->\n\n\t<DL>');
```

That might look more organized, but each of those method calls means a little more work for the JavaScript engine. Think about it. What would you rather do: make five trips to and from the store and buy things a little at a time, or go to the store once and buy it all the first time? Just pass a lengthy text string separated with + signs, and be done with it.

Both buttons call function `formatResults()` when the user clicks them. The only difference is the arguments that they pass, representing different result subsets. Both buttons are similar under the hood. They look different because of the **VALUE** attribute. Here is the beginning of the "Prev" button at lines 155–156:

```
docObj.writeln('<INPUT TYPE=BUTTON VALUE="Prev ' + offset + ' Results" ' +
```

Now the "Next" button at lines 164–165:

```
docObj.writeln('<INPUT TYPE=BUTTON VALUE="Next ' + trueTop + ' Result' +
    howMany
```

Both lines contain the **TYPE** and **VALUE** attributes of the form button plus a number indicating how many previous or next results. Since the number of previous results is always the same (*offset*), the "Prev" button value displays that number, for example, "Prev 10 Results." The number of next results can vary, however. It is either *offset* or the number remaining if the final subset is less than *offset*. To address that, variable *trueTop* is set to that value, whichever it is.

Notice how the value of the "Prev" button always contains the word "Results." This makes sense. The *showMatches* never changes throughout the app. In this case it is and always will be 10. So the user can always count on seeing 10 previous results. However, that isn't always the case for the amount of "Next" results. Suppose the last subset contains only one record. The user shouldn't see a button labeled "Next 1 Results." That's incorrect grammar. To clean this up, **prevNextResults()** contains a local variable named *howMany* that uses the ternary operator once again. You'll find it at line 163:

```
var howMany = (trueTop > 1 ? "s" : "");
```

If *trueTop* is greater than 1, *howMany* is set to the string s. If *trueTop* equals 1, *howMany* is set to an empty string. As you can see at line 165, *howMany* is printed immediately after the word "Result." If there is only one record in the subset, the word "Result" appears unchanged. If there are more, however, the user sees "Results."

The final step in both buttons is "telling" them what to do when they are clicked. I mentioned earlier that the *onClick* events of both buttons call `formatResults()`. Lines 157–158 and 166–167 dynamically write the call to `formatResults()` in the *onClick* event handler of either button. Here is the first set (the latter half of the `document.writeln()` call):

```
'onClick="' + parent.frames[0].formatResults(parent.frames[0].copyArray, ' +
    (reference - offset) + ', ' + offset + ')">');
```

The arguments are determined with the aid of the ternary operator and written on the fly. Notice the three arguments passed (once the JavaScript generates the code) are *copyArray*, *reference – offset*, and *offset*. The "Prev" button will always get these three arguments. By the way, notice how `formatResults()` and *copyArray* are written:

```
parent.frames[0].formatResults(...);
```

and:

```
parent.frames[0].copyArray
```

That may seem strange at first, but remember that the call to `formatResults()` does not happen from *nav.html* (`parent.frames[0]`). It happens from the results frame `parent.frames[1]`, which has no function named `formatResults()` and no variable named *copyArray*. Therefore, functions and variables need this reference.

The "Next" button gets a similar call in the *onClick* event handler, but wait a sec. Don't we have to deal with the possibility of less than *offset* results in the last results subset of *copyArray* just as we did in `formatResults()` when displaying the range of currently viewed results? Nope. Function `formatResults()` takes care of that decision process; all we do is add *reference* to *offset* and pass it in. Take a look at lines 166–167, again the latter half of the `document.writeln()` method call:

```
'onClick="parent.frames[0].formatResults(parent.frames[0].copyArray, ' +
(reference + offset) + ', ' + offset + ')">');
```

JavaScript Technique: The Ternary Operator

After that section, you must have seen this one coming. The ternary operator is pretty helpful, so here's my sermon. Ternary operators require three operands, and they are used throughout this app as a one-line if-else statement. Here's the syntax straight from Netscape's *JavaScript Guide for Communicator 4.0*, Chapter 9:

```
(condition) ? val1 : val2
```

This conditional operator, when properly populated, acts upon `val1` if *condition* evaluates to true, and `val2` otherwise. I'm making all the fuss about it because in many cases I find it makes code easier to read and there is usually less to write. This operator can be especially helpful if you're coding within several nested statements.

The ternary operator is not the cure for everything. If you have multiple things that need to happen if *condition* is true or false, take the if-else route. Otherwise, give this a try in your code.

The HTML

nav.html has very little static HTML. Here it is again, starting with line 174:

```
</HEAD>
<BODY BGCOLOR="WHITE">
<TABLE WIDTH="95%" BORDER="0" ALIGN="CENTER">
<TR>
  <TD VALIGN=MIDDLE>
  <FONT FACE="Arial">
  <B>Client-Side Search Engine</B>
  </TD>

  <TD VALIGN=ABSMIDDLE>
  <FORM NAME="search"
    onsubmit="validate(document.forms[0].query.value); return false;">
  <INPUT TYPE=TEXT NAME="query" SIZE="33">
  <INPUT TYPE=HIDDEN NAME="standin" VALUE="">
  </FORM>
  </TD>

  <TD VALIGN=ABSMIDDLE>
  <FONT FACE="Arial">
  <B><A HREF="main.html" TARGET="main">Help</A></B>
  </TD>
</TR>
</TABLE>
</BODY>
</HTML>
```

There aren't really any surprises. You have a form embedded in a table. "Submitting" the form executes the code we've been covering. The only question you might have is: "How can the form be submitted without a button?" As of the HTML 2.0 specification, most browsers (including Navigator and MSIE) have enabled form submission with a single text field form.

There's no law saying you have to do it this way. Feel free to add a button or image to jazz it up.

Building Your Own JavaScript Database

Eventually you'll want to replace the records I've provided with your own records. You can do this in three easy steps.

1. Open *records.js* in your text editor.

2. Remove the records already there so that the file looks like this:

   ```
   var profiles = new Array(

       );
   ```

3. For each record you want to add, use the following syntax:

```
"Your_Page_Title|Your_Page_Description|http://your_page_url/file_name.html",
```

Add as many of these elements between the parentheses as you want. Be sure to include the comma at the end of each record—*except the last one*. Notice also the page title, description, and URL are each separated by | (the pipe character). Don't use any of those in your titles, descriptions, or URLs. That will cause JavaScript errors. Remember, too that if you include double quotes (") other than the ones on the outside, be sure to escape them with a backslash (e.g., use \" instead of just ").

Potential Extensions

The search engine is pretty useful the way it is. What's even better is that you can make some significant improvements or changes. Here are some possibilities:

- Make it JavaScript 1.0 compatible
- Make it harder to break
- Display banner ads
- Add refined search capabilities
- Develop cluster sets

JavaScript 1.0 Compatibility

You know it, and I know it. Both of the major browsers are in the latter 4.x or early 5.x versions. Both are free. But there are still people out there clunking along with MSIE 3.02 or NN 2.x. I still get a surprising hit count of visitors with those credentials to HotSyte—The JavaScript Resource (*http://www.serve.com/hotsyte/*).

Since a search engine is pretty much a core feature of a web site, you might consider converting this app for JavaScript 1.0. Fortunately, all you have to do is go through the code listed earlier, line by line, figure out which features aren't supported in JavaScript 1.0, and change *all* of them.

OK. I already did that, but admit it: I had you going. Actually, you'll find the modified version in */ch01/js1.0/*. Open *index.html* in your browser just like you did with the original. In this section, we'll take a quick look at what will make the app work in JavaScript 1.0 browsers. There are three changes:

- No JavaScript source file (a browser issue really)
- No array sorting (with the `sort()` method)
- A workaround for the `split()` method

NN 2.x and MSIE 3.x do not support *.js* source files.* The workaround for this is to embed the profiles array in *nav.html*. The second change eliminates the call to `resultSet.sort()` in line 90. That means your results will not be sorted in dictionary order, but by the way you have them chronologically listed in *profiles.* The last change is eliminating the `split()` method. JavaScript 1.0 does not support that either; the workaround takes care of that, but it degrades performance.

TANSTAAFL

That's what my economics professor wrote on the chalkboard my freshman year at Florida State University. The translated acronym: Thar' Ain't No Such Thang As A Free Lunch. In other words, these changes give you older browser version compatibility, but cost you in functionality and code management.

Without support for *.js* files, you have to dump that profiles array into your *nav. html*. That will be quite unsightly and more unmanageable if you want to include those records in other searches.

The `sort()` method, while not critical to the operation, is a great feature. People might have to view all subsets of matched records because the records are in no particular order. Of course, you could place the results in the array alphabetically, but that's no picnic either. Or you write your own sort method for JavaScript 1.0. The `split()` method is arguably the least of your troubles. The JavaScript 1.0 version of the app has a workaround, so it really isn't an issue.

Make It Harder to Break

As it stands, you can pass the pipe character as part of the search query. Why not add the functionality to remove any characters from the query used as the string delimiters? That makes the app harder to break.

Display Banner Ads

If your site gets a lot of traffic, why not use it to make some extra money?

How? Try this. Suppose you want to randomly display five banner ads (no particular order in this case). If you have several ad image URLs in an array, you could pick one to load at random. Here's the array.

```
var adImages = new Array("pcAd.gif", "modemAd.gif", "webDevAd.gif");
```

Then you might randomly display one on the results page like so:

```
document.writeln('<IMG SRC=' + ads[Math.floor(Math.random(ads.length))] +
    '>');
```

---

* Actually that's a stretch. Some versions of MSIE 3.02 do support JavaScript source files.

Add Refined Search Capabilities

You can have some great programming fun with this concept. For example, suppose the user could select from array elements to search. Then the user could narrow seach results accordingly.

Consider displaying a set of checkboxes under the text field in *nav.html.* Maybe like this:

```
<INPUT TYPE=CHECKBOX NAME="group" VALUE="97">1997 Records<BR>
<INPUT TYPE=CHECKBOX NAME="group" VALUE="98">1998 Records<BR>
<INPUT TYPE=CHECKBOX NAME="group" VALUE="99">1999 Records<BR>
```

Use this checkbox group to determine which arrays to search, in this case *profiles97, profiles98,* or *profiles99.*

There are many things you can add to increase the user's ability to refine searches. One easy one is to offer case-sensitive and case-insensitive queries. As it stands now, case does not matter, but you can change that by adding a checkbox allowing either style.

You could also expand search refinement by broadening Boolean searches from the current *AND* and *OR* searches to *AND, OR, NOT, ONLY,* even *LIKE.* Here is a breakdown of the general meanings:

AND
> Record must contain both terms on the left and right of AND.

OR
> Record can contain either of the terms on the left and right of OR.

NOT
> Record must not contain the term(s) to the right of NOT.

ONLY
> Record must contain this and only this record.

LIKE
> Record can contain term(s) spelled like or sounding like.

This takes some work (especially *LIKE*), but users would be quite amazed at your wizardry.

Cluster Sets

Another popular and useful technique is to establish cluster sets. Cluster sets are predefined word groups that automatically return predefined results. For example, if a user includes the term "mutual funds" anywhere in the query string, you could automatically generate results containing records featuring your company's financial products. This technique takes a bit more planning, but it would be a great feature in a search application.

2

The Online Test

The online test application is a boilerplate for just about any multiple-choice test you'd like to administer over the Web. You have significant flexibility in the following ways:

- You determine the number of test questions the user takes.

- The questions and answers are randomly jumbled each time the application is loaded or the test is retaken, virtually guaranteeing each user a unique test.

- You can add or subtract test questions anywhere in the question set; the application adjusts the shuffling, the administration, the grading, and the ranking.

- You can easily remove the answers from the application to prevent cheating, and forward user answers to the server-side application of your choice for grading.

You can load the application by opening *ch02/index.html* in your browser. Figure 2-1 shows the opening screen. Now who would have guessed that the test questions included here deal with JavaScript? Try the test. It is a 50-question test that most folks find challenging. Questions cover many JavaScript issues: core JavaScript, client-side and server-side JavaScript, LiveConnect, known bugs, and more. It isn't easy, but it is fun. (I have documentation that supports all the test questions and answers. Nonetheless, if you think one or more of the questions are inaccurate, send me email.)

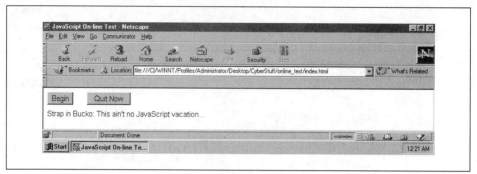

Figure 2-1. Are you ready for this?

Once you begin the test, you'll see that each question offers four possible answers. As soon as you make your choice, the application auto-advances to the next question. You can't go back to change your answers. Each question is a one-time deal. Figure 2-2 shows the question-answer format.

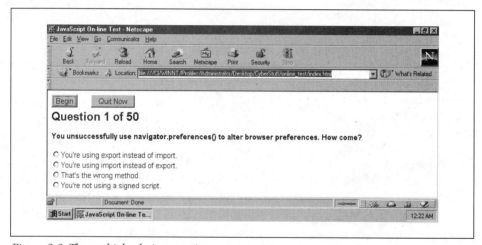

Figure 2-2. The multiple-choice questions

When you answer the last test question, your choices are compared with the answers; your performance, ranked; and the results, displayed. Figure 2-3 shows the results. Notice how each question and its accompanying four choices are written to the screen along with the answer you selected. If you answered correctly, your text is green. Otherwise, you get the shameful red text.

To better understand the questions that he or she missed, the user can view an explanation of the question choices by passing the mouse pointer arrow over the red text of any incorrect question. Notice the text explanation at the top right of the screen in Figure 2-4.

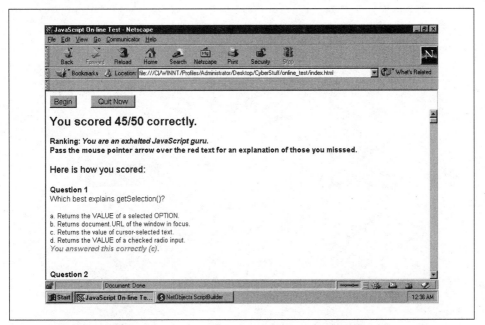

Figure 2-3. Test results

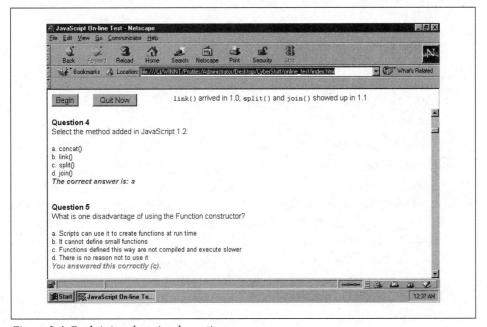

Figure 2-4. Explaining the missed questions

OK. That's the application at first pass. Indeed, it seems fairly straightforward, but
the diagram in Figure 2-5 will give you a better idea of the application flow from

the user perspective. Dashed lines indicate optional user action or waiting-for-user action status. Follow along with the following five-step process.

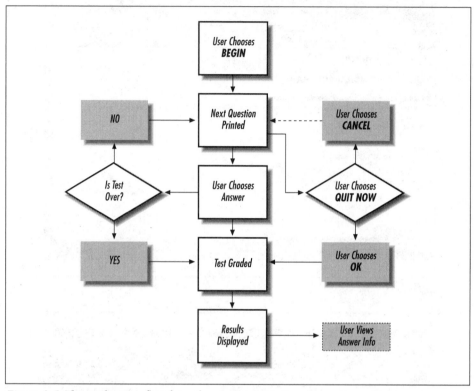

Figure 2-5. The application flow from the user's perspective

Here is the process:

1. The user chooses the "Begin" button. This action writes the first question and waits for the user to select an answer or choose the "Quit Now" button.

2. If the user selects an answer, the application records that selection, then decides whether the test has ended or to print another question. If the test is finished (the user has answered the last question), it's on to step 4 (grading the test). Otherwise, the next question is printed.

3. If the user, however, chooses "Quit Now", he or she is prompted to confirm that choice. Should the user choose "OK", the test is graded (though prematurely) in step 4. Should the user choose "Cancel" instead, the application resumes the test.

4. When the test is over (or aborted), the user's choices are compared with the correct answers, and then the results are printed to the screen.

5. As the user scans the results display, he or she can pass the mouse pointer arrow over any of the red text (indicating an incorrectly answered question) for more information about the question content.

Execution Requirements

This is all JavaScript 1.1, so Navigator 3.x and up and MSIE 4.x and up fit the bill. As far as scalability goes, there are currently 75 test questions in the application. I stopped testing after 400 questions. Since no one will probably use this to administer a bar exam or the SAT, I felt 400 was plenty.

The Syntax Breakdown

Figure 2-5 shows a flowchart indicating how the user proceeds through the application from beginning to end. A good way to understand what is really happening here is to start with a more comprehensive flowchart that deals with the JavaScript flow, and then examine the files and supporting code from there.

Figure 2-6 illustrates the JavaScript flow. Dashed-line boxes indicate processes that occur before or after the test (such as during the loading of the pages). Dashed-line arrows indicate optional user action or a return to a waiting-for-user action status. The function associated with each process is listed in italics.

Associated functions are italicized. Compare the chart in Figure 2-5 with the one in Figure 2-6, and you'll catch on quickly. You basically have the same flow, except that there is a bit going on before and after the user takes the test.

index.html—The Frameset

This application has three files: *index.html*, *administer.html*, and *questions.js*. Since *index.html* is the frameset, let's start there. Example 2-1 leads the way.

Example 2-1. The index.html Source Code

```
 1 <HTML>
 2 <HEAD>
 3 <TITLE>JavaScript On-line Test</TITLE>
 4 <SCRIPT LANGUAGE="JavaScript1.1">
 5 <!--
 6 var dummy1 = '<HTML><BODY BGCOLOR=WHITE></BODY></HTML>';
 7 var dummy2 = '<HTML><BODY BGCOLOR=WHITE><FONT FACE=Arial>' +
 8   'Strap in Bucko: This ain\'t no JavaScript vacation...</BODY></HTML>';
 9 //-->
10 </SCRIPT>
11 </HEAD>
12 <FRAMESET ROWS="90,*" FRAMEBORDER=0 BORDER=0>
13   <FRAMESET COLS="250,*">
```

Example 2-1. The index.html Source Code (continued)

```
14      <FRAME SRC="administer.html" SCROLLING=NO>
15      <FRAME SRC="javascript: self.dummy1">
16    </FRAMESET>
17    <FRAME NAME="questions" SRC="javascript: self.dummy2">
18  </FRAMESET>
19  </HTML>
```

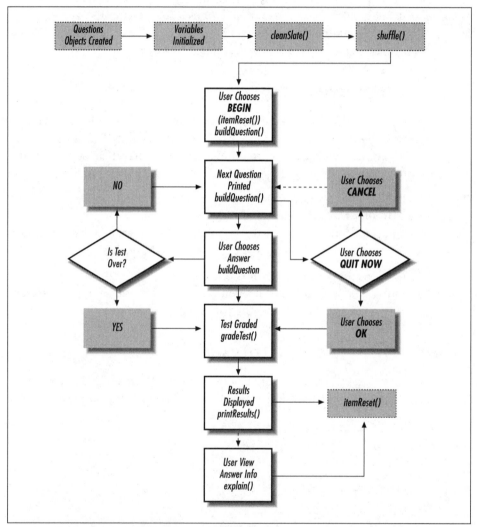

Figure 2-6. The JavaScript flow

As you probably noticed, this isn't your average run-of-the-web frameset. First of all, it's nested. That is, a frameset within a frameset. The outer frameset in line 12 defines two rows—the first 90 pixels high, and the second filling the rest of the available window height.

The 90-pixel frame also contains a frameset; this one declares two columns—the first 250 pixels wide and the second filling the remaining available window width. Figure 2-7 shows how the parent window is divided among frames. The SRC attribute of each frame is also listed.

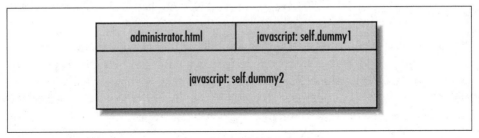

Figure 2-7. The nested frameset layout of index.html

administer.html makes sense as a SRC for a FRAME tag, but what about the other two? The two dummy variables implicitly define HTML pages. That means *dummy1* and *dummy2* represent HTML pages with no filename. Each exists only within the realm of the application. The dummy variables are defined in lines 7 and 8. Notice that each contains a small amount of HTML. Not much, but it will work. *index.html* uses the `javascript:` protocol to evaluate the expressions contained in *dummy1* and *dummy2*, then returns each as the content of a URL for the SRC attribute. Check out the "JavaScript Technique: Cheating the SRC Attribute" sidebar for more info.

The frameset is now in place. You have filled three frames using only one HTML page (*administer.html*). Talk about economy.

questions.js—The JavaScript Source File

Let's continue with *questions.js*, the JavaScript source file called by *administer. html*, shown in Example 2-2.

Example 2-2. The Beginning of the questions.js Source Code

```
 1 function question(answer, support, question, a, b, c, d) {
 2   this.answer = answer;
 3   this.support = support;
 4   this.question = question;
 5   this.a = a;
 6   this.b = b;
 7   this.c = c;
 8   this.d = d;
 9   return this;
10   }
11 var units = new Array(
12   new question("a", "The others are external objects.",
13   "Choose the built-in JavaScript object:",   "Image", "mimeType",
14   "Password", "Area"),
```

Example 2-2. The Beginning of the questions.js Source Code (continued)

```
15 // and so on ...
16  }
```

This is, of course, an abbreviated version of the file. Array *units* is much longer (75 elements in all), but this shows you that each element of *units* is a question object as defined in function `question()` in lines 1-10.

This application is based on user-defined JavaScript objects (objects that you and I declare). If the concept of JavaScript objects seems obscure, check Netscape's documentation at *http://developer.netscape.com/docs/manuals/communicator/jsguide4/ model.htm*. It will help you better understand the JavaScript Object Model. In the meantime, use the next few paragraphs as a crash course.

An object is a set of structured data. Each object can own or have associated with it two types of entities—properties and methods. Properties *have* something, such as the number 6, the expression a * b, or the string "Jimmy." Methods *do* something, such as calculate the circumference of a circle or change the color of your document background. Consider the JavaScript *document* object. Each document has things (*document.bgColor, document.fgColor*, etc.) and does things (*document. open(), document.write(), document.close()*). Properties *have*. Methods *do*.

JavaScript Technique: Cheating the SRC Attribute

Setting the SRC attribute equal to a JavaScript evaluation might seem a bit confusing. Let's back up. Suppose you open your text editor and copy the following code into a fresh clean text file:

```
<BODY BGCOLOR=WHITE>
<FONT FACE=Arial>
Better strap in, Bucko. This ain't no JavaScript vacation...
</FONT>
</BODY>
```

Then you name that file *bucko.html* and load it in your browser. You'll no doubt know what to expect. What's happening in *index.html* is basically the same thing, except variable *dummy2* has been set to the same text above, and the `javascript:` protocol evaluates *dummy2*. The SRC attribute at line 20 is set equal to the `javascript:` protocol evaluation; in this case, the value of *dummy2*. For more about the `javascript:` protocol, see the "JavaScript Technique: The javascript: Protocol" sidebar later in this chapter.

What you have is an anonymous HTML page. I call this technique cheating the SRC. We'll get some serious mileage out of it later in the chapter.

You can create objects by first creating a constructor function, like so:

```
function myFirstConstructor(arg1, arg2, argn) {
    this.property1 = arg1;
    this.property2 = arg2;
    this.propertyn = argn;
    return this;
    }
```

This looks similar to just about any function you might create, except that it utilizes the **this** keyword to refer to itself. Any arguments you pass in can be assigned to properties or manipulated in other ways. Once you have your constructor, you need only instantiate variables with the new operator:

```
var myFirstObject    = new myFirstConstructor(6, a*b, "Jimmy"),
var mySecondObject   = new myFirstConstructor(6, a*b, "Jimmy"),
var myThirdObject    = new myFirstConstructor(6, a*b, "Jimmy"),
```

For our script, object implementation is that easy. The objects we create, instances of the constructor function **question()**, have only properties. Lines 2–8 identify seven properties of each **question()**: an answer, an explanation, a question (the text), and four multiple-choice possibilities: a, b, c, and d. Here are lines 1–10:

```
function question(answer, support, question, a, b, c, d) {
    this.answer = answer;
    this.support = support;
    this.question = question;
    this.a = a;
    this.b = b;
    this.c = c;
    this.d = d;
    return this;
    }
```

Properties and methods are assigned to objects by using the **this** notation. So, each element of *units* uses the **new** operator to create a new instance of **question()**, which is passed the seven parameters that will be assigned to the properties. Line 9 uses the following syntax:

```
    return this;
```

That line returns a reference to the instantiated variable (in our case, each of the **units** elements). Think of it as sealing the deal to make things official. Now each element in *units* is a **question**. This is a convenient way of creating, deleting and otherwise managing questions for the test. You can add questions at will by using the same syntax as the other *units* elements:

```
new question("your_answer_letter", "your_explanation",
    "your_question_text", "option_a", "option_b", "option_c", "option_d");
```

In case you're wondering, I put the answer as the first argument of the function because it seems easier to have the one-character string at the front of the argument list instead of the back. Some of those questions are pretty long. It just makes it easier to find and change.

Creating a question object for each question might seem unnecessary, but it makes life considerably easier when it comes time to work with the data in each question's properties. We'll get into that when we examine *administer.html.*

 If you don't use JavaScript objects in your applications, consider changing your style. Objects have significant advantages. They tend to make your code more elegant and manageable. Objects also have the advantage of inheritance, the transfer of properties from an original object to another object that is constructed from the original object. You can download a PDF file or read the documentation about JavaScript and object inheritance online at *http://developer. netscape.com:80/docs/manuals/communicator/jsobj/contents.htm.*

administer.html

The objects are now in place. Let's put them to work for us. This is another application where the JavaScript brains reside in the upper frame, and the lower frame is used for interaction. You can break down the application into a series of processes. Table 2-1 lists and describes these processes and includes the JavaScript variables and functions associated with each.

Table 2-1. Test Processes and Associated JavaScript Functions

Process	Description	Associated JavaScript
Setting the environment	Declare and initialize global variables, shuffle the question-answer sets.	variables `qIdx`, `correct`, `howMany`, `stopOK`, `nextQ`, `results`, `aFrame`, `qFrame` arrays `keeper`, `rank`, `questions`, `answers` functions `itemReset()`, `shuffle()`
Administering the test	Write each question-answer set to the window, record each user choice.	functions `buildQuestion()`, `makeButton()`, possibly `chickenOut()`
Grading the test	Compare student answers with correct answers.	function `gradeTest()`
Printing out results	Print out all answers, right and wrong, to the window along with a ranking.	function `printResults()`
Displaying explanations	Printing and clearing explanations to `parent.frame[1]`.	functions `explain()` and `show()`.

Table 2-1. Test Processes and Associated JavaScript Functions (continued)

Process	Description	Associated JavaScript
Resetting the environment	Set all necessary variables to their original values.	variables `qIdx`, `correct`, `stopOK` array `keeper` functions `cleanSlate()`, `shuffle()`

We'll look at each of these in a moment. For now, check out the code for *administer.html* in Example 2-3.

Example 2-3. The administer.html Source Code

```
 1 <HTML>
 2 <HEAD><TITLE>On-line JavaScript Test</TITLE>
 3 <SCRIPT LANGUAGE="JavaScript1.1" SRC="questions.js"></SCRIPT>
 4 <SCRIPT LANGUAGE="JavaScript1.1">
 5 var qIdx     = 0;
 6 var correct  = 0;
 7 var howMany  = 50;
 8 var keeper   = new Array();
 9 var rank     = new Array('No offense, but you need help.',
10    'Ummm... Well... Few have done worse.',
11    'Ehhh... You know some. Keep at it.',
12    'You seem to have a working knowledge.',
13    'Better than the average bear.','You are an adequate JavaScripter.',
14    'You are a formidable JavaScripter.',
15    'You are an excellent JavaScripter.',
16    'You are an exhalted JavaScript guru.'
17    );
18 var stopOK = false;
19 var nextQ     = '';
20 var results   = '';
21 var aFrame = parent.frames[1];
22 var qFrame = parent.frames[2];
23 function shuffle() {
24    for (var i = 0; i < units.length; i++) {
25      var j = Math.floor(Math.random() * units.length);
26      var tempUnit = units[i];
27      units[i] = units[j];
28      units[j] = tempUnit;
29      }
30    }
31 function itemReset() {
32    qIdx    = 0;
33    correct    = 0;
34    stopOK    = false;
35    keeper    = new Array();
36    shuffle();
37    }
38 function buildQuestion() {
39    if (qIdx == howMany) {
40      gradeTest();
41      return;
42      }
```

Example 2-3. The administer.html Source Code (continued)

```
43    nextQ = '<HTML><BODY BGCOLOR=WHITE><FONT FACE=Arial>' +
44    '<H2>Question ' + (qIdx + 1) + ' of ' + howMany + '</H2>' +
45    '<FORM>' + '<B>' + units[qIdx].question + '</B><BR><BR>' +
46    makeButton("a", units[qIdx].a) +
47    makeButton("b", units[qIdx].b) +
48    makeButton("c", units[qIdx].c) +
49    makeButton("d", units[qIdx].d) +
50    '</FORM></BODY></HTML>';
51    qFrame.location.replace("javascript: parent.frames[0].nextQ");
52    qIdx++;
53    if(qIdx >= 2 && !stopOK) { stopOK = true; }
54    }
55 function makeButton(optLtr, optAnswer) {
56    return   '<INPUT TYPE=RADIO NAME="answer" VALUE="' + optLtr +
57      '" onClick="parent.frames[0].keeper[parent.frames[0].qIdx - 1] =
58      this.value; parent.frames[0].buildQuestion()">' + optAnswer + '<BR>';
59    }
60 function chickenOut() {
61    if(stopOK && confirm('Stopping early? Are you really a ' +
62      'JavaScript Chicken?')) {
63      gradeTest();
64      }
65    }
66 function gradeTest() {
67    for (var i = 0; i < qIdx; i++) {
68      if (keeper[i] == units[i].answer) {
69        correct++;
70        }
71      }
72    var idx = Math.ceil((correct/howMany) * rank.length - 1) < 0 ? 0 :
73      Math.ceil((correct/howMany) * rank.length - 1);
74    printResults(rank[idx]);
75    itemReset();
76    }
77 function printResults(ranking) {
78    results = '<HTML><BODY BGCOLOR=WHITE LINK=RED VLINK=RED ALINK=RED>' +
79      '<FONT FACE=Arial>' +
80      '<H2>You scored ' + correct + '/' + howMany + ' correctly.</H2>' +
81      '<B>Ranking: <I>' + ranking +
82      '</I><BR>Pass the mouse over the red text for an explanation of ' +
83      'those you misssed.</B>' +
84    '<BR><BR><FONT SIZE=4>Here is how you scored: </FONT><BR><BR>';
85    for (var i = 0; i < howMany; i++) {
86      results += '\n\r\n\r\n\r<B>Question ' + (i + 1) + '</B><BR>' +
87        units[i].question + '<BR><BR>\n\r<FONT SIZE=-1>' +
88        'a. ' + units[i].a + '<BR>' +
89        'b. ' + units[i].b + '<BR>' +
90        'c. ' + units[i].c + '<BR>' +
91        'd. ' + units[i].d + '<BR></FONT>';
92      if (keeper[i] == units[i].answer) {
93        results += '<B><I><FONT COLOR=GREEN>' +
94          'You answered this correctly (' + keeper[i] + '). ' +
95          '</FONT></I></B>\n\r<BR><BR><BR>';
```

Example 2-3. The administer.html Source Code (continued)

```
 96        }
 97     else {
 98       results += '<FONT FACE=Arial><B><I>' + '
 99         '<A HREF=" " onMouseOver="parent.frames[0].show();' +
100         parent.frames[0].explain(\'' + units[i].support + '\'); ' +
101         'return true" onMouseOut="parent.frames[0].explain(\' \');"' +
102         'onClick="return false;">' +
103         'The correct answer is: ' + units[i].answer +
104         '</A></FONT></I></B>\n\r<BR><BR><BR>';
105       }
106     }
107   results += '\n\r</BODY></HTML>';
108   qFrame.location.replace("javascript: parent.frames[0].results");
109   }
110 function show() { parent.status = ''; }
111 function explain(str) {
112   with (aFrame.document) {
113     open();
114     writeln('<HTML><BODY BGCOLOR=WHITE><FONT FACE=Arial>' + str +
115       '</FONT></BODY></HTML>');
116     close();
117     }
118   }
119 function cleanSlate() {
120   aFrame.location.replace('javascript: parent.dummy1');
121   qFrame.location.replace('javascript: parent.dummy2');
122   }
123 </SCRIPT>
124 </HEAD>
125 <BODY BGCOLOR=WHITE onLoad="cleanSlate();">
126 <FONT FACE="Arial">
127   <FORM>
128   <INPUT TYPE=BUTTON VALUE="Begin"
129     onclick="itemReset(); buildQuestion();">
130        
131   <INPUT TYPE=BUTTON VALUE="Quit Now" onclick="chickenOut();">
132   </FORM>
133 </FONT>
134 </BODY>
135 </HTML>
```

This long file can be broken into four sections. First the source file *questions.js* is called. Next some of global variables are defined. Then come the functions. Finally, we have a few lines of HTML. Let's look at the HTML first, since it is short and sweet.

HTML Body

When *administer.html* finishes loading, function **cleanSlate()** is called at line 125:

```
<BODY BGCOLOR=WHITE onLoad="cleanSlate();">
```

`cleanSlate()` uses the `replace()` method of the location object to replace the current URLs of `parent.frames[1]` (alias `aFrame`) and `parent.frames[2]` (alias `qFrame`) with the contents of the value of the *dummy1* and *dummy2* variables defined earlier in *index.html*. See lines 119–122:

```
function cleanSlate() {
    aFrame.location.replace('javascript: parent.dummy1');
    qFrame.location.replace('javascript: parent.dummy2');
    }
```

We just did that in *index.html*, right? Indeed, we did. This, however, ensures that if the user reloads *administer.html* for any reason, the top right frame will always begin as a blank white page, that the bottom frame will always start with the opening "bucko" message, and that the previous contents of the page, perhaps a test question, won't be accessible any longer and possibly run things awry.

The rest of the HTML is simply a form with two buttons. This part won't take long. *administer.html* has a form with two buttons. Each button has calls to different functions when clicked. Here is the code at lines 127–132:

```
<FORM>
  <INPUT TYPE=BUTTON VALUE="Begin"
    onclick="itemReset(); buildQuestion();">
       
  <INPUT TYPE=BUTTON VALUE="Quit Now" onclick="chickenOut();">
</FORM>
```

Notice that the "Begin" button calls `itemReset()` and `buildQuestion()`, and the "Quit Now" button calls `chickenOut()`. We'll get to all three functions in the "Functions" section.

Global Variables

Just after the code to embed the JavaScript source file *questions.js* at line 4, you'll see the global variables used in this application. Here they are in lines 5–22:

```
var qIdx     = 0;
var correct  = 0;
var howMany  = 50;
var keeper   = new Array();
var rank     = new Array('No offense, but you need help.',
     'Ummm... Well... Few have done worse.',
     'Ehhh... You know some. Keep at it.',
     'You seem to have a working knowledge.',
     'Better than the average bear.',
     'You are an adequate JavaScripter.',
     'You are a formidable JavaScripter.',
     'You are an excellent JavaScripter.',
     'You are an exhalted JavaScript guru.'
     );
var stopOK = false;
var nextQ    = '';
```

```
var results    = '';
var aFrame = parent.frames[1];
var qFrame = parent.frames[2];
```

The following list describes the function of each global variable. We'll have a closer look at them in the function discussion.

qIdx

A variable used to monitor the current question that is displayed on the screen

correct

A variable used to track the number of correct answers while the test is graded

howMany

A static number you set to determine how many questions you want the user to answer (out of the number available in the *units* array)

keeper

An initially empty array that holds the user's answer choices

rank

An array of strings indicating various levels of performance

stopOK

A variable containing a Boolean value indicating whether to permit stopping the test early

nextQ

An empty string repeatedly set to the value of the HTML that represents each test question

results

An empty string later set to the value of the HTML that represents the test results

aFrame

An easy reference to the second frame

qFrame

A easy reference to the third frame

Functions

Next we come to the functions. We start with `itemReset()`.

itemReset()

The first of our functions to get the call in this application is `itemReset()`. It happens when the user chooses the "Begin" button (lines 128–129):

```
<INPUT TYPE=BUTTON VALUE="Begin"
onclick="itemReset(); buildQuestion();">
```

`itemReset()` sets the values of the global variables to their original values and shuffles the question object array elements (more on shuffling shortly). Have a look at lines 31–37:

```
function itemReset() {
  qIdx      = 0;
  correct   = 0;
  stopOK    = false;
  keeper    = new Array();
  shuffle();
}
```

Note that the user hasn't even seen the first question, and JavaScript is already hard at work resetting the global variables. Why? Well, suppose you've already taken the test, and you only got two questions right. You might choose the "Begin" button to retake the test. After the first test, however, many global variables no longer have their original values. `itemReset()` takes care of that and gives you fresh new values.

Notice that variable *howMany* is not included. Its value stays the same for the duration of the application. Variables *nextQ* and *results* originally start as empty strings, but their values are not reset. There is no need. Check lines 43 and 86, respectively, and you'll see that these variables are set on the fly.

With the variables properly set, how about the call to `shuffle()` at line 36?

shuffle()

This little function gives the test administrator a lot of flexibility. This function randomly orders the questions, almost guaranteeing each test taker a unique version. Just to give you an idea of the possibilities, consider that the number of possible combinations (different orders) of test questions is $n(n - 1)$, where n is the number of questions. So a measly 10-question test has 10 (10 – 1) or 90 possible combinations. A 20-question test has 380 possible arrangements. This 50-question test has a significant 2,450 combinations. That could be a cheater's worst nightmare.

The test is also made unique because though the *units* array has 75 questions available, variable *howMany* is set to 50. When the shuffling is finished, the test uses the first 50. Since there are 75, there is a strong possibility that users will not receive the same 50 questions. Therefore, this test gives you thousands of combinations of different test questions. Amazingly, the shuffle process is pretty easy.

Here are lines 23–30:

```
function shuffle() {
  for (var i = 0; i < units.length; i++) {
    var j = Math.floor(Math.random() * units.length);
    var tempUnit = units[i];
```

```
        units[i] = units[j];
        units[j] = tempUnit;
        }
    }
```

For each element in the *units* array:

1. Pick a random integer between 0 and `units.length - 1`.

2. Set the value of local variable *tempUnit* equal to the element of the current index (`units[i]`).

3. Set the value of the element of the current index (`units[i]`) to the value of the element of the random integer index (`units[j]`).

4. Set the value of the element of the random integer index to the value of local variable *tempUnit*.

In other words, systematically iterate through all elements of the array, and swap each value for the value of another randomly chosen element, then set the value of the randomly chosen element to the value of the currently counted array element.

The questions are jumbled in random fashion and now awaiting the user.

buildQuestion()

This function acts as the test administrator. As you probably noticed in the last flowchart, `buildQuestion()` is mentioned in several places. It has a lot of responsibility. Here it is starting at line 38 and ending at line 54:

```
function buildQuestion() {
   if (qIdx == howMany) {
     gradeTest();
     return;
     }
   nextQ = '<HTML><BODY BGCOLOR=WHITE><FONT FACE=Arial>' +
   '<H2>Question ' + (qIdx + 1) + ' of ' + howMany + '</H2>' +
   '<FORM>' + '<B>' + units[qIdx].question + '</B><BR><BR>' +
   makeButton("a", units[qIdx].a) +
   makeButton("b", units[qIdx].b) +
   makeButton("c", units[qIdx].c) +
   makeButton("d", units[qIdx].d) +
   '</FORM></BODY></HTML>';
   qFrame.location.replace("javascript: parent.frames[0].nextQ");
   qIdx++;
   if(qIdx >= 2 && !stopOK) { stopOK = true; }
   }
```

From the top, `buildQuestion()` checks to see if variable *qIdx* is equal to variable *howMany*. If so, the user has just answered the last question, and it is time for grading. Function `gradeTest()` is called at line 40.

JavaScript Technique: Shuffling and Array Manipulation

This test rearranges the array elements in random order. That is the desired effect for this application, but other, more controlled shuffling schemas aren't that hard to write either. The following function accepts a copy of an array object to shuffle and an integer indicating the multiple by which you want to shuffle:

```
function shakeUp(formObj, stepUp) {
  stepUp = (Math.abs(parseInt(stepUp)) > 0 ?
    Math.abs(parseInt(stepUp)) : 1);
  var nextRound = 1;
  var idx = 0;
  var tempArray = new Array();
  for (var i = 0; i < formObj.length; i++) {
    tempArray[i] = formObj[idx];
    if (idx + stepUp >= formObj.length) {
      idx = nextRound;
      nextRound++;
      }
    else {
      idx += stepUp;
      }
    }
  formObj = tempArray;
  }
```

For example, if your array has 10 elements, and you want them sorted by multiples of 2 (elements 0, 2, 4, 6, 8, then 1, 3, 5, 7, 9), then you call **shakeUp(yourArrayObj, 2)**. If you pass 0, the increment defaults to 1. You'll find more functions like these in Chapter 6, *Implementing JavaScript Source Files*.

If the test is not over, **buildQuestion()** proceeds to—you guessed it—build the next question by generating a string that represents an entire HTML page. This happens in lines 43 through 50. If you examine *nextQ*, you'll see that the forthcoming HTML page contains a question number indicator and the total number of test questions. That is line 44:

```
'<H2>Question ' + (qIdx + 1) + ' of ' + howMany + '</H2>'
```

Next you'll see an opening **FORM** tag followed by question text. The question text, if you'll recall, is stored in the *question* property of each *units* element. It's no surprise, then, to see line 45 like so:

```
'<FORM>' + '<B>' + units[qIdx].question
```

And where there is a FORM tag, form elements aren't too far behind. Actually, that is all that remains in the making of the HTML page. This form has only four elements, each a radio button. Rather than hardcoding the HTML within the function to write the radio buttons (which are almost identical), function makeButton() generates them. You need only pass the choice letter and the choice text, which are provided in each call in lines 46 through 49. Here is function makeButton() in lines 55–59:

```
function makeButton(optLtr, optAnswer) {
    return  '<INPUT TYPE=RADIO NAME="answer" VALUE="' + optLtr +
    '" onClick="parent.frames[0].keeper[parent.frames[0].qIdx - 1] =
    this.value; parent.frames[0].buildQuestion()">' + optAnswer + '<BR>';
    }
```

This function simply returns a string representing a radio button with a custom-set VALUE attribute—equal to a, b, c, or d—and the choice answer printed immediately to the right. The VALUE attribute comes from *optLtr*, and the choice text comes from *optAnswer*.

Keep in mind that this test is user-driven, so it auto-advances as soon as the user makes a choice. In JavaScript-ese, that means a couple of things happen by associating expressions with the *onClick* event handler in each radio button.

The first thing that happens is that the array *keeper* stores the letter associated with the user's answer. To determine which element to assign to the current user choice, we use:

```
parent.frames[0].qIdx - 1
```

Variable *qIdx* keeps track of the current question count, so it is perfect for helping assign the next element to the current user choice.

The next thing that happens is for JavaScript to call buildQuestion() to print the next question, or grade the test if it is finished. Notice that both *keeper* and buildQuestion() are referred to starting from parent.frames[0]. Since this information will be written to parent.frames[1], we need to access them from the upper frame.

With the form properly built, all that remains (as far as the HTML is concerned) is to close the tags and load the content into the window. See lines 50–51:

```
'</FORM></BODY></HTML>';
    qFrame.location.replace("javascript: parent.frames[0].nextQ");
```

This loads the value of *nextQ* into the bottom frame. Notice that the application uses the replace() method of the location object, instead of setting the location.href property or even using document.write() to print the test questions to the page. In this application, that makes an important difference. replace() loads the specified URL into the browser (in our case, the URL is a string of HTML evaluated by the `javascript:` protocol), but replaces the current page in the history. This prevents users from going back to view previous questions or change previous answers. If a user chooses the "Back" button, the browser loads the page loaded prior to *index.html.*

The last thing to do before leaving `buildQuestion()` is take care of a little housecleaning at lines 52–53.

```
qIdx++;
if(qIdx >= 2 && !stopOK) { stopOK = true; }
```

Incrementing *qIdx* by 1 sets things up for the next call to `buildQuestion()`. Remember in line 39 that if *qIdx* is greater than the number of questions on the test (in variable *howMany*), then it is time for grading. The *if* statement at line 53 determines whether the user is eligible to stop the test. The current code requires that the user answer at least one question before being allowed to end the test early by choosing the "Quit Now" button. Adjust it to your fancy.

JavaScript Technique: The javascript: Protocol

You've seen it a lot so far in this book; you can count on seeing it more. The `javascript:` protocol allows JavaScript to evaluate any expressions following it. It has multiple uses. For example, if you want something to happen other than loading a new page into the browser after a user clicks on a link, use it in the `HREF` attribute of the `<A>` tag:

```
<A HREF="javascript: alert('You found the alert dialog!');">Click me</A>
```

You can also set `SRC` attributes of other HTML tags. See "JavaScript Technique: Cheating the SRC Attribute" earlier in this chapter for details.

One word of caution: If you use the protocol within a JavaScript function you defined, don't try to use it to evaluate variables local to the function. It won't work. The `javascript:` protocol maintains a global scope, and therefore can only "see" and access global variables, global objects, and the like. Line 51 is a classic example:

```
qFrame.location.replace("javascript: parent.frames[0].nextQ");
```

The variable *nextQ* could well have been defined locally. After all, it is only used with `buildQuestion()`. However, since line 55 uses the `javascript:` protocol, the following won't work:

```
qFrame.location.replace("javascript: nextQ");
```

If *nextQ* is local, `javascript:` won't be able to evaluate it.

gradeTest()

`gradeTest()` performs two functions. First it compares the user's answers to the correct answers, keeping a running tab of correct user choices. Second, `gradeTest()` calculates a ranking index and response based on the number of correct user answers. Here is `gradeTest()` in its entirety, lines 66–76:

```
function gradeTest() {
  for (var i = 0; i < qIdx; i++) {
    if (keeper[i] == units[i].answer) {
      correct++;
      }
    }
  var idx = Math.ceil((correct/howMany) * (rank.length - 1)) < 0 ? 0 :
    Math.ceil((correct/howMany) * (rank.length - 1));
  printResults(idx);
  itemReset();
  }
```

Array *keeper* contains each letter (a, b, c, or d) associated with the answer that the user chose for each question. Each element of the *units* array is a question object that contains an *answer* property—also a, b, c, or d. `gradeTest()` iterates through each *keeper* element and compares its value to the *answer* property of the corresponding *units* element. If there is a match, variable *correct* is incremented by 1.

Note that this function does not keep track of which answers are correct. That never actually happens in this application. The function only determines the number of correct answers and delivers a ranking based on that number. We'll pay the *keeper* array another visit when we examine `printResults()` shortly. Also note that `gradeTest()` does not iterate through *howMany* questions. It doesn't matter how many questions are on the test, only how many the user answered.

Once the results are in, the *correct* variable holds the value of how many correct answers the user gave. `gradeTest()` need only determine the user's ranking, or how well he or she did. Lines 72–73 take care of this:

```
var idx = Math.ceil((correct/howMany) * (rank.length - 1)) < 0 ? 0 :
  Math.ceil((correct/howMany) * (rank.length - 1));
```

Here's how this works. We want to assign one of the rankings from the elements in the *rank* array on line 9. To choose an element, we need an integer between 0 and `rank.length - 1`. Function `gradeTest()` chooses an integer using a three-step process:

1. Calculate the percentage of correct answers (`correct / howMany`).

2. Multiply that percentage by (`rank.length - 1`).

3. Round that product to the next highest integer.

The result of the process is set to local variable *idx*, which is an integer proportional to the user's performance between 0 and `rank.length`. In other words, no matter how many test questions there are, the user will always receive a ranking based more or less on how many he or she answer correctly. The following example should help. Suppose you have the *rank* array set as follows:

```
var rank = new Array( "I've seen better", "So-so", "Good", "Very Good"
"Excellent");
```

`rank.length` is 5, so if your test has 50 questions, the grading scale is as follows:

Questions Correct	Calculated Integer	Ranking (rank[int])
0–9	0	"I've seen better"
10–19	1	"So-so"
20–29	2	"Good"
30–39	3	"Very Good"
40–50	4	"Excellent"

There are, then, approximately `howMany` / `rank.length` answers per ranking (except the highest ranking, such as 40–50 in the previous table). Doesn't matter if it is 2 or 200 questions. It works the same.

This grade system has the advantage of being effective, but the disadvantage of being fairly crude. Grading systems are usually more complex. Most schools use something to the effect of 90% and above is an A, 80–89% is a B, 70–79% is a C, 60–69% is a D, and everything below 60% is an F. Perhaps you want to use some type of curve. See the "Potential Extensions" section in this chapter for some novel ideas.

`gradeTest()` has basically finished its job. Variable *rank[idx]* is passed to function `printResults()` for display; then `itemReset()` is called for clean up.

printResults()

The application knows how well the user performed; it is time to show the user. Function `printResults()` does so by displaying the following items:

- The number of correct answers out of the number of total questions
- The user's ranking based on the calculation passed from `gradeTest()`
- Each test question, including the four answer choices
- The user's choice if it was correct or the correct answer if not
- Linked text that allows users to view additional information about incorrectly answered questions

Lines 77 through 84 take care of the first two:

```
function printResults(ranking) {
   results = '<HTML></HEAD><BODY BGCOLOR=WHITE LINK=RED VLINK=RED ALINK=RED>'+
      '<FONT FACE=Arial>' +
      '<H2>You scored ' + correct + '/' + howMany + ' correctly.</H2>' +
      '<B>Ranking: <I>' + ranking +
      '</I><BR>Pass the mouse over the red text for an explanation of ' +
      'those you misssed.</B>' +
      '<BR><BR><FONT SIZE=4>Here is how you scored: </FONT><BR><BR>';
```

Variables *correct* and *howMany* represent the number of correct answers and total test questions, respectively, and `rank[rankIdx]` represents the string indicating user performance. As for the test question and the four corresponding choices, this happens from lines 85 through 91. It's no surprise that it happens within a *for* loop:

```
for (var i = 0; i < howMany; i++) {
   results += '<B>Question ' + (i + 1) + '</B><BR>' +
   units[i].question + '<BR><BR><FONT SIZE=-1>' +
   'a. ' + units[i].a + '<BR>' +
   'b. ' + units[i].b + '<BR>' +
   'c. ' + units[i].c + '<BR>' +
   'd. ' + units[i].d + '<BR></FONT>';
```

For every iteration from 0 through **howMany** − 1, *results* is given a string containing the question number (`i + 1`), the question text (`units[i].question`), and the corresponding four answer choices (`units[i].a`, `units[i].b`, `units[i].c`, and `units[i].d`). The surrounding HTML jazzes it up a little.

The last piece of the print-out puzzle is displaying the user's answer in green text if he or she chose wisely, or linked red text otherwise. Here are lines 92 through 106:

```
if (keeper[i] == units[i].answer) {
      results += '<B><I><FONT COLOR=GREEN>' +
      'You answered this correctly (' + keeper[i] + '). ' +
      '</FONT></I></B>\n\r<BR><BR><BR>';
   }
   else {
      results += '<FONT FACE=Arial><B><I>' + '
      '<A HREF=" " onMouseOver="parent.frames[0].show();' +
      parent.frames[0].explain(\'' + units[i].support + '\'); ' +
      'return true" onMouseOut="parent.frames[0].explain(\' \');"' +
      'onClick="return false;">' +
      'The correct answer is: ' + units[i].answer +
      '</A></FONT></I></B>\n\r<BR><BR><BR>';
   }
}
```

For each question, the user either chose the right answer or the wrong answer. It's no shock, then, to see this facilitated by an if-else statement. If **keeper[i]** equals

units[i].answer, the user chose correctly. Therefore, the green text indicates the user is correct and prints his or her answer (**keeper[i]**). If the two are not equal, the red text indicates the correct answer and offers the option to view additional information about the question in **parent.frames[1]**. This frame, which has not been used for anything significant, so far, is finally put to use.

Those questions that the user answered correctly are displayed simply as text. You can see, however, that incorrectly answered questions are displayed as linked text. The *onMouseOver* event in each link calls two functions before returning true: **show()** and **explain()**. Function **show()** is very easy. It prints an empty string to the status bar to prevent any unnecessary distractions caused by the *onMouseOver* event. Here is the code at line 110.

```
function show() { parent.status = ''; }
```

Function **explain()** accepts a string argument and utilizes the **document. write()** method to display HTML to the patiently waiting **parent.frames[1]**. Check out lines 111—118:

```
function explain(str) {
  with (aFrame.document) {
    open();
    writeln('<HTML><BODY BGCOLOR=WHITE><FONT FACE=Arial>' + str +
      '</FONT></BODY></HTML>');
    close();
    }
  }
```

Even though the *onMouseOver* event has been taken care of, **explain()** still has a little more work. Notice that **explain()** is called again in line 101 in the *onMouseOut* event handler. This time, however, function **explain()** is passed an empty string, so *aFrame* will appear to have been cleared out after each *onMouseOut* event.

The only thing left to do is prevent anything from happening if the user clicks the links used for the mouse-over capabilities. Line 102 contains **onClick="return false;"**. This cancels the loading of any document URL listed in the **HREF** attribute.

Keep in mind that this is still within the *for* loop. The above process happens for every answer from 0 through **howMany** - 1. After the *for* loop runs its course, variable *results* is one big string containing the number of correctly answered questions, the total number of test questions, all the question text and four choices, and the user's choice or the correct answer. Lines 107-109 add some closing HTML, load the string into the bottom frame, and close out the function.

```
results += '\n\r</BODY></HTML>';
  qFrame.location.replace("javascript: parent.frames[0].results");
  }
```

chickenOut()

There is that one small matter of the user quitting early. It certainly isn't necessary, and you might want to remove it from any of your implementations. I added it just to give the user a little extra functionality. Here's the code at lines 60–65:

```
function chickenOut() {
  if(stopOK && confirm('Stopping early? Are you really a ' +
    'JavaScript Chicken?')) {
    gradeTest();
    }
  }
```

If the user is eligible and confirms the desire to quit early, `gradeTest()` is called. Remember that a user becomes eligible to stop early after answering at least one question. Variable *stopOK*, originally set to **false**, is set to **true** after *qIDx* is greater than 1. See line 53.

The catch is that `gradeTest()` compares answers to all the questions, even if the user didn't answer them. This tends to do tremendous damage to the user ranking, but that's the price you pay for quitting early.

Potential Extensions

This application can be modified in a number of ways. The two obvious extensions I see, however, are making it cheat-proof by performing the grading on the server, and changing the application to administer a survey instead of a test.

Making It Cheat-Proof

One of the first things you might have thought after tinkering with the application for a while is, "Users can check the answers by downloading and opening the JavaScript source file." It would be a pain to go through each question and find the letter, but it can be done.

You can remove the "Peeping Tom" factor by simply not sending the answers with the application and requiring the user to submit his or her test results to a server for grading. We won't get into grading the test on the server, but it won't be much more involved than `gradeTest()`. Maybe a little more involved, but the principles will be the same.

To remove the grading feature and add the server-side submission feature, you'll need to do the following:

- Remove any data representing the answers from the object and array logic in *questions.js*.

- Remove `gradeTest()` and replace the call to it in `buildQuestion()` with `printResults()`.

- Modify `printResults()` so that the user can view his or her answers, and embed the answer data within an HTML form to send the waiting server.

Removing the answers from the array logic

Remove `this.answer` and `this.support` from the question constructor in *question.js*. Change this:

```
function question(answer, support, question, a, b, c, d) {
  this.answer = answer;
  this.support = support;
  this.question = question;
  this.a = a;
  this.b = b;
  this.c = c;
  this.d = d;
  return this;
  }
```

to this:

```
function question(question, a, b, c, d) {
  this.question = question;
  this.a = a;
  this.b = b;
  this.c = c;
  this.d = d;
  return this;
  }
```

Notice that variables *answer* and *support* have also been removed. Now that you have removed these from the constructor, you can remove them from each call to the *new* operator in each element of *units*. In other words, remove the first two arguments from each element in *units*.

Removing gradeTest() and modifying buildQuestion()

Since the answers and explanations no longer exist, there is no reason to grade the test or display any results. That means you can get rid of function `gradeTest()`. Just delete lines 66–76 in *administer.html*. This also means that you can get rid of the call to `gradeTest()` in `buildQuestion()` at line 40. Actually, you'll want to replace it with a call to `printResults()` so that the user can see his or her answers and the answers can be embedded in an HTML form.

Lines 39–42 are changed from this:

```
if (qIdx == howMany) {
  gradeTest();
  return;
  }
```

to this:

```
if (qIdx == howMany) {
  printResults();
  return;
  }
```

Modifying printResults()

`printResults()` is where most of the new work happens. Line 84 in *administer. html* currently looks like this:

```
'<BR><BR><FONT SIZE=4>Here is how you scored: </FONT><BR><BR>';
```

Change it to this:

```
'<BR><BR><FONT SIZE=4>Here is how you scored: </FONT><BR><BR>' +
'<FORM ACTION="your_server_script_URL" METHOD=POST>';
```

And replace lines 92–105 with the following:

```
results += '<INPUT TYPE=HIDDEN NAME="question' + (i + 1) + '" VALUE="' +
  keeper[i] + '"><B><I><FONT>COLOR=GREEN>You chose ' + keeper[i] +
  '</I></B></FONT><BR><BR><BR>';
```

That removes the decision-making portion of the function that determines whether users answered correctly and then displays the appropriate green or red text. Lastly, line 107 currently looks like this:

```
results += '\n\r</BODY></HTML>';
```

Change it to this:

```
results += '<INPUT TYPE=SUBMIT VALUE="Submit"> </FORM></BODY></HTML>';
```

Those few changes added opening and closing **FORM** tags, a uniquely named hidden field with a value of each of the user's answers, and a **SUBMIT** button. The **FORM** tags and the submit button are static, but the hidden fields involve a bit more.

Each answer is written as the value of a hidden field, which is named according to its question number. Iterative variable *i* is used to create a unique name for each hidden field and also associates the proper question number with the proper user answer. Each time variable *i* is incremented in the update portion of the *for* loop (i++), a new hidden field can be made. The fields will follow the pattern of *question1*, *question2*, *question3*, ad infinitum.

The changes in `printResults()` still display the questions, four choices, and the user's answers. The test isn't graded, however. All the user has to do is choose "Submit" to send the answers off for a grading.

Converting to a Survey

Since surveys theoretically don't have right and wrong answers, converting the application to administer a survey requires the same changes you just saw, plus one more easy one—adjusting the content. Simply change the *units* elements to reflect survey questions with multiple choice options, and you're in business. Thanks to the changes above, the user can view the results before he or she sends them in for marketing analysis.

3

The Interactive Slideshow

This application allows users to view groups of slides, in any order, or consecutively in auto-pilot mode according to a timed interval you choose. Each slide is a DHTML layer that contains an image and descriptive text. Your slides could conceivably contain almost any combination of text, graphics, DHTML, and the like. These slides give the user a fictitious tour of the wild animal kingdom. Figure 3-1 shows the opening screen.

Notice the slides in the center of the screen and the two graphics labeled "Automate" and "<Guide>" at the top left of the screen. The arrows of the "<Guide>" image (< and >) allow the user to navigate slide by slide, forward or backward in the slideshow.

Users can also move to any slide in the show by clicking "Guide." This reveals a slide menu that automatically moves the user to the desired slide by passing the cursor over the corresponding slide name. Clicking "Guide" once again conceals the slide menu. Figure 3-2 shows the slide menu.

In the two previous chapters, the applications follow a beginning-to-end process. That is, the user always starts at the same place (say, entering search text or answering question one) and ends at the same place (say, a page of matching search results or getting test results after answering the last question). The slide-show is different. Users can jump in almost anywhere and take advantage of the

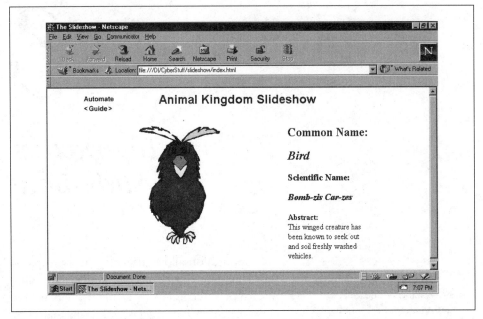

Figure 3-1. The opening slide

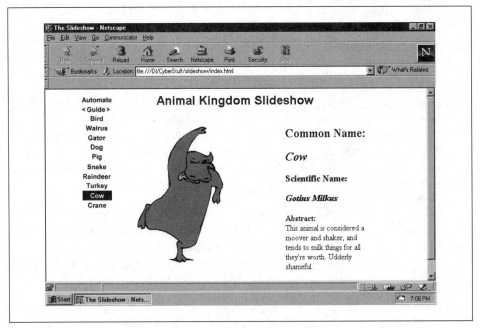

Figure 3-2. The highlighted name indicates the slide currently in view

application features. Therefore, it is better to describe the application code in terms of its features instead of describing the code from top to bottom. That's exactly how we'll go through it in this chapter.

Execution Requirements

The moment you utter the "D" in DHTML, you can bet that you're talking about MSIE 4.x and Navigator 4.x and up. It's the same story here. All the slides are DHTML-based entities. As far as scalability, there's no reason why you couldn't fit hundreds of slides into your online presentation. However, this application pre-loads *all* the images (except for two small ones), so I doubt you want to spend your time preloading hundreds of images.

The Syntax Breakdown

The script is included in one file, *index.html*. You'll find it in your zip file at *ch03/index.html*. Example 3-1 has the code.

Example 3-1. index.html

```
 1 <HTML>
 2 <HEAD>
 3 <TITLE>The Slideshow</TITLE>
 4
 5 <STYLE TYPE="text/css">
 6 #menuConstraint { height: 800; }
 7 </STYLE>
 8
 9 <SCRIPT LANGUAGE="JavaScript1.2">
10 <!--
11 var dWidLyr  = 450;
12 var dHgtLyr  = 450;
13 var curSlide = 0;
14 var zIdx        = -1;
15 var isVis       = false;
16
17 var NN      = (document.layers ? true : false);
18 var sWidPos = ((NN ? innerWidth  : screen.availWidth)  / 2) -
19    (dWidLyr / 2);
20 var sHgtPos = ((NN ? innerHeight : screen.availHeight) / 2) -
21    (dHgtLyr / 2);
22 var hideName = (NN ? 'hide' : 'hidden');
23 var showName = (NN ? 'show' : 'visible');
24
25 var img = new Array();
26 var imgOut = new Array();
27 var imgOver = new Array();
28 var imgPath = 'images/';
29
```

Example 3-1. index.html (continued)

```
30 var showSpeed = 3500;
31 var tourOn = false;
32
33 function genLayer(sName, sLeft, sTop, sWdh, sHgt, sVis, copy) {
34   if (NN) {
35     document.writeln('<LAYER NAME="' + sName + '" LEFT=' + sLeft +
36       ' TOP=' + sTop + ' WIDTH=' + sWdh + ' HEIGHT=' + sHgt +
37       ' VISIBILITY="' + sVis + '"' + ' Z-INDEX=' + (++zIdx)  + '>' +
38       copy + '</LAYER>');
39     }
40   else {
41     document.writeln('<DIV ID="' + sName +
42       '" STYLE="position:absolute; overflow:none;left:' + sLeft +
43       'px; top:' + sTop + 'px; width:' + sWdh + 'px; height:' + sHgt +
44       'px;' + ' visibility:' + sVis + '; z-Index=' + (++zIdx) + '">' +
45       copy + '</DIV>');
46     }
47   }
48
49 function slide(imgStr, scientific, copy) {
50   this.name    = imgStr;
51   imagePreLoad(imgStr);
52   this.copy    = copy;
53   this.structure =
54     '<TABLE WIDTH=500 CELLPADDING=10><TR><TD WIDTH=60% VALIGN=TOP>' +
55     '<IMG SRC=' + imgPath + imgStr + '.gif></TD>' +
56     '<TD WIDTH=40% VALIGN=TOP><H2>Common Name:</H2><H2><I>' +
57     camelCap(imgStr) + '</I></H2><H3>Scientific Name: </H3><H3><I>' +
58     scientific + '</I></H3>' + '<B>Abstract:</B><BR>' + copy +
59     '</TD></TR></TABLE>';
60
61   return this;
62   }
63
64 function imagePreLoad(imgStr) {
65   img[img.length]  = new Image();
66   img[img.length - 1].src = imgPath + imgStr + '.gif';
67
68   imgOut[imgOut.length] = new Image();
69   imgOut[imgOut.length - 1].src = imgPath + imgStr + 'out.gif';
70
71   imgOver[imgOver.length] = new Image();
72   imgOver[imgOver.length - 1].src = imgPath + imgStr + 'over.gif';
73   }
74
75 var slideShow  = new Array(
76   new slide('bird', 'Bomb-zis Car-zes', 'This winged creature has been
77     known to seek out and soil freshly-washed vehicles.'),
78   new slide('walrus', 'Verius Clueless', 'These big fellas good fishers,
79     but toothbrushing is another story.'),
80   new slide('gator', 'Couldbeus Luggajus', 'These reptiles often play
81     mascots for large college sporting events.'),
```

Example 3-1. index.html (continued)

```
82   new slide('dog', 'Makus Messus', 'Man\'s best friend? Yeah, right.
83     No wonder these mammals get a bad rep.'),
84   new slide('pig', 'Oinkus Lotsus', 'Humans with questionable eating
85     habits are often compared to these farm creatures.'),
86   new slide('snake', 'Groovius Dudis', 'Slick and sly with a
87     watchful eye.'),
88   new slide('reindeer', 'Redius Nosius', 'Though co-workers used to
89     laugh and call him names, he eventually won the respect of the entire
90     team.'),
91   new slide('turkey', 'Goosius Is Cooktis', 'Celebrated and revered for
92     an entire year, then served as dinner shortly after.'),
93   new slide('cow', 'Gotius Milkus', 'This animal is considered a moover
94     and shaker, and tends to milk things for all they\'re worth. Udderly
95     shameful.'),
96   new slide('crane', 'Whooping It Upus', 'Not to be confused with a
97     piece of heavy construction equipment. Rumored as the source of the
98     nickname <I>birdlegs</I>.')
99   );
100
101  function camelCap(str) {
102    return str.substring(0, 1).toUpperCase() + str.substring(1);
103  }
104
105  function genScreen() {
106    var menuStr = '';
107    for (var i = 0; i < slideShow.length; i++) {
108      genLayer('slide' + i, sWidPos, sHgtPos, dWidLyr, dHgtLyr,
109        (i == 0 ? true : false), slideShow[i].structure);
110      menuStr += '<A HREF="" onMouseOver="hideStatus(); if(!tourOn)
111        { setSlide(' + i + ');' +
112        ' imageSwap(\'' + slideShow[i].name + '\', ' + i + ', true)};' +
113            return true;"' +
114        ' onMouseOut="if(!tourOn) { setSlide(' + i + ');' +
115        ' imageSwap(\'' + slideShow[i].name + '\', ' + i + ', false)};' +
116            return true;"' +
117        ' onClick="return false;"><IMG NAME="' + slideShow[i].name +
118        '" SRC="' + imgPath + slideShow[i].name +
119            'out.gif" BORDER=0></A><BR>';
120    }
121
122    genLayer('automation', sWidPos - 100, 11, 100, 200, true,
123      '<A HREF="javascript: autoPilot();" onMouseOver="hideStatus();
124          return true;">' +
125      '<IMG SRC="' + imgPath + 'automate.gif" BORDER=0></A>'
126    );
127
128    genLayer('guide', sWidPos - 100, 30, 100, 200, true,
129      '<A HREF="javascript: if(!tourOn) { changeSlide(-1); }"
130          onMouseOver="hideStatus(); return true;">' +
131      '<IMG SRC="' + imgPath + 'leftout.gif" BORDER=0></A>' +
132      '<A HREF="javascript: if(!tourOn) { menuManager(); }"
133          onMouseOver="hideStatus(); return true;">' +
```

Example 3-1. index.html (continued)

```
134      '<IMG SRC="' + imgPath + 'guideout.gif" BORDER=0></A>' +
135      '<A HREF="javascript: if(!tourOn) { changeSlide(1); }"
136          onMouseOver="hideStatus(); return true;">' +
137      '<IMG SRC="' + imgPath + 'rightout.gif" BORDER=0></A>'
138      );
139
140  genLayer('menu', sWidPos - 104, 43, 100, 200, false,
141      '<DIV ID="menuConstraint"><TABLE><TD>' +
142          menuStr + '</TD></TABLE></DIV>'
143      );
144  }
145
146 function refSlide(name) {
147   if (NN) { return document.layers[name]; }
148   else { return eval('document.all.' + name + '.style'); }
149   }
150
151 function hideSlide(name) {
152   refSlide(name).visibility = hideName;
153   }
154
155 function showSlide(name) {
156   refSlide(name).visibility = showName;
157   }
158
159 function menuManager() {
160   if (isVis) { hideSlide('menu'); }
161   else { showSlide('menu'); }
162   isVis = !isVis;
163   }
164
165 function changeSlide(offset) {
166   hideSlide('slide' + curSlide);
167   curSlide = (curSlide + offset < 0 ? slideShow.length - 1 :
168     (curSlide + offset == slideShow.length ? 0 : curSlide + offset));
169   showSlide('slide' + curSlide);
170   }
171
172 function setSlide(ref) {
173   if (tourOn) { return; }
174   hideSlide('slide' + curSlide);
175   curSlide = ref;
176   showSlide('slide' + curSlide);
177   }
178
179 function imageSwap(imagePrefix, imageIndex, isOver) {
180   if (isOver) { document[imagePrefix].src = imgOver[imageIndex].src; }
181   else { document[imagePrefix].src = imgOut[imageIndex].src; }
182   }
183
184 function hideStatus() { window.status = ''; }
185
```

Example 3-1. index.html (continued)

```
186 function autoPilot() {
187   if (tourOn) {
188     clearInterval(auto);
189     imageSwap(slideShow[curSlide].name, curSlide, false);
190     }
191   else {
192     auto = setInterval('automate()', showSpeed);
193     imageSwap(slideShow[curSlide].name, curSlide, true);
194     showSlide('menu');
195     visible = true;
196     }
197   tourOn = !tourOn;
198   }
199
200 function automate() {
201   imageSwap(slideShow[curSlide].name, curSlide, false);
202   changeSlide(1);
203   imageSwap(slideShow[curSlide].name, curSlide, true);
204   }
205
206 //-->
207 </SCRIPT>
208 </HEAD>
209 <BODY BGCOLOR=WHITE>
210 <CENTER>
211 <FONT FACE=Arial>
212 <H2>Animal Kingdom Slideshow</H2>
213 </FONT>
214 </CENTER>
215 <SCRIPT LANGUAGE="JavaScript1.2">
216 <!--
217 genScreen();
218 //-->
219 </SCRIPT>
220 </FONT>
221 </BODY>
222 </HTML>
```

Application Variables

Let's look first at the variables and other details; then we'll get into the functions. Here are lines 5–7:

```
<STYLE TYPE="text/css">
#menuConstraint { height: 800; }
</STYLE>
```

This defines a cascading style sheet ruled with the name *menuConstraint* and only one property, a height of 800 pixels. This is applied to every slide created to ensure that users have enough page real estate to view the slides. In other words, if the user has a monitor resolution set to less than a height of 800 pixels, this style sheet forces vertical scrollbars. This is especially helpful if your images are long or you have a lot of copy. At least, users can scroll to see the rest. Lines 11–31 show the variables:

```
var dWidLyr   = 450;
var dHgtLyr   = 450;
var curSlide  = 0;
var zIdx      = -1;
var isVis     = false;

var NN        = (document.layers ? true : false);
var sWidPos   = ((NN ? innerWidth  : screen.availWidth)  / 2) -
   (dWidLyr / 2);
var sHgtPos   = ((NN ? innerHeight : screen.availHeight) / 2) -
   (dHgtLyr / 2);
var hideName  = (NN ? 'hide' : 'hidden');
var showName  = (NN ? 'show' : 'visible');

var img       = new Array();
var imgOut    = new Array();
var imgOver   = new Array();
var imgPath   = 'images/';

var showSpeed = 3500;
var tourOn    = false;
```

The variables are divided into four groups:

- DHTML layer defaults

- Browser-determined variables

- Image-related variables

- Autopilot-related variables

DHTML Layer Defaults

Variables *dWidLyr* and *dHgtLyr* simply declare the default width and height of the slides. Variable *curSlide* always holds the array index value of the current slide in view. Variable *zIdx* assigns a z-index value to each layer created, and *isVis* holds a Boolean value indicating whether the layer is currently visible.

 I generally refer to the slides as DHTML layers or just layers. Don't confuse them with Netscape's proprietary LAYER tag, which is used to create these layers in Navigator. In other words, a layer is a LAYER in Navigator, but not in MSIE.

Browser-Determined Variables

The next five variables, *NN*, *sWidPos*, *sHgtPos*, *showName*, and *hideName* are determined according to the browser in which the application is loaded. Variable *NN* at line 17 is set to true if the *layers* property of the *document* object exists. In other words, it's Netscape Navigator 4.x. Netscape's current implementation of the document object model supports a *layers* object:

```
var NN = (document.layers ? true : false);
```

Otherwise the script assumes the user has MSIE 4.x, and sets *NN* to false. Microsoft's object model references layers in the *styles* object of *document.all*. Variables *sWidPos* and *sHgtPos* hold the values of the x and y coordinates of the top left corner, where the layer will be positioned so that it is in the center of the browser window (not the screen). These are determined not only by the value of *NN*, but also by the values of variables *dWidLyr* and *dHgtLyr*. Here are lines 18–21:

```
var sWidPos  = ((NN ? innerWidth  : screen.availWidth)  / 2) -
   (dWidLyr / 2);
var sHgtPos  = ((NN ? innerHeight : screen.availHeight) / 2) -
   (dHgtLyr / 2);
```

How would you find the values of the x and y coordinates? You can easily calculate the center coordinates by dividing the browser window width by 2 for the x coordinate, then the browser window height by 2 for the y coordinate. In other words, the center of the window coordinates equals (window width in pixels / 2, window height in pixels / 2).

Now you know the coordinates for the center of the window. Since these coordinates will also be the center of each of the layers, you can get the x and y coordinates by subtracting half of *dWidLyr* from the center x coordinate and half of *dHgtLyr* from the center y coordinate.

The remaining two browser-determined variables are strings that hold the correct name of visible or hidden status of layers according to the DOM utilized. Here are lines 22 and 23:

```
var hideName = (NN ? 'hide' : 'hidden');
var showName = (NN ? 'show' : 'visible');
```

According to the Netscape DOM, hidden layers have the *visibility* property set to **hide**, while the Microsoft DOM has the *visibility* set to **hidden**. Conversely, the Netscape layers property *visibility* of those in view is set to **show**, and Microsoft to **visible**.

Also according to the Netscape DOM, the window width and height are contained in *window* object properties *innerWidth* and *innerHeight*, while Microsoft stores these values in the *screen* object properties *availWidth* and *availHeight*. Since variable *NN* has been set for just this purpose, JavaScript knows which properties to reference.

Image-Related Variables

The next group of variables consists of arrays that will manage the images. Check out lines 25–28:

```
var img = new Array();
var imgOut = new Array();
var imgOver = new Array();
var imgPath = 'images/';
```

These are fairly straightforward. The images stored in the *img* array represent the slide images. Those stored in the *imgOut* array are used as the slide menu images. The images stored in the *imgOver* array are used for the menu rollover images. We'll get more involved with image rollovers when we cover the `swapImage()` function shortly.

The last variable, *imgPath*, contains the value of the path to where all the images are kept on your web server. You can make this path absolute or relative. An absolute path contains the entire location of files, from the host and domain name or IP address of the web server (such as *http://www.oreilly.com/*) or local drive (such as `C:\`) to the directory containing the files. Here are two examples.

```
var imgPath = 'http://www.serve.com/hotsyte/';
var imgPath = 'C:\\Winnt\\Profiles\\Administrator\\Desktop\\';
```

You'll have to use two backslashes (\\) to produce a single escaped backslash with any Windows OS. If you don't, JavaScript will think you mean:

```
C:WinntProfilesAdministratorDesktop;
```

That's not only wrong, it's a syntax error.

Automated Slideshow Variables

The last two variables, *showSpeed* and *tourOn*, represent the speed at which the slides change and whether the autopilot is on. Here they are at lines 30–31:

```
var showSpeed = 3500;
var tourOn = false;
```

Variable *showSpeed* is expressed in milliseconds. You can increase the time between changes, to say, 10 seconds by setting it to `10000`, for slides with more information. You can also make it blindingly fast by setting it to, say, `10`. When the page first loads, the automated slideshow isn't on. So, *tourOn*, not surprisingly, is set to `false`.

The Application Functions

The slideshow functions fall into three categories: layer creation, image handling, and navigation/display. Table 3-1 describes each of the functions and the category in which it belongs.

Table 3-1. Slideshow Functions and Descriptions

Function Name	Category	Description
genLayer()	Layers	Generates the slides
slide()	Layers	The object constructor for each slide
imagePreLoad()	Images	Preloads images for the slides and the navigation bar
camelCap()	Layers	Capitalizes the first letter of the slide name
genScreen()	Layers	Calls genLayer() and positions all layers
hideSlide()	Layers	Hides layers
showSlide()	Layers	Reveals layers
refSlide()	Layers	Returns a reference to layers based on browser
menuManager()	Layers	Hides and reveals the slide menu
changeSlide()	Layers	Changes slide currently in view via Guide arrows or autopilot
setSlide()	Layers	Changes slide currently in view via mouse events
imageSwap()	Images	Performs image rollovers for the slide menu
hideStatus()	Navigation	Sets the window status bar value equal to ""
autoPilot()	Navigation	Manages the autopilot mode
automate()	Navigation	Performs the advance of slides automatically

Layer-Related Functions

Since most of the slideshow setup relies on layer-related functions, it makes sense to start with them.

genLayer()

This function is cross-browser DHTML central. Anything you want displayed in the slideshow, no matter how big, small, multicolored, or image-intensive, passes through here. Take a good look at lines 33–47:

```
function genLayer(sName, sLeft, sTop, sWdh, sHgt, sVis, copy) {
  if (NN) {
    document.writeln('<LAYER NAME="' + sName + '" LEFT=' + sLeft +
      ' TOP=' + sTop + ' WIDTH=' + sWdh + ' HEIGHT=' + sHgt +
      ' VISIBILITY="' + sVis + '"' + ' z-Index=' + (++zIdx) + '>' +
      copy + '</LAYER>');
  }
  else {
```

```
    document.writeln('<DIV ID="' + sName +
      '" STYLE="position:absolute; overflow:none; left:' + sLeft +
      'px; top:' + sTop + 'px; width:' + sWdh + 'px; height:' + sHgt +
      'px;' + ' visibility:' + sVis + '; z-Index=' + (++zIdx) + '">' +
      copy + '</DIV>');
  }
}
```

This function contains a lone if-else statement. Actually `genLayer()` performs the same basic operation in both blocks of code. One works for Netscape; the other, for MSIE. Until the document object model is straightened out, this is the way things will have to be.

Line 34 uses the *NN* variable to determine whether the user's browser is Netscape Navigator or (presumably) Microsoft Internet Explorer. If *NN* is `true`, then the browser is Navigator. Otherwise, it is assumed that the user has MSIE.

Note the arguments expected in line 33. They are *sName, sLeft, sTop, sWdh, sHgt, sVis,* and *copy.* Regardless of browser, all of them do pretty much the same thing. `sName` represents a name you'd like to associate with the layer. *sLeft* specifies the number of pixels from the left of the screen to position the layer. *sTop* specifies the number of pixels from the top of the browser window to position the layer. *sWdh* and *sHgt,* as you can imagine, hold pixel values for the layer dimensions. *sVis* contains `true` or `false`, which determines whether the layer is visible (true). *copy* contains a string you want to display as the contents of the layer. Content is presumably HTML, but plain text never hurt anyone.

Whichever the browser may be, function `genLayer()` calls the `document.writeln()` method and constructs a `LAYER` tag for Navigator or a `DIV` tag for IE.

slide()

`slide()` is an object constructor. Instances of `slide()` contain important details about each slide, such as the animal name, descriptive text, and HTML content. Have a look at lines 49–62:

```
function slide(imgStr, scientific, copy) {
  this.name     = imgStr;
  imagePreLoad(imgStr);
  this.copy     = copy;
  this.structure =
    '<TABLE WIDTH=500 CELLPADDING=10><TR><TD WIDTH=60% VALIGN=TOP>' +
    '<IMG SRC=' + imgPath + imgStr + '.gif></TD>' +
    '<TD WIDTH=40% VALIGN=TOP><H2>Common Name:</H2><H2><I>' +
    camelCap(imgStr) + '</I></H2><H3>Scientific Name: </H3><H3><I>' +
    scientific + '</I></H3>' + '<B>Abstract:</B><BR>' + copy +
    '</TD></TR></TABLE>';

  return this;
}
```

JavaScript Technique:
The First Step to Cross-Browser DHTML

Before the proliferation of the 4.x browsers and DHTML, web developers had to be content with whining about MSIE 3.x not being JavaScript 1.1 compatible. Among other things, that meant basically no image rollovers, barely any support for JavaScript source files, and having to implement workarounds accordingly.

However, now there can be peace, by simply making our pages cross-browser compatible. Here is one of your most powerful weapons: *document.all*.

For simpler applications, an if-else statement is all that is required:

```
if (document.all) {  // It's MSIE
                     // Use the Jscript equivalent
                     // e.g., document.all.styles, etc.

   }

else {               // It's NN
                     // Stick with JavaScript
                     // e.g., document.layers, etc.

   }
```

Function `slide()` accepts three arguments—*imgStr, scientific,* and *copy. imgStr* represents the name of the "wild" animal depicted on the slide. *imgStr* is in many ways the backbone of each slide. Now is a good time to look at the application's naming convention. The name associated with each *slide* object is set in line 50.

```
this.name  = imgStr;
```

imgStr pops up a few more times. Check out lines 53–59. This is where the *structure* property of the slide is set:

```
this.structure =
  '<TABLE WIDTH=500 CELLPADDING=10><TR><TD WIDTH=60% VALIGN=TOP>' +
  '<IMG SRC=' + imgPath + imgStr + '.gif></TD>' +
  '<TD WIDTH=40% VALIGN=TOP><H2>Common Name:</H2><H2><I>' +
  camelCap(imgStr) + '</I></H2><H3>Scientific Name: </H3><H3><I>' +
  scientific + '</I></H3>' + '<B>Abstract:</B><BR>' + copy +
  '</TD></TR></TABLE>';
```

To dynamically create the slide image, `slide()` concatenates the required HTML for an <IMG> tag with variables *imgPath* and *imgStr*, followed by `'gif'`. If *imgStr* were equal to *pig*, the slide image HTML would look like this:

```
<IMG SRC='images/pig.gif'>
```

The *structure* property defines the slide content as an HTML table, each with one row and two data cells. The left data cell contains the slide image, and the right

---

JavaScript Technique:
Using Well-Constructed Naming Conventions

It pops up almost everywhere in this book. Naming conventions. Consider how the slideshow application leverages a lot of referencing power with simple words such as *cow*, *bird*, and *dog*. Of course, none of these applications is made for an enormous enterprise with complex data warehousing, but you can get a surprising amount from very little. This isn't really a JavaScript technique; you can use it with nearly any language. Consider the simplicity of the naming convention used here with parameter *imgStr*.

imgStr is the name of an animal. Let's say a pig. So *imgStr* equals *pig*. That seems innocent enough, but that string also defines the name of the animal, the base name of the slide image, and the two images used for the rollovers in the slide menu (we'll get there soon). Four JavaScript members and one animal name based on a single string. That's getting your money's worth. The following table illustrates how *pig* and other *imgStrs* are central to their respective slides.

imgStr	Animal Name	Slide Image	Menu Image	Menu Image Rollover
pig	pig	*pig.gif*	*pigout.gif*	*pigover.gif*
cow	cow	*cow.gif*	*cowout.gif*	*cowover.gif*
snake	snake	*snake.gif*	*snakeout.gif*	*snakeover.gif*

---

cell contains the descriptive text. Line 57 makes use of *imgStr* again to assign a common name to the animal.

```
camelCap(imgStr)
```

Function `camelCap()` in lines 88–90 simply returns whatever text string it is passed with the first character in uppercase. This is a formatting issue and simply makes things look a bit nicer. Notice also that argument *scientific* is set as the scientific name of the animal. Of course, after you read some of the "scientific" names I came up with, you may question (or laugh at) scientific research in general.

Just when it seems *imgStr* has been worked to the bone, `slide()` passes it to function `preLoadImages()` for another round. See line 51. This function preloads all those slide images. We'll get to that shortly.

genScreen()

Function `genScreen()` utilizes the application's layer-creating ability to get things on the screen. It is by far the function with the most code. Here are lines 105–144.

`genScreen()` not only manages slide creation and positioning, but also defines the navigational features of the application with dynamic JavaScript.

```
function genScreen() {
  var menuStr = '';
  for (var i = 0; i < slideShow.length; i++) {
    genLayer('slide' + i, sWidPos, sHgtPos, dWidLyr, dHgtLyr,
      (i == 0 ? true : false), slideShow[i].structure);
    menuStr += '<A HREF="" onMouseOver="hideStatus();' if(!tourOn)
      { setSlide(' + i + '); +
      ' imageSwap(\'' + slideShow[i].name + '\', ' + i + ', true)};
          return true;"' +
      ' onMouseOut="if(!tourOn) { setSlide(' + i + ');' +
      ' imageSwap(\'' + slideShow[i].name + '\', ' + i + ', false)};
          return true;" +
      ' onClick="return false;"><IMG NAME="' + slideShow[i].name +
      '" SRC="' + imgPath + slideShow[i].name +
      'out.gif" BORDER=0></A><BR>';
  }

  genLayer('automation', sWidPos - 100, 11, 100, 200, true,
    '<A HREF="javascript: autoPilot();" onMouseOver="hideStatus();' +
    ' return true;">' +
    '<IMG SRC="' + imgPath + 'automate.gif" BORDER=0></A>'
    );

  genLayer('guide', sWidPos - 100, 30, 100, 200, true,
    '<DIV ID="menuConstraint">' +
    '<A HREF="javascript: if(!tourOn) { changeSlide(-1); }" ' +
    'onMouseOver="hideStatus(); return true;">' +
    '<IMG SRC="' + imgPath + 'leftout.gif" BORDER=0></A>' +
    '<A HREF="javascript: if(!tourOn) { menuManager(); }" ' +
    'onMouseOver="hideStatus(); return true;">' +
    '<IMG SRC="' + imgPath + 'guideout.gif" BORDER=0></A>' +
    '<A HREF="javascript: if(!tourOn) { changeSlide(1); }" ' +
    'onMouseOver="hideStatus(); return true;">' +
    '<IMG SRC="' + imgPath + 'rightout.gif" BORDER=0></A></DIV>'
    );

  genLayer('menu', sWidPos - 104, 43, 100, 200, false,
    '<DIV ID="menuConstraint"><TABLE><TD>' +
    menuStr + '</TD></TABLE></DIV>'
    );
}
```

It is this function's responsibility to manage the creation of all the slide layers plus three more for the navigation links (one for the slide menu, one for the "<Guide>" images, and one for the "Automate" image). The *for* loop in lines 106–120 takes care of the layers and generates the content for the slide menu layer:

```
var menuStr = '';
for (var i = 0; i < slideShow.length; i++) {
  genLayer('slide' + i, sWidPos, sHgtPos, dWidLyr, dHgtLyr,
    (i == 0 ? true : false), slideShow[i].structure);
  menuStr += '<A HREF="" onMouseOver="hideStatus();' +
```

```
        'if(!tourOn) { setSlide(' + i + '); imageSwap(\'' +
        slideShow[i].name + '\', ' + i + ', true)}; return true;"' +
        ' onMouseOut="if(!tourOn) { setSlide(' + i + ');' +
        ' imageSwap(\'' + slideShow[i].name + '\', ' + i + ', false)}; ' +
        'return true;" onClick="return false;"><IMG NAME="' +
        slideShow[i].name + '" SRC="' + imgPath + slideShow[i].name +
        'out.gif" BORDER=0></A><BR>';
    }
```

By iterating through all the elements of the *slideShow* array, creating each layer slide happens rather easily with one call to **genLayer()**. Here is a closer look:

```
genLayer('slide' + i, sWidPos, sHgtPos, dWidLyr, dHgtLyr,
        (i == 0 ? true : false), slideShow[i].structure);
```

That's a hefty load of values to pass as arguments. Table 3-2 lists and describes each.

Table 3-2. Arguments for genLayer()

Value	Description
`'slide' + i`	Creates a unique, but indexed name for each slide, such as *slide0*, *slide1*, etc.
`sWidPos`	The pixel distance from the left of the window for positioning the slide.
`sHgtPos`	The pixel distance from the top of the window for positioning the slide.
`dWidLyr`	Default slide width, in this case 450.
`dHgtLyr`	Default slide height, in this case 450.
`(i == 0 ? true : false)`	Determines whether to show (**true**) or hide (**false**) the slide. All slides begin hidden except the first, when *i* is equal to 0.
`slideShow[i].structure`	This is the content of the slide, including text and graphics, embedded in a table. It came from the slide constructor. See lines 54–59.

Function **genLayer()** is called **slideShow.length** times, to create a layer for each slide. It doesn't matter if you have 6 slides or 106 slides: this one line handles them all. Surprisingly enough, the rest of the code within **genScreen()** is devoted to getting three navigational layers on the screen, but let's get a little more use out of that *for* loop before moving on. Check out the rest of it:

```
menuStr += '<A HREF="" onMouseOver="hideStatus();' +
    'if(!tourOn) { setSlide(' + i + '); imageSwap(\'' +
    slideShow[i].name + '\', ' + i + ', true)}; return true;"' +
    ' onMouseOut="if(!tourOn) { setSlide(' + i + '); imageSwap(\'' +
    slideShow[i].name + '\', ' + i + ', false)}; return true;"' +
    ' onClick="return false;"><IMG NAME="' + slideShow[i].name +
    '" SRC="' + imgPath + slideShow[i].name +
    'out.gif" BORDER=0></A><BR>';
```

I snuck it in at line 110, but variable *menuStr*, previously initialized to an empty string, is going to be set to an HTML string containing code for an image rollover pair for each slide. See Figure 3-2 for a look at the slide menu rollover effect.

For every slide, *menuStr* is set equal to itself plus a linked image corresponding with the slide. Before you try to match those single and double quotes, consider what each linked image rollover pair needs.

1. An opening <A HREF> tag

2. Code for the *onMouseOver* event handler when the user passes the mouse pointer arrow over the linked image

3. Code for the *onMouseOut* event handler when the user removes the mouse pointer arrow from the linked image

4. Code for the *onClick* event handler to prevent anything from happening if the user clicks on the linked image (you can easily change this, though)

5. An <IMG> tag with a unique NAME and SRC

6. A closing </A> tag

Item 1 is straightforward; just input it.

Item 2 is a bit more involved. To eliminate any annoying status bar text, the first thing that the *onMouseOver* event handler does is set the value of the status bar to an empty string with a call to hideStatus(). You can see this one-line function at line 184.

Next, but if and only if the user is not running the show on autopilot, the *onMouseOver* event needs to call function setSlide() (discussed shortly). For now just remember that the value of *i* is passed in.

As if *onMouseOver* won't have enough to do, the last thing we need to add code for is function imageSwap(). This function handles the image rollovers and will be discussed shortly as well. In the meantime, remember that the JavaScript coded here has three values passed in slideShow[i].name, the value of *i*, and the Boolean value true.

Item 3 has the same requirements for the *onMouseOut* event handler except that no call will be made to hideStatus() because the status bar is already clear, and the last coded value passed to *imageSwap* is the Boolean false instead of true.

Item 4 is easy: just add onClick="false". This cancels any clicking the user might do.

Here is how to satisfy the requirement in Item 5:

```
'<IMG NAME="' + slideShow[i].name + '" SRC="' + imgPath +
  slideShow[i].name + 'out.gif" BORDER=0>'
```

The `<IMG>` tag will get a unique name from `slideShow[i].name`. `slide-Show[i].name` is also used with variable *imgPath* and the string `"out.gif"` to create the proper source for the `<IMG>`.

Item 6 is simple. Add a `<BR>` tag to the end, and you're done.

Variable *menuStr* is set to itself plus the string that comes from the aforementioned code each iteration of the *for* loop.

Now what happens to *menuStr?* Since *menuStr* contains the HTML and JavaScript contents of the slide menu, it is passed in as an argument in the call to `genLayer()` in lines 140–143:

```
genLayer('menu', sWidPos - 104, 43, 100, 200, false,
  '<DIV ID="menuConstraint"><TABLE><TD>' +
  menuStr + '</TD></TABLE></DIV>'
  );
```

I saved the call for last in this function simply because the other two navigation layers created are positioned above the slide menu, and I thought it made more sense to generate them in the code in that order. Notice the use of the `<DIV>` tag with the `ID` attribute set to `menuConstraint`. This provides the assurance of 800 pixels of height for the slideshow.

We need to make two other calls to `genLayer()` to finish the slideshow layout. One is to display a linked image to start and stop the autopilot feature, the other is for the linked image that reveals and conceals the slide menu with forward and backward arrows to navigate slides one at a time. There's not much to creating the layer for the linked image of the autopilot feature. See lines 122–126:

```
genLayer('automation', sWidPos - 100, 11, 100, 200, true,
  '<A HREF="javascript: autoPilot();" onMouseOver="hideStatus();' +
  'return true;"><IMG SRC="images/automate.gif" BORDER=0></A>'
  );
```

You've already seen just about everything here. The `javascript:` protocol will be used in the `HREF` attribute to call the `autoPilot()` function, and the *onMouseOver* event handler calls `hideStatus()`. As you yearn for something more challenging, take a look at the last layer code. The call to `genLayer()` in lines 128–138 creates the final layer. It contains three images: two arrows and the word "Guide." It looks like this: `<Guide>`.

```
genLayer('guide', sWidPos - 100, 30, 100, 200, true,
  '<A HREF="javascript: if(!tourOn) { changeSlide(-1); }" ' +
  'onMouseOver="hideStatus(); return true;">' +
  '<IMG SRC="' + imgPath + 'leftout.gif" BORDER=0></A>' +
  '<A HREF="javascript: if(!tourOn) { menuManager(); }" ' +
  'onMouseOver="hideStatus(); return true;">' +
  '<IMG SRC="' + imgPath + 'guideout.gif" BORDER=0></A>' +
  '<A HREF="javascript: if(!tourOn) { changeSlide(1); }" ' +
  'onMouseOver="hideStatus(); return true;">' +
```

```
'<IMG SRC="' + imgPath + 'rightout.gif" BORDER=0></A>'
);
```

The code for each image looks almost identical. Again you've seen much of the code in the linked images before. Clicking the left and right arrow image links, however, conditionally calls `changeSlide()`. The –1 passed causes the slide-show to move to the previous slide. The 1 causes the slideshow to advance to the next slide. We'll cover `changeSlide()` soon. All the linked `<Guide>` image does is show or hide the slide menu, handled by function `menuManager()`.

Before we put `genScreen()` to rest, notice that it is called within the `<BODY>` tags before the page is loaded. MSIE can't create layers after the document has loaded, so we need to fire it up before then. Here are lines 215–219:

```
<SCRIPT LANGUAGE="JavaScript1.2">
<!--
genScreen();
//-->
</SCRIPT>
```

The elements of slideShow

You may have already noticed the array variable *slideShow*. Each element contains the building blocks (properties) of a single *slide* object. Here is the *slideShow* array in lines 75-98. There are 10 elements, and hence, 10 slides of animals:

```
var slideShow  = new Array(
    new slide('bird', 'Bomb-zis Car-zes', 'This winged creature has ' +
        'been known to seek out and soil freshly-washed vehicles.'),
    new slide('walrus', 'Verius Clueless', 'These big fellas ' +
        'good fishers, but toothbrushing is another story.'),
    new slide('gator', 'Couldbeus Luggajus', 'These reptiles ' +
        'often play mascots for large college sporting events.'),
    new slide('dog', 'Makus Messus', 'Man\'s best friend? Yeah, right. ' +
        'No wonder these mammals get a bad rep.'),
    new slide('pig', 'Oinkus Lotsus', 'Humans with questionable eating ' +
        'habits are often compared to these farm creatures.'),
    new slide('snake', 'Groovius Dudis', 'Slick and sly with a ' +
        'watchful eye.'),
    new slide('reindeer', 'Redius Nosius', 'Though co-workers used to ' +
        'laugh and call him names, he eventually won the respect of the ' +
        'entire team.'),
    new slide('turkey', 'Goosius Is Cooktis', 'Celebrated and revered ' +
        'for an entire year, then served as dinner shortly after.'),
    new slide('cow', 'Gotius Milkus', 'This animal is considered a ' +
        'moover and shaker, and tends to milk things for all they\'re ' +
        'worth. Udderly shameful.'),
    new slide('crane', 'Whooping It Upus', 'Not to be confused with a ' +
        'piece of heavy construction equipment. Rumored as the source of the ' +
        'nickname <I>birdlegs</I>.')
);
```

Compare the values passed in each call to the *slide* constructor with the arguments expected. The first is the name of the animal (and image); next is the "technical" name; and each wraps up with some descriptive text. Notice that line 85 has some HTML included in the text. There is certainly no reason why you couldn't build on this concept, even defining layers in the slides themselves. See "Potential Extensions" later in the chapter for more possibilities.

If your list gets too long, consider putting this array into a JavaScript source file to clean up the code somewhat. Since there are only 10, I kept it in this file.

Image-Related Functions

With the slide functions under our belts, let's take a look at how to handle the images.

preLoadImages()

This function does what its name implies. Here are lines 64–73:

```
function imagePreLoad(imgStr) {
  img[img.length]   = new Image();
  img[img.length - 1].src = imgPath + imgStr + '.gif';

  imgOut[imgOut.length] = new Image();
  imgOut[imgOut.length - 1].src = imgPath + imgStr + 'out.gif';

  imgOver[imgOver.length] = new Image();
  imgOver[imgOver.length - 1].src = imgPath + imgStr + 'over.gif';
  }
```

This function creates new *Image* objects and preloads their sources three at a time. While this increases your original load time for the application, users will be spared having to wait for images to download as they navigate through the slideshow.

Variables *imgPath* and *imgStr* are concatenated together with *.gif, out.gif,* and *over.gif,* respectively, to make the necessary images associated with each slide. For example, the slide named *cow* has images *cow.gif, cowout.gif,* and *cowover.gif* associated with it.

imageSwap()

This function performs the image rollovers, whether users call it "manually" by passing the mouse pointer arrow over or away from the linked images in the slide menu, or whether it happens in autopilot mode. Not much to it, but lines 179–182 make all the difference:

```
function imageSwap(imagePrefix, imageIndex, isOver) {
   if (isOver) { document[imagePrefix].src = imgOver[imageIndex].src; }
```

```
        else { document[imagePrefix].src = imgOut[imageIndex].src; }
    }
```

Many rollover scripts, including the one on my site, perform the rollover with two separate functions: one for *onMouseOver* and the other for *onMouseOut*. You can combine the operations into one function, however, by passing in a few handy arguments.

Called *imagePrefix*, *imageIndex*, and *isOver*, these arguments represent the base string used to name the image (*imgStr* again), the index of the desired image (this is the value of *i* from the *for* loop in `genScreen()`), and a Boolean value used to indicate whether to use the images from array *imgOver* or array *imgOut*.

To make this a bit clearer, revisit lines 105–120 in function `genScreen()`. Notice the dynamic JavaScript created in line 112:

```
    imageSwap(\'' + slideShow[i].name + '\', ' + i + ', true)};
```

When this is written to the document and *i* equals 0, it will look like this:

```
    imageSwap('bird', 0, true);
```

Once the function is called, you can see where things are headed. Since *isOver* is `true`, then:

```
    document[bird].src = imgOver[0].src;
```

And `imgOver[0].src` is *images/birdover.gif*. If *isOver* is `false`, the image is set to `imgOut[0].src`, which is *images/birdout.gif*.

Navigational Functions

The slide function created the slides and the controls for viewing them. The image functions enable preloading and rollovers. Now let's look at what makes this slideshow a slideshow—the navigational functions.

refSlide(), hideSlide(), showSlide(), and menuManager()

The slides have been created, and the images have been loaded. Now we want to do things with the slides—namely, show the one we want and keep the other ones hidden. Before we can manipulate them, we need to be able to reference them. That's normally pretty easy, right? Just reference the layer name. Well, yes and no. You'll have to use the name of the layer, but remember that Navigator and MSIE reference layers differently in their document object models. Function `refSlide()` takes care of that in lines 146–149:

```
    function refSlide(name) {
      if (NN) { return document.layers[name]; }
      else { return eval('document.all.' + name + '.style'); }
    }
```

If the user has Navigator, `refSlide()` returns a reference to the `document.layers[name]`. If the user has MSIE, however, `refSlide()` returns a reference using `eval('document.all.' + name + '.style')`. This allows us to change the visibility of the layer no matter which browser. It's no surprise, then, to see these two functions in lines 151–157.

Not only is that simple, but all those members will be very easy to access later.

```
function hideSlide(name) {
  refSlide(name).visibility = hideName;
  }

function showSlide(name) {
  refSlide(name).visibility = showName;
  }
```

JavaScript Technique: The Power of eval()

As Netscape puts it, `eval()` "Evaluates a string of JavaScript code without reference to a particular object." It might not sound like much, but this function is available to all objects, and it means good news for us coders. Suppose you need to reference an object, but you're not sure of its index number (if it's an array) or you need to de-reference a string to properly access the object. That is the case for this application:

```
eval("document.all.styles." + name + ".visibility");
```

Here's another example:

```
eval("document.forms[0]." + elementName + ".value");
```

This will come in handy for many situations including constructing form objects and image rollovers, and performing mathematic calculations, all using strings as input. Make sure you add `eval()` to your arsenal. Visit Netscape's DevEdge Online for more information about `eval()` at: *http://developer. netscape.com/docs/manuals/communicator/jsref/glob8.htm.*

Both functions call `refSlide()` and pass in the name argument that they receive. This code might look a bit strange at first. How can `refSlide()` have the *visibility* property? In fact, it does not. Remember, however, that `refSlide()` returns a *reference* to a layer, each of which has the *visibility* property. If we want to hide a particular slide, we reference it with `refSlide()` and set the *visibility* property of the returned object to *hideName*, which, if you recall, was set to either the string *hide* or *hidden* back in line 22, depending on the browser. The same goes for showing a slide, except that the *visibility* property of the returned layer is set to the value of *showName*, also set depending on the browser in line 23.

hideSlide() and showSlide() are used to hide and reveal not only the slides, but also the slide menu. The functions are not called directly; instead, they are called by function menuManager() shown here:

```
function menuManager() {
    if (isVis) { hideSlide('menu'); }
    else { showSlide('menu'); }
    isVis = !isVis;
}
```

Whenever the slide menu is in view, variable *isVis* is set to true; it is false otherwise. So menuManager() shows the slide menu if *isVis* is false and hides it if it is currently true, then sets *isVis* to its opposite for the next time around.

changeSlide()

Now that we can reference the slides correctly regardless of browser and we have functions to hide and show the slides (and the slide menu), we need a function to actually change the slides from one to the next. Actually, there are two functions: changeSlide() and setSlide().

I hope I haven't been leading you on with this hiding and showing business. Changing from one slide to the next actually involves three steps:

1. Hide the current slide.

2. Determine which slide to show next.

3. Show that slide.

Steps 1 and 3 may seem painfully obvious by now, but step 2 is more involved than you might suspect. There are two situations in which you want to change slides. The first happens when you want to change slides one by one, forward or backward, in sequence. This type occurs when you use the < and > arrows to move through the slideshow. The second occurs when the autopilot advances through the slides. Function changeSlide() was crafted to handle both cases. See lines 165–170:

```
function changeSlide(offset) {
    hideSlide('slide' + curSlide);
    curSlide = (curSlide + offset < 0 ? slideShow.length - 1 :
        (curSlide + offset == slideShow.length ? 0 : curSlide + offset));
    showSlide('slide' + curSlide);
}
```

The first thing that happens is that hideSlide() is called with the value of the expression 'slide' + curSlide. Variable *curSlide* was originally set to 0 in line 13. Since that is the slide currently in view, function hideSlide() will conceal *slide0*, which is the bird slide. Fair enough. Now which slide should be revealed?

Recall that changeSlide() expects a parameter named *offset*. *offset* is either 1 or
−1. The 1 causes the next highest slide of the slideShow array to be revealed.
Since *curSlide* is the integer representing the current index of the slide in view,
adding 1 to it changes its value to 1, then 2, then 3, etc. The −1 causes the next
lowest slide of the *slideShow* array to be revealed. Not surprisingly, if *curSlide*
were 3, adding −1 to it would yield 2, then 1, then 0.

Everything seems fine, until you try hiding a slide named 'slide' + -1 or
'slide'+slideShow.length. Those slides don't exist, and you can bank on syntax errors. So how do you prevent *curSlide* from dipping below zero and creep-
ing above slideShow.length − 1?

Lines 167–168 provide the answer:

```
curSlide = (curSlide + offset < 0 ? slideShow.length - 1 :
   (curSlide + offset == slideShow.length ? 0 : curSlide + offset));
```

The value of *curSlide* is determined by using a set of nested ternary operators.
Here is the pseudo-code translation:

```
IF curSlide + offset is less than 0, THEN curSlide equals slideShow.length −1
   ELSE
      IF curSlide + offset equals slideShow.length THEN curSlide equals 0
      ELSE curSlide equals curSlide + offset
```

If adding *offset* to *curSlide* makes *curSlide* too low, *curSlide* is set to slideShow.
length − 1. If adding *offset* to *curSlide* makes *curSlide* too high, *curSlide* is simply set to 0. Otherwise, *curSlide* can safely be set equal to itself plus *offset*.

Once *curSlide* has been determined, the call to showSlide() in line 169 can
safely be made.

setSlide()

changeSlide() is one of two functions used to change the slides. Whereas
changeSlide() changes slides +/- 1 in relation to the current slide shown, function setSlide() hides the current slide in view, then shows whatever slide is associated with the index number it receives as an argument. Here are lines 172-177:

```
function setSlide(ref) {
   if (tourOn) { return; }
   hideSlide('slide' + curSlide);
   curSlide = ref;
   showSlide('slide' + curSlide);
   }
```

The first line checks *tourOn* to determine whether the autopilot mode is running,
and if so, returns immediately. If autopilot is on, there is no reason to do any slide
changing; it's done automatically for you.

Just like changeSlide(), setSlide() hides the slide currently in view. However, unlike changeSlide(), setSlide() doesn't care what the current value of *curSlide* is. setSlide() assigns the value of parameter *ref* to *curSlide* anyway, then shows the current slide associated with that number.

autoPilot()

As you can likely imagine, autoPilot() controls the autopilot feature of the slideshow. autoPilot() is turned on or off from the same link of the slideshow screen. Have a look at lines 186–198:

```
function autoPilot() {
  if (tourOn) {
    clearInterval(auto);
    imageSwap(slideShow[curSlide].name, curSlide, false);
  }
  else {
    auto = setInterval('automate()', showSpeed);
    imageSwap(slideShow[curSlide].name, curSlide, true);
    showSlide('menu');
    visible = true;
  }
  tourOn = !tourOn;
}
```

autoPilot() "knows" whether the autopilot feature is on or off by the value of variable *tourOn*. If *tourOn* is **false**, then the autopilot feature is not currently running. Therefore, the function uses the **setInterval()** method of the *window* object to call function **automate()** (discussed next) every *showSpeed* milliseconds.

It would be nice to see the slide menu advancing with the slides, highlighting the current slide menu image along the way. Since the user had to click the "Automate" image link to call autoPilot(), the autoPilot() takes care of both showing the slide menu (if it isn't showing already) and highlighting the current slide menu image the first time. Function automate() takes care of the rest, so it needs to be done only once.

If, however, autopilot is currently running (i.e., *tourOn* is **false**), autoPilot() utilizes the **clearInterval()** method, also of the *window* object, to cancel the **setInterval()** call associated with variable *auto*. To keep things neat, a last call to **imageSwap()** is made to roll the currently highlighted slide menu image back to its unhighlighted image like the others.

The last thing autoPilot() does is to change the current value of *tourOn* to its opposite. Obviously, if you click to turn it on, the next time you click, you'll want to turn it off, and so on.

JavaScript Technique:
Introducing setInterval() and clearInterval()

Window methods `setInterval()` and `clearInterval()` are an upgrade from their JavaScript 1.0 cousins `setTimeout()` and `clearTimeout()`. Whereas the `setTimeout()` runs the code within its first argument only once, `setInterval()` runs its code indefinitely. To get the same effect, you had to call `setTimeout()` and the function in which it is contained recursively, like this:

```
y = 50;

function overAndOver() {
    // Do something
    y = Math.log(y);

    // Call it again, Sam
    setTimeout("overAndOver()", 250);
    }
```

The function **overAndOver()** can be called as follows:

```
<BODY onLoad="overAndOver()";>
```

`setInterval()` takes care of the recursion implicitly and can take care of this in one call.

```
y = 50;

function overAndOver() {
    // Do something
    y = Math.log(y);
    }
```

The *onLoad* event handler can also produce this code. Just make sure you "turn off" the operation(s) performed with `clearInterval()`.

---

automate()

`automate()` is a small function that runs the slideshow by performing the following three operations:

1. Simulates an *onMouseOut* event to cause the currently highlighted image in the slide menu to roll back to the unhighlighted image. This happens with a call to **imageSwap()**.

2. Advances to the next slide with a call to **changeSlide()**.

3. Simulates an *onMouseOver* event to cause the next unhighlighted image in the slide menu to rollover to the highlighted images. This happens with a call to **imageSwap()**.

Here are lines 200–204. That's about all there is to it.

```
function automate() {
  imageSwap(slideShow[curSlide].name, curSlide, false);
  changeSlide(1);
  imageSwap(slideShow[curSlide].name, curSlide, true);
  }
```

One final note. Both calls to `imageSwap()` pass in the value of *curSlide*, giving the illusion that the same slide menu image might be rolled over and rolled back. Keep in mind, though, that the call to `changeSlide()` changes the value of *curSlide*. So the second call to `imageSwap()` causes the rollover to happen on the correct slide menu image.

Potential Extensions

As with nearly any application using DHTML, you can add dozens of things to make the slideshow snappier. I'll try to keep the list short.

Change Random Slides in AutoPilot

Why not mix things up a bit? Generate a random integer between 0 and `slideShow.length-1`. Then call `setSlide()`. Here is what the function might look like:

```
function randomSlide() {
  var randIdx = Math.floor(Math.rand() * slideShow.length);
  setSlide(randIdx);
  }
```

Instead of calling `changeSlide()` in function `automate()`, call `randomSlide()`:

```
function automate() {
  imageSwap(slideShow[curSlide].name, curSlide, false);
  randomSlide();
  imageSwap(slideShow[curSlide].name, curSlide, true);
  }
```

Animated GIFs or Image Rollovers in the Slides

These may be obvious improvements, but they certainly help. Users really like the added interactivity; anything with cool moves and color on a web page (this excludes the pitiful `BLINK` tag) can spice up the look.

Animate the Slides Themselves

Every slide created in this application remains in one place. At times, you have the "now you see it, now you don't" slides. But the layers remain in the same place throughout the entire show. Why not have the slides move in from the left or exit right? Or the top and bottom?

I'm opening the door to an entire new application within an application, so I won't get into the code, but I'll tell you where you can get a JavaScript toolkit to perform loads of layer effects. Netscape has a library file awaiting your download.

You can find it at *http://developer.netscape.com/docs/technote/dynhtml/csspapi/ xbdhtml.txt.*

Notice it has a *.txt* extension. Whenever you save the document as a local file, change the extension to *.js*.

Scratching the Surface

This book does not go crazy with DHTML. There are plenty of resources available if you want to explore slideshow extensions. Here are a few of my favorites:

Netscape's Dynamic HTML In Netscape Communicator:

> *http://developer.netscape.com/docs/manuals/communicator/dynhtml/ index.htm*

Microsoft's DHTML References:

> *http://msdn.microsoft.com/developer/sdk/inetsdk/help/dhtml/references/ dhtmlrefs.htm*

World Wide Web Consortium HTML 4.0 Specification:

> *http://www.w3.org/TR/REC-html40/*

Macromedia's DHTMLZone:

> *http://www.dhtmlzone.com/*

Dynamic Drive:

> *http://dynamicdrive.com/*

The Multiple Search Engine Interface

Application Features

- Frames-Based Multiple Search Engine
- Single-Click Searching
- Simple Search Engine Management

JavaScript Techniques

- Reusing Your Code
- Foregoing OO
- Math Versus Memory
- Using escape()

Multiple search engine apps written in Java-Script abound on the Net. This kind of application is one of the coolest and potentially easiest things to develop in JavaScript. And why not? You can capitalize on OPD (other people's data) to make your web site a portal to the network universe. This is my version. There are certainly more robust applications out there, but this one gives you significant advantages fairly easily. Figure 4-1 shows the first look as you open *ch04/index.html* in your browser.

Using this application isn't complicated. The user enters query text in the bottom left corner, then uses the arrows to advance through a layer-based menu of available search engines. All the user needs to do is click on the button of the search engine he or she wants to send the query text to, and the results show up in the center frame. I searched the Image Surfer database for the term "andromeda" and received the results shown in Figure 4-2.

That's really all there is to it. Notice the search results frame is surrounded by a black border. That's my award-winning attempt at web page design. It's a personal preference and easy to change to a more basic two-frame (top and bottom) layout.

By the way, if you've been following the chapters in order, you'll soon notice that this one is different in that it doesn't present entirely new code. Actually, I'll show you how to get extra mileage out of the code we covered in Chapter 3, *The Interactive Slideshow*. This will be a great way to see how you can reapply code that you already have to save time.

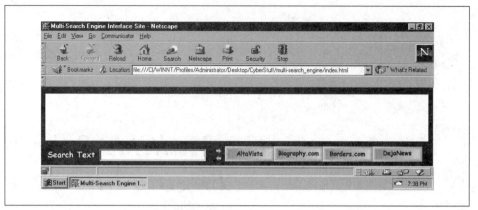

Figure 4-1. The multiple search engine interface

Figure 4-2. Image Surfer returns pictures in its database associated with the term "andromeda"

Execution Requirements

This application uses DHTML, so you'll need NN or MSIE 4.x to use it. I included 20 search engines. The number of search engines you use can easily reach the hundreds. But that's probably more than the average user will ever need. Keep in mind, too, that this application might run really well on your local machine, but, as with the slideshow, lots of graphics will increase the load time for Internet users.

The Syntax Breakdown

This application involves two files: *index.html* and *multi.html. index.html,* shown in Example 4-1, utilizes nested framesets to achieve the surrounding border effect.

Example 4-1. index.html

```
 1 <HTML>
 2 <HEAD>
 3 <TITLE>Multi-Search Engine Interface Site</TITLE>
 4 <SCRIPT LANGUAGE="JavaScript1.2">
 5 <!--
 6 var black = '<BODY BGCOLOR=BLACK></BODY>';
 7 var white = '<BODY BGCOLOR=WHITE></BODY>';
 8 //-->
 9 </SCRIPT>
10 </HEAD>
11 <FRAMESET ROWS="15,*,50" FRAMEBORDER=0 BORDER=0>
12 <FRAME SRC="javascript: parent.black;" SCROLLING=NO>
13 <FRAMESET COLS="15,*,15"  FRAMEBORDER=0 BORDER=0>
14   <FRAME SRC="javascript: parent.black;"SCROLLING=NO>
15   <FRAME SRC="javascript: parent.white;">
16   <FRAME SRC="javascript: parent.black;"
17     SCROLLING=NO>
18   </FRAMESET>
19 <FRAME SRC="multi.html" SCROLLING=NO>
20 </FRAMESET>
21 </HTML>
```

The two JavaScript variables *black* and *white* at lines 6 and 7 are evaluated as HTML strings in the SRC attribute of the frames in lines 12 and 14–16. We reviewed this in the "JavaScript Technique: Cheating The SRC Attribute" sidebar in Chapter 2, *The Online Test.* If you've been following along in order, this shouldn't be rocket science. The only frames that see any real action are frames[2], which displays the search results, and frames[4], which houses the search engine interface. The rest are purely for show. Let's move on to *multi.html,* shown in Example 4-2.

Example 4-2. multi.html

```
 1 <HTML>
 2 <HEAD>
 3 <TITLE>Multi-Engine Menu</TITLE>
 4 <SCRIPT LANGUAGE="JavaScript1.2">
 5 <!--
 6
```

Example 4-2. multi.html (continued)

```
 7 parent.frames[2].location.href  = 'javascript: parent.white';
 8
 9 var NN      = (document.layers ? true : false);
10 var curSlide   = 0;
11 var hideName   = (NN ? 'hide' : 'hidden');
12 var showName   = (NN ? 'show' : 'visible');
13 var perLyr   = 4;
14 var engWdh   = 100;
15 var engHgt   = 20;
16 var left     = 375;
17 var top      = 10;
18 var zIdx     = -1;
19 var imgPath   = 'images/';
20 var arrayHandles = new Array('out', 'over');
21
22 for (var i = 0; i < arrayHandles.length; i++) {
23   eval('var ' + arrayHandles[i] + ' = new Array()');
24   }
25
26 var engines = new Array(
27   new Array('HotBot',
28     'http://www.hotbot.com/?MT=',
29     'http://www.hotbot.com/'),
30   new Array('InfoSeek',
31     'http://www.infoseek.com/Titles?col=WW&sv=IS&lk=noframes&qt=',
32     'http://www.infoseek.com/'),
33   new Array('Yahoo',
34     'http://search.yahoo.com/bin/search?p=',
35     'http://www.yahoo.com/'),
36   new Array('AltaVista',
37     'http://www.altavista.com/cgi-bin/query?pg=q&kl=XX&q=',
38     'http://www.altavista.digital.com/'),
39   new Array('Lycos',
40     'http://www.lycos.com/cgi-bin/pursuit?matchmode=and&cat=lycos' +
41       '&query=',
42     'http://www.lycos.com/'),
43   new Array('Money.com',
44     'http://jcgi.pathfinder.com/money/plus/news/searchResults.oft?' +
45       'vcssortby=DATE&search=',
46     'http://www.money.com/'),
47   new Array('DejaNews',
48     'http://www.dejanews.com/dnquery.xp?QRY=',
49     'http://www.dejanews.com/'),
50   new Array('Insight',
51     'http://www.insight.com/cgi-bin/bp/870762397/web/result.html?' +
52      'a=s&f=p&t=A&d=',
53     'http://www.insight.com/'),
54   new Array('Scientific American',
55     'http://www.sciam.com/cgi-bin/search.cgi?' +
56     'searchby=strict&groupby=confidence&docs=100&query=',
57     'http://www.sciam.com/cgi-bin/search.cgi'),
58   new Array('Image Surfer',
```

Example 4-2. multi.html (continued)

```
59      'http://isurf.interpix.com/cgi-bin/isurf/keyword_search.cgi?q=',
60      'http://www.interpix.com/'),
61    new Array('MovieFinder.com',
62      'http://www.moviefinder.com/search/results/1,10,,00.html?' +
63        'simple=true&type=movie&mpos=begin&spat=',
64      'http://www.moviefinder.com/'),
65    new Array('Monster Board',
66      'http://www.monsterboard.com/pf/search/USresult.htm? ' +
67        'loc=&EmploymentType=F&KEYWORDS=',
68      'http://www.monsterboard.com/'),
69    new Array('MusicSearch.com',
70      'http://www.musicsearch.com/global/search/search.cgi?QUERY=',
71      'http://www.musicsearch.com/'),
72    new Array('ZD Net',
73      'http://xlink.zdnet.com/cgi-bin/texis/xlink/xlink/search.html?' +
74        'Utext=',
75      'http://www.zdnet.com/'),
76    new Array('Biography.com',
77      'http://www.biography.com/cgi-bin/biomain.cgi?search=FIND&field=',
78      'http://www.biography.com/'),
79    new Array('Entertainment Weekly',
80      'http://cgi.pathfinder.com/cgi-bin/ew/cg/pshell?venue=pathfinder&q=',
81      'http://www.entertainmentweekly.com/'),
82    new Array('SavvySearch',
83      'http://numan.cs.colostate.edu:1969/nph-search?' +
84        'classic=on&Boolean=OR&Hits=10&Mode=MakePlan&df=normal' +
85        '&AutoStep=on&KW=',
86      'http://www.savvysearch.com/'),
87    new Array('Discovery Online',
88      'http://www.discovery.com/cgi-bin/searcher/-?' +
89        'output=title&exclude=/search&search=',
90      'http://www.discovery.com/'),
91    new Array('Borders.com',
92      'http://www.borders.com:8080/fcgi-bin/db2www/search/' +
93        'search.d2w/QResults?doingQuickSearch=1&srchPage=QResults' +
94        '&mediaType=Book&keyword=',
95      'http://www.borders.com/'),
96    new Array('Life Magazine',
97      'http://cgi.pathfinder.com/cgi-bin/life/cg/pshell?' +
98        'venue=life&pg=q&date=all&x=15&y=16&q=',
99      'http://www.life.com/')
100       );
101
102 engines = engines.sort();
103
104 function imagePreLoad(imgName, idx) {
105   for(var j = 0; j < arrayHandles.length; j++) {
106     eval(arrayHandles[j] + "[" + idx + "] = new Image()");
107     eval(arrayHandles[j] + "[" + idx + "].src = '" + imgPath +
108     imgName + arrayHandles[j] + ".jpg'");
109     }
110   }
```

Example 4-2. multi.html (continued)

```
111
112 function engineLinks() {
113    genLayer('sliderule', left - 20, top + 2, 25, engHgt, true,
114       '<A HREF="javascript: changeSlide(1);" ' +
115       'onMouseOver="hideStatus(); return true;">' +
116       '<IMG SRC="' + imgPath + 'ahead.gif" BORDER=0></A><BR>' +
117       '<A HREF="javascript: changeSlide(-1);" ' +
118       'onMouseOver="hideStatus(); return true;">' +
119       '<IMG SRC="' + imgPath + 'back.gif" BORDER=0></A>');
120    lyrCount = Math.ceil
121    (engines.length / perLyr);
122    for (var i = 0; i < lyrCount; i++) {
123    var engLinkStr = '<TABLE BORDER=0 CELLPADDING=0 CELLSPACING=0><TR>';
124    for (var j = 0; j < perLyr; j++) {
125      var imgIdx   = (i * perLyr) + j;
126      if (imgIdx == engines.length) { break; }
127      var imgName  = nameFormat(engines[imgIdx][0]);
128      imagePreLoad(imgName, imgIdx);
129      engLinkStr += '<TD><A HREF="javascript: ' +
130         'callSearch(document.forms[0].elements[0].value, ' +
131         imgIdx + ');" onMouseOver="hideStatus(); imageSwap(\'' +
132         imgName + '\', ' + imgIdx + ', 1); return true" ' +
133         'onMouseOut="imageSwap(\'' + imgName + '\', ' + imgIdx +
134         ', 0);"><IMG NAME="' + imgName + '" SRC="' + imgPath + imgName +
135         'out.jpg' + '" BORDER=0></A></TD>';
136       }
137    engLinkStr += '</TR></TABLE>';
138    genLayer('slide' + i, left, top, engWdh, engHgt, false, engLinkStr);
139    }
140  }
141
142 function genLayer(sName, sLeft, sTop, sWdh, sHgt, sVis, copy) {
143   if (NN) {
144     document.writeln('<LAYER NAME="' + sName + '" LEFT=' + sLeft +
145       ' TOP=' + sTop + ' WIDTH=' + sWdh + ' HEIGHT=' + sHgt +
146       ' VISIBILITY=' + sVis + ' z-Index=' + (++zIdx) + '>' +
147       copy + '</LAYER>');
148    }
149   else {
150     document.writeln('<DIV ID="' + sName +
151       '" STYLE="position:absolute; overflow:none;left: ' +
152       sLeft + 'px; top:' + sTop + 'px; width:' + sWdh + 'px; height:' +
153       sHgt + 'px; visibility:' + sVis + ' z-Index=' + (++zIdx) +
154       '">' + copy + '</DIV>');
155    }
156  }
157
158 function nameFormat(str) {
159   var tempArray = str.split(' ');
160   return tempArray.join('').toLowerCase();
161  }
162
```

Example 4-2. multi.html (continued)

```
163 function hideSlide(name) { refSlide(name).visibility = hideName; }
164
165 function showSlide(name) { refSlide(name).visibility = showName; }
166
167 function refSlide(name) {
168   if (NN) { return document.layers[name]; }
169   else { return eval('document.all.' + name + '.style'); }
170   }
171
172 function changeSlide(offset) {
173   hideSlide('slide' + curSlide);
174   curSlide = (curSlide + offset < 0 ? slideShow.length - 1 :
175     (curSlide + offset == slideShow.length ? 0 : curSlide + offset));
176   showSlide('slide' + curSlide);
177   }
178
179 function imageSwap(imagePrefix, imageIndex, arrayIdx) {
180   document[imagePrefix].src = eval(arrayHandles[arrayIdx] +
181     "[" + imageIndex + "].src");
182   }
183
184 function callSearch(searchTxt, idx) {
185   if (searchTxt == "") {
186     parent.frames[2].location.href = engines[idx][2] +
187       escape(searchTxt);
188     }
189   else {
190     parent.frames[2].location.href = engines[idx][1] +
191       escape(searchTxt);
192     }
193   }
194
195 function hideStatus() { window.status = ''; }
196
197 //-->
198 </SCRIPT>
199
200 </HEAD>
201 <BODY BGCOLOR="BLACK" onLoad="showSlide('slide0');">
202 <SCRIPT LANGUAGE="JavaScript1.2">
203 <!--
204 engineLinks();
205 //-->
206 </SCRIPT>
207 <FORM onSubmit="return false;">
208 <TABLE CELLPADDING=0>
209   <TR>
210     <TD>
211     <FONT FACE=Arial>
212     <IMG SRC="images/searchtext.jpg">
213     </TD>
214     <TD>
```

Example 4-2. multi.html (continued)

```
215     <INPUT TYPE=TEXT SIZE=25>
216     </TD>
217   </TR>
218 </TABLE>
219 </FORM>
220 </BODY>
221 </HTML>
```

More than 200 lines of code, but you've seen most of it already. This shouldn't be that bad. Let's begin at line 7.

```
parent.frames[2].location.href ='javascript: parent.white';
```

If you count the frames in *index.html*, you'll see that `frames[2]` is where the search results show up. Setting the `location.href` property in this frame makes things a bit smoother if you decide to reload the application. This automatically sets the results document content to some "local" HTML so that you don't have to wait for any previous search queries to reload.

By the way, even though you get a neat display of search engine results in `frames[2]`, once you follow a search results link, you're at the mercy of the search engine designers. Some will let you follow the links while staying in the same frame. Others, unfortunately, like InfoSeek, will force the document into the top window of the browser.

Strolling down Memory Lane

Let's take a trip down Memory Lane (RAM, in case you're wondering). As you examine the variables below, you'll see some newcomers, but several will bear a striking resemblance to those you've worked with in Chapter 3. Look, there's *NN* and *curSlide!* And they brought *hideName* and *showName*, too. Not to mention *imagePath* and *zIdx*:

```
var NN           = (document.layers ? true : false);
var curSlide     = 0;
var hideName     = (NN ? 'hide' : 'hidden');
var showName     = (NN ? 'show' : 'visible');
var perLyr       = 4;
var engWdh       = 100;
var engHgt       = 20;
var left         = 375;
var top          = 10;
var zIdx         = -1;
var imgPath      = 'images/';
var arrayHandles = new Array('out', 'over');
```

These variables all have the same function they did in Chapter 3. They just pick up where they left off. As for the new ones, *perLyr* defines the number of search engines you want to display per layer. Variables *engWdh* and *engHgt* define default width and height values for each layer, respectively. Variables *left* and *top* hold values for positioning the layers. Variable *arrayHandles* contains an array used for dynamically preloading images. Hold that thought for just a bit; we'll go over it shortly.

Talking about family reunions, the variables aren't the only familiar code. Check out the functions from way back when.

Lines 142–156:

```
function genLayer(sName, sLeft, sTop, sWdh, sHgt, sVis, copy) {
  if (NN) {
    document.writeln('<LAYER NAME="' + sName + '" LEFT=' + sLeft +
      ' TOP=' + sTop + ' WIDTH=' + sWdh + ' HEIGHT=' + sHgt +
      ' VISIBILITY=' + sVis + ' z-Index=' + (++zIdx) + '>' +
      copy + '</LAYER>');
  }
  else {
    document.writeln('<DIV ID="' + sName +
      '" STYLE="position:absolute; overflow:none;left: ' +
      sLeft + 'px; top:' + sTop + 'px; width:' + sWdh + 'px; height:' +
      sHgt + 'px; visibility:' + sVis + ' z-Index=' + (++zIdx) +
      '">' + copy + '</DIV>');
  }
}
```

Lines 163–177:

```
function hideSlide(name) { refSlide(name).visibility = hideName; }

function showSlide(name) { refSlide(name).visibility = showName; }

function refSlide(name) {
  if (NN) { return document.layers[name]; }
  else { return eval('document.all.' + name + '.style'); }
}

function changeSlide(offset) {
  hideSlide('slide' + curSlide);
  curSlide = (curSlide + offset < 0 ? slideShow.length - 1 :
    (curSlide + offset == slideShow.length ? 0 : curSlide + offset));
  showSlide('slide' + curSlide);
}
```

Five functions: `genSlide()`, `refSlide()`, `hideSlide()`, `showSlide()`, and `changeSlide()`. All of them operate the same way they did in Chapter 3; if you're not clear on how any of them works, flip back a chapter and check them out. There are actually two more functions, `imagePreLoad()` and `imageSwap()`, which perform the same operations as well, but they've been modified enough to merit new discussion.

Dynamically Preloading Images

One of the big web paradigms is performing conventionally static operations dynamically. Why do something statically when you can manage it more easily on the fly? That's what the following code does with image preloading. What's the typical modus operandi when you want to preload images to perform rollovers? It might look something like this:

```
var myImage1On = new Image();
myImage1On.src = 'images/myImgOn1.gif';
var myImage1Off = new Image();
myImage1Off.src = 'images/myImgOff1.gif';
```

Simple enough. But that's four lines of code for one pair of image rollovers. What if you have five or ten pairs? That's 20 or 40 lines. If you ever have to make changes, that'll get messy in no time. The Multiple Search Engine Interface introduces a way to pull off the same preloading, no matter how many (theoretically) image pairs you have. We'll need three things:

1. An array of *Image* objects for each set of images you'll need. This application uses one array for the images used when the mouse pointer arrow is over the link and one array for the images that roll back when the mouse pointer arrow moves out of the link.

2. A simple naming convention for the images. The *myImg1On.gif/myImgOff1.gif* convention will work fine. See the "JavaScript Technique: The Advantage of Simple Naming Conventions" sidebar in Chapter 3 for more information. The naming convention must incorporate the names of the arrays in step 1.

3. The `eval()` method.

For step 1, this application will use two arrays. One will be named *out* and will contain *Image* objects of those images that roll over when the mouse-pointer arrow is outside the linked image. The other will be named *over* and will contain *Image* objects of those images that roll over when the mouse-pointer arrow is over the linked image. Those variables will be represented for now in an array of strings called *arrayHandles*, line 20:

```
var arrayHandles = new Array('out', 'over')
```

For step 2, we'll use a very simple naming convention. All image pairs will have the same prefix followed by either *out.jpg* or *over.jpg*, depending on the image. For example, the image rollovers associated with InfoSeek are named *infoseekout.jpg* and *infoseekover.jpg*.

For step 3, we'll first iterate through each element of *arrayHandles* and use `eval()` to create the arrays soon to hold the *Image* objects. Enter lines 22–24:

```
for (var i = 0; i < arrayHandles.length; i++) {
  eval('var ' + arrayHandles[i] + ' = new Array()');
  }
```

Performing the above *for* loop is equivalent to hardcoding this:

```
var out   = new Array();
var over  = new Array();
```

To polish off the preloading, we use `eval()` again in function `preLoadImages()` to dynamically create *Image* objects and assign the SRC property of each. Here is the function in lines 104–110:

```
function imagePreLoad(imgName, idx) {
  for(var j = 0; j < arrayHandles.length; j++) {
    eval(arrayHandles[j] + "[" + idx + "] = new Image()");
    eval(arrayHandles[j] + "[" + idx + "].src = '" + imgPath +
      imgName + arrayHandles[j] + ".jpg'");
    }
  }
```

`imagePreLoad()` accepts two arguments, a name prefix (e.g., *Infoseek*) and an integer used to assign the appropriate array element to a new *Image* object. Once again, a *for* loop iterates through *arrayHandles*, utilizing each element string to access one of the arrays just created and assign it a unique reference. For example. Calling `imagePreLoad('infoseek', 0)` is equivalent to hardcoding the following:

```
out[0]      = new Image();
out[0].src  = 'images/infoseekout.jpg';
over[0]     = new Image();
over[0].src = 'images/infoseekover.jpg';
```

But that's four lines of code, exactly what I wanted to avoid doing over and over. Every time I want a new image rollover pair, I can make a call to `preLoad-Images()`. And that is working smarter, not harder.

Start Your Engines

Variable *engines* at lines 26–100 represents an array of elements, each containing another array of elements with specific search engine information. Variable *engines* has 20 fairly long elements, so let's takes a look at just the first one as shown in lines 27–29:

```
new Array('HotBot',
          'http://www.hotbot.com/?MT=',
          'http://www.hotbot.com/'),
```

Element 0 identifies the search engine name, HotBot. Element 1 identifies the URL with the query string, which, when included with query text, will call the search engine and return the results page. Element 2 represents the URL of the search engine home page. This is used in place of Element 1 if the user attempts a null search (searching with an empty string).

JavaScript Technique: Reusing Your Code

It's not really a JavaScript technique, per se. You can apply this to just about any language. If you take a higher level approach when coding, particularly when creating objects and functions, you'll find that you can use the same code in multiple situations. Consider the functions `genSlide()`, `refSlide()`, `hideSlide()`, and `showSlide()`. They perform very basic, but necessary operations. The following list explains.

- To create cross-browser DHTML layers, use `genSlide()`

- To reference cross-browser DHTML layers, use `refSlide()`

- To hide cross-browser DHTML layers, use `hideSlide()`

- To show cross-browser DHTML layers, use `showSlide()`

Think of all the mileage we got from those functions in the last chapter. We'll also see them again later in the book. If you haven't already, consider building a JavaScript source file library with your reusable code. Chapter 6, *Implementing JavaScript Source Files*, tells you all about it. When you devise a great function or object that you're sure to use again, drop it into a wisely named *.js* file for easy future access.

---

engineLinks( )

Function `engineLinks()` is similar to function `genScreen()` in Chapter 3 because it is responsible for managing the creation of the layers. It does have its differences, though. Examine lines 112–140.

Managing layers

The first thing this function takes care of is generating the layer containing the navigation links:

```
genLayer('sliderule', left - 20, top + 2, 25, engHgt, true,
  '<A HREF="javascript: changeSlide(1);" '+
  'onMouseOver="hideStatus(); return true;"><IMG SRC="' +
  imgPath + 'ahead.gif" BORDER=0></A><BR><A HREF="javascript: ' +
  'changeSlide(-1);" onMouseOver="hideStatus(); return true;">' +
  '<IMG SRC="' + imgPath + 'back.gif" BORDER=0></A>');
```

This happens with a simple call to `genLayer()`. There are no real surprises here. The layer will contain two linked images: a forward and a backward arrow. Notice that the left and top pixel values passed in are relative to the left and top positions, `left - 20` and `top + 2`, of the soon-to-be created engine link layers.

Next up, variable *lyrCount* determines the number of layers of search engine buttons to create, depending on the number of buttons you want per layer and the

JavaScript Technique: Foregoing OO

After taking a good look at the *engines* array, you might be wondering why we don't have a *searchEngine* constructor. Wouldn't this be a great place to have a *searchEngine* constructor? You know, something like this:

```
function searchEngine(name, searchURL, homePage) {
  this.name = name;
  this.searchURL = searchURL;
  this.homePage = homePage;
  return this;
  }
```

Then *engines* would look like this:

```
var engines = new Array(
    new searchEngine('HotBot',
      'http://www.hotbot.com/?MT=',
      'http://www.hotbot.com/')
  // etc., etc,
```

That is the route I would take except for that one little technicality at line 102:

```
engines = engines.sort();
```

The fact is, I want to present the search engines in alphabetical order. Users will appreciate being able to find their favorite search engines faster. If you take the OO (object oriented) route, the **sort()** method won't change the order of the elements. The array of arrays in lines 26–100, however, will be sorted based upon the first element of each array. That's why the search engine name is the first element in each new array. As it stands right now, JavaScript will sort according to the first element. Objects don't have a first element, per se. This is the same thing that happened in Chapter 1, *The Client-Side Search Engine*. The search results are displayed in alphabetical order, so all the records are coded the same way. Don't get me wrong. I'm still keen on OO. This was just an application that didn't need it.

number of engines you have allotted in the *engines* array. It is really pretty easy. Divide the number of search engines (**engines.length**) by the number of engines you want to display per layer (*perLyr*). If the remainder is anything but 0, you'll need one more layer.

Let's use the values of the application. **engines.length** is 20, and *perLyr* is 4. Therefore, variable *lyrCount* is 5. If I had used 21 engines, 21 / 4 = 5.25. A remainder of .25 indicates the need for an extra layer, so *lyrCount* would be set to 6. Here is the code again:

```
lyrCount = Math.ceil(engines.length / perLyr);
```

The conditional operator performs exactly as described above. If the remainder is 0, set *lyrCount* to `engines.length/perLyr`. Otherwise set *lyrCount* to `Math.ceil(engines.length/perLyr)`. Determining *lyrCount* is important. Once determined, `engineLinks()` creates *lyrCount* layers in lines 122–136:

```
for (var i = 0; i < lyrCount; i++) {
   var engLinkStr = '<TABLE BORDER=0 CELLPADDING=0 CELLSPACING=0><TR>';
   for (var j = 0; j < perLyr; j++) {
      var imgIdx  = (i * perLyr) + j;
      if (imgIdx >= engines.length) { break; }
      var imgName  = nameFormat(engines[imgIdx][0]);
      imagePreLoad(imgName, imgIdx);
      engLinkStr += '<TD><A HREF="javascript: ' +
        callSearch(document.forms[0].elements[0].value, ' + imgIdx +
        ');" onMouseOver="hideStatus(); imageSwap(\'' + imgName + '\', ' +
        imgIdx + ', 1); return true" onMouseOut="imageSwap(\'' + imgName +
        '\', ' + imgIdx + ', 0);"><IMG NAME="' + imgName + '" SRC="' +
        imgPath + imgName + 'out.jpg' + '" BORDER=0></A></TD>';
   }
```

For each layer, `engineLinks()` declares local variable *engLinkStr*, which will contain the code for each slide. After creating *engLinkStr*, which as you can see in line 123 starts the table that will encapsulate the images, a nested *for* loop makes *perLyr* iterations to create the table cells that will contain the image.

For each *perLyr* iteration, local variable *imgIdx* is assigned the value `(i * perLyr) + j`. That expression is simply an integer that starts at 0 and is incremented by 1 at the beginning of every iteration. *imgIdx* will be used to identify the prefix of the images (which is the name of the search engine in element 0 in each array in *engines*) and then preload the images as discussed earlier. Table 4-1 offers a quick multiplication scheme when *perLyr* is 4.

Table 4-1. Calculating Layers to Display (perLayer is 4)

When i is . . .	And j values at . . .	(i * perLyr) + j keeps rising by 1 . . .
0	0, 1, 2, 3	0, 1, 2, 3
1	0, 1, 2, 3	4, 5, 6, 7
2	0, 1, 2, 3	8, 9, 10, 11
3	0, 1, 2, 3	12, 13, 14, 15
4	0, 1, 2, 3	16, 17, 18, 19

There are 20 integers, 0–19.

Now that we know the value of *imgIdx*, we have to make sure we haven't gone too far. Line 126 handles that:

```
if (imgIdx == engines.length) { break; }
```

JavaScript Technique: Math Versus Memory

Instead of some unnecessary expression such as (`i` * `perLyr`) + `j`, why not just set a variable—named, for example, *count*—set it to 0, and increment it every iteration, like **++count**? Well, you certainly can. But why allocate more memory resources in declaring an extra variable, even if it's local?

JavaScript already has the necessary values in *i*, *perLyr*, and *j*, to perform the desired calculation. It might seem like a small issue here, but this can conserve precious memory when coding larger applications.

Since the value of *imgIdx* is incremented unconditionally each iteration, once it reaches the **engines.length**, there are no more search engines to display links for, so the function will "break" out of the *for* loop.

Preloading images

The time has come to preload the pair of images for each search engine. Before that happens, we need to know the image prefix. Simply enough, the prefix is the lowercase version of the search engine name. That is, the "InfoSeek" image prefix is *infoseek*; the HotBot image prefix is *hotbot*, and so on. Variable *imgIdx* identifies the correct image prefix in line 127:

```
var imgName = nameFormat(engines[imgIdx][0]);
```

Element 0 of each array in *engines* contains the search engine name. Variable *imgIdx* identifies the correct element index in *engines*, which returns that search engine name. All that is left is to convert all the letters to lowercase. Function **nameFormat()** does the trick at lines 158–161:

```
function nameFormat(str) {
  var tempArray = str.split(' ');
  return tempArray.join('').toLowerCase();
  }
```

All whitespace is removed by splitting the string passed by whitespaces into array elements, then joined. Now *imgName* has a lowercase, whitespace-free image prefix. It is ready to be passed with *imgIdx* to **imagePreload()** in line 128.

Building the link

Time to build a linked image with appropriate rollover code for each search engine. Enter lines 129–135:

```
engLinkStr += '<TD><A HREF="javascript: ' +
  'callSearch(document.forms[0].elements[0].value, ' + imgIdx + ');" ' +
  'onMouseOver="hideStatus(); imageSwap(\'' + imgName + '\', ' + imgIdx +
```

```
', 1); return true" onMouseOut="imageSwap(\'' + imgName + '\', ' +
   imgIdx + ', 0);"><IMG NAME="' + imgName + '" SRC="' + imgPath +
   imgName + 'out.jpg' + '" BORDER=0></A></TD>';
```

Let's consider this. Each search engine link will need the same four requirements:

1. Code that calls the appropriate search engine when the user clicks on the image

2. Code for the *onMouseOver* event handler that rolls over the image

3. Code for the *onMouseOut* event handler that rolls the image back

4. An `IMG` tag with a unique `NAME` and the `SRC` attribute set to the corresponding image path

Dissecting the string set to *engLinkStr* will reveal how each requirement is satisfied.

The first requirement is satisfied with the following code:

```
HREF="javascript: callSearch(document.forms[0].elements[0].value, ' +
   imgIdx + ');"
```

You can see that the link created, upon being clicked, will call function `callSearch()`, in which `document.forms[0].elements[0].value` will be passed in along with the corresponding value of *imgIdx*. More on `callSearch()` soon. For now it's safe to say that requirement 1 is in the bag.

The second requirement is satisfied by the following code:

```
'onMouseOver="hideStatus(); imageSwap(\'' + imgName + '\', ' + imgIdx +
   ', 1); return true" ' +
```

This code handles creating the call to `hideStatus()` for clearing the status bar of annoying URLs, then the call to `imageSwap()`, passing in the three necessary parameters *imgName*, *imgIdx*, and an integer (1) corresponding to the element in *arrayHandles*.

The third requirement is remedied like so:

```
'onMouseOut="imageSwap(\'' + imgName + '\', ' + imgIdx + ', 0);">' +
```

Not much of a change. The only appreciable difference is passing in 0 instead of 1.

And now for the fourth requirement:

```
'<IMG NAME="' + imgName + '" SRC="' + imgPath + imgName + 'out.jpg' +
   '" BORDER=0></A></TD>';
```

The name of each image is set to the value of *imgName*. That is how it will be referenced in function `imageSwap()`. The `SRC` attribute is set to the concatenation of *imgPath*, *imgName*, and *out.jpg*. Since the images will start in the mouse-arrow pointer *out* position, the `SRC` tag is set to the images corresponding with the *out.jpg* substring. For example, the opening image for HotBot is located at *images/hotbotout.jpg*.

Lines 137–138 add the finishing touches:

```
engLinkStr += '</TR></TABLE>';
genLayer('slide' + i, left, top, engWdh, engHgt, false, engLinkStr);
```

That is, *engLinkStr* receives the HTML to close the table, and all that remains is to create the layer with **genLayer()**. Notice that all calls to **genLayer()** here pass in false. Remember that passing in **false** hides the layer from view. All the layers are hidden until the page is loaded. Then *slide0* is revealed in the *onLoad* event handler at line 201.

imageSwap()

You saw it Chapter 3, but this version is a bit different. Consider lines 179–182:

```
function imageSwap(imagePrefix, imageIndex, arrayIdx) {
  document[imagePrefix].src = eval(arrayHandles[arrayIdx] + "[" +
  imageIndex + "].src");
}
```

This function performs the image rollovers. Argument *imagePrefix* identifies the source of the image to be switched. Arguments *imageIndex* and *arrayIdx* are integers that properly access the correct *Image* object in *arrayHandles*.

callSearch()

When the HTML form and the layers are in place, the user needs only enter search text and click the search engine of choice. When users click a search engine image, function **callSearch()** gets the call. Here it is in lines 184–193:

```
function callSearch(searchTxt, idx) {
  if (searchTxt == "") {
    parent.frames[2].location.href = engines[idx][2] +
      escape(searchTxt);
  }
  else {
    parent.frames[2].location.href = engines[idx][1] +
      escape(searchTxt);
  }
}
```

callSearch() expects two arguments. *searchTxt* contains the text entered in the text field, and *idx* contains an integer that corresponds with the search engine information in the engines array. The application loads one of two documents in **frames[2]**. If the user enters no search text, **frames[2]** is loaded with the default home page of the search engine. This URL is contained in element 2 of each array in engines. If, however, the user enters search text, the application loads **frames[2]** with the URL and query string of the search engine, plus the escaped version of the text the user entered.

JavaScript Technique: Using escape() and unescape()

escape() is a built-in function in JavaScript that converts the non-alpha-numeric characters of a string to their hexadecimal equivalents. This ensures that reserved or disallowed characters don't interfere with processing the string. For example, the ampersand (&) is already used to separate name-value pairs of form fields. So every & the user enters is replaced with %26. escape() is commonly used to format strings that you want to submit as part of a URL query string. Whenever you submit a form, your browser takes care of the work for you. Since this application doesn't use form submission, char-acter conversion must be added.

unescape() is handy when writing cookies. The plus sign (+) and equals sign (=) are reserved to assign values to cookie attributes, such as *name, domain,* and *expires.* The unescape() method, as you might guess, converts the hexadecimal representations back to their ASCII equivalents.

You might be wondering where I got those lengthy query strings in element 1 of each array in *engines.* Where could I possibly come up with those values?

Actually, I checked the source code of each search page and built the query string based on the HTML form used to submit search text. Let's start with an easy exam-ple. MusicSearch.com has a single text field for searching. The ACTION attribute of the form is *http://www.musicsearch.com/global/search/search.cgi.* The name of the field is *QUERY.* Therefore, the URL with query string should look like this:

```
http://www.musicsearch.com/global/search/search.cgi?QUERY= +
    escape(searchTxt);
```

That's pretty easy. One name-value pair. Search engines can have *plenty* of options, though. Consider the meta-search engine (one that searches other organi-zations' databases instead of its own) SavvySearch. With SavvySearch, you enter search text, and then can use checkboxes to choose which media to search, such as search engines, newsgroups, etc. You can also impose Boolean search rules, set the number of results to return from each database, and choose the amount of information displayed about each search result.

The ACTION attribute of the SavvySearch form is *http://numan.cs.colostate. edu:1969/npb-search.* Here is a list of the required form elements:

- The name of the select list for Boolean searches is *Boolean*

- The name of the results count select list is *Hits*

- The name of the result amount radio buttons is *df*

- The name of the text field is *KW*

I set the *Boolean* select list value to OR, the *Hits* select list value to 10, the results display button *df* value to `normal`, and the search text field *KW* to `escape(searchTxt)`. I didn't invent values OR, 10, and `normal`. Those are either option values in the select lists or radio button values, all of which are in the HTML source code.

The form also contains two hidden fields, one with the name *Mode,* and the other with the name *AutoStep.* The *Mode* HIDDEN field has the value `MakePlan`. The HIDDEN field *AutoStep* has the value `on`. I'm not sure what purpose they serve, but that's not important. All you have to do is add them to the query string. Submitting a query to SavvySearch, then, requires the following URL:

```
http://numan.cs.colostate.edu:1969/nph-search? ' +
    classic=on&Boolean=OR&Hits=10&Mode=MakePlan&df=normal&AutoStep=on&KW= +
    escape(searchTxt)
```

Another nice thing about "decrypting" the query strings is that the order of the name-value pairs generally doesn't matter. As long as they are in the query string, things will work fine.

Potential Extension: Adding User Control

As mentioned earlier, this application leaves users at the "mercy" of the search engine defaults. That is, users have little or no control over customizing their searches. The only thing the user has to enter is the query text. You can code it so that users can also effect such features as the number of results to return per page, the amount of information displayed with each result, or perhaps whether to impose Boolean search rules with terms such as AND, OR, LIKE, and NOT LIKE. In this section, I'll use the HotBot search engine as an example.

Perhaps the easiest way to extend functionality is to increase the number of results per page. You'll need the name-value pair associated with the results per page for each search engine. Table 4-2 lists a few names and possible values for several search engines.

Table 4-2. Search Engines and Variables for Determining the Result Count

Search Engine	Field name	Possible values	Example
HotBot	DC	10, 25, 50, 100	DC=10
InfoSeek Advanced Search	Numberresults	10, 20, 25, 50	Numberresults=10
Scientific American	Docs	10, 25, 50, 100	Docs=10
Yahoo!	N	10, 20, 50, 100	n=10

I pulled these field names from the source code of each search page. Some of the fields come from the search engine's advanced search pages, so the URLs in the *engines* array might not work. Keep in mind, too, that the number of results might not be adjustable. The search engine coders may have it set to a fixed number. If you don't see a select list on the search page that allows you to change the number of results, you might contact the organization and ask someone if the results (and other features, while you're at it) can be modified. Otherwise, you'll have to add some type of default that doesn't pass in a results field for certain search engines.

Notice also that the possible values vary among search engines. You'll have to add code to compensate for that. It's not difficult, though. Use the following procedure to add a search-results select list to your application. Then use it as a general guideline to add other feature controls.

1. Add a select list to the frame containing the text field.

2. Add an extra element in each new array containing the name of the results field for each corresponding search engine in the engine array.

3. And an extra **new Array()** containing possible values of the corresponding search engine to each new array in the *engines* array.

4. Remove the predefined name-value pair from the query string (if the name-value pair exists in the query string) .

5. Adjust the code in function **callSearch()** to correctly concatenate the query string for each search engine.

Let's stick with the HotBot example.

Step 1

Adding the select list shouldn't be a problem. It might be wise to choose values most common to all the search engines in your application. Here is the code using 10, 25, 50, and 100:

```
<SELECT NAME="docs">
<OPTION VALUE="10">10
<OPTION VALUE="25">25
<OPTION VALUE="50">50
<OPTION VALUE="100">100
</SELECT>
```

Step 2

As it stands, each instance of **new Array()** in the *engines* array defines a search engine with three elements: element 0 is the search engine name; element 1 is the search engine query string; and element 2 is the search engine home page. Here is the HotBot record again:

```
new Array('HotBot',
   'http://www.hotbot.com/?MT=',
   'http://www.hotbot.com/')
```

Set element 3 to the name of the field associated with HotBot. Recalling the previous table, the field name is *DC*. Now the HotBot record looks like this:

```
new Array('HotBot',
  'http://www.hotbot.com/?MT=',
  'http://www.hotbot.com/',
  'DC')
```

If one or more of your search engines doesn't have a results count (and, hence, a name-value pair) that you can set, place null in element 3.

Step 3

Now that you have identified the respective name, add another array containing all the allowable values. Do so by defining the new array in element 4. Referring again to the previous table, the HotBot record would look like this:

```
new Array('HotBot',
  'http://www.hotbot.com/?MT=',
  'http://www.hotbot.com/',
  'DC',
  new Array(10, 25, 50, 100))
```

Step 4

This step applies only if the default query string in element 2 contains the name-value pair of the results setting. Here is the query string for HotBot in element 2:

```
http://www.hotbot.com/?MT=
```

Since *DC* isn't there, we can skip step 4. Just as an example though, the search engine for *Scientific American* does contain the name-value pair, which is docs=100. Take a look:

```
http://www.sciam.com/cgi-bin/search.cgi?' +
  'searchby=strict&groupby=confidence&docs=100&query=
```

You would need to take that out so it looks like this:

```
http://www.sciam.com/cgi-bin/search.cgi?' +
  'searchby=strict&groupby=confidence&query=
```

If one or more of your search engines doesn't have a results count (and, hence, a name-value pair) that you can set, don't create a value for element 4.

Step 5

The last item to handle is the decision-making code that constructs the query string before passing it to the awaiting search engine. You can do this all in function callSearch(). Here is the original code:

```
function callSearch(searchTxt, idx) {
  if (searchTxt == "") {
    parent.frames[2].location.href = engines[idx][2] +
      escape(searchTxt);
  }
```

```
    else {
      parent.frames[2].location.href = engines[idx][1] +
        escape(searchTxt);
      }
    }
```

If the user enters nothing in the query text form field, the application should still redirect the user to the search engine home page. So the *if* block can stay the same. It's in the *else* block that we need to focus attention:

```
else {
  if(engines[idx][3] != null) {
    for (var i = 0; i < engines[idx][4].length; i++) {
      var selRef = parent.frames[4].document.forms[0].docs;
      if (selRef.options[selRef.selectedIndex].value =
        engines[idx][4][i].toString()) {
        parent.frames[2].location.href = engines[idx][1] +
          escape(searchTxt) + '&' + engines[idx][3] + '=' +
          engines[idx][4][i];
        return;
        }
      }
    }
  parent.frames[2].location.href = engines[idx][1] +
    escape(searchTxt);
  }
```

Here is the line that adds the appropriate name-value pair to the query string:

```
parent.frames[2].location.href = engines[idx][1] +
  escape(searchTxt) + '&' + engines[idx][3] + '=' +
  engines[idx][4][i];
```

What you have here is the search engine URL plus the escaped *searchTxt* plus the name (`engines[idx][3]`) plus the value the user chose. However, this happens only after two conditions are satisfied. If not, the search is set to the default query string defined in element `engines[idx][1]`. First, the search engine must have a results feature that you can change. If so, the field is defined as the string in `engines[idx][3]`. Otherwise, that element is set to null. This happens in step 3. The following *if* statement verifies that `engines[idx][3]` is not null:

```
if(engines[idx][3] != null) {
```

If the value is equal to null, the first condition has failed. Therefore, the default query string is used. If `engines[idx][3]` does not equal null, Java-Script then iterates through the number of acceptable values defined in the array at `engines[idx][4]`. If the number chosen in the select list, which is represented by `selRef.options[selRef.selectedIndex].value`, matches one of the acceptable values in the array, JavaScript concatenates the user search engine URL and query text with the name-value pair, then loads `frames[2]` with the document result, and stops executing.

If the loop iterates through all acceptable values without encountering a match, the second condition has failed, and the default query string is used instead.

5

ImageMachine

Application Features

- Dynamic Image Rollover Code Generator and Viewer
- Code Accommodates Lesser JavaScript Browsers
- Flexible and Extensible HTML Attribute Settings
- Supports Image Rollovers for MouseDown Events

JavaScript Techniques

- JavaScripting Defensively
- The Power of Global Variables
- Search and Replace in JavaScript 1.1 and 1.2

Everywhere you look in these chapters, the applications are designed with one person in mind: the user. You know, the ones we want to arrive like lemmings to our web sites, then bump up our traffic, buy our stuff, and download our software. This application breaks the mold. This one's for you: the developer, webmaster, or designer.

Although DHTML has enhanced the capabilities of what can happen when we put our mouse-pointer arrows over some frame, widget, button or stylesheet, the image rollover is still one of the hottest and most widely used techniques on the Net.

Generating the JavaScript to enable the rollovers isn't rocket science, but it sure would make life easier to have an application that spews nicely formatted image rollover code. That way, we coders can just drop it in our pages. Enter ImageMachine. Figure 5-1 shows the opening look as you open *ch05/index.html*.

The app is fairly easy to use. You just have to make a few decisions about your images. As Figure 5-1 indicates:

1. Choose the number of image pairs you want.

2. Set the default width, height, and border for all the images. (You can make individual adjustments later).

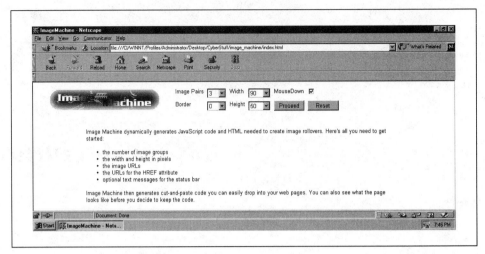

Figure 5-1. ImageMachine ready for action

3. Check the "MouseDown" option if you want to specify a third image for the *onMouseDown* state. Otherwise, leave it blank.

4. Choose "Proceed" to continue or "Reset" to start over.

Once you've reached this point, ImageMachine generates a template as shown in Figure 5-2.

If you didn't select the "MouseDown" option, you'll have two HTML file fields for each image group: one for the primary image and one for the rollover image. If you selected the "MouseDown" option, an extra corresponding file field will also appear. Each image also comes with fields to enter the HREF attribute for each link and any status text to be displayed in the status bar when users pass the mouse-pointer arrows over the link. Finally, three small text fields contain the value of the default width, height, and border values of each image group—yours for the changing. Take the final few steps to get the code you need:

1. Enter the paths of each primary image (the one displayed when the pointer arrow is elsewhere) in the file fields. They are file fields instead of text fields because your images might be on your local machine. You can change the URL info once you're satisfied with the code. Do the same for each rollover image and mousedown image, if you have any.

2. Enter a relative or absolute URL in the text field associated with HREF for each image group.

3. In the "Status Bar" text field, enter any status bar text you want displayed when the user passes the mouse pointer arrow over the link.

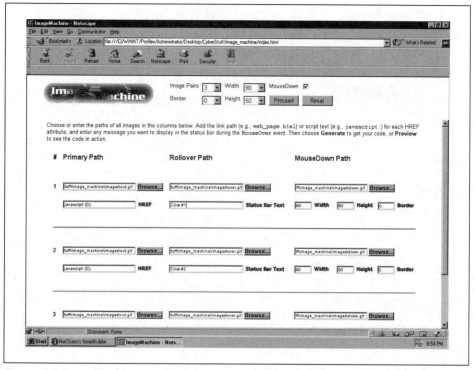

Figure 5-2. ImageMachine generates a custom template according to the options you select

4. Make any adjustments to the individual width, height, and border attributes in their respective text fields.

5. Choose "Generate" to see the code or "Preview" to see how the code works in your browser.

Figure 5-3 shows ImageMachine after "Generate" is chosen. Check out the Java-Script and HTML, all well commented. Notice that for each image group you specify, ImageMachine generates the code to preload the images and set them up for the rollover. The ensuing HTML includes corresponding A HREF and IMG tags, fully loaded with event handlers and image attributes.

You'll notice two more buttons at the bottom of the screen. "Preview" lets you see the code in action. "Change Info" lets you go back to the template and make changes. Figure 5-4 shows the interpreted code displaying the images and their preloaded rollover counterparts.

One of the most powerful things about this generated code is that it reduces performance according to the JavaScript capability of the browser in which it is viewed. In other words, browsers that support JavaScript 1.2 and higher will perform both *onMouseOver-*, *onMouseOut-*, and *onMouseDown-*related rollovers. JavaScript 1.1 capable browsers will fire only the *onMouseOut-* and *onMouseOver-*

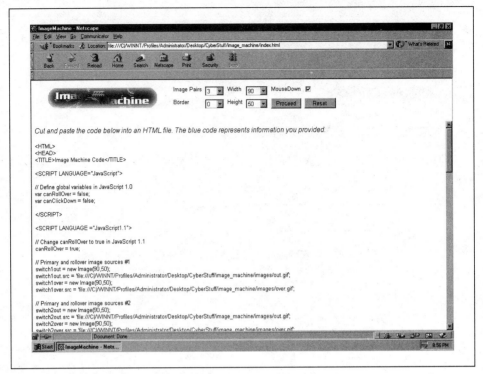

Figure 5-3. See the code you just created

related rollovers. JavaScript 1.0 capable browsers execute only the code for setting the status bar text.

And how's this for bandwidth-friendly? Only the images that will actually be used are downloaded. If the browser can't use it, it won't have to download it. Java-Script 1.1 browsers won't preload any images associated with the *onMouseDown* event. JavaScript 1.0 capable browsers won't preload any of the images!

Execution Requirements

Although the code generated will run in any JavaScript-capable browser, you, the developer, must use a JavaScript 1.2-capable browser. Some string replacement and other code requires 1.2. As far as scalability goes, you can create the code for as many rollovers as your system resources can accommodate. The maximum is currently set to 50 groups, which is more than I think I'll ever have on one page, but to each his own.

By the way, the interface is designed to be viewed with a monitor resolution of at least 1024 × 768. The requirements of both the image template and the code demand the extra page width.

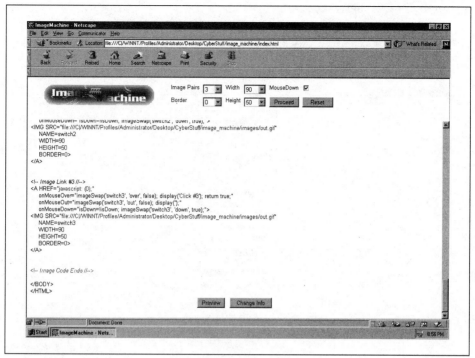

Figure 5-4. Choose "Preview" or "Change Info" for more options

The Syntax Breakdown

Before we consider any code, it might be a good idea to get a visual sense of the program flow. Figure 5-5 illustrates the basic flow from beginning to end. Basically, you begin by creating your image form and setting the specs for each rollover. Then you can toggle back and forth between previewing, making changes, and generating the code. When you see what you like, copy and paste the generated code.

ImageMachine has three files: a frameset page and two content pages. The frameset is named *index.html*, and contains files *nav.html* and *base.html. index. html* has neither JavaScript nor any surprises. Brace yourself; here are all nine staggering lines, shown in Example 5-1.

Example 5-1. index.html

```
1 <HTML>
2 <HEAD>
3 <TITLE>ImageMachine</TITLE>
4 </HEAD>
5 <FRAMESET ROWS="105, *" FRAMEBORDER="0" BORDER="0">
```

Example 5-1. index.html (continued)

```
6    <FRAME SRC="nav.html" NAME="nav" SCROLLING=NO>
7    <FRAME SRC="base.html" NAME="base">
8    </FRAMESET>
9 </HTML>
```

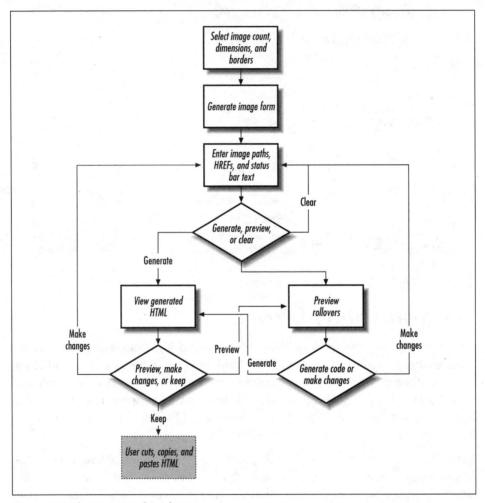

Figure 5-5. The ImageMachine logic

If you look at *base.html*, you'll see more static HTML. Before we get to *nav.html*, shown in Example 5-2, it's important to understand a few things about the code you're about to see. It's long (400+ lines) and somewhat hard to read, but not all that complicated.

Example 5-2. nav.html

```
 1 <HTML>
 2 <HEAD>
 3 <TITLE>ImageMachine</TITLE>
 4 <SCRIPT LANGUAGE="JavaScript1.2">
 5
 6 var platform = navigator.platform;
 7 var lb = (platform.indexOf("Win" != -1) ? "\n\r" :
 8   (platform.indexOf("Mac" != -1) ? "\r" : "\n"));
 9 var fontOpen = '<FONT COLOR=BLUE>';
10 var fontClose = '</FONT>';
11
12 function genSelect(name, count, start, select) {
13   var optStr = "";
14   for (var h = start; h <= count; h++) {
15     optStr += "<OPTION VALUE=" + h +
16       (h == select ? " SELECTED" : "") + ">" + h;
17   }
18   document.write("<SELECT NAME=" + name + ">" + optStr + "</SELECT>");
19 }
20
21 function captureDefaultProfile(formObj) {
22   setArrays();
23   imgDefaults    = formObj;
24   var imgQty     = (imgDefaults.imgnumber.selectedIndex + 1);
25   var imgHeight  = (imgDefaults.pxlheight.selectedIndex);
26   var imgWidth   = (imgDefaults.pxlwidth.selectedIndex);
27   var imgBorder  = (imgDefaults.defbdr.selectedIndex);
28   for (var i = 0; i < imgQty; i++) {
29     imgPrim[i] = "";
30     imgRoll[i] = "";
31     imgDown[i] = "";
32     imgLink[i] = "";
33     imgText[i] = "";
34     imgWdh[i]  = imgWidth;
35     imgHgt[i]  = imgHeight;
36     imgBdr[i]  = imgBorder;
37   }
38   generateEntryForm();
39 }
40
41 function setArrays() {
42   imgPrim = new Array();
43   imgRoll = new Array();
44   imgDown = new Array();
45   imgLink = new Array();
46   imgText = new Array();
47   imgWdh  = new Array();
48   imgHgt  = new Array();
49   imgBdr  = new Array();
50 }
51
52
```

Example 5-2. nav.html (continued)

```
53 function generateEntryForm() {
54   with(parent.frames[1].document) {
55   open();
56     writeln("<HTML><BODY BGCOLOR=FFFFEE><FONT FACE=Arial SIZE=2>" +
57       "<BLOCKQUOTE>Choose or enter the paths of all images in the " +
58       "columns below. Add the link path (e.g., <FONT FACE=Courier>" +
59       "web_page.html</FONT>) or script text (e.g., <FONT FACE=Courier>" +
60       "javascript:</FONT>) for each HREF attribute, and  enter any " +
61       "message you want to display in the status bar during the " +
62       "<FONT FACE=Courier>MouseOver</FONT> event. Then choose " +
63       "<B>Generate</B> to get your code, or <B>Preview</B> to see the " +
64       "code in action.</BLOCKQUOTE><FORM NAME='imgProfile' " +
65       "onSubmit='return false;'><CENTER><TABLE BORDER=0 ALIGN=CENTER " +
66       "CELLSPACING=5 CELLPADDING=5><TH ALIGN=LEFT><FONT FACE=Arial>#" +
67       "<TH ALIGN=LEFT><FONT FACE=Arial>Primary Path" +
68       "<TH ALIGN=LEFT><FONT FACE=Arial>Rollover Path" +
69       (imgDefaults.mousedown.checked ? "<TH ALIGN=LEFT>" +
70       "<FONT FACE=Arial>MouseDown Path" : "") +
71       "<TR><TD><BR></TD></TR>");
72     }
73
74   for (i = 0; i < imgPrim.length; i++) {
75     with(parent.frames[1].document) {
76       writeln("<TR>" +
77       "<TD><FONT FACE=Arial SIZE=2><CENTER><B>" + (i + 1) +
78       "</B></CENTER><TD VALIGN=BOTTOM><FONT FACE=Arial SIZE=2>" +
79       "<INPUT TYPE=FILE NAME='prim" + i + "' VALUE='" + imgPrim[i] +
80       "'><TD VALIGN=BOTTOM><FONT FACE=Arial SIZE=2><INPUT TYPE=FILE " +
81       "NAME='seci" + i + "' VALUE='" + imgRoll[i] + "'>" +
82       (imgDefaults.mousedown.checked ? "<TD VALIGN=BOTTOM><FONT " +
83       "FACE=Arial SIZE=2><INPUT TYPE=FILE NAME='down" + i + "' VALUE='" +
84       imgDown[i] + "'>" : "") + "<TR><TD VALIGN=BOTTOM><FONT " +
85       "FACE=Arial SIZE=2>   </TD>" +
86       "<TD VALIGN=BOTTOM><FONT FACE=Arial SIZE=2><INPUT TYPE=TEXT " +
87       "NAME='href" + i + "' VALUE='" + imgLink[i] + "'> " +
88       "<IMG SRC='images/href.jpg'><TD VALIGN=BOTTOM><FONT FACE=Arial " +
89       "SIZE=2><INPUT TYPE=TEXT NAME='stat" + i + "' VALUE='" +
90       imgText[i] + "'><IMG SRC='images/statusbar.jpg'> " +
91       (!imgDefaults.mousedown.checked ?"<TR>" : "") +
92       "<TD VALIGN=BOTTOM><FONT FACE=Arial SIZE=2>" +
93       (!imgDefaults.mousedown.checked ?
94       "</TD><TD VALIGN=BOTTOM><FONT FACE=Arial SIZE=2>" : "") +
95       "<INPUT TYPE=TEXT NAME='wdh" + i + "' VALUE='" +
96       imgWdh[i] + "' SIZE=3> <IMG SRC='images/wdh.jpg'> " +
97       "   <INPUT TYPE=TEXT NAME='hgt" + i + "' VALUE='" +
98       imgHgt[i] + "' SIZE=3><IMG SRC='images/hgt.jpg'>  " +
99       (!imgDefaults.mousedown.checked ?
100      "<TD VALIGN=BOTTOM><FONT FACE=Arial SIZE=2>" : "") +
101      "<INPUT TYPE=TEXT NAME='bdr" + i + "' VALUE='" + imgBdr[i] +
102      "' SIZE=3> <IMG SRC='images/bdr.jpg'>" +
103      "<TR><TD VALIGN=BOTTOM COLSPAN=" +
104      (!imgDefaults.mousedown.checked ? "3" : "4") +
```

Example 5-2. nav.html (continued)

```
105       "><BR><HR NOSHADE><BR></TD></TR>");
106       }
107    }
108
109    with(parent.frames[1].document) {
110      writeln("</TABLE><CENTER><INPUT TYPE=BUTTON " +
111        "onClick='parent.frames[0].imgValid8(this.form, true);' " +
112        "VALUE='Generate'><INPUT TYPE=BUTTON " +
113        "onClick='parent.frames[0].imgValid8(this.form, false);' " +
114        "VALUE='Preview'> <INPUT TYPE=RESET VALUE='   Clear   '>" +
115        "</FORM></BODY></HTML>");
116      close();
117    }
118  }
119
120  function imgValid8(imgTemplate, mimeType) {
121    for (var  i = 0; i < imgPrim.length; i++) {
122      if (imgTemplate['prim' + i].value == "" ||
123        imgTemplate['seci' + i].value == "" ||
124        imgTemplate['href' + i].value == "") {
125        alert("All images and HREF attributes must have URLs.");
126        return;
127      }
128      if (imgDefaults.mousedown.checked) {
129        if(imgTemplate['down' + i].value == "") {
130          alert("All images and HREF attributes must have URLs.");
131          return;
132        }
133      }
134    }
135    genJavaScript(imgTemplate, mimeType);
136  }
137
138  function genJavaScript(imgTemplate, mimeType) {
139    imageLinks = '';
140
141    if (mimeType) {
142      lt    = "&lt;";
143      gt    = "&gt;";
144      br    = "<BR>";
145      HTML  = true;
146      nbsp  = "     ";
147    }
148    else {
149      lt    = "<";
150      gt    = ">";
151      br    = lb;
152      HTML  = false;
153      nbsp  = "      ";
154    }
155
156    if(imgTemplate != null) {
```

Example 5-2. nav.html (continued)

```
157    setArrays();
158    for (var i = 0; i < (imgDefaults.imgnumber.selectedIndex + 1); i++) {
159      imgPrim[i] = purify(imgTemplate['prim' + i].value);
160      imgRoll[i] = purify(imgTemplate['seci' + i].value);
161      if (imgDefaults.mousedown.checked) {
162        imgDown[i] = purify(imgTemplate['down' + i].value);
163        }
164      imgLink[i] = purify(imgTemplate['href' + i].value);
165      imgText[i] = purify(imgTemplate['stat' + i].value);
166      imgWdh[i]  = purify(imgTemplate['wdh' + i].value);
167      imgHgt[i]  = purify(imgTemplate['hgt' + i].value);
168      imgBdr[i]  = purify(imgTemplate['bdr' + i].value);
169      }
170    }
171
172  if (HTML) {
173    primJavaScript = "<HTML><HEAD><TITLE>Image Machine Code</TITLE>" +
174      "</HEAD><BODY BGCOLOR=FFFFEE><FONT FACE=Arial>" +
175      "<I>Cut and paste the code below into an HTML file. The blue " +
176      "code represents information you provided.</I>" +
177      "<BR><BR></FONT><FONT SIZE=2 FACE=Arial>" +
178      lt + "HTML" + gt + "<BR>" + lt + "HEAD" + gt + "<BR>" +
179      lt + "TITLE" + gt + "Image Machine Code" + lt + "/TITLE" + gt;
180    }
181  else {
182    primJavaScript = "<HTML><HEAD><TITLE>Image Machine Code</TITLE>";
183    }
184
185  primJavaScript += br + br + lt + "SCRIPT LANGUAGE=\"JavaScript\"" +
186    gt + br + br + "// Define global variables in JavaScript 1.0" + br +
187    "var canRollOver = false;" + br + "var canClickDown = false;" + br +
188    br + lt + "/SCR" + "IPT" + gt + br + br + lt +
189    "SCRIPT LANGUAGE =\"JavaScript1.1\"" + gt + br + br +
190    "// Change canRollOver to true in JavaScript 1.1" + br +
191    "canRollOver = true;" + br + br;
192
193  secJavaScript = lt + "SCRIPT LANGUAGE=\"JavaScript1.2\"" + gt + br +
194    br + "// Change canClickDown to true in JavaScript 1.2" + br +
195    "canClickDown = true;" + br + br;
196
197  for (var j = 0; j < imgPrim.length; j++) {
198    primJavaScript += "// Primary and rollover image sources #" +
199      (j + 1) + br +"switch" + (j + 1) + "out = new Image(" +
200      (HTML ? fontOpen : "") + imgWdh[j] +
201      (HTML ? "</FONT>," : ", ") +
202      (HTML ? fontOpen : "") + imgHgt[j]  +
203      (HTML ? fontClose : "") + "); " + br + "switch" + (j + 1) +
204      "out.src = '" +
205      (HTML ? fontOpen : "") +
206      (imgPrim[j].indexOf(":\\") != -1 ? pathPrep(imgPrim[j]) :
207        imgPrim[j]) +
208      (HTML ? fontClose : "") + "';" + br + "switch" + (j + 1) +
```

Example 5-2. nav.html (continued)

```
209        "over = new Image(" +
210        (HTML ? fontOpen : "") + imgWdh[j]  +
211        (HTML ? "</FONT>," : ", ") +
212        (HTML ? fontOpen : "") + imgHgt[j] +
213        (HTML ? fontClose : "") + "); " + br + "switch" + (j + 1) +
214        "over.src = '" +
215        (HTML ? fontOpen : "") +
216        (imgRoll[j].indexOf(":\\") != -1 ? pathPrep(imgRoll[j]) :
217          imgRoll[j]) +
218        (HTML ? fontClose : "") + "';" + br + br;
219
220     if (imgDefaults.mousedown.checked) {
221       secJavaScript += "// MouseDown image source #" + (j + 1) + br +
222          "switch" + (j + 1) + "down = new Image(" +
223          (HTML ? fontOpen : "") + imgWdh[j] +
224          (HTML ? "</FONT>," : ", ") +
225          (HTML ? fontOpen : "") + imgHgt[j]  +
226          (HTML ? fontClose : "") + "); " + br + "switch" +
227          (j + 1) + "down.src = '" +
228          (HTML ? fontOpen : "") +
229          (imgPrim[j].indexOf(":\\") != -1 ? pathPrep(imgDown[j]) :
230            imgDown[j]) +
231          (HTML ? fontClose : "") + "';" + br + br;
232       }
233
234     imageLinks += lt + "!-- <I> Image Link #" + (j + 1) +
235        " </I>//--" + gt + br + lt + "A HREF=\"" +
236        (HTML ? fontOpen : "") + imgLink[j] +
237        (HTML ? fontClose : "") + "\" " + br + nbsp +
238        "onMouseOver=\"imageSwap('switch" + (j + 1) +
239        "', 'over', false); display('" +
240        (HTML ? fontOpen : "") + imgText[j] +
241        (HTML ? fontClose : "") + "'); return true;\"" + br +
242        nbsp + "onMouseOut=\"imageSwap('switch" +
243        (j + 1) + "', 'out', false); display('');\"" +
244        (imgDefaults.mousedown.checked ?
245          br + nbsp + "onMouseDown=\"isDown=!isDown; imageSwap('switch" +
246          (j + 1) + "', 'down', true);\"" : "") +
247        gt + br + lt + "IMG SRC=\"" +
248        (HTML ? fontOpen : "") + pathPrep(imgPrim[j]) +
249        (HTML ? fontClose : "") + "\"" + br + nbsp +
250        "NAME=switch" + (j + 1) + br + nbsp + "WIDTH=" +
251        (HTML ? fontOpen : "") + imgWdh[j] +
252        (HTML ? fontClose : "") + br + nbsp + "HEIGHT=" +
253        (HTML ? fontOpen : "") + imgHgt[j] +
254        (HTML ? fontClose : "") + br + nbsp + "BORDER=" +
255        (HTML ? fontOpen : "") + imgBdr[j] +
256        (HTML ? fontClose : "") +
257        gt + "" + lt + "/A" + gt + br + br + br;
258     }
259
260   scriptClose = br + lt + "/SCR" + "IPT" + gt + br + br;
```

Example 5-2. nav.html (continued)

```
261
262    swapCode = br + lt + "/SCR" + "IPT" + gt + br + br +
263      lt + "SCRIPT LANGUAGE =\"JavaScript\"" + gt + br + br +
264      (imgDefaults.mousedown.checked ?
265        "var isDown = false;" + br + br : "") +
266      "// Conditionally perform the rollovers in JavaScript 1.0" + br +
267      "function imageSwap(imageName, imageSuffix) {" + br +
268      nbsp + "if (!canRollOver) { return; }" + br + nbsp +
269      (imgDefaults.mousedown.checked ?
270        "if (!isDown) { " + br + nbsp + nbsp : "") +
271      "document[imageName].src = " +
272      "eval(imageName + imageSuffix + \".src\");" + br + nbsp +
273      (imgDefaults.mousedown.checked ? nbsp + "}" + br + nbsp +
274      "else if (canClickDown) {" + br +
275      nbsp + nbsp + "document[imageName].src = " +
276      eval(imageName + imageSuffix + \".src\");" + br +
277      nbsp + nbsp + "}" + br + nbsp : "") + "}" + br + br +
278      "function display(stuff) { window.status = stuff; }" +
279      br + br + lt + "/SCR" + "IPT" + gt + br;
280
281    primHTML = br + lt + "/HEAD" + gt + br +
282      lt + "BODY BGCOLOR=FFFFEE" +
283      gt + br + br + (HTML ? "<FONT COLOR=RED>" : "") + lt +
284      "!-- <I> Image Code Begins </I> //--" + gt + br +
285      (HTML ? fontClose : "") + br + br;
286
287    secHTML = (HTML ? "<FONT COLOR=RED>" : "") +
288      lt + "!-- <I> Image Code Ends</I> //--" + gt +
289      (HTML ? fontClose : "") + br + br +
290      (HTML ? lt + "/BODY" + gt + br + lt + "/HTML" + gt : "") +
291      br + br + "<CENTER><FORM>" + br +
292      "<INPUT TYPE=BUTTON onClick='parent.frames[0].genJavaScript(null, " +
293      (HTML ? "false" : "true") + ");' VALUE='" +
294      (HTML ? 'Preview' : 'Generate') + "'>   " +
295      "<INPUT TYPE=BUTTON " +
296      "onClick='parent.frames[0].generateEntryForm();' " +
297      "VALUE='Change Info'>" + br + "</FORM></CENTER>" + br + br +
298      "</BODY></HTML>";
299
300    agregate = primJavaScript +
301      (imgDefaults.mousedown.checked ? scriptClose + secJavaScript : "") +
302      swapCode + primHTML + imageLinks + secHTML;
303
304    parent.frames[1].location.href =
305      "javascript: parent.frames[0].agregate";
306    }
307
308  function purify(txt) { return txt.replace(/\'|\"/g, ""); }
309
310  function pathPrep(path) {
311    if (path.indexOf(":\\") != -1) {
312      path = path.replace(/\\/g, "/");
```

Example 5-2. nav.html (continued)

```
313     path = path.replace(/:\//, "|/");
314     return "file:///" + path;
315     }
316   else { return path; }
317   }
318
319 </SCRIPT>
320 </HEAD>
321 <BODY BGCOLOR=FFFFEE>
322 <FORM>
323 <TABLE BORDER="0">
324   <TR>
325     <TD VALIGN=MIDDLE>
326     <IMG SRC="images/image_machine.gif" WIDTH=275 HEIGHT=56 HSPACE=25>
327     </TD>
328     <TD>
329     <!-- Create a the default template //-->
330     <TABLE BORDER="0" ALIGN="CENTER">
331       <TR>
332         <TD VALIGN="TOP">
333         <FONT FACE="Arial" SIZE=2>
334         Image Pairs
335         </TD>
336         <TD VALIGN="TOP">
337         <FONT FACE="Arial" SIZE=2>
338         <SCRIPT LANGUAGE="JavaScript1.2">
339         <!--
340         genSelect("imgnumber", 50, 1, 1);
341         //-->
342         </SCRIPT>
343         </TD>
344         <TD VALIGN="TOP">
345         <FONT FACE="Arial" SIZE=2>
346         Width
347         </TD>
348         <TD VALIGN="TOP">
349         <FONT FACE="Arial" SIZE=2>
350         <SCRIPT LANGUAGE="JavaScript1.2">
351         <!--
352         genSelect("pxlwidth", 250, 0, 90);
353         //-->
354         </SCRIPT>
355         </TD>
356         <TD VALIGN="TOP">
357         <FONT FACE="Arial" SIZE=2>
358         MouseDown
359         </TD>
360         <TD VALIGN="TOP">
361         <FONT FACE="Arial" SIZE=2>
362         <INPUT TYPE=CHECKBOX NAME="mousedown">
363         </TD>
364       </TR>
```

Example 5-2. nav.html (continued)

```
365      <TR>
366          <TD VALIGN="TOP">
367          <FONT FACE="Arial" SIZE=2>
368          Border
369          </TD>
370          <TD VALIGN="TOP">
371          <FONT FACE="Arial" SIZE=2>
372          <SCRIPT LANGUAGE="JavaScript1.2">
373          <!--
374          genSelect("defbdr", 10, 0, 0);
375          //-->
376          </SCRIPT>
377          </TD>
378          <TD VALIGN="TOP">
379          <FONT FACE="Arial" SIZE=2>
380          Height
381          </TD>
382          <TD VALIGN="TOP">
383          <FONT FACE="Arial" SIZE=2>
384          <SCRIPT LANGUAGE="JavaScript1.2">
385          <!--
386          genSelect("pxlheight", 250, 0, 50);
387          //-->
388          </SCRIPT>
389          </TD>
390          <TD VALIGN="TOP">
391          <FONT FACE="Arial" SIZE=2>
392          <INPUT TYPE=BUTTON VALUE="Proceed"
393            onClick="captureDefaultProfile(this.form);">
394          </TD>
395          <TD VALIGN="TOP">
396          <FONT FACE="Arial" SIZE=2>
397          <INPUT TYPE=RESET VALUE="  Reset  ">
398          </TD>
399        </TR>
400      </TABLE>
401      </TD>
402    </TR>
403 </TABLE>
404 </CENTER>
405 </FORM>
406 </BODY>
407 </HTML>
```

That's the most code per application so far. Some of this looks confusing, but it isn't as bad as it seems. To best understand ImageMachine, let's run through the application from a typical user experience. Consider this five-step scenario:

1. The pages load.

2. The user enters the image pairs and defaults, then chooses "Proceed."

3. The user fills in the image paths, HREF attributes, etc, then chooses "Generate" to see the code.

4. The user chooses "Preview" to watch the code in action.

5. The user chooses "Change Info" to make changes.

Step 1: The Pages Load

Everything seems fairly normal. A frameset named *index.html*, and two frame fillers named *nav.html* and *base.html*. JavaScript, however, is going to do some work even before the user has a chance to do anything. I call your attention to lines 323–403. Here you'll see the code for a table with several JavaScript function calls in the data cells. For example:

```
<TD VALIGN="TOP">
<FONT FACE="Arial" SIZE=2>
Image Pairs
</TD>
<TD VALIGN="TOP">
<FONT FACE="Arial" SIZE=2>
<SCRIPT LANGUAGE="JavaScript1.2">
<!--
genSelect("imgnumber", 50, 1, 1);
//-->
</SCRIPT>
</TD>
<TD VALIGN="TOP">
<FONT FACE="Arial" SIZE=2>
Width
</TD>
<TD VALIGN="TOP">
<FONT FACE="Arial" SIZE=2>
<SCRIPT LANGUAGE="JavaScript1.2">
<!--
genSelect("pxlwidth", 250, 0, 90);
//-->
</SCRIPT>
</TD>
```

The calls to function `genSelect()` use JavaScript to dynamically create select lists. Each of the select lists allows you to set default values for the image attributes. Select lists work better here than text fields because you don't have to worry about form validation as much. The user can't enter an incorrect value (such as a non-numeric value) for a border or image width because he or she must select from the numbers provided in the lists. But who wants to hard-code a select list with 250 or 300 different options, one for each number? Suppose you had to change the number of options. JavaScript can help with a call to `genSelect()` for each select list we want to make. Look at lines 12–19:

```
function genSelect(name, count, start, select) {
  var optStr = "";
  for (var h = start; h <= count; h++) {
    optStr += "<OPTION VALUE=" + h +
```

```
        (h == select ? " SELECTED" : "") + ">" + h;
    }
  document.write("<SELECT NAME=" + name + ">" + optStr + "</SELECT>");
  }
```

`genSelect()` expects four arguments—a string containing a name for the select list, the number of the highest valued option, the integer at which to start displaying the numbers (incrementing by 1 thereafter), and a number specifying which option to be selected. `genSelect()` simply iterates from *start* to *count*, creating a string of <OPTION> tags. When that ends, JavaScript writes that string between the <SELECT> tags to the document. Now the pages are loaded and ready to go. Let's see what happens when the user enters the defaults.

Step 2: Entering the Image Pairs and Defaults

Notice in Figure 5-1 that the user sets the defaults with four select lists and a checkbox. The most important setting is the number of image pairs. Image-Machine allows you to choose from 1 to 50 pairs. I doubt you'll ever need 50, but a little overkill never hurt anyone.

The user can then select the default pixel width and height for all of the image pairs. Each of these select lists has pixel ranges from 1 to 250. You might want to change this later, but it'll work for now. The default width and height selected are 90 and 50, respectively. This is a nice rectangle size for a button.

The last of the select lists is used to set the border, which ranges from 0 to 10 pixels. Most people will always want it set at 0, but I've seen rollovers with image borders.

Checking the checkbox allows the user to add an image rollover feature for the *onMouseDown* event handler, supported in JavaScript 1.2 and the later DOMs of NN and MSIE. All the user has to do is choose "Proceed" to generate an image template according to the information he or she has just provided.

Step 3: Filling in Image Paths, HREF Attributes, and More

Once the user chooses "Proceed," ImageMachine generates a custom image template as shown in Figure 5-2. ImageMachine utilizes three functions to create the custom template: `captureDefaultProfile()`, `setArrays()`, and `generateEntryForm()`.

captureDefaultProfile()

Function `captureDefaultProfile()` is called first when the user chooses "Proceed." Here are lines 21–39:

```
function captureDefaultProfile(formObj) {
  setArrays();
  imgDefaults    = formObj;
  var imgQty     = (imgDefaults.imgnumber.selectedIndex + 1);
  var imgHeight  = (imgDefaults.pxlheight.selectedIndex);
  var imgWidth   = (imgDefaults.pxlwidth.selectedIndex);
  var imgBorder  = (imgDefaults.defbdr.selectedIndex);
  for (var i = 0; i < imgQty; i++) {
    imgPrim[i] = "";
    imgRoll[i] = "";
    imgDown[i] = "";
    imgLink[i] = "";
    imgText[i] = "";
    imgWdh[i]  = imgWidth;
    imgHgt[i]  = imgHeight;
    imgBdr[i]  = imgBorder;
  }
  generateEntryForm();
}
```

The first action that `captureDefaultProfile()` takes is to call function `setArrays()`. Shown in lines 41–50 below, `setArrays()` declares and initializes eight arrays. Each array is responsible for holding the specific attribute values of each image group. For example, *imgPrim* contains the image paths for all the primary image rollovers. *imgRoll* contains all the image paths for the rollover images (for the *onMouseOver* event handler), and so on. If the arrays have not already been declared, `setArrays()` takes care of that. If the arrays have been already declared (the user has generated image code before), this resets the arrays to containing zero elements.

```
function setArrays() {
  imgPrim = new Array();
  imgRoll = new Array();
  imgDown = new Array();
  imgLink = new Array();
  imgText = new Array();
  imgWdh  = new Array();
  imgHgt  = new Array();
  imgBdr  = new Array();
}
```

After `setArrays()` returns, `captureDefaultProfile()` continues by copying the form object *formObj* to variable *imgDefaults*. This is important: *imgDefaults* is global. It doesn't "die" like the many other local variables in this application, so it keeps a copy of the user's defaults if he or she wants to toggle between previewing or generating the code, or changing the image attributes. This is the only place in the application where *imgDefaults* is set. That means the only way users can change their defaults is to choose "Proceed" again.

Once ImageMachine has a copy of the user defaults, `captureDefaultProfile()` declares four local variables. Here they are:

```
var imgQty      = (imgDefaults.imgnumber.selectedIndex + 1);
var imgHeight   = (imgDefaults.pxlheight.selectedIndex);
var imgWidth    = (imgDefaults.pxlwidth.selectedIndex);
var imgBorder   = (imgDefaults.defbdr.selectedIndex);
```

imgQty represents the number of rollovers that the user wants. *imgHeight*, *imgWidth*, and *imgBorder* represent the default width, height, and border settings. These variables enable the function to assign values to those arrays declared in `setArrays()`. Here are lines 28–37:

```
for (var i = 0; i < imgQty; i++) {
   imgPrim[i] = "";
   imgRoll[i] = "";
   imgDown[i] = "";
   imgLink[i] = "";
   imgText[i] = "";
   imgWdh[i]  = imgWidth;
   imgHgt[i]  = imgHeight;
   imgBdr[i]  = imgBorder;
}
```

The *for* loop makes as many iterations as the user wants rollovers, assigning attributes to each of the declared arrays. *imgPrim* holds the paths for the *MouseOut* events. *imgRoll* holds the values of the *MouseOver* events, and *imgDown* holds the paths for the *MouseDown* events. *imgLink* and *imgText* hold the values of the `HREF` attributes and the status bar text, respectively. Since the user will set the value for the first five elements individually in the image template, each element in these five arrays initially receives an empty string.

All elements in the remaining three arrays will be set alike. The default width is the same for all images. So are the default height and border. The user can change these later, but for now they are set equally.

generateEntryForm()

The last thing to do in the function is to call `generateEntryForm()`. That's where the real fun begins. This function is solely responsible for creating a custom image template in HTML for the user to enter specific data about each image group. Take a look at lines 53–118.

Sixty-six lines of code for one function. That probably violates every programmer's size limits for a function. However, `generateEntryForm()` still performs only one operation: making the image template. It's pretty easy if you break the function into three chunks of HTML—the table headers (`TH`), the form text fields, and the buttons. This entire function is really a series of calls to `document.writeln()`. That's it. Here is the code that writes the headers in lines 54–72:

```
with(parent.frames[1].document) {
  open();
    writeln("<HTML><BODY BGCOLOR=FFFFEE><FONT FACE=Arial SIZE=2>" +
      "<BLOCKQUOTE>Choose or enter the paths of all images in the " +
      "columns below. Add the link path (e.g., <FONT FACE=Courier>" +
      "web_page.html</FONT>) or script text (e.g., <FONT FACE=Courier>" +
      "javascript:</FONT>) for each HREF attribute, and  enter any " +
      "message you want to display in the status bar during the " +
      "<FONT FACE=Courier>MouseOver</FONT> event. Then choose " +
      "<B>Generate</B> to get your code, or <B>Preview</B> to see the " +
      "code in action.</BLOCKQUOTE><FORM NAME='imgProfile' " +
      "onSubmit='return false;'><CENTER><TABLE BORDER=0 ALIGN=CENTER " +
      "CELLSPACING=5 CELLPADDING=5><TH ALIGN=LEFT><FONT FACE=Arial>#" +
      "<TH ALIGN=LEFT><FONT FACE=Arial>Primary Path" +
      "<TH ALIGN=LEFT><FONT FACE=Arial>Rollover Path" +
      (imgDefaults.mousedown.checked ? "<TH ALIGN=LEFT>" +
      "<FONT FACE=Arial>MouseDown Path" : "") +
      "<TR><TD><BR></TD></TR>");
}
```

Notice that the image template form is embedded in a table. Everything in this block is static, except for the code in lines 69–70. Using the ternary operator, Java-Script adds an extra header if the user checked the "MouseDown" checkbox, and adds nothing otherwise. Take a closer look:

```
(imgDefaults.mousedown.checked ? "<TH ALIGN=LEFT><FONT FACE=Arial>" +
  "MouseDown Path" : "")
```

Here's the real payoff: if you understand this, you're going to fly through the rest of the function because `generateEntryForm()` makes *all* coding decisions based on whether the user checked the "MouseDown" checkbox. Look at the text field chunk in lines 74–107.

For as many elements as there are in *imgPrim* (and hence the number of roll-overs), ImageMachine adds a new TR that includes TDs of two (or three) FILE fields, a text field for the HREF attributes, status bar text, and the width, height, and border pixel settings. If you look closely, you'll see that each element of index *i* in the arrays declared in `setArrays()` is assigned to a value in a corresponding text field.

Remember that *imgPrim, imgRoll, imgDown, imgLink,* and *imgText* were origi-nally set to empty strings? Up to this point, the user hasn't had a chance to enter any values for these. It makes sense, then, that the values of these text fields are set to an empty string. The default values for width, height, and border, however, have been set. Therefore, it makes sense that the corresponding elements of index *i* from arrays *imgWidth, imgHeight,* and *imgBorder* are assigned to their respec-tive text field values.

Notice the recurring code:

```
(imgDefaults.mousedown.checked ?
```

Each instance comes at a point in the form where if the user checked the "Mouse-Down" checkbox, the additional code to accommodate the additional image is added.

The headers and the form text fields have been taken care of. The only thing left for the image template is to create the buttons: "Generate," "Preview," and "Clear."

```
with(parent.frames[1].document) {
  writeln("</TABLE><CENTER><INPUT TYPE=BUTTON " +
    "onClick='parent.frames[0].imgValid8(this.form, true);' " +
    "VALUE='Generate'><INPUT TYPE=BUTTON " +
    "onClick='parent.frames[0].imgValid8(this.form, false);' " +
    "VALUE='Preview'> <INPUT TYPE=RESET VALUE='   Clear   '>" +
    "</FORM></BODY></HTML>");
  close();
  }
```

The "Clear" button is your basic **RESET** button, so we'll focus on the other two. Notice that both buttons call function **imgValid8()** when clicked. Both pass a copy of the form to the function, but one passes **true** and the other **false**. This makes all the difference in whether ImageMachine creates the printed code or the interpreted code. We'll get to that shortly.

By the way, you might want to scan each line of **generateEntryForm()** to see how the HTML for the form comes about. You'll see how one big string creates a form that takes the user to the next step. Function **generateEntryForm()** makes the form to be filled out by the user, who then, according to our four-step procedure at the beginning of this chapter, chooses "Generate." Doing so as seen in the code above, calls **imgValid8()**. Here it is in lines 120–136:

```
function imgValid8(imgTemplate, mimeType) {
  for (var i = 0; i < imgPrim.length; i++) {
    if (imgTemplate['prim' + i].value == "" ||
      imgTemplate['seci' + i].value == "" ||
      imgTemplate['href' + i].value == "") {
      alert("All images and HREF attributes must have URLs.");
      return;
      }
    if (imgDefaults.mousedown.checked) {
      if(imgTemplate['down' + i].value == "") {
        alert("All images and HREF attributes must have URLs.");
        return;
        }
      }
    }
  genJavaScript(imgTemplate, mimeType);
  }
```

This function makes sure that the user has entered values for each of the image paths. Remember that the "Generate" button passes a copy of the form with all the image info.

This copy is assigned to *imgTemplate*. Once again, using the length of *imgPrim*, Image-Machine iterates through the text fields containing the image paths. The fields containing the primary image paths are named `prim + i`, where `i` is a number from 0 to `imgPrim.length - 1`. The fields containing the rollover image paths are named similarly, except using *seci* instead of *prim*. If the user included images for the *MouseDown* event, these text fields are named with *down*.

genJavaScript()

If any of the inspected fields is empty, the user is alerted, and the function returns. If each has at least some text, ImageMachine calls function `genJavaScript()`, passing in `imgTemplate` and the as-of-yet unexamined Boolean value contained in `mimeType`. As you can guess, `genJavaScript()` is responsible for creating the JavaScript code of the web page to the screen. The function is very long, but performs similar work to that of `generateEntryForm()`. See lines 138–306.

JavaScript Technique: JavaScripting Defensively

It's no accident that there are `SCRIPT` tags in the generated code with several different `LANGUAGE` attribute settings. You'll see some code within the `<SCRIPT LANGUAGE="JavaScript">` `</SCRIPT>` tags at line 185. Other code within the `<SCRIPT LANGUAGE="JavaScript1.1">` `</SCRIPT>` tags at line 189, and finally yet more code between within the `<SCRIPT LANGUAGE= "JavaScript1.2">` `</SCRIPT>` tags at line 193.

This keeps browsers of varying JavaScript compatibility from executing code they won't support, and hence causing application-stopping errors. For example, the `Image()` object isn't supported in JavaScript 1.0. Therefore, you won't see any `Image()` object code unless it is embedded in a `<SCRIPT>` tag with "JavaScript 1.1" (or higher) as the `LANGUAGE` attribute.

You can code defensively like this by using control variables, setting their values according to the `<SCRIPT>` tag in which they reside. When it comes time to run a function with questionably supported code, run that code only if the conditions of the control variables are met. You can see this in variables *can-RollOver* for the *Image* object code and variable *canClickDown* for the *onMouseDown* event handler code.

Notice also that scripting this way can also reduce download times. For example, browsers that don't support JavaScript 1.2 won't execute any code within the `<SCRIPT LANGUAGE="JavaScript1.2">` `</SCRIPT>` tags. That's good news because the browser won't have to request images used for the rollovers associated with the *onMouseDown* event.

And you thought `generateEntryForm()` was long! It's still the same deal, though. `genJavaScript()` performs a single task: it generates the rollover code, which is mostly JavaScript.

The first thing that `genJavaScript()` does is to reset global variable *imageLinks*. More on these code-holding globals in a moment. Next up, `genJavaScript()` sets a handful of global "specification" variables according to the value of *mime-Type*. Here are lines 141–154:

```
if (mimeType) {
   lt       = "&lt;";
   gt       = "&gt;";
   br       = "<BR>";
   HTML     = true;
   nbsp     = "     ";
   }
else {
   lt       = "<";
   gt       = ">";
   br       = lb;
   HTML     = false;
   nbsp     = "     ";
   }
```

If *mimeType* is `true`, the globals will be set to string values that force the code to be printed. Variables *lt* and *gt* are set to < and > respectively. Variable *br* is then set to the string value of <BR>. *HTML* is a Boolean variable, indicating that the user wants the code interpreted (instead of displayed on the screen). This will come into play shortly when generating the code. Variable *nbsp* is set to a string of HTML non-breaking spaces. *nbsp* is used for the HTML equivalent of emulating the Tab key.

If *mimeType* proves `false`, the globals will be set to force the code to be interpreted. Variables *lt* and *gt* are set to < and > respectively. Variable *br* is then set to the string value of *lb*. The value of *lb* was set all the way back in lines 6–8. Here it is:

```
var platform = navigator.platform;
var lb = (platform.indexOf("Win") != -1) ? "\n\r" :
   (platform.indexOf("Mac") != -1) ? "\r" : "\n"));
```

As you can see, variables *platform* and *lb* work together. *platform* contains a string of the value of the operating system for which the browser was compiled. Variable *lb* is set according to the value of *platform*. Windows (DOS) represents the line break, equivalent to pressing the Enter or Return key, by \n\r. Macintosh does so with \r, and Unix operating systems use \n. This use of line breaks keeps the generated code from being jammed into two or three mile-long lines. This isn't vital to the application, but when ImageMachine prints the HTML and JavaScript, viewing the source code will be much easier.

JavaScript Technique: The Power of Global Variables

This application reaps the benefits of global variables. ImageMachine generates printed code or executable code. You look at one and run the other. Both types of code, however, are almost the same except that the executed code utilizes HTML brackets < and >, whereas the printed code utilizes the character entities of HTML brackets, < and >. Global variables *lt* and *gt* are set to either the HTML brackets or the character entities, depending whether you choose the "Generate" button or the "Preview" button.

Variables *br* and *nbsp* are assigned similarly. This is the power of global variables: simply changing their value yields strings that perform distinctly different but equally useful purposes.

Moving on, *HTML*, set to **false**, is a Boolean variable, indicating that the user wants to have the code interpreted. This will come into play shortly when generating the code. Variable *nbsp* is set to a string of whitespace.

Now ImageMachine has the information from the text field in the template, and whether the user has selected printed code or interpreted code. Generating the JavaScript truly begins at line 185 and works until the end of the function.

As you scan the code, you'll see several calls to function **pathPrep()**. This function reformats the image path string if the path appears to be an absolute local path on a Windows machine (see Chapter 3 for facts about paths). Why all the fuss? Remember that Windows uses backslash notation (\) to separate directories. Browsers use the forward slash (/). So do Unix machines. Therefore, it will be necessary to convert backslashes to forward slashes. Actually, some browsers make the conversion on the fly.

The catch is that JavaScript interprets the backslash character as part of an escaped character. Therefore, JavaScript would perceive *C:\My_Directory\My.File* as *C:My_DirectoryMy.File*. The **pathPrep()** function takes care of it. Here are lines 310–317:

```
function pathPrep(path) {
  if (path.indexOf(":\\") != -1) {
    path = path.replace(/\\/g, "/");
    path = path.replace(/:\//, "|/");
    return "file:///" + path;
    }
  else { return path; }
  }
```

Browsers also open local documents with the file protocol, which means we'll need *file:///* attached to the front of the URL and a pipe (|) in place of the colon (:) to conform to the specification.

Decision time

Things are now set up to generate code according to a printed or interpreted specification. Before ImageMachine builds the code, though, it needs to "know" whether to generate code based on new data from the image template or use information already stored in the arrays. According to our user cycle, described earlier, the user just finished entering information in the image template. The other situation arises when the user has *already* generated code and is toggling back and forth between "Generate" and "Preview." We'll cover that shortly.

If the information will be coming from the image template (in our case), `genJavaScript()` resets all *img* arrays by calling `setArrays()` so that the new information from the image template can be assigned. ImageMachine determines whether to call `setArrays()` and reassign values by evaluating *imgTemplate*. `genJavaScript()` can be called in one of three ways, from buttons "Generate," and "Preview," and from function *imgValid8()*. Calling `genJavaScript()` from "Generate" and "Preview" passes a null value to `imgTemplate`. Therefore, if *imgTemplate* is not equal to null, `genJavaScript()` knows to clear the arrays and make way for new information. Otherwise, the elements in the *img* arrays won't be modified. Study lines 156–170 carefully and see how this checks out:

```
if(imgTemplate != null) {
  setArrays();
  for (var i = 0; i < (imgDefaults.imgnumber.selectedIndex + 1); i++) {
    imgPrim[i] = purify(imgTemplate['prim' + i].value);
    imgRoll[i] = purify(imgTemplate['seci' + i].value);
    if (imgDefaults.mousedown.checked) {
      imgDown[i] = purify(imgTemplate['down' + i].value);
      }
    imgLink[i] = purify(imgTemplate['href' + i].value);
    imgText[i] = purify(imgTemplate['stat' + i].value);
    imgWdh[i]  = purify(imgTemplate['wdh' + i].value);
    imgHgt[i]  = purify(imgTemplate['hgt' + i].value);
    imgBdr[i]  = purify(imgTemplate['bdr' + i].value);
    }
  }
```

If the array elements are modified, the string values assigned to them go through a quick, dangerous character removal process by way of function `purify()` at line 308. Here you go:

```
function purify(txt) { return txt.replace(/\'|\"/g, ""); }
```

This removes all single and double quotes from your values. They certainly aren't illegal, but JavaScript has to use both single and double quotes to generate the code. Unless they're properly escaped with a backslash, this will mean trouble for your generated code. `purify()` removes them from the string it is passed, then returns the fresh new string.

Generate the code

Once that is complete, it is time to generate the long-awaited code. This occurs in lines 185–305 by assigning all the generated code equal to several "code-holding" variables. The variables are as follows:

PrimJavaScript
> Holds the HTML tags such as `HTML`, `HEAD`, and `TITLE`. Also contains the preliminary JavaScript and rollover code associated with the *MouseOver* and *MouseOut* events.

secJavaScript
> Holds rollover code associated with the JavaScript 1.2 *MouseDown* event.

imageLinks
> Holds HTML code that displays the links.

scriptClose
> Holds a closing `SCRIPT` tag.

swapCode
> Holds the JavaScript functions that will perform the image rollovers.

primHTML
> Holds the `BODY` tag and some HTML comments.

secHTML
> Holds closing HTML tags plus the "Form" buttons displayed after the code is generated (either "Generate" and "Change Info" or "Preview" and "Change Info").

aggregate
> This variable is the concatenation of all the other variables just mentioned.

The *for* loop at line 197 once again iterates `imgPrim.length` times. For each iteration, variables *primJavaScript, secJavaScript* (if the user chose *MouseDown* option), and *imageLinks* have added to them code corresponding with the next image group in the iteration.

Variables *scriptClose, swapCode, primHTML,* and *secHTML* are not part of the *for* loop. Their content can be set once by using the ternary operator in conjunction with variable *HTML* and *imgDefaults.mousedown.checked*.

Once the *for* loop has finished and the other variables have been accordingly set, the last thing to do is get the content to the page. It all happens at lines 300–305:

```
agregate = primJavaScript +
  (imgDefaults.mousedown.checked ? scriptClose + secJavaScript : "") +
  swapCode + primHTML + imageLinks + secHTML;

parent.frames[1].location.href =
  "javascript: parent.frames[0].agregate";
```

Step 4: Choosing "Preview" to Watch the Code in Action

If you're mentally drained by now, I don't blame you. Fortunately, the last two steps are pretty quick and painless. Suppose the user has viewed the generated code and now wants to see it in action. A quick click of "Preview" will do. Remember that clicking "Preview" calls `genJavaScript()`, but *mimeType* is false instead of true with the "Generate" button. That's the only difference. The "specification" variables in lines 141–154 are simply reset to reflect interpreted code instead of printed code as before. Everything else happens the same as with the "Generate" button.

Step 5: Choosing "Change Info" to Make Changes

Now you've seen the generated code and the code in action. Suppose the user wants to make some changes. Choose "Change Info," and the image template with the information reappears. Widths, heights, status text . . . everything you entered *except* the image URLs. Wait a minute . . . why not?

The effect happens because the image path URLs are stored in a *FileUpload* object (i.e., `<INPUT TYPE=FILE>`). For security reasons, the *FileUpload* object is read-only. In other words, you must manually populate the field by entering a value with the keyboard or selecting a file from the dialog box with the mouse. The good news is that this is very easy to change. Just swap `TYPE=FILE` for `TYPE=TEXT` in `generateEntryForm()`. You'll find it there three times. The only problem is that you'll lose the ability to seek local files with the mouse and the dialog box. Use the arrangement that is most convenient for you. Once you've made your changes, you can choose "Generate" or "Preview" and check out the new code.

Potential Extension: Adding Attributes to the Template

Big applications can always be made bigger. This section is devoted to showing you how to add attributes to the image template, giving you greater control over the generated code. For the sake of simplicity, I'll show you how to add the `IMG` attributes `HSPACE` and `VSPACE`. The procedure involves these six steps:

1. Add the new fields in the default template.
2. Create an array for its values in `setArrays()`.
3. Capture the new default values.
4. Add text fields in the image template in `generateEntryForm()`.

5. Reference and assign the new attribute values in `genJavaScript()`.

6. Generate the HTML required to display the attributes in `genJavaScript()`.

JavaScript Technique: String Replacement with JavaScript 1.1 and 1.2

JavaScript 1.2 brought with it many cool new features. One of those is the ability to use regular expressions for string matching and replacing. Functions `pathPrep()` and `purify()` perform a simple but powerful method of replacing, using JavaScript 1.2. This is a great for JavaScript 1.2 capable browsers, but Netscape 3.x is still used in significant numbers. Here is a function that performs string replacement in JavaScript 1.1 using methods of the *Array* object:

```
function replacev11(str, oldSubStr, newSubStr) {
  var newStr = str.split(oldSubStr).join(newSubStr);
  return newStr;
  }
```

This function takes a string, creates an array of elements `split()` according to the substring you want to remove (*oldSubStr*), then returns a string made by using `join()` to hook up the array with the new substring (*newSubStr*). Not pretty, but it works.

Step 1: Adding the Fields

```
<TD VALIGN="TOP">
<FONT FACE="Arial" SIZE=2>
HSpace
</TD>
<TD VALIGN="TOP">
<FONT FACE="Arial" SIZE=2>
<SCRIPT LANGUAGE="JavaScript1.2">
<!--
genSelect("hspace", 25, 0, 0);
//-->
</SCRIPT>
</TD>
<TD VALIGN="TOP">
<FONT FACE="Arial" SIZE=2>
VSpace
</TD>
<TD VALIGN="TOP">
<FONT FACE="Arial" SIZE=2>
<SCRIPT LANGUAGE="JavaScript1.2">
<!--
genSelect("vspace", 25, 0, 0);
//-->
</SCRIPT>
</TD>
```

Step 2: Creating Arrays in setArrays()

```
function setArrays() {
  imgPrim = new Array();
  imgRoll = new Array();
  imgDown = new Array();
  imgLink = new Array();
  imgText = new Array();
  imgWdh  = new Array();
  imgHgt  = new Array();
  imgBdr  = new Array();
  imgHSpace  = new Array();  // For the HSPACE
  imgVSpace  = new Array();  // For the VSPACE
  }
```

That makes room to store the new default values. That brings us to the next step— filling those new arrays.

Step 3: Capturing the New Default Values

In `captureDefaultProfile()`, we will add two local variables named *imgHspace* and *imgVspace*, then assign their values to the values chosen in the default template. Now `captureDefaultProfile()` looks like this:

```
function captureDefaultProfile(formObj) {
  setArrays();
  imgDefaults     = formObj;
  var imgQty      = (imgDefaults.imgnumber.selectedIndex + 1);
  var imgHeight   = (imgDefaults.pxlheight.selectedIndex);
  var imgWidth    = (imgDefaults.pxlwidth.selectedIndex);
  var imgBorder   = (imgDefaults.defbdr.selectedIndex);
  var imgHspace   = (imgDefaults.hspace.selectedIndex);
  var imgVspace   = (imgDefaults.vspace.selectedIndex);
  for (var i = 0; i < imgQty; i++) {
    imgPrim[i] = "";
    imgRoll[i] = "";
    imgDown[i] = "";
    imgLink[i] = "";
    imgText[i] = "";
    imgWdh[i]  = imgWidth;
    imgHgt[i]  = imgHeight;
    imgBdr[i]  = imgBorder;
    imgHSpace[i] = imgHspace;  // For HSPACE
    imgVSpace[i] = imgVspace;  // For VSPACE
    }
  generateEntryForm();
  }
```

ImageMachine will now be able to include the default values for **HSPACE** and **VSPACE** in the image template.

Step 4: Adding Text Fields in generateEntryForm()

Now you can add the strings of HTML in `generateEntryForm()` to accommodate the two new text fields. Let's put them in their own `TR` under all the others. You can adjust it later to make it look better. Lines 103-106 currently look like this:

```
"<TR><TD VALIGN=BOTTOM COLSPAN=" +
(!imgDefaults.mousedown.checked ? "3" : "4") +
"><BR><HR NOSHADE><BR></TD></TR>");
```

Adding the two text fields to the end looks like this:

```
"<TR><TD VALIGN=BOTTOM><INPUT TYPE=TEXT NAME='hsp " + i +
"' VALUE='" + imgHspace[i] + "' SIZE=3> HSPACE </TD>" +
"<TR><TD VALIGN=BOTTOM><INPUT TYPE=TEXT NAME='vsp" + i +
"' VALUE='" + imgVspace[i] + "' SIZE=3> VSPACE </TD></TR>" +
"<TR><TD VALIGN=BOTTOM COLSPAN=" +
(!imgDefaults.mousedown.checked ? "3" : "4") + ">" +
"<BR><HR NOSHADE><BR></TD></TR>");
```

This code adds two extra text fields for every image group and displays the default value in each. The user can change this later, just like the others.

Step 5: Referencing and Assigning the New Values in genJavaScript()

Once the user chooses to generate the code, ImageMachine needs to grab the information from the new text fields in the image template. Just add the code in lines 158-169, which now looks like this:

```
for (var i = 0; i < (imgDefaults.imgnumber.selectedIndex + 1); i++) {
  imgPrim[i] = purify(imgTemplate['prim' + i].value);
  imgRoll[i] = purify(imgTemplate['seci' + i].value);
  if (imgDefaults.mousedown.checked) {
    imgDown[i] = purify(imgTemplate['down' + i].value);
  }
  imgLink[i] = purify(imgTemplate['href' + i].value);
  imgText[i] = purify(imgTemplate['stat' + i].value);
  imgWdh[i]  = purify(imgTemplate['wdh' + i].value);
  imgHgt[i]  = purify(imgTemplate['hgt' + i].value);
  imgBdr[i]  = purify(imgTemplate['bdr' + i].value);
  imgHSpace[i] = purify(imgTemplate['hsp' + i].value);
  imgVSpace[i] = purify(imgTemplate['vsp' + i].value);
}
```

The last two lines in the block show ImageMachine assigning the form values from the image template to elements in *imgHSpace* and *imgVSpace*. We're almost there. The only thing left is to make sure the new attributes are included in the code generation, printed or interpreted.

Step 6: Generating the Additional HTML in genJavaScript( )

The new code will be added to the variable *imageLinks*. The last few lines of the string are as follows:

```
(HTML ? fontClose : "") + br + nbsp + "HEIGHT=" +
(HTML ? fontOpen : "") + imgHgt[j] +
(HTML ? fontClose : "") + br + nbsp + "BORDER=" +
(HTML ? fontOpen : "") + imgBdr[j] +
(HTML ? fontClose : "") +
gt + "" + lt + "/A" + gt + br + br + br;
```

All you need to do is copy a few lines, and change HEIGHT to HSPACE, imgHgt to imgHSpace, BORDER to VSPACE, and imgBdr to imgVSpace. Here is the new version:

```
(HTML ? fontClose : "") + br + nbsp + "HEIGHT=" +
(HTML ? fontOpen : "") + imgHgt[j] +
(HTML ? fontClose : "") + br + nbsp + "BORDER=" +
(HTML ? fontOpen : "") + imgBdr[j] +
(HTML ? fontClose : "") + br + nbsp + "HSPACE=" +
(HTML ? fontOpen : "") + imgHSpace[j] +
(HTML ? fontClose : "") + br + nbsp + "VSPACE=" +
(HTML ? fontOpen : "") + imgVSpace[j] +
(HTML ? fontClose : "") +
gt + "" + lt + "/A" + gt + br + br + br;
```

That adds two new attributes for your images. You might also consider adding an ALT tag for image content. There's no need to limit this type of modification to the IMG tag. There is plenty to do in the <A> tag; you can customize it for image maps, and so on.

6

Implementing
JavaScript Source Files

If you've been following along since the beginning (in order) you've been poring through code trying to understand how the functions and variables work together so that those applications actually do something. I thought it might be a nice break to look at something that could make life easier for all your applications.

This chapter doesn't contain any applications. Rather, it documents several dozen functions contained in JavaScript source files. Though you may not find all of them useful, there are probably a handful that you can use right away and many others that you can customize to make useful.

I didn't include these files to imply that I could hand you a bunch of functions and say, "OK, coders, this is all you'll ever need." That's ludicrous. This chapter is designed to encourage you to beef up your own JavaScript library with reusable code. Then you won't have to re-invent the wheel every time you code a new application. The following list shows the *.js* files, in alphabetical order, and the purpose of each.

arrays.js

Contains array manipulation functions. Some of the functions allow you to perform the equivalent JavaScript 1.2 operations in lesser browsers.

cookies.js

> This awesome library, mostly from JavaScript veteran Bill Dortch, makes leveraging cookie power a snap.

dhtml.js

> You've seen all of these functions in Chapter 3, *The Interactive Slideshow*, and Chapter 4, *The Multiple Search Engine Interface*. This is a nice package to create, show, and hide cross-browser DHTML layers.

events.js

> This source file contains code that will enable and disable capturing *mousemove* and *keypress* events in both NN and MSIE.

frames.js

> These functions help keep your web pages in or out (whichever you prefer) of other framesets.

images.js

> Rollover code, which you've probably seen in earlier chapters, makes for a neat package here.

navbar.js

> Contains code that generates a dynamic navigation bar based on the current document loaded. Impressive.

numbers.js

> Contains code to correct JavaScript rounding errors and provide number formatting.

objects.js

> Contains code for generic object creation and object inspection.

strings.js

> This file contains a few string manipulation functions.

Except for *navbar.js*, each *.js* file has a correspondingly named HTML document (for example, *arrays.html* goes with *arrays.js*). The functions aren't explained in as much detail here as they are in the applications. In most cases that's because it's just not necessary, although exceptions are noted. As you make your way through the chapter, think about how each function can solve a common problem you have. If it won't work for you as it is, consider how you can change it to make it do so.

Each section that describes a *.js* file starts with the file name, its practical uses, the version of JavaScript required, and a list of the functions contained in the file.

arrays.js

Practical use

Array manipulation

Version requirement

JavaScript 1.2

Functions

avg(), high(), low(), jsGrep(), truncate(), shrink(), integrate(), reorganize()

These functions take your arrays, manipulate them, and return other useful information, including other arrays. Figure 6-1 shows *arrays.html*. Nothing exciting to look at, but you can see that each function is demonstrated.

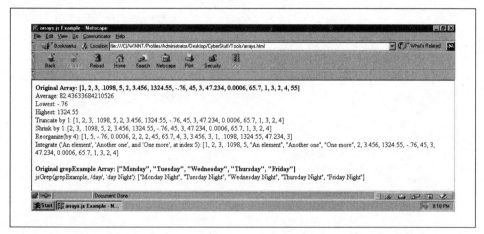

Figure 6-1. Showing off the power of arrays.js

Here is the laundry list of functions of *arrays.js* and their uses:

avg()

Returns the average value of all the numbers in the array

high()

Returns the highest number value of the array

low()

Returns the lowest value of the array

jsGrep()

Performs string matching and replacement on all array elements

truncate()

Returns a copy of the array without the last element

`shrink()`

Returns a copy of the array without the first element

`integrate()`

Combines the elements of two arrays starting with an index you define

`reorganize()`

Reorders the array elements according to a multiple you choose

Now look at the code for *arrays.html,* shown in Example 6-1. Not much here. Just a call to `document.write()`. The string displayed contains the results of all the function calls with sample arrays—`someArray()` and `grepExample()`.

Example 6-1. arrays.html

```
 1 <HTML>
 2 <HEAD>
 3 <TITLE>arrays.js Example</TITLE>
 4 <SCRIPT LANGUAGE="JavaScript1.2" SRC="arrays.js"></SCRIPT>
 5 </HEAD>
 6 <BODY>
 7 <SCRIPT LANGUAGE="JavaScript1.2">
 8 <!--
 9
10 var someArray = new Array(1,2,3,.1098,5,2,3.456,1324.55,-0.76,45,3,47.234,.
   00060,65.7,1,3,2,4,55);
11 var grepExample = new Array('Monday', 'Tuesday', 'Wednesday',
12   'Thursday', 'Friday');
13 document.write("<B>Original Array: " + someArray + "</B><BR>" +
14   "Average: " + avg(someArray) + "<BR>" +
15   "Lowest: " + low(someArray) + "<BR>" +
16   "Highest: " + high(someArray) + "<BR>" +
17   "Truncate by 1: " + truncate(someArray) + "<BR>" +
18   "Shrink by 1: " + shrink(someArray) + "<BR>" +
19   "Reorganize(by 4): " + reorganize(someArray, 4) + "<BR>" +
20   "Integrate ('An element', 'Another one', and 'One more', " +
21   "at index 5): integrate(someArray, new Array('An element', " +
22   "'Another one', 'One more'), 5) + "<BR><BR><B>Original grepExample " +
23   "Array: " + grepExample + "</B><BR> " +
24   "jsGrep(grepExample, /day/, \'day Night\'): " +
25   jsGrep(grepExample, /day/, 'day Night') + "<BR>");
26
27 //-->
28 </SCRIPT>
29 </BODY>
30 </HTML>
```

You might have noticed that both `SCRIPT` tags require JavaScript 1.2. The only reason for this is the function `jsGrep()`, which utilizes JavaScript 1.2 string-matching and replacement features. More on `jsGrep()` in a moment. You can include JavaScript 1.1 browsers by removing (or rewriting) `jsGrep()`. Now that

you see how the functions are called, look at the functions themselves; in
Example 6-2, *arrays.js*.

Example 6-2. arrays.js

```
 1   var sum = 0;
 2   for (var i = 0; i < arrObj.length; i++) {
 3     sum += arrObj[i];
 4     }
 5   return (sum / i);
 6   }
 7
 8 function high(arrObj) {
 9   var highest = arrObj[0];
10   for (var i = 1; i < arrObj.length; i++) {
11     highest = (arrObj[i] > highest ? arrObj[i] : highest);
12     }
13   return (highest);
14   }
15
16 function low(arrObj) {
17   var lowest = arrObj[0];
18   for (var i = 1; i < arrObj.length; i++) {
19     lowest = (arrObj[i] < lowest ? arrObj[i] : lowest);
20     }
21   return (lowest);
22   }
23
24 function jsGrep(arrObj, regexp, subStr) {
25   for (var i = 0; i < arrObj.length; i++) {
26     arrObj[i] = arrObj[i].replace(regexp, subStr);
27     }
28   return arrObj;
29   }
30
31 function truncate(arrObj) {
32   arrObj.length = arrObj.length - 1;
33   return arrObj;
34   }
35
36
37 function shrink(arrObj) {
38   var tempArray = new Array();
39   for(var p = 1; p < arrObj.length; p++) {
40     tempArray[p - 1] = arrObj[p];
41     }
42   return tempArray;
43   }
44
45
46 function integrate(arrObj, elemArray, startIndex) {
47   startIndex = (parseInt(Math.abs(startIndex)) < arrObj.length ?
48     parseInt(Math.abs(startIndex)) : arrObj.length);
```

Example 6-2. arrays.js (continued)

```
49    var tempArray = new Array();
50    for( var p = 0; p < startIndex; p++) {
51      tempArray[p] = arrObj[p];
52      }
53    for( var q = startIndex; q < startIndex + elemArray.length; q++) {
54      tempArray[q] = elemArray[q - startIndex];
55      }
56    for( var r = startIndex + elemArray.length; r < (arrObj.length +
57      elemArray.length); r++) {
58      tempArray[r] = arrObj[r - elemArray.length];
59      }
60    return tempArray;
61    }
62
63 function reorganize(formObj, stepUp) {
64    stepUp = (Math.abs(parseInt(stepUp)) > 0 ?
65      Math.abs(parseInt(stepUp)) : 1);
66    var nextRound = 1;
67    var idx = 0;
68    var tempArray = new Array();
69    for (var i = 0; i < formObj.length; i++) {
70      tempArray[i] = formObj[idx];
71      if (idx + stepUp >= formObj.length) {
72        idx = nextRound;
73        nextRound++;
74        }
75      else {
76        idx += stepUp;
77        }
78      }
79    return tempArray;
80    }
```

Functions `avg()`, `high()`, and `low()` don't seem all that shocking. `avg()` adds up all the values, then divides that sum by `arrObj.length` and returns that quotient. The other two functions iterate through the passed array, comparing the elements with one another to determine the highest or lowest valued element.

Function `jsGrep()` iterates through the elements of an array and executes string matching or replacement. Anyone familiar with Perl has probably used the subroutine `grep()` plenty of times. Perl's `grep()` is much more powerful, but works much the same way.

Functions `truncate()` and `shrink()` are simple JavaScript 1.1 equivalents of JavaScript 1.2 array function `pop()` and `shift()`. Actually, `pop()` and `shift()` are also named after the similarly named and performing subroutines in Perl.

Function `integrate()` is also a JavaScript 1.1 equivalent for the JavaScript 1.2 array method `slice()`.

`slice()` is also named after the Perl subroutine. This function is fairly simple. Although there are three *for* loops, the total number of iterations is always `arrObj.length + elemArray.length`.

Function `reorganize()` reorders array elements by a multiple you select. In other words, if you "reorganize" a 10-element array (that starts out as 0, 1, 2, 3, 4, 5, 6, 7, 8, 9) by 3, the new order comes out as 0, 3, 6, 9, 1, 4, 7, 2, 5, 8.

cookies.js

Practical uses
    Individual hit counters, form repopulation, user preferences settings

Version requirement
    JavaScript 1.1

Functions
    `getCookieVal()`, `GetCookie()`, `DeleteCookie()`, `SetCookie()`

You want client-state management? How about cool web site greetings for repeat visitors? Need to set up a language switching interface or other user preferences? This code makes setting and getting cookie information really easy. Figures 6-2, 6-3, and 6-4 show *cookies.html* in action. Notice in Figure 6-2 that the first time the page is loaded, the user is prompted to provide a name. Figure 6-3 displays the greeting that the first-time visitor receives. Figure 6-4 shows that repeat visitors are welcomed back warmly with a personalized hit count.

Figure 6-2. First timers fill in their name once . . .

This is definitely a simple example of cookie power. Chapter 7, *Cookie-Based User Preferences,* applies this same code to "remember" user preferences. By the way, if you haven't fully digested the concept of a cookie, check out the Unofficial Cookie FAQ at *http://www.cookiecentral.com/unofficial_cookie_faq.htm.* As unofficial as it

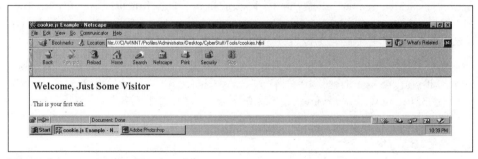

Figure 6-3. ... get a newcomer's welcome . . .

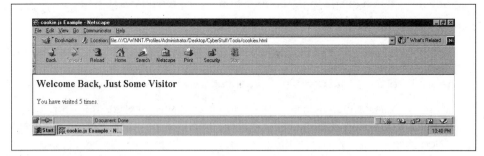

Figure 6-4. ... then become one of the gang

is, you'll get the low-down on *all* your cookie questions. Also, we'll go into more detail in Chapter 7.

File *cookies.html* works like this: when the user loads the page, it checks for a cookie of the name *user_id*. If the name does not exist (equals null), it prompts the user for his or her name. Then it sets the cookie *user_id* to the value of the user's name, and cookie *hit_count* to 2 (the number of times the user will have visited on next return).

If *user_id* does exist, it grabs its value and the value of *hit_count*. If the *user_id* cookie exists, the user has been to the site before. It's safe to say, then, the cookie *hit_count* has also been set. It displays the name and the number of times the user has come to the site, then resets the value of *hit_count* to a string equivalent of hit_count+1. Take a look at *cookies.js*, in Example 6-3, to see what all this setting and getting is about.

Example 6-3. cookies.js

```
1 var today = new Date();
2 var expiry = new Date(today.getTime() + 365 * 24 * 60 * 60 * 1000);
3
4 function getCookieVal (offset) {
5   var endstr = document.cookie.indexOf (";", offset);
```

Example 6-3. cookies.js (continued)

```
 6   if (endstr == -1) { endstr = document.cookie.length; }
 7   return unescape(document.cookie.substring(offset, endstr));
 8   }
 9
10 function GetCookie (name) {
11   var arg = name + "=";
12   var alen = arg.length;
13   var clen = document.cookie.length;
14   var i = 0;
15   while (i < clen) {
16     var j = i + alen;
17     if (document.cookie.substring(i, j) == arg) {
18       return getCookieVal (j);
19       }
20     i = document.cookie.indexOf(" ", i) + 1;
21     if (i == 0) break;
22     }
23   return null;
24   }
25
26 function DeleteCookie (name,path,domain) {
27   if (GetCookie(name)) {
28     document.cookie = name + "=" +
29     ((path) ? "; path=" + path : "") +
30     ((domain) ? "; domain=" + domain : "") +
31     "; expires=Thu, 01-Jan-70 00:00:01 GMT";
32     }
33   }
34
35 function SetCookie (name,value,expires,path,domain,secure) {
36   document.cookie = name + "=" + escape (value) +
37     ((expires) ? "; expires=" + expires.toGMTString() : "") +
38     ((path) ? "; path=" + path : "") +
39     ((domain) ? "; domain=" + domain : "") +
40     ((secure) ? "; secure" : "");
41   }
```

There are four functions here, but you'll only need to call three: `SetCookie()`, `GetCookie()`, and `DeleteCookie()`. `getCookieVal()` is an internal function. You never need to call it directly.

Creating cookies with `SetCookie()` is easy. You need only pass in a cookie name (to access it later with `GetCookie()`), the information you want to store (such as a username or hit count), and an expiration date, in that order. You must provide the first two parameters. The expiration date, however, is provided by way of variables *today* and *expiry*. Variable *expiry* is set to a date one year from the day the user loads the page. This happens by instantiating variable *today* to a new *Date* object and using the `getTime()` method. Here's how it works.

Variable *today* is a *Date* object. So `today.getTime()` returns the current time in terms of milliseconds (since 1970 at 00:00:00, Greenwich Mean Time). That brings us to the present time in milliseconds, but we want an expiration date of one year from now. There are 365 days in a year, 24 hours in a day, 60 minutes in an hour, 60 seconds in a minute and 1,000 milliseconds in a second. Just multiply them together and add the product (which is 3.1536e10 milliseconds) to the return of `getTime()`.

The syntax for `GetCookie()` and `DeleteCookie()` are even easier. All you do is pass in the name associated with the cookie. `GetCookie()` will return the value of the cookie (or null if it isn't found), and `DeleteCookie()` deletes the cookie associated with the name passed in. Deleting simply means setting the cookie with an expiration date in the past.

dhtml.js

Practical use
   DHTML layer creation, hiding, and revealing

Version requirement
   JavaScript 1.2

Functions
   `genLayer()`, `hideSlide()`, `showSlide()`, `refSlide()`

If you've been reading the book in order, you've seen this code in two previous applications (the slideshow and the multiple search engine interface). Figures 6-5 and 6-6 show the code that has created a layer and allows you to hide and show it at will.

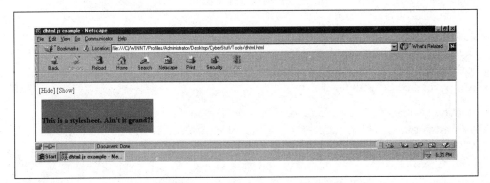

Figure 6-5. "Eye-catching" DHTML: Now you see it

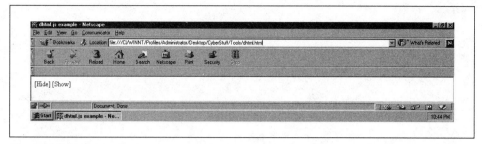

Figure 6-6. Now you don't

Example 6-4 shows the contents of *dhtml.js*. I haven't changed a thing. Check Chapters 3 and 5 for the code details.

Example 6-4. dhtml.js

```
 1 var NN       = (document.layers ? true : false);
 2 var hideName = (NN ? 'hide' : 'hidden');
 3 var showName = (NN ? 'show' : 'visible');
 4 var zIdx     = -1;
 5 function genLayer(sName, sLeft, sTop, sWdh, sHgt, sVis, copy) {
 6   if (NN) {
 7     document.writeln('<LAYER NAME="' + sName + '" LEFT=' + sLeft +
 8       ' TOP=' + sTop +
 9       ' WIDTH=' + sWdh + ' HEIGHT=' + sHgt + ' VISIBILITY="' + sVis +
10       '" z-Index=' + zIdx + '>' + copy + '</LAYER>');
11   }
12   else {
13     document.writeln('<DIV ID="' + sName +
14       '" STYLE="position:absolute; overflow:none;left:' + sLeft +
15       'px; top:' + sTop + 'px; width:' + sWdh + 'px; height:' + sHgt +
16       'px; visibility:' + sVis + ' z-Index=' + (++zIdx) + '">' + copy +
17       '</DIV>');
18   }
19 }
20
21 function hideSlide(name) {
22   refSlide(name).visibility = hideName;
23 }
24
25 function showSlide(name) {
26   refSlide(name).visibility = showName;
27 }
28
29 function refSlide(name) {
30   if (NN) { return document.layers[name]; }
31   else { return eval('document.all.' + name + '.style'); }
32 }
```

events.js

Practical uses

Cross-browser event handler assignment, mouse movement tracking

Version requirement

JavaScript 1.2

Functions

`enableEffects()`, `showXY()`, `keepKeys()`, `showKeys()`

If you haven't experimented with cross-browser event handling scripts, this might be just the primer for you. This example utilizes three event handlers: *onclick, onmousemove,* and *onkeypress.* When you first click anywhere in the document space, the JavaScript captures the initial x and y coordinates of the mouse-pointer arrow with respect to the browser window. After that, the status bar displays the x and y coordinates as the user moves the pointer arrow around. Clicking once again "turns off" the coordinate tracking and calculates the pixel distance between the point the user first clicked and current location. You can see this in Figure 6-7 and Figure 6-8.

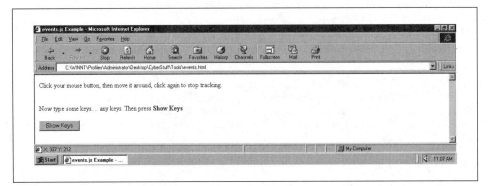

Figure 6-7. x and y mouse coordinates in the status bar

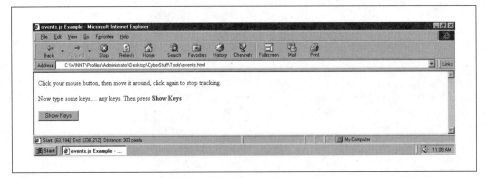

Figure 6-8. The pixel distance between the two points

Independent of the mouse action, you can also type any sequence of keys on your keyboard. The status bar will then display each of the individual keys you type. When you finish, choose the "Show Keys" button, and you'll get a JavaScript alert dialog box that displays the cumulative sequence of keys you entered up to that point. Figure 6-9 shows this. Choose "OK," and you start again from scratch.

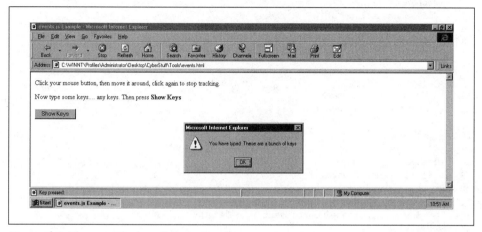

Figure 6-9. These are the keys the user typed

By now you're familiar with the intricacies of coding cross-browser stylesheets. You know: LAYER tags in one browser, DIV tags in the other.* Things don't change much for the good when it comes to the event models, either. If you check the source code in *events.html,* you'll find the following two lines of JavaScript:

```
document.onclick = enableEffects;
document.onkeypress = keepKeys;
```

The *onclick* event handler is associated with function **enableEffects()**, and the *onkeypress* event handler is associated with function **keepKeys()**. Both functions are shown below. Notice that neither function has any parentheses in the syntax. That is, the code does not look like this:

```
document.onclick = enableEffects();
document.onkeypress = keepKeys();
```

Using parentheses would call each method the moment each line was interpreted. You don't want that: the event handlers are associated by a *reference* to the functions, instead. Look at the code in Example 6-5.

---

* Actually, you can use DIV tags for positioning in Netscape Navigator 4.x as long as you include a value for "position" in the STYLE attribute. However, until Netscape comes on board with the document object model, using the LAYER tag gives you access to all the properties of the *Layer* object.

Example 6-5. events.js

```
 1 var keys = '';
 2 var change = true;
 3 var x1, x2, y1, y2;
 4
 5 function enableEffects(ev) {
 6   if(change) {
 7     if(document.layers) {
 8       x1 = ev.screenX;
 9       y1 = ev.screenY;
10       document.captureEvents(Event.MOUSEMOVE);
11       }
12     else {
13       x1 = event.screenX;
14       y1 = event.screenY;
15       }
16     document.onmousemove = showXY;
17     }
18   else {
19     if (document.layers) {
20       x2 = ev.screenX;
21       y2 = ev.screenY;
22       document.releaseEvents(Event.MOUSEMOVE);
23       }
24     else {
25       x2 = event.screenX;
26       y2 = event.screenY;
27       document.onmousemove = null;
28       }
29     window.status = 'Start: (' + x1 + ',' + y1 +
30       ') End: (' + x2 + ',' + y2 + ') Distance: ' +
31       (Math.round(Math.sqrt(Math.pow((x2 - x1), 2)+ Math.pow((y2 - y1), 2))))
          + ' pixels';
32     }
33   change = !change;
34   }
35
36 function showKeys() {
37   if (keys != '') {
38     alert('You have typed: ' + keys);
39     window.status = keys = '';
40     }
41   else { alert('You have to type some keys first.'); }
42   }
43
44 function showXY(ev) {
45   if (document.all) { ev = event; }
46   window.status = 'X: ' + ev.screenX + ' Y: ' + ev.screenY;
47   }
48
49 function keepKeys(ev) {
50   if (document.layers) {
51     keys += String.fromCharCode(ev.which);
```

Example 6-5. events.js (continued)

```
52      window.status = 'Key pressed: ' + String.fromCharCode(ev.which);
53      }
54   else {
55      keys += String.fromCharCode(event.keyCode);
56      window.status = 'Key pressed: ' + String.fromCharCode(event.keyCode);
57      }
58   }
```

Function `enableEffects()` is the epicenter for the *click* and *mouseover* events. I call your attention to lines 6, 18, and 33:

```
if (change) { ....

else { ....

change = !change;
```

The variable *change* starts as `true` and is changed to its opposite (i.e., to `false`, back to `true`, and so forth) during every call. Since clicking calls `enableEffects()` and *change* is `true` the first time, that brings lines 7–15, shown here, into effect:

```
if(document.layers) {
  x1 = ev.screenX;
  y1 = ev.screenY;
  document.captureEvents(Event.MOUSEMOVE);
  }
else {
  x1 = event.screenX;
  y1 = event.screenY;
  }
```

These lines capture x and y coordinates and enable the *onmousemove* event handler. If `document.layers` exists, the user has Navigator. The event object created on the fly is reflected in the argument passed to the function, named *ev* in this case. Global variables *x1* and *y1* are set to the respective x and y coordinates where the user first clicks (contained in *screenX* and *screenY*). Then the call to the document method `captureEvents()` causes the *mousemove* event to be intercepted.[*]

If `document.layers` does not exist, the script assumes the user has Internet Explorer and takes appropriate actions to do the same as above. Microsoft's event model, however, defines an event object as *event*. That's where properties *screenX* and *screenY* will be waiting. No additional method calls are required for event capturing in MSIE, which leads us to line 16:

```
document.onmousemove = showXY;
```

---

[*] At least some versions of NN4.x seem to respond only intermittently to the mouse clicks. That is, sometimes you have to click twice to start or stop the tracking. I haven't found any supporting documentation about such a bug.

The *onmousemove* event handler is then assigned by reference to function
showXY() in both browsers. Let's have a quick look at showXY():

```
function showXY(ev) {
  if (document.all) { ev = event; }
  window.status = 'X: ' + ev.screenX + ' Y: ' + ev.screenY;
  }
```

The call to showXY() each time the mouse moves displays the x and y coordinates of the mouse-pointer arrow. The x and y values are referenced in the same
cross-browser manner as before. showXY() is called repeatedly as the user moves
the mouse around. This happens until the user decides to click again, which puts
in another call to enableEffects(). However, variable *change* is false this time
around, so lines 19–31 get the call:

```
if (document.layers) {
  x2 = ev.screenX;
  y2 = ev.screenY;
  document.releaseEvents(Event.MOUSEMOVE);
  }
else {
  x2 = event.screenX;
  y2 = event.screenY;
  document.onmousemove = null;
  }
window.status = 'Start: (' + x1 + ',' + y1 +
  ')  End: (' + x2 + ',' + y2 + ')  Distance: ' +
  (Math.round(Math.sqrt(Math.pow((x2 - x1), 2)+ Math.pow((y2 - y1), 2)))
    + ' pixels';
```

Variables *x1* and *y1* hold the values of the starting click location. Now variables *x2*
and *y2* are set to the values of the stopping click location. There is no longer a
need to keep processing the *onmousemove* event handler. So with Navigator, the
releaseEvents() method is called to cease interception of the *mousemove*
event. The same result is performed by setting document.onmousemove equal to
null in MSIE.

All that remains is to display the distance between the starting and stopping
points. Do you recall the distance formula? You may have used it in ninth grade
Geometry class. That's the same formula here in lines 29–31.

That takes care of the *onclick* and *onmouseover* event handlers, leaving only
onkeypress. Remember that document.onkeypress was set to call function
keepKeys() during the loading of *events.html*. Here is keepKeys(), lines 49–58:

```
function keepKeys(ev) {
  if (document.layers) {
    keys += String.fromCharCode(ev.which);
    window.status = 'Key pressed: ' + String.fromCharCode(ev.which);
    }
```

```
      else {
        keys += String.fromCharCode(event.keyCode);
        window.status = 'Key pressed: ' + String.fromCharCode(event.keyCode);
        }
     }
```

Using the same browser detection technique, empty string variable *keys* is set to itself plus the string equivalent of the key pressed. This happens with `String.fromCharCode()`, regardless of browser. JavaScript 1.2, however, represents the keystrokes as ISO Latin-1 characters. JScript uses Unicode representations. The number in JavaScript is stored in the *which* property of the event object. The number for JScript is reflected in the *event.keyCode* property. So the user types a number of keys, then selects the "Show Keys" button. This function alerts the value of *keys*, then sets it to an empty string.

A Word About the Dueling Event Models

The Navigator 4 and MSIE 4 event models have some things in common, thank goodness. As of this writing, however, there are still significant differences worth your investigation. Perhaps the greatest difference is that while Navigator events move down the object hierarchy (e.g., from *window* to *frame* to *document* to *form* to *field*). MSIE events bubble up (e.g., from *field* to *form* to *document* to *frame* to *window*). You can find out more about both models at the URLs below. This info is vital if you plan to do any complex, cross-browser event handling.

For Navigator, visit:

http://developer.netscape.com/docs/manuals/communicator/jsguide4/evnt.htm

For MSIE, see:

http://msdn.microsoft.com/developer/sdk/inetsdk/help/dhtml/doc_object/event_model.htm#dom_event

---

frames.js

Practical use
    Forced frame loading

Version requirement
    JavaScript 1.1

Functions
    `keepIn()`, `keepOut()`

This source file contains only two functions. One keeps your documents in a particular frameset. The other keeps your documents out of them. *frames.js* requires multiple HTML pages for its examples. For example, try to load *ch06\frameset. html* in your browser. This file is a frameset with two frames. One of the frames has file *frames.html* as the source. *frames.html* utilizes *frames.js* to ensure that *frames.html* is always loaded in the top window. That's why loading *frameset.html* gives you the results shown in Figure 6-10 and Figure 6-11 (the browser loaded *frames.html*).

Conversely, those who want to make certain that their files aren't loaded unless they are in a particular frameset can use *frames.js* as well. Check out Figure 6-10, which shows what happens when you try to load *ch06\frames2.html*. You'll get an alert stating the frameset violation, then the browser loads the corresponding frameset containing *frames2.html*. You can see this in Figure 6-11.

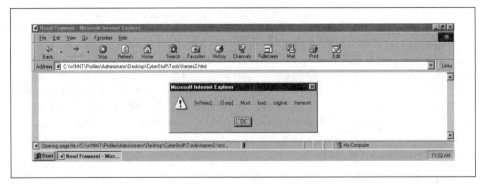

Figure 6-10. Busted by the frameset police

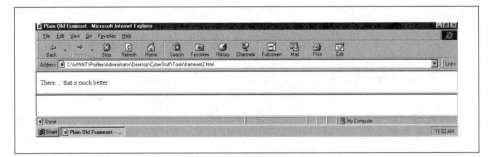

Figure 6-11. That's better

The code to accommodate this functionality is short and sweet. Function `keepOut()` compares document URL in the top window with the document URL of the current frame. If the `location.href` properties don't match, `keepOut()` protests with an alert dialog box and loads the document in its own top window. Function `keepIn()` performs the exact opposite comparison and loads the URL contained in the argument passed if the comparison fails. Example 6-6 shows the code for *frames.js*.

Example 6-6. frames.js

```
 1 function keepOut() {
 2   if (top.location.href != self.location.href) {
 3     alert('This document bows to no frameset.');
 4     top.location.href = self.location.href;
 5     }
 6   }
 7
 8 function keepIn(parentHREF) {
 9   if (top.location.href == self.location.href) {
10     alert('[Wheez]. . .  [Gasp]. . . Must. . . load. . . ' +
11       'original. . . frameset.');
12     top.location.href = parentHREF;
13     }
14   }
```

images.js

Practical use
> Image rollovers

Version requirement
> JavaScript 1.1

Functions
> `imagePreLoad()`, `imageSwap()`, `display()`

Just like the functions in *dhtml.js*, the code in *images.js* was presented in earlier chapters. Chapters 3, 4, and 5 have various versions of the code listed in Example 6-7. You can preload images and use them for mouse rollovers.

Example 6-7. images.js

```
 1 var imgPath    = 'images/';
 2 var arrayHandles = new Array('out', 'over');
 3
 4 for (var i = 0; i < arrayHandles.length; i++) {
 5   eval('var ' + arrayHandles[i] + ' = new Array()');
 6   }
 7
 8 for (var i = 0; i < imgNames.length; i++) {
 9   imagePreLoad(imgNames[i], i);
10   }
11
12 function imagePreLoad(imgName, idx) {
13   for(var j = 0; j < arrayHandles.length; j++) {
14     eval(arrayHandles[j] + "[" + idx + "] = new Image()");
15     eval(arrayHandles[j] + "[" + idx + "].src = '" + imgPath + imgName +
```

Example 6-7. images.js (continued)

```
16        arrayHandles[j] + ".gif'");
17      }
18   }
19
20 function imageSwap(imagePrefix, imageIndex, arrayIdx) {
21    document[imagePrefix].src = eval(arrayHandles[arrayIdx] + "[" +
22      imageIndex + "].src");
23   }
24 function display(stuff) { window.status = stuff; }
```

Since you know the procedure for image rollovers, I haven't included any graphics here to illustrate the difference.

navbar.js

Practical use
> Dynamic page navigation

Version requirement
> JavaScript 1.1

Function
> `navbar()`

This source file contains only one function, but it's a good one. Suppose you have on your web site several pages of content, each with a navigation bar of links to all the other pages. Wouldn't it be great if JavaScript could make a smart nav bar that included links to all other pages on the site except the one currently loaded? Figure 6-12 shows *ch06\astronomy.html*. The nav bar contains links to the other pages on the site: *Other Sciences, Sports, Musicians' Corner,* and *Cool People.* Figure 6-13 shows the document that loads after following the People link. Now look at the nav bar: *Astronomy, Other Sciences, Sports,* and *Musicians' Corner.* There's no link for *People* because it's already loaded. You can do this for as many pages as you like, and if documents change, you need to make changes only in *navbar.js.* This will save plenty of time.

The code for this is surprisingly basic. Just populate array *navURLs* with the filenames of your web pages, and array *linkText* with the text you want to display in your links. Function `navbar()` iterates through all the filenames and generates a link with corresponding text for all those that do not appear in the *location.href* property of the current document. It's that easy. Check out the code in Example 6-8.

Example 6-8. navbar.js

```
1 var navURLs  = new Array('astronomy.html', 'science.html', 'sports.html',
2   'music.htm', 'people.htm');
3 var linkText = new Array('Astronomy', 'Other Sciences', 'Sports',
4   'Musicians\' Corner', 'Cool People');
5
6 function navbar() {
7   var navStr= '';
8   for (var i = 0; i < navURLs.length; i++) {
9     if (location.href.indexOf(navURLs[i]) == -1) {
10      navStr += ' <B>[</B><A HREF="' + navURLs[i] + '">' + linkText[i] +
11        '</A><B>]</B> ';
12    }
13  }
14  document.writeln('<BR><BR>' + navStr);
15  }
```

You can extend this functionality dramatically. There is no reason you can't use images (with rollovers) in place of the text links. If you have a ton of links and don't want to list them across the page, why not embed them in a select list? Then you can really pile on the links and save precious real estate.

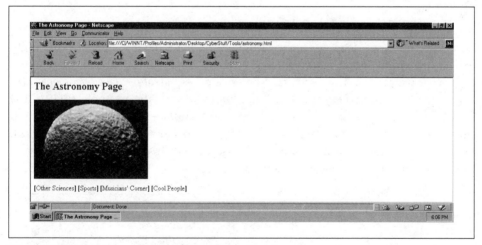

Figure 6-12. The astronomy page with no links to astronomy

numbers.js

Practical uses

Correcting rounding errors and number formatting for shopping cart programs

Version requirement

JavaScript 1.1

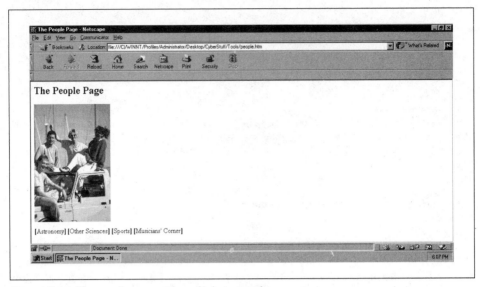

Figure 6-13. The people page with no links to people

Functions

     `twoPlaces()`, `round()`, `totals()`

JavaScript performs floating point arithmetic a little differently than we might expect; the result is that many of our calculations also come out slightly different than what we expect. The DevEdge Newsgroup FAQ at *http://developer1.netscape. com:80/support/faqs/champions/javascript.html#2-2* uses the example 0.119 * 100 = 11.899999. It's also common to want to display number in terms of dollars and cents. The functions in *numbers.js* are designed to help with both situations. All three functions included are based on those at *http://www.irt.org/script/number. htm* maintained by Martin Webb. Figure 6-14 shows *ch06\numbers.html* loaded.

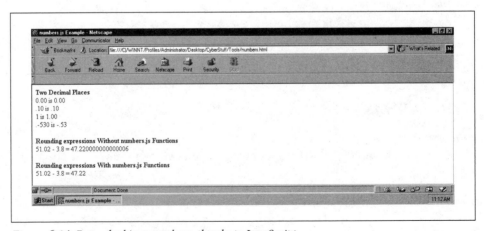

Figure 6-14. Better looking numbers, thanks to JavaScript

The numbers displayed under the "Two Decimal Places" heading shows how function `twoPlaces()` formats numbers to place them in a dollars and cents format. The other two headings display the difference between the expression 51.02 - 3.8 both without and with function `round()` and `totals()`, the latter of which is the desired effect. Example 6-9 shows *numbers.js*.

Example 6-9. number.js

```
 1 function twoPlaces(amount) {
 2   return (amount == Math.floor(amount)) ? amount + '.00' :
 3     ((amount*10 == Math.floor(amount*10)) ? amount + '0' : amount);
 4   }
 5
 6 function round(number,X) {
 7   X = (!X ? 2 : X);
 8   return Math.round(number * Math.pow(10,X)) / Math.pow(10,X);
 9   }
10
11 function totals(num) {
```

Function `twoPlaces()` returns the string value of the number it receives with either 0 or `.00` appended, or nothing if the number is already correctly formatted. That huge conditional expression translates to English as:

- If the number is equal to its greatest lower integer (`Math.floor(amount)`), return it as a string with `.00` appended.

- Otherwise, if the number times 10 equals its greatest lower integer times 10 (`Math.floor(amount) * 10`), return it as a string with .0 appended.

- Otherwise, return the number as a string, because it is fine the way it is.

As for the rounding errors listed below the "Two Decimal Places" list, function `round()` returns the number received rounded to the precision of integer x decimal places. x defaults to 2. Therefore, the default is rounding to two places if you don't pass in a value for x.

objects.js

Practical uses
> Generic object creation, object inspection

Version requirement
> JavaScript 1.1

Functions

    makeObj(), parseObj(), objProfile()

Now JavaScript objects. So many things to do with them, so little time to try them all. *objects.js* provides two utilities. One is a generic object constructor, the other is a basic object inspector. Open *ch06\objects.html* in your browser. Figure 6-15 shows you what you get.

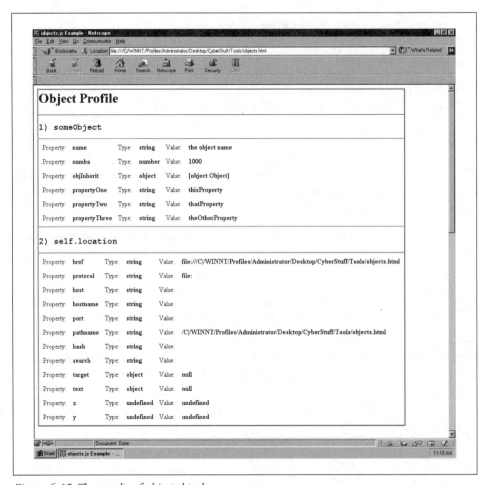

Figure 6-15. The results of objects.html

Object inspector functions parseObj() and objProfile() reveal the properties of two objects: one represented by variable *someObject*; the other is the location object of the window. Have a look at *objects.html* in Example 6-10 to see how this gets under way.

Example 6-10. objects.html

```
 1 <HTML>
 2 <HEAD>
 3 <TITLE>objects.js Example</TITLE>
 4 <STYLE type="text/css">
 5 <!--
 6 td { font-family: courier new; font-size: 14}
 7 -->
 8 </STYLE>
 9 <SCRIPT LANGUAGE="JavaScript1.1" SRC="objects.js"></SCRIPT>
10 </HEAD>
11 <BODY>
12 <SCRIPT LANGUAGE="JavaScript1.1">
13 <!--
14
15 function plainOldObject() {
16   this.name = 'some name';
17   this.numba = 1000;
18   this.objInherit = new makeObj('propertyOne', 'thisProperty',
19     'propertyTwo', 'thatProperty', 'propertyThree', 'theOtherProperty');
20   return this;
21   }
22
23 var someObject = new plainOldObject();
24
25 document.write(objProfile('someObject', 'self.location'));
26 //-->
27 </SCRIPT>
28
29 </BODY>
30 </HTML>
```

Notice line 23 sets variable *someObject* equal to a new `plainOldObject()`. The `plainOldObject()` constructor has several properties, including *name, numba,* and *objInherit. objInherit* represents an object made from the generic object constructor `makeObj()` found in *objects.js*. Take a look at the source file in Example 6-11.

Example 6-11. objects.js

```
 1 function makeObj() {
 2   if (arguments.length % 2 != 0) {
 3     arguments[arguments.length] = "";
 4     }
 5   for ( var i = 0; i < arguments.length; i += 2 ) {
 6     this[arguments[i]] = arguments[i + 1] ;
 7     }
 8   return this;
 9   }
10
11 function parseObj(obj) {
12   var objStr = '';
```

Example 6-11. objects.js (continued)

```
13    for (prop in obj) {
14      objStr += '<TR><TD>Property: </TD><TD><B>' + prop +
15        '</B></TD><TD>Type: </TD><TD><B>' + typeof(obj[prop]) +
16        '</B></TD><TD>Value: </TD><TD><B>'  + obj[prop] +
17        '</B></TD></TR>';
18      if (typeof(obj[prop]) == "object") {
19        objStr += parseObj(obj[prop]);
20        }
21      }
22    return objStr;
23    }
24
25 function objProfile() {
26    var objTable = '<TABLE BORDER=2 CELLSPACING=0><TR><TD><H1>' +
27      'Object Profile</H1></TD></TR>';
28    for (var i = 0; i < arguments.length; i++) {
29      objTable += '<TR><TD><BR><BR><H2><TT>' + (i + 1) + ') ' +
30        arguments[i] +  '</H2></TD></TR>';
31      objTable += '<TR><TD><TT><TABLE CELLPADDING=5>' +
32        parseObj(eval(arguments[i])) + '</TABLE></TD></TR>';
33      }
34    objTable += '</TABLE><BR><BR><BR>';
35    return objTable;
36    }
```

Let's first have a look at **makeObj**(); here are lines of the source file:

```
function makeObj() {
  if (arguments.length % 2 != 0) {
    arguments[arguments.length] = "";
    }
  for ( var i = 0; i < arguments.length; i += 2 ) {
    this[arguments[i]] = arguments[i + 1] ;
      }
  return this;
  }
```

This constructor builds properties by assigning pairs of arguments passed in. If there is an odd number of arguments passed (meaning one argument won't make a pair), **makeObj**() assigns an additional element of empty string value to the *arguments* array. Now every argument element has a buddy. **makeObj**() then iterates through the arguments elements by twos, assigning the first element of the pair as an object property name, and the second element of the pair as the value of the previously named property. That is, calling **makeObj**(**'name'**, **'Madonna'**, **'occupation'**, **'singer/songwriter'**) would return a reference to an object with the following properties:

```
this.name = 'Madonna';
this.occupation = 'singer/songwriter';
```

Therefore, variable *objInherit* now refers to an object and has the following properties:

```
objInherit.propertyOne    = 'thisProperty';
objInherit.propertyTwo    = 'thatProperty';
objInherit.propertyThree  = 'theOtherProperty';
```

Note that all the properties have strings as values. You can certainly pass in numbers, objects, and the like. Function makeObj() is great for creating multiple objects, each with different properties, *without* having to define a constructor for each.

The other object inspected is the location object. Pretty straightforward, but how does the inspection work? Functions objProfile() and parseObj() work together recursively to "drill down" into object properties and create a table of results. Each table row identifies the object property name, the property object type, and the value to which it is associated. Let's begin with objProfile():

```
function objProfile() {
  var objTable = '<TABLE BORDER=2 CELLSPACING=0><TR><TD><H1>' +
    'Object Profile</H1></TD></TR>';
  for (var i = 0; i < arguments.length; i++) {
    objTable += '<TR><TD><BR><BR><H2><TT>' + (i + 1) + ') ' +
      arguments[i] +  '</H2></TD></TR>';
    objTable += '<TR><TD><TT><TABLE CELLPADDING=5>' +
      parseObj(eval(arguments[i])) + '</TABLE></TD></TR>';
    }
  objTable += '</TABLE><BR><BR><BR>';
  return objTable;
  }
```

objProfile() is the function you call and pass parameters. See line 25 in *objects. html*:

```
document.write(objProfile('someObject', 'self.location'));
```

The arguments passed in aren't objects at all. They're strings. They'll reflect objects soon. Passing in the string equivalent allows JavaScript to display these objects by name to the page. Once the necessary table TRs and TDs are created, these string arguments passed in to objProfile() are iteratively de-referenced with the eval() method in line 32 and passed to parseObj(). Watch what happens then:

```
function parseObj(obj) {
  var objStr = '';
    for (prop in obj) {
      objStr += '<TR><TD>Property: </TD><TD><B>' + prop +
        '</B></TD><TD>Type: </TD><TD><B>' + typeof(obj[prop]) +
        '</B></TD><TD>Value: </TD><TD><B>'  + obj[prop] +
        '</B></TD></TR>';
      if (typeof(obj[prop]) == "object") {
        objStr += parseObj(obj[prop]);
        }
```

```
    }
    return objStr;
}
```

Each dereferenced string arrives as an object and is called *obj*. Using the *for ... if* loop, `parseObj()` iterates through all properties in *obj*, accumulating a string of its property, type, and value along with appropriate table tags. `parseObj()` accesses the object type with the `typeof()` operator. Once the property, type and value have been added to the string, `parseObj()` checks to see whether the type of that particular property is an object. If so, `parseObj()` calls itself and passes in the property (which is an *obj* object). This recursion allows the "drill down" effect to get to the bottom of, and reveal, a top-level object's internal hierarchy.

When `parseObj()` has no more objects to parse, the entire string of properties, types, values, and table tags, reflected in variable *objStr,* is eventually returned to function `objProfile()`. `objProfile()` then concatenates this string to the other table rows and cells that it created. This string, reflected in variable *objTable,* is finally written to the page in line 25 of *objects.html.*

These object inspection functions are designed for relatively small objects, such as user-created objects. Both Navigator and IE will choke on the script if there is too much recursion. For example, try changing line 25 of *objects.html* from this:

```
document.write(objProfile('someObject', 'self.
location'));
```

to this:

```
document.write(objProfile('document'));
```

Now load the document into MSIE. You'll no doubt receive a stack overflow message. Try this in line 25 with Navigator:

```
document.write(objProfile('window'));
```

You get this in the JavaScript console: `JavaScript Error: too much recursion`

---

strings.js

Practical uses
    String manipulation, alphabetization, frequency counting

Version requirement
    JavaScript 1.2

Functions
    `camelCaps()`, `prepStr()`, `wordCount()`, `reorder()`

The functions give you a taste of what you can do with strings, most likely from user input. Open *ch06\string.html* in your browser and Figure 6-16 is what you'll see.

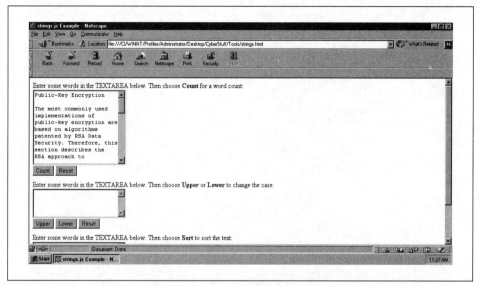

Figure 6-16. Three forms to crunch string data, starting with word count

What you have here are three forms that demonstrate three functions. The first form contains a TEXTAREA to enter text. After the user enters text and presses the "Count" button, function wordCount() generates a new page with a table. The table list each of the "words" typed in the TEXTAREA and the number of times the word was encountered. You can see the results in Figure 6-17.

The second form contains a TEXTAREA for entering text, too. The user can then choose "Upper" or "Lower" to convert the first character of each word to upper- or lowercase. Function camelCaps() takes care of this. You might find this function handy for form validation, perhaps when users have to enter names and addresses. Check out the case change in Figure 6-18.

Not to be outdone, the last form has a TEXTAREA, which, after the user types in his or her text, can sort each instance of the words. This is a good alphabetization script. Have a look at Figure 6-19 to see the results. Choosing "Sort" multiple times renders the text between ascending and descending sort orders. You've seen the puppet show; now its time to see who's pulling the strings.

Example 6-12 has the code for *strings.js*.

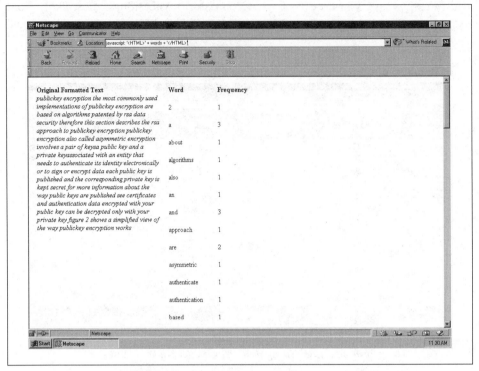

Figure 6-17. The table of words and their respective counts

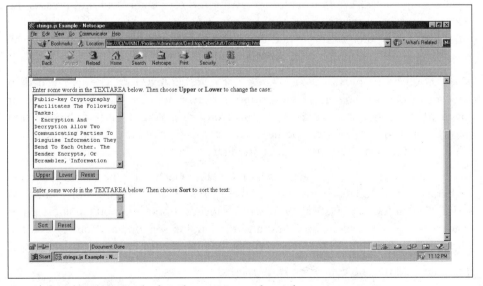

Figure 6-18. Capitalizing the first character or each word

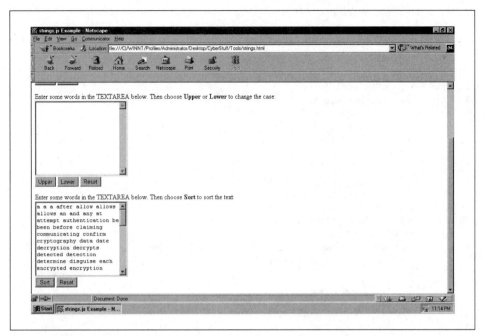

Figure 6-19. Alphabetizing the words

Example 6-12. strings.js

```
1  function wordCount(str, output) {
2    var wordArray = new Array();
3    str = prepStr(str);
4    var tempArray = str.split(' ').sort();
5    var count = 1;
6    for (var i = 0; i < tempArray.length; i++) {
7      if (wordArray[tempArray[i]]) {
8        wordArray[tempArray[i]]++;
9        }
10     else { wordArray[tempArray[i]] = 1; }
11     }
12   if (output) { return wordArray; }
13   else {
14     var arrStr = '';
15     for (word in wordArray) {
16       if (word != "") {
17         arrStr += '<TR><TD>' + word + '</TD><TD>' + wordArray[word] +
18           '</TD></TR>';
19         count++;
20         }
21       }
22     return '<TABLE BORDER=0><TR><TD WIDTH=300 VALIGN=TOP ROWSPAN=' +
23       count + '><B>Original Formatted Text</B><BR><I>' + str +
24       '</I><TD><B>Word</B><TD><B>Freqency</B></TR>' + arrStr +
```

Example 6-12. strings.js (continued)

```
25        '</TABLE>';
26    }
27  }
28
29 function prepStr(str) {
30    str = str.toLowerCase();
31    str = str.replace(/['"-]/g, "");
32    str = str.replace(/\W/g, " ");
33    str = str.replace(/\s+/g, " ");
34    return str;
35  }
36
37 function camelCaps(str, theCase) {
38    var tempArray = str.split(' ');
39    for (var i = 0; i < tempArray.length; i++) {
40      if (theCase) {
41        tempArray[i] = tempArray[i].charAt(0).toUpperCase() +
42          tempArray[i].substring(1);
43      }
44      else {
45        tempArray[i] = tempArray[i].charAt(0).toLowerCase() +
46          tempArray[i].substring(1);
47      }
48    }
49    return tempArray.join(' ');
50  }
51
52 var order = true;
53
54 function reorder(str) {
55    str = prepStr(str);
56    str = str.replace(/\d/g, "");
57    order = !order;
58    if(!order) { str = str.split(' ').sort().join(' '); }
59    else { str = str.split(' ').sort().reverse().join(' '); }
60    return str.replace(/^\s+/, "");
61  }
```

To generate a word count using the first form, **wordCount()** accomplishes the following steps:

1. Removes any characters that aren't letters, numbers (or underscores) or single whitespaces

2. Creates an array of all the words in the text

3. Counts the number of occurrences of each word

4. Displays the results in table format

Step 1 is accomplished with another function, **prepStr()**. Here it is at lines 29–35:

```
function prepStr(str) {
  str = str.toLowerCase();
  str = str.replace(/['"-]/g, "");
  str = str.replace(/\W/g, " ");
  str = str.replace(/\s+/g, " ");
  return str;
}
```

The string is first converted to all lowercase (no need to count "Boat" and "boat" as two separate words). Then the function performs a series of string replacements. Quotation marks and dashes are eliminated in line 31. Any characters that are not letters, numbers, or underscores are converted to single whitespaces in line 32. Finally, one or more adjacent whitespaces are converted to a single whitespace. This cleans up the text a bit and keeps the ensuing code from counting such entries as ? or "string" (quotes included) as a word.

Back to `wordCount()`. `prepStr()` returns a string of words delimited by whitespace. This makes for an easy `split()` to wrap up step 2 from above. Step 3 happens in lines 6–11:

```
for (var i = 0; i < tempArray.length; i++) {
  if (wordArray[tempArray[i]]) {
    wordArray[tempArray[i]]++;
    }
  else { wordArray[tempArray[i]] = 1; }
  }
```

In the second form, the text the user typed is passed to the function `camelCaps()` as a string. `camelCaps()` also accepts a second argument, a Boolean value indicating whether the case conversion is upper- or lowercase. Here's another look:

```
function camelCaps(str, theCase) {
  var tempArray = str.split(' ');
  for (var i = 0; i < tempArray.length; i++) {
    if (theCase) {
      tempArray[i] = tempArray[i].charAt(0).toUpperCase() +
        tempArray[i].substring(1);
      }
    else {
      tempArray[i] = tempArray[i].charAt(0).toLowerCase() +
        tempArray[i].substring(1);
      }
    }
  return tempArray.join(' ');
  }
```

Local variable *tempArray* is set to an array containing all the words in the text. A "word," in this case, refers to any text between whitespace. Now it's a matter of iterating through all the words and replacing the first character of each with its upper- or lowercase equivalent. When all first letters have been changed, the function returns a string of these new words joined by a whitespace. Function camelCaps() is essentially returning the whitespace that it removed during the split().

For the last form, function reorder() performs either a sort() or a reversed sort(). See for yourself:

```
var order = true;

function reorder(str) {
  str = prepStr(str);
  str = str.replace(/\d/g, "");
  order = !order;
  if(!order) { str = str.split(' ').sort().join(' '); }
  else { str = str.split(' ').sort().reverse().join(' '); }
  return str.replace(/^\s+/, "");
}
```

Just as in wordCount(), prepStr() formats the string passed in. For this function, though, I also removed the digits with a call to str.replace(/\d/g, ""). This keeps the focus on words as opposed to numbers. Variable order is changed to its opposite, which determines the sort order and sets up things for the next click of the "Sort" button. Now, consider what must happen if the words are sorted traditionally or in reverse. For a traditional sort:

1. The text is split into an array.

2. Those array elements are sorted.

3. That array is joined to make a string.

In the case of a reverse sort, there is an extra step:

1. The text is split into an array.

2. Those array elements are sorted.

3. The elements are reversed.

4. That array is joined to make a string.

Lines 58–59 of *strings.js* use the value of order to determine which of the two routes to take. Afterwards, the string is returned (less any leading whitespace that may have been created by the join()).

Potential Extensions

The sky is really the limit here. Of course, you can add cool functions to these files or even make the existing functions better. In all honesty, though, I doubt you'll want to keep your functions in these same source files. Maybe you're designing a handful of web sites, and you want to name *.js* files by site name.

Great. Insert the functions that you need, and you just made a toolkit. (How about naming it *toolkit.js?*) The important thing to remember is that you need to come up with a system that works best for you. Don't let your *.js* files manage you. Keep it the other way around. I'd really like to know what you come up with.

7

Cookie-Based User Preferences

This chapter contains a worthless application, but don't flip to the next one yet. Did I mention that the code in this one can help you add some of the coolest functionality to your web site? I'm talking about setting user preferences. Consider this. What's the one word every user has on his or her mind while surfing the Web?

"Me."

Yes, users are a selfish bunch, always thinking about their concerns and interests, rather than yours. Whatever people do, they always tend to seek things that remind them of themselves. That's why DHTML freaks hang out at the Dynamic HTML Zone (*http://www.dhtmlzone. com/*), shoppers go to Shopping.com (*http:// www.shopping.com/ibuy/*), and astronomy geeks (that would be me. See? I'm doing it right now) visit the Sky & Telescope site (*http://www.skypub.com/*). Marketers, advertisers, and salespeople have capitalized on this for centuries. The Web is no different. Using a fictitious application, this chapter shows you how to add personalization of functionality to your site, even if it's as simple as remembering a username. Using JavaScript cookies, visitors will be able to customize their experience on your web site.

Say you've developed a site for Internet investors who have a little extra spending cash. Visitors get a free membership at this fictitious Wall Street cybercenter, called Take-A-Dive Brokerage $ervices. They can't do any trading here, but they can get their own customized home page with a choice of favorite links to other financial-related web sites and e-news. Figure 7-1 shows what happens when the user first visits the soon-to-be-customized page (*\ch07\dive.html*). This is the user's first time, so he or she is redirected to the user preferences page.

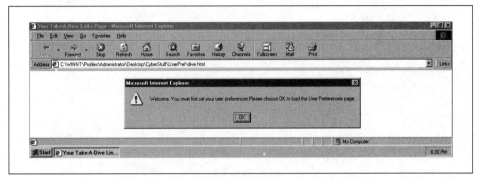

Figure 7-1. First timers go directly to the user preferences screen

Figure 7-2 shows the user preferences page (*\ch07\prefs.html*). It's a long form that allows the user to enter name, age, occupation, and category of investment strategy. A series of checkboxes allow the user to choose which (if any) of the available finance-related links to put on the customized home page.

The form winds up with a series of select lists, with which the user chooses a background image, font size, and font family from the provided thumbnail images. When everything is chosen, clicking "Save" writes the selections to the resident browser cookie file. The user is then asked to review the changes, as shown in Figure 7-3. Choosing "OK" directs the user to *dive.html*, a page that reflects everything the user selected—the personal info, the background, even the font stuff.

Pretty cool, but what if the user wants to make changes? Simply choose the "Set Preferences" link, and you're back at *prefs.html*. Notice that the user's choices are also maintained here. All the personal information remains intact. The most recently checked checkboxes are still selected. Even the background images and font details are in place. Now the user can experiment with the background images and font specs to see which works best. Figure 7-4 shows one of the many possible combinations.

Execution Requirements

This application has JavaScript 1.2 written all over it. Stylesheets and string replacement make it so. Users will need to have at least version 4 of Navigator or Internet Explorer. This application can be significantly extended; it makes use of a

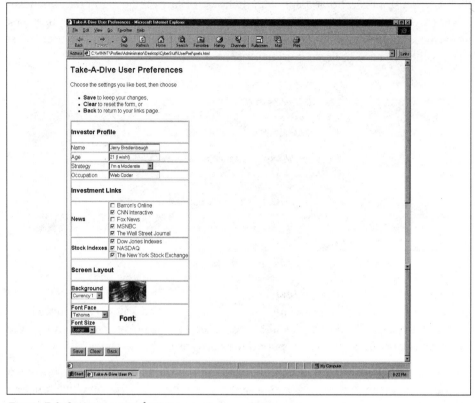

Figure 7-2. Setting user preferences

very simple stylesheet. The only limitations are those imposed by your ability to utilize DHTML (in other words, not many).

This is a cookies-based application, so you are limited to the cookie specifications of each browser. You can find those at the URLs listed below.

Netscape Navigator:

http://developer1.netscape.com:80/docs/manuals/communicator/jsguide4/cookies.htm

MSIE:

http://msdn.microsoft.com/msdn-online/workshop/author/dhtml/reference/properties/cookie.asp

Don't worry, though. This application stays well within the cookie limits of both NN and MSIE 4.x browsers.

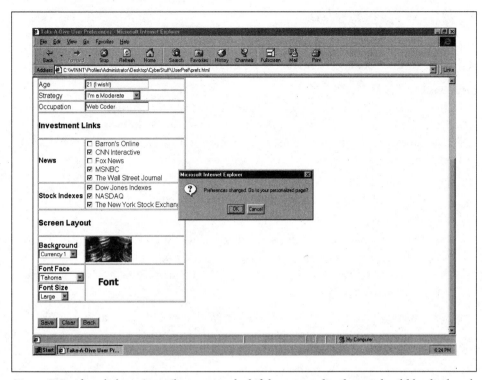

Figure 7-3. After clicking Save, the user is asked if the personalized page should be displayed

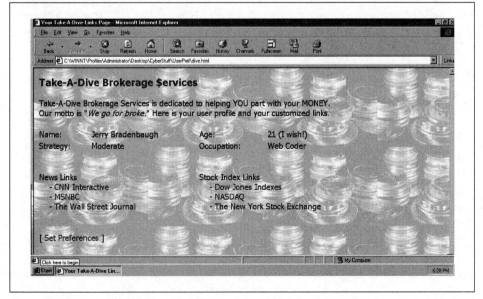

Figure 7-4. The customized page, including font and background image

Syntax Breakdown

This application consists of two HTML pages (*prefs.html* and *dive.html*) and a Java-Script source file, *cookies.js*. The following list describes each file:

prefs.html
> This is the page is used to set the preferences for *dive.html*. This page is also affected by the extracted cookie info, as the cookie information is used to determine which settings the user has already selected, and to populate a form accordingly.

dive.html
> This page is custom-designed by the information extracted from the cookie.

cookies.js
> This file contains the functions used to write the user preferences to and extract the preferences from the cookie. *cookies.js* is embedded in both HTML files. The `GetCookie()` and `SetCookie()` functions, which you'll see in the other two files come from here.

The files *prefs.html* and *dive.html* are both new, but *cookies.js* is a source file that was included in Chapter 6, *Implementing JavaScript Source Files*. You can find a discussion of its functionality there.

prefs.html

Although the sequence of screen captures leads you through the true progression of events (i.e., the user begins with no preference settings), let's assume the user has previously set user preferences and is returning to *prefs.html* to make changes. I think you'll find it much easier to follow. Example 7-1 shows *prefs.html*.

Example 7-1. prefs.html

```
 1  <HTML>
 2  <HEAD>
 3  <TITLE>Take-A-Dive User Preferences</TITLE>
 4  <STYLE type="text/css">
 5    BODY, TD { font-family: Arial; }
 6  </STYLE>
 7  <SCRIPT LANGAUGE="JavaScript1.2" SRC="cookies.js"></SCRIPT>
 8  <SCRIPT LANGUAGE="JavaScript1.2">
 9
10  var imagePath = 'images/';
11  var newsNames = new Array(
12    new Array('The Wall Street Journal','http://www.wsj.com/'),
13    new Array('Barron\'s Online','http://www.barrons.com/'),
14    new Array('CNN Interactive','http://www.cnn.com/'),
15    new Array('MSNBC','http://www.msnbc.com/'),
```

Example 7-1. prefs.html (continued)

```
16    new Array('Fox News','http://www.foxnews.com/')
17    );
18
19 var indexNames = new Array(
20    new Array('The New York Stock Exchange','http://www.nyse.com/'),
21    new Array('NASDAQ','http://www.nasdaq.com/'),
22    new Array('Dow Jones Indexes','http://www.dowjones.com/')
23    );
24
25 var strategy = new Array(
26    new Array('Cheap', 'I\'m Really Cheap'),
27    new Array('Stingy', 'I\'m Pretty Stingy'),
28    new Array('Conservative', 'I\'m Conservative'),
29    new Array('Moderate', 'I\'m a Moderate'),
30    new Array('Agressive', 'I\'m Aggressive'),
31    new Array('Willing to sell mother', 'I\'d Sell My Mother!')
32    );
33
34 var background = new Array(
35    new Array(imagePath + 'goldthumb.gif', 'Gold Bars'),
36    new Array(imagePath + 'billsthumb.gif', 'Dollar Bills'),
37    new Array(imagePath + 'fistthumb.gif', 'Fist of Cash'),
38    new Array(imagePath + 'currency1thumb.gif', 'Currency 1'),
39    new Array(imagePath + 'currency2thumb.gif', 'Currency 2')
40    );
41
42 var face = new Array(
43    new Array('times', 'Times Roman'),
44    new Array('arial', 'Arial'),
45    new Array('courier', 'Courier New'),
46    new Array('tahoma', 'Tahoma')
47    );
48
49 var size = new Array(
50    new Array('10', 'Small'),
51    new Array('12', 'Medium'),
52    new Array('14', 'Large'),
53    new Array('16', 'X-Large')
54    );
55
56 indexNames = indexNames.sort();
57 newsNames = newsNames.sort();
58
59 var allImages = new Array();
60
61 var imageNames = new Array(
62    'courier10', 'courier12', 'courier14', 'courier16',
63    'arial10', 'arial12', 'arial14', 'arial16',
64    'times10', 'times12', 'times14', 'times16',
65    'tahoma10', 'tahoma12', 'tahoma14', 'tahoma16',
66    'goldthumb','billsthumb','fistthumb','currency1thumb','currency2thumb',
```

Example 7-1. prefs.html (continued)

```
 67    'blank'
 68    );
 69
 70 for (var i = 0; i < imageNames.length; i++) {
 71    allImages[i] = new Image();
 72    allImages[i].src = imagePath + imageNames[i] + '.gif';
 73    }
 74
 75 function makePath(formObj) {
 76    var fontName = imagePath +
 77      formObj.face.options[formObj.face.selectedIndex].value +
 78      formObj.size.options[formObj.size.selectedIndex].value + '.gif';
 79    swapImage("fontImage", fontName);
 80    }
 81
 82 function swapImage(imageName, imageBase) {
 83    document[imageName].src = imageBase;
 84    }
 85
 86 function genSelect(name, select, onChangeStr) {
 87    var optStr = "";
 88    var arrObj = eval(name);
 89    for (var i = 0; i < arrObj.length; i++) {
 90      optStr += '<OPTION VALUE="' + arrObj[i][0] +
 91        (i == select ? '" SELECTED' : '"') + '>' + arrObj[i][1];
 92      }
 93    return '<SELECT NAME="' + name + '"' + (onChangeStr ? ' onChange="' +
 94      onChangeStr + ';"' : '') + '>' + optStr + '</SELECT>';
 95    }
 96
 97 function genBoxes(handle, arrObj) {
 98    var boxStr = '';
 99    for (var i = 0; i < arrObj.length; i++) {
100      boxStr += '<INPUT TYPE=CHECKBOX NAME="' + handle + i + '" VALUE="' +
101        arrObj[i][0] + ',' + arrObj[i][1] + '"> ' + arrObj[i][0] + '<BR>';
102      }
103    return boxStr;
104    }
105
106 function getPrefs(formObj) {
107    var prefStr = GetCookie('userPrefs');
108    if (prefStr == null) { return false; }
109    var prefArray = prefStr.split('-->');
110    for (var i = 0; i < prefArray.length; i++) {
111      var currPref = prefArray[i].split('::');
112      if (currPref[1] == "select") {
113        formObj[currPref[0]].selectedIndex = currPref[2];
114        }
115      else if (currPref[1] == "text") {
116        formObj[currPref[0]].value = currPref[2];
117        }
```

Example 7-1. prefs.html (continued)

```
118      else if (currPref[1] == "checkbox") {
119         formObj[currPref[0]].checked = true;
120         }
121      }
122   return true;
123   }
124
125 function setPrefs(formObj) {
126   var prefStr = '';
127   var htmlStr = '';
128   for (var i = 0; i < formObj.length; i++) {
129      if (formObj[i].type == "select-one") {
130         prefStr += formObj[i].name + '::select::' +
131         formObj[i].selectedIndex + '-->';
132         htmlStr += formObj[i].name + '=' +
133            formObj[i].options[formObj[i].selectedIndex].value + '-->';
134         }
135      else if (formObj[i].type == "text") {
136         if (formObj[i].value == '') { formObj[i].value = "Not Provided"; }
137            prefStr += formObj[i].name + '::text::' +
138            safeChars(formObj[i].value) + '-->';
139            htmlStr += formObj[i].name + '=' + formObj[i].value + '-->';
140         }
141      else if (formObj[i].type == "checkbox" && formObj[i].checked) {
142            prefStr += formObj[i].name + '::checkbox::' + '-->';
143            htmlStr += formObj[i].name + '=' + formObj[i].value + '-->';
144         }
145      }
146   SetCookie('userPrefs', prefStr, expiry);
147   SetCookie('htmlPrefs', htmlStr, expiry);
148   if (confirm('Preferences changed. Go to your personalized page?')) {
149      self.location.href = "dive.html";
150      }
151   }
152
153 function safeChars(str) {
154   return str.replace(/::|=|-->/g, ':;');
155   }
156
157 function populateForm(formObj) {
158   if (getPrefs(formObj)) {
159      makePath(formObj);
160      swapImage('bkgImage',
161       formObj.background.options[formObj.background.selectedIndex].value);
162      }
163   else { resetImage(document.forms[0]); }
164   }
165
166 function resetImage(formObj) {
167   swapImage('bkgImage', formObj.background.options[0].value);
168   swapImage('fontImage', imagePath + formObj.face.options[0].value +
```

Example 7-1. prefs.html (continued)

```
169       formObj.size.options[0].value + '.gif');
170    }
171
172  </SCRIPT>
173  </HEAD>
174
175  <BODY BGCOLOR=FFFFFF onLoad="populateForm(document.forms[0]);">
176  <DIV ID="setting">
177  <H2>Take-A-Dive User Preferences</H2>
178  Choose the settings you like best, then choose<BR>
179  <UL>
180    <LI><B>Save</B> to keep your changes,
181    <LI><B>Clear</B> to reset the form, or
182    <LI> <B>Back</B> to return to your links page.
183  </UL>
184
185  <FORM>
186  <TABLE BORDER=1 CELLBORDER=0 CELLPADDING=0 CELLSPACING=1>
187    <TR>
188      <TD COLSPAN=2>
189      <BR>
190      <H3>Investor Profile</H3>
191      </TD>
192    </TR>
193    <TR>
194      <TD>Name</TD>
195      <TD><INPUT TYPE=TEXT NAME="investor"></TD>
196    </TR>
197    <TR>
198      <TD>Age</TD>
199      <TD><INPUT TYPE=TEXT NAME="age"></TD>
200    </TR>
201    <TR>
202      <TD>Strategy</TD>
203      <TD>
204        <SCRIPT LANGUAGE="JavaScript1.2">
205        document.write(genSelect('strategy', 3));
206        </SCRIPT>
207      </TD>
208    </TR>
209    <TR>
210      <TD>Occupation</TD>
211      <TD>
212        <INPUT TYPE=TEXT NAME="occupation">
213      </TD>
214        <TR>
215          <TD COLSPAN=2>
216            <BR>
217            <H3>Investment Links</H3>
218          </TD>
219        </TR>
```

Example 7-1. prefs.html (continued)

```
220        <TR>
221          <TD><B>News<B></TD>
222          <TD>
223            <SCRIPT LANUAGE="JavaScript1.2">
224            document.write(genBoxes('newsNames'));
225            </SCRIPT>
226          </TD>
227        </TR>
228        <TR>
229          <TD><B>Stock Indexes</B></TD>
230          <TD>
231            <SCRIPT LANUAGE="JavaScript1.2">
232            document.write(genBoxes('indexNames'));
233            </SCRIPT>
234          </TD>
235        </TR>
236        <TR>
237         <TD COLSPAN=2>
238         <BR>
239         <H3>Screen Layout</H3>
240         </TD>
241        </TR>
242        <TR>
243          <TD>
244          <B>Background</B>
245          <BR>
246          <SCRIPT LANGUAGE="JavaScript1.2">
247           document.write(genSelect('background', 0,
248             "swapImage('bkgImage',
249             this.options[this.selectedIndex].value)"));
250          </SCRIPT>
251          </TD>
252          <TD>
253          <IMG SRC="images/blank.gif"
254            NAME="bkgImage" WIDTH=112 HEIGHT=60>
255          </TD>
256        </TR>
257         <TR>
258          <TD>
259          <B>Font Face</B>
260          <BR>
261          <SCRIPT LANGUAGE="JavaScript1.2">
262          document.write(genSelect('face', 0, "makePath(this.form)"));
263          </SCRIPT>
264          </TD>
265          <TD ROWSPAN=2>
266            <IMG SRC="images/blank.gif" NAME="fontImage"
267              WIDTH=112 HEIGHT=60>
268          </TD>
269
270        </TR>
```

Example 7-1. prefs.html (continued)

```
271        <TR>
272          <TD>
273            <B>Font Size</B>
274            <BR>
275            <SCRIPT LANGUAGE="JavaScript1.2">
276            document.write(genSelect('size', 0, "makePath(this.form)"));
277            </SCRIPT>
278          </TD>
279        </TR>
280 </TABLE>
281 <BR><BR>
282 <INPUT TYPE=BUTTON VALUE="Save" onClick="setPrefs(this.form);">
283 <INPUT TYPE=RESET VALUE="Clear" onClick="resetImage(this.form);">
284 <INPUT TYPE=BUTTON VALUE="Back" onClick="location.href='dive.html';">
285 <!--
286 <INPUT TYPE=BUTTON VALUE="Show"
287   onClick="alert(GetCookie('userPrefs'));alert(GetCookie('htmlPrefs'));">
288 <INPUT TYPE=BUTTON VALUE="Erase"
289   onClick="DeleteCookie('userPrefs'); DeleteCookie('htmlPrefs');">
290 //-->
291 </FORM>
292 </DIV>
293 </BODY>
294 </HTML>
```

Lines 10–68 are fairly academic. Other than identifying a path location for the images (line 10), the variables here are dedicated to configuring the layout for *dive.html*. Each of the variables is set to the value of a "multidimensional" array. A multidimensional array is essentially an array of arrays. For example, here is a one-dimensional array:

```
var oneDimension = new Array("This", "That", "The Other");
```

You can easily reference any element by using one set of brackets and the corresponding index, such as **oneDimension[0]**. In a "multidimensional" array, each element is an array of more elements, like so:

```
var twoDimension =
  new Array(
    new Array(1,2,3),
    new Array(4,5,6),
    new Array(7,8,9)
    );
```

Now **twoDimension[0]** refers to **new Array(1,2,3)** instead of a string, such as *This*. To refer to values 1, 2, or 3, you must use a second set of brackets, like this:

```
twoDimension[0][0]    // Refers to 1
twoDimension[0][1]    // Refers to 2
twoDimension[0][2]    // Refers to 3
twoDimension[1][0]    // Refers to 4
```

```
twoDimension[2][1]    // Refers to 5
twoDimension[3][2]    // Refers to 6
```

I use the term "multidimensional" in quotes because JavaScript technically doesn't create multidimensional arrays. It only emulates them. Getting back to the script, each of the variables declared in lines 11-68 is set to an array of information as described in Table 7-1.

Table 7-1. Variables with Information About the User's Page

Array Name	Contains...
newsNames	The names and URLs of several online financial news resources
indexNames	The names and URLs of several online stock indexes
strategy	The name and type of investment strategy users can classify themselves with
background	The names and URLs of available background images
face	The image handle (more on that shortly) and the names of the available font families
size	The image handle and the names of the available font sizes
allImages	A currently empty array used later to store the preloaded images for easy access
imageNames	An array containing image handles; these strings help preload the images

As the term *multidimensional array* implies, each element of the array is itself a two-element array. Basically, one element contains a string for display; the other contains a string for behind-the-scenes work. For example, `size[0][0]` equals 10. That value will be used to set the pixel size of the font. However, `size[0][1]` equals *Small*, which is the description printed on the page. Users will have an easier time relating to "small" letters than 10-point letters. It works basically the same for all the other arrays.

Lines 56–57 are calls to the *Array* object's `sort()` method to neatly arrange the news and stock index links. Not necessary, but two more lines won't hurt anybody. *prefs.html* utilizes a handful of graphics, so it's a good idea to preload them. Lines 70–73 handle this:

```
for (var i = 0; i < imageNames.length; i++) {
    allImages[i] = new Image();
    allImages[i].src = imagePath + imageNames[i] + '.gif';
    }
```

Each of the elements in *imageNames* is a string. This image handle, when concatenated between variable *imagePath* and the string *.gif*, make it possible to iterate through the elements of *imageNames* and preload everything necessary. By the way, make a mental note that the image handles (such as *courier10*) aren't named arbitrarily. The naming convention has a utility that we'll explore a little later.

If you scan the rest of the code within the SCRIPT tags, you'll see that everything else is defined in terms of functions. So, any code that executes is called elsewhere. This happens twice:

- As the HTML content is loading

- In the *onLoad* event handler of the BODY tag

Let's have a look, then, at the HTML following the JavaScript, lines 174–294. See Example 7-1 for this code.

Preferences Form

The interface is a form containing a text field, checkbox, and select list elements with which users specify preferences. Creating text fields is a matter (at least in this case) of hardcoding each and setting the names as desired. This happens in lines 195, 199, and 212 for name, age, and occupation.

The next thing to decide on is the type of investment strategy the user employs. Categories range from very conservative ("Stingy") to very aggressive ("Willing to Sell Mother"). The user doesn't fill in a text field as before, but instead chooses from a list of options. Instead of hardcoding each OPTION tag, we can use a JavaScript function to write the lists on the fly. The function genSelect() comes in handy in lines 205, 247–249, 262, and 276. Line 205 takes care of the investment strategy list, while other calls accommodate lists for the background, font face, and font size. Look at the genSelect() in lines 86–95:

```
function genSelect(name, select, onChangeStr) {
  var optStr = "";
  var arrObj = eval(name);
  for (var i = 0; i < arrObj.length; i++) {
    optStr += '<OPTION VALUE="' + arrObj[i][0] +
    (i == select ? '" SELECTED' : '"') + '>' + arrObj[i][1];
  }
  return '<SELECT NAME="' + name + '"' + (onChangeStr ? ' onChange="' +
  onChangeStr + ';"' : '') + '>' + optStr + '</SELECT>';
}
```

You may have seen a similar genSelect() in Chapter 5, *ImageMachine*. That function generated select lists based strictly on using integers as string values. This version generates OPTION tags not based on numbers, but rather on an array of elements. Let's take the call to genSelect() at line 205:

```
document.write(genSelect('strategy', 3));
```

The function receives two arguments: the string *strategy* and the number 3. You might be thinking. "Wait a minute . . . there's an array named *strategy*. Why pass in a string with the same name?"

Indeed, there is an array named *strategy*. It makes sense to pass a copy of the *strategy* array, except for the fact that each select list needs a name to be referenced when setting the user preferences. To keep things simple, each select list assumes the name of the associated array. That's why the string equivalent is passed in.

Then variable *arrObj* is set to the de-referenced value of the string. That is, `eval(name)` equals `eval('strategy')` equals a reference to the *strategy* array. Now `genSelect()` has both an array (*arrObj*) to reference for the `OPTION` items and a name (*name*) to assign the select list.

The second argument passed in is an integer, assigned to *select*. This value determines the option that will be selected by default. If the value of *i* is equal to *select*, then the `OPTION` tag associated with *select* will have the `SELECTED` attribute in its tag. If *select* equals 0, then the first option will be the default; if *select* equals 1, then the second option is selected by default, and so on. You can see this in line 91 in the conditional expression:

```
(i == select ? '" SELECTED' : '"')
```

After iterating through all the elements in *strategy* and building *optStr* with all the `OPTION` tags, a simple concatenation in lines 93–94 puts together all the `OPTION` tags with surrounding `SELECT` tags.

Now, what about that third expected argument defined in `genSelect()`? It's called *onChangeStr* and is not used in this particular call. However, you can see it elsewhere. For example, check out lines 247–249:

```
document.write(genSelect('background', 0,
  "swapImage('bkgImage',
  this.options[this.selectedIndex].value)"));
```

In this call, argument *name* is assigned the string *background,* argument *select* is assigned the value 0, and argument *onChangeStr* is assigned the value `swapImage('bkgImage',this.options[this.selectedIndex].value)`. When `genSelect()` receives an argument for *onChangeStr*, the string is added to the *onChange* event handler in the soon-to-be select list. Otherwise, no *onChange* event handler is added. The lists in lines 247–249, 262, and 276 utilize the *onChange* event handler to roll over images that correspond with the option currently selected. As you move from "Small" to "Medium" to "Large" to "X-Large" in the font size category, a larger and larger image rolls over to reflect the larger size.

Select lists aren't the only dynamically created elements created with JavaScript in this form. Function `genBoxes()` creates two groups of checkboxes—one for news links, the other for stock index links—with calls at lines 224 and 232.

Here is **genBoxes()**, lines 97–104:

```
function genBoxes(name) {
  var boxStr = '';
  var arrObj = eval(name);
  for (var i = 0; i < arrObj.length; i++) {
    boxStr += '<INPUT TYPE=CHECKBOX NAME="' + handle + i + '" VALUE="' +
    arrObj[i][0] + ',' + arrObj[i][1] + '"> ' + arrObj[i][0] + '<BR>'
    }
  return boxStr;
  }
```

Here, things happen much as they do in **genSelect()**. The string equivalent of the desired array is passed in and de-referenced to yield the desired array. Iterating through the elements produces a string of checkboxes, which is returned and finally written to the document.

Loading Stored Preferences

Once all the HTML is loaded, the empty form can be populated with the user's previous settings (if there are any). The *onLoad* event handler in the BODY tag summons function **populateForm()** and passes in a copy of the empty form to work on. Here is **populateForm()** at lines 157–164:

```
function populateForm(formObj) {
  if (getPrefs(formObj)) {
    makePath(formObj);
    swapImage('bkgImage', formObj.background.options
    [formObj.background.selectedIndex].value);
        }
    else { resetImage(document.forms[0]); }
    }
```

populateForm() is just a function manager, calling others to do the work. It operates like this: if preferences have been previously set, fill in the appropriate form fields with the info gleaned from the cookie. Then set the background and font image to match the selected OPTION tags in the screen layout section. If no preferences have been set, do nothing. **populateForm()** checks for user preferences in the cookie with function **getPrefs()**. Here it is in lines 106–123:

```
function getPrefs(formObj) {
  var prefStr = GetCookie('userPrefs');
  if (prefStr == null) { return false; }
  var prefArray = prefStr.split('-->');
  for (var i = 0; i < prefArray.length; i++) {
    var currPref = prefArray[i].split('::');
    if (currPref[1] == "select") {
      formObj[currPref[0]].selectedIndex = currPref[2];
      }
```

```
      else if (currPref[1] == "text") {
        formObj[currPref[0]].value = currPref[2];
        }
      else if (currPref[1] == "checkbox") {
        formObj[currPref[0]].checked = true;
        }
      }
    return true;
    }
```

`getPrefs()` also has a little decision-making to do. It works like so: get the cookie information associated with the name *userPrefs*. If it has a null value, return false. That means the **document.cookie** property *userPrefs* has not been set. If, however, *userPrefs* does not equal null, this indicates that there are previous user settings. For our example, *userPrefs* equals null, but now is a good time to see what happens when *userPrefs* contains usable information.

If *userPrefs* contains the desired goodies, `getPrefs()` creates an array by splitting the value of *prefStr* according to the delimiter used to concatenate each setting in `setPrefs()`. The string is -->. Now the elements in *prefsArray* contain strings delimited by :: that indicate the type of form element and the value associated with it. Assigning the associated values to the form elements is a matter of iterating through the *prefsArray* elements and assigning each according to the type of form element. Lines 110–121 explain it better:

```
  for (var i = 0; i < prefArray.length; i++) {
    var currPref = prefArray[i].split('::');
    if (currPref[1] == "select") {
      formObj[currPref[0]].selectedIndex = currPref[2];
      }
    else if (currPref[1] == "text") {
      formObj[currPref[0]].value = currPref[2];
      }
    else if (currPref[1] == "checkbox") {
      formObj[currPref[0]].checked = true;
      }
    }
```

Remember that the user sets preferences in three ways:

- Selecting an option from a select list

- Entering text in a text field

- Checking a checkbox

Therefore, the values in *prefsArray* each contain a form element type identifier (*text, checkbox,* or *select-one*) and another string that represents the value of the form element, both of which are separated by :: as a delimiter. This will become clearer shortly. The following list shows some examples of *prefsArray* elements.

`strategy::select::0`

> This indicates that the form element named *strategy* is a select list and has `OPTION` 0 selected.

`newsNames0::checkbox::Barron's Online,http://www.barrons.com/`

> This indicates that the form element named `newsNames0` is a checkbox and has the value `Barron's Online, http://www.barrons.com/`.

`investor::text::Jerry Bradenbaugh`

> This indicates that the form element named *investor* is a text field and has the value `Jerry Bradenbaugh`.

As the *for* loop at line 110 iterates the elements of *prefsArray*, local variable *currPref* is set to an array by splitting `prefsArray[i]` at every instance of `::`. That means *currPref* will have three elements (two for checkbox elements). Since `currPref[1]` contains the form element type identifier, checking it determines what `getPrefs()` does with `currPref[0]` and `currPref[2]`.

If `currPref[1]` equals *select*, `getPrefs()` utilizes line 113 to assign the select list of the name in `currPref[0]` to the option associated with the `selectedIndex` in `currPref[2]`—actually `parseInt(currPref[2])`, but JavaScript knows to convert the string to a number.

If `currPref[1]` equals *text*, `getPrefs()` utilizes line 116 to assign the text field of the name in `currPref[0]` the value in `currPref[2]`.

Finally, if `currPref[1]` equals *checkbox*, `getPrefs()` imposes line 119 to set the `checked` property of the checkbox of the name in `currPref[0]` to `true`. There is no `currPref[2]` for this one. If the checkbox comes up in the cookie info, that's the only indication necessary to check it.

This happens for each element of *prefsArray*. Once that has finished, the user has a form that reflects all the information last set. So `getPrefs()` has done its job and returns true to indicate to `populateForm()` that all went well.

Laying Out Images

That leaves only one more challenge—synchronizing the background and font images with the options selected in the form. Notice that the `SRC` attributes of both graphics in the HTML are set to *images/blank.gif*. That is merely a transparent placeholder until the images change according to the information from the cookie. Function `populateForm()` keeps things going at lines 159–161. Have a look:

```
makePath(formObj);
swapImage('bkgImage',
    formObj.background.options[formObj.background.selectedIndex].value);
```

Upholding its reputation as a function manager, `populateForm()` calls `make-Path()` and `swapImage()` to do the image rollovers. Actually, `swapImage()` is the only function that does any rollovers; `makePath()` just manipulates a couple of strings to make a path suitable to send to `swapImage()`. Let's examine the simpler of the two, the call to `swapImage()`. After you see that `swapImage()` expects two arguments, which are passed in at lines 160-161, have a look at the code, lines 82–84:

```
function swapImage(imageName, imageBase) {
    document[imageName].src = imageBase;
    }
```

Argument *imageName* represents the name of the *Image* object whose source will be rolled over. Argument *imageBase* is a URL of an image to which we want to roll over. Check out the argument passed in:

```
formObj.background.options[formObj.background.selectedIndex].value
```

That is a pretty big argument, but it is nothing more than the value of the selected `OPTION` tag. Since `getPrefs()` just finished setting all the select lists to the options previously selected by user, the image will certainly match. To get a better idea, look at Table 7-2. It contains the `OPTION` tag's value, the `OPTION` text (the text that the user sees), and the argument to pass to `swapImage()`.

Table 7-2. OPTIONs for the Background

OPTION Value	OPTION Text	Argument for swapImage()
images/goldthumb.gif	Gold Bars	*images/goldthumb.gif*
images/billsthumb.gif	Dollar Bills	*images/billsthumb.gif*
images/fistthumb.gif	Fist of Cash	*images/fistthumb.gif*
images/currency1thumb.gif	Currency 1	*images/currency1thumb.gif*
images/currency2thumb.gif	Currency 2	*images/currency2thumb.gif*

That seems pretty easy. `swapImage()` receives the value of the `OPTION` currently selected. It's already a URL, so the rollover happens in a snap. Incidentally, this is the same code used when the user changes the options in the background select list. The rollovers happen just the same. Here is the HTML generated when you load the page, and look: those two arguments going to `swapImage()` bear a striking resemblance to those we just saw in line 161:

```
<SELECT NAME="background" onChange="swapImage('bkgImage', this.options[this.
selectedIndex].value);">
```

The background image has been set. What about the font image graphic? That's a bit more involved. With the background image, there is one image to rollover using one select list. With the font image, there is still one image to roll over, but the rollover image is based on the selected `OPTION` tags of two select lists. See for yourself how the image URLs are made. Table 7-3 shows the OPTION values and corresponding text for the two select lists.

Table 7-3. OPTIONs for Font Family and Size

Face OPTION Value	Size OPTION Value	Face OPTION Text	Size OPTION Text
Timesroman	10	Times Roman	Small
Arial	12	Arial	Medium
Courier	14	Courier	Large
Tahoma	16	Tahoma	X-Large

Now watch what happens when the OPTION values from each are combined. Look at all the possible combinations of font face and size.

timesroman10	*arial10*	*courier10*	*tahoma10*
timesroman12	*arial12*	*courier12*	*tahoma12*
timesroman14	*arial14*	*courier14*	*tahoma14*
timesroman16	*arial16*	*courier16*	*tahoma16*

Now don't those look just like the elements used to preload the images in the array *imageNames* at line 61? Indeed, they do. This is turning out to be a pretty cool application after all. Now we know that we have to construct a composite URL. That's a URL made from several strings. We still need to call swapImage(), but before doing so, we'll have to make a URL from scratch using the combinations in the earlier table. That's where function makePath() comes in. populateForm() gives it the call at line 159. Here is the real thing at lines 75–80:

```
function makePath(formObj) {
    var fontName = imagePath +
       formObj.face.options[formObj.face.selectedIndex].value +
       formObj.size.options[formObj.size.selectedIndex].value + '.gif';
    swapImage("fontImage", fontName);
}
```

makePath() accepts a copy of the form object as an argument. It is from *formObj* that we reference both values of the two selected OPTION tags, then add *.gif*. Now local variable *fontName* is a string pointing to a legitimate image. The call to swapImage() at line 79 seals the deal. Of course, all this assumes that the user has previously set preferences. If getPrefs() returns false, populateForm() calls function resetImage() at line 163 to roll over the background and font images to the images associated with OPTION tag 0 in the background and font select lists. See the forthcoming section "Resetting the Form" for details.

Let's take a moment and review:

- The form elements have been written to the page, some with calls to genSelect() and genBoxes().

- The gleaned cookie information has been used to set every form element to a value with `getPrefs()`.

- The background and font images have been synchronized to the selected OPTION tags with functions `swapImage()` and `makePath()`.

Making Changes

The user now sees a user preferences page that "remembered" what settings were last set. Let's see what happens when the user wants to make changes.

For the user, making changes is as easy as entering new text in the text fields, selecting other options from the select lists, and checking or unchecking a new combination of checkboxes. He or she can then choose "Save," and it's done. While the user's work is done, your work is just beginning. Have a look at the code for the "Save" button at line 282:

```
<INPUT TYPE=BUTTON VALUE="Save" onClick="setPrefs(this.form);">
```

Looks pretty typical. This calls function `setPrefs()` and passes a copy of the form as an argument. The fun begins at lines 125–151:

```
function setPrefs(formObj) {
  var prefStr = '';
  var htmlStr = '';
  for (var i = 0; i < formObj.length; i++) {
    if (formObj[i].type == "select-one") {
      prefStr += formObj[i].name + '::select::' + formObj[i].
      selectedIndex + '-->';
      htmlStr += formObj[i].name + '=' + formObj[i].options[formObj[i].
      selectedIndex].value + '-->';
    }
    else if (formObj[i].type == "text") {
      if (formObj[i].value == '') { formObj[i].value = "Not Provided"; }
      prefStr += formObj[i].name + '::text::' +
      safeChars(formObj[i].value) + '-->';
      htmlStr += formObj[i].name + '=' + formObj[i].value + '-->';
    }
    else if (formObj[i].type == "checkbox" && formObj[i].checked) {
      prefStr += formObj[i].name + '::checkbox::' + '-->';
      htmlStr += formObj[i].name + '=' + formObj[i].value + '-->';
    }
  }
  SetCookie('userPrefs', prefStr, expiry);
  SetCookie('htmlPrefs', htmlStr, expiry);
    if (confirm('Preferences changed. Go to your personalized page?')) {
      self.location.href = "dive.html";
    }
}
```

`setPrefs()` generates two strings—one is set to local variable *prefStr*, the other to local variable *htmlStr*. We really need two cookies—one for this page to populate the preferences form, the other to generate the layout and links for *dive.html*, the user's custom links page. The information stored is almost identical, except that each has its own way of representing the data. You'll see in a moment. Here is the basic modus operandi for `setPrefs()`, in order:

1. Iterate through *formObj*, building two cookie strings based on the values of the FORM elements.

2. Write both cookies to the user's cookie file(s).

3. Offer the user the option of being redirected to *dive.html* right away to see the new changes.

Step 1: Iterating through formObj

This shouldn't be a problem. Since the beginning of the book, there have been hordes of *formObj* iterations to this point. It's the same thing here, except `setPrefs()` needs to know what to look for.

Look at the preferences form again. Notice that each element (besides the buttons at the bottom) is a text field, a select list, or a checkbox. Therefore, `setPrefs()` only needs to know what type of action to take when `formObj[i]` is one of those element types. The code in lines 129-144 sets the guidelines.

```
if (formObj[i].type == "select-one") {
    prefStr += formObj[i].name + '::select::' +
     formObj[i].selectedIndex + '-->';
    htmlStr += formObj[i].name + '=' +
     formObj[i].options[formObj[i].selectedIndex].value + '-->';
    }
else if (formObj[i].type == "text") {
    if (formObj[i].value == '') { formObj[i].value = "Not Provided"; }
    prefStr += formObj[i].name + '::text::' +
     safeChars(formObj[i].value) + '-->';
    htmlStr += formObj[i].name + '=' + formObj[i].value + '-->';
    }
else if (formObj[i].type == "checkbox" && formObj[i].checked) {
    prefStr += formObj[i].name + '::checkbox::' + '-->';
    htmlStr += formObj[i].name + '=' + formObj[i].value + '-->';
    }
```

One of the cool and underused properties of a form element is the *type* property, which contains a string identifying the kind of form element. `setPrefs()` needs only to be on the lookout for three of them—*select-one, text,* and *checkbox*. The compound *if* statement in the previous code takes a slightly different action for each type. Regardless of the type, though, `setPrefs()` is going to do the following in one way or another:

- Concatenate the form element name, the string equivalent of the form element type, and possibly the form element value or selected index, separated by a delimiter.

- Concatenate the string to the existing value of *prefStr* and *htmlStr*.

If the element type is a select list, the selected index is added to the string. If the element is a checkbox, the checkbox name is added to the string. If the element is a text field, its name and value are added to the strings. Notice that the function `safeChars()` operates on the value of all text fields. This happens because the values associated with select lists and checkboxes are predetermined. Since the user can enter anything, it's possible to enter one of the strings reserved as delimiters (in this case, `::`, `-->`, and `=`). That would cause plenty of undesired results the next time the application tried to acquire and parse the cookie info. Here is the function in lines 153–155:

```
function safeChars(str) {
    return str.replace(/::|=|-->/g, ':;');
}
```

Function `safeChars()` simply removes the reserved strings from anything the user enters and returns the string. Each name/type or value or selected index string is delimited by `-->`. Each section of the string in variable *prefStr* is delimited by `::`. *htmlStr* uses `=`. Those don't have to be the delimiters, but they're both pretty simple. Here is an example of what the two might look like when building strings with the same form.

prefStr might look like this:

```
investor::text::Not Provided-->age::text::Not Provided-->strategy::
select::3-->occupation::text::Not Provided-->newsNames0::checkbox::-->
newsNames1::checkbox::-->newsNames2::checkbox::-->newsNames4::checkbox::
-->indexNames0::checkbox::-->indexNames2::checkbox::-->background::select
::2-->face::select::3-->size::select::2-->
```

and *htmlStr* might look like this:

```
investor=Not Provided-->age=Not
Provided-->strategy=Moderate-->occupation
=Not Provided-->newsNames0=Barron's Online,http://www.barrons.com/-->
newsNames1=CNN Interactive,http://www.cnn.com/-->newsNames2=Fox News,
http://www.foxnews.com/-->newsNames4=The Wall Street Journal,
http://www.wsj.com/-->indexNames0=Dow Jones Indexes,
http://www.dowjones.com/-->indexNames2=The New York Stock Exchange,
http://www.nyse.com/-->background=images/fistthumb.gif-->face=tahoma-->
size=14-->
```

Remember that `-->` separates the form element entries from one another in both *prefStr* and *htmlStr*, while `::` and `=` separate the individual form element pieces in the two variables, respectively. Just so you know, I grabbed this info by uncommenting lines 286-289. These extra buttons allow you to display the variable values with "Show" and delete the cookie info with "Erase." Your users won't need them, but they might help you out of a debugging bind.

If the above code looks like an ugly variable, don't fret. We'll get to the deconstruction of *htmlStr* when we tackle the code in *dive.html*. Fortunately, we've already been through "decoding" the value of *prefStr* with function `getPrefs()`. It might be a good idea to review that section. Comparing how `setPrefs()` puts the cookie info together and how `getPrefs()` parses that cookie data will surely increase your comprehension of how this thing works as a whole.

Step 2: Writing the information to the cookie file(s)

Once *prefStr* and *htmlStr* have been loaded with great user preferences info, the calls to `SetCookie()` in lines 146–147 store the information to a cookie file.

Netscape Navigator keeps cookie-related information in a file called *cookies.txt*. Here is part of mine:

```
.hotwired.com   TRUE    /    FALSE   2145917529   p_uniqid
    2sfurM4NNMfDKAqQ8A
.hotbot.com    TRUE    /    FALSE   946739221    p_uniqid
    3MarneJsXGwNqxWbFA
www.allaire.com  FALSE   /    FALSE   2137622729   CFTOKEN   97611446
```

MSIE 4.x15.x, on the other hand, keeps cookie info stored as separate files. Cookie files are named according to the domain from which the cookie came and the name of the user logged on when the cookie was set. Here's a partial list of the MSIE cookie files on my WinNT machine right now. I'm logged on as the administrator.

```
Cookie:administrator@altavista.com
Cookie:administrator@amazon.com
Cookie:administrator@builder.com
Cookie:administrator@cnn.com
Cookie:administrator@dejanews.com
Cookie:administrator@hotbot.com
Cookie:administrator@infoseek.com
```

Step 3: Offering users a peek at new choices

The last job for `setPrefs()` is redirecting the user to *dive.html* to see the effects the changes have on the layout. Here is the code at lines 148–150.

```
if (confirm('Preferences changed. Go to your personalized page?')) {
    self.location.href = "dive.html";
    }
```

That encompasses the functionality of *prefs.html*. There is, however, one more item that in most circumstances can be overlooked—resetting the form.

Resetting the Form

Wouldn't a simple `<INPUT TYPE=RESET>` button take care of this? Yes, a reset button sets the text field values to an empty string, unchecks all the checkboxes, and returns the option selected for each select list to `OPTION 0`. That's super, but those background and font images haven't moved. They need to roll over to the images associated to `OPTION 0` in both cases. That's why line 283 looks like this:

```
<INPUT TYPE=RESET VALUE="Clear" onClick="resetImage(this.form);">
```

Not only does choosing "Clear" reset the form, it also calls function `resetImage()`. Here are lines 166-170.

```
function resetImage(formObj) {
  swapImage('bkgImage', formObj.background.options[0].value);
  swapImage('fontImage', imagePath + formObj.face.options[0].value +
    formObj.size.options[0].value + '.gif');
}
```

This is another function-calling function, which calls `swapImage()` twice. The first call to `swapImage()` rolls over the background image associated with `OPTION 0`, a.k.a. `formObj.background.options[0].value`. The next call does the same thing, but creates the image path associated with `OPTION 0`. Similar to the logic in `makePath()`, `resetImages()` makes the image URL with variable *imagePath*, the `OPTION` values of both font-related select lists (though this time 0 is used in place of `selectedIndex`), followed by the faithful string *.gif*. These two calls set the images where they need to be.

That brings us to the end of the functionality in *prefs.html*. Let's forge ahead to *dive.html*.

dive.html

The user preferences have been changed. The time has come to see how to convert those recorded changes into visual realities. The process isn't long, but the details can get a bit sticky. It's probably obvious by now that the information will come from information stored in a cookie. That extracted information is used in three ways.

- As a URL for a background image
- As URLs and display text for links
- As part of a stylesheet declaration for font family and size

We'll encounter each use as we go. For now, soak in the code for *dive.html*, coming right up in Example 7-2.

Example 7-2. dive.html

```
 1 <HTML>
 2 <HEAD>
 3 <TITLE>
 4 Your Take-A-Dive Links Page
 5 </TITLE>
 6 <SCRIPT LANGAUGE="JavaScript1.2" SRC="cookies.js"></SCRIPT>
 7 <SCRIPT LANGUAGE="JavaScript1.2">
 8 <!--
 9
10 var newsNames = new Array();
11 var indexNames = new Array();
12
13 function getAttributes() {
14   var htmlStr = GetCookie('htmlPrefs');
15   if (htmlStr == null) {
16     alert('Welcome. You must first set your user preferences.' +
17     'Please choose OK to load the User Settings page.');
18     self.location.href = 'prefs.html';
19   }
20   var htmlArray = htmlStr.split('-->');
21   for (var i = 0; i < htmlArray.length; i++) {
22     var tagInfo = htmlArray[i].split('=');
23     if (tagInfo[0] != "") {
24       if (tagInfo[0].indexOf('newsNames') == 0) {
25         newsNames[newsNames.length] = tagInfo[1];
26       }
27       else if (tagInfo[0].indexOf('indexNames') == 0) {
28         indexNames[indexNames.length] = tagInfo[1];
29       }
30       else { eval(tagInfo[0] + ' = "' + tagInfo[1] + '"'); }
31     }
32   }
33 }
34
35 getAttributes();
36
37 function genLinks(linkArr) {
38   var linkStr = '';
39   for (var i = 0; i < linkArr.length; i++) {
40     var linkParts = linkArr[i].split(',')
41     linkStr += '    - <A HREF="' + linkParts[1] + '"> ' +
42       linkParts[0] + '</A><BR>'
43   }
44   return linkStr;
45 }
46
47 //-->
48 </SCRIPT>
```

Example 7-2. dive.html (continued)

```
49 <SCRIPT LANGUAGE="JavaScript1.2">
50   document.write('<STYLE type="text/css"> TD ' +
51     { font-family: ' + face + '; font-size: ' + size + 'pt; } </STYLE>');
52 </SCRIPT>
53 </HEAD>
54 <SCRIPT LANGUAGE="JavaScript">
55   document.write('<BODY BACKGROUND="' +
56     background.replace(/thumb/, "") + '">');
57 </SCRIPT>
58 <TABLE BORDER=0>
59   <TR>
60     <TD VALIGN=TOP COLSPAN=4>
61     <H2>Take-A-Dive Brokerage $ervices</H2>
62     </TD>
63   </TR>
64   <TR>
65     <TD VALIGN=TOP COLSPAN=4>
66     Take-A-Dive Brokerage Services is dedicated to helping YOU part with
67     your MONEY. <BR> Our motto is "<I>We go for broke.</I>"
68     Here is your user profile
69     and your customized links.
70     <BR><BR>
71     </TD>
72   </TR>
73   <TR>
74     <TD VALIGN=TOP>
75     Name:</TD>
76     <TD VALIGN=TOP>
77       <SCRIPT LANGUAGE="JavaScript1.2">document.write(investor);</SCRIPT>
78         <TD VALIGN=TOP>
79         </TD>
80         Age:
81         <TD VALIGN=TOP>
82         <SCRIPT LANGUAGE="JavaScript1.2">document.write(age);</SCRIPT>
83         </TD>
84     </TR>
85     <TR>
86         <TD VALIGN=TOP>
87         Strategy:
88         </TD>
89         <TD VALIGN=TOP>
90         <SCRIPT LANGUAGE="JavaScript1.2">
91           document.write(strategy);
92         </SCRIPT>
93         </TD>
94         <TD VALIGN=TOP>
95         Occupation:
96         </TD>
97         <TD VALIGN=TOP>
98         <SCRIPT LANGUAGE="JavaScript1.2">
99           document.write(occupation);
```

Example 7-2. dive.html (continued)

```
100                </SCRIPT>
101                </TD>
102          </TR>
103          <TR>
104             <TD VALIGN=TOP COLSPAN=2>
105             <BR><BR>
106             News Links<BR>
107             <SCRIPT LANGUAGE="JavaScript1.2">
108               document.writeln(genLinks(news));
109             </SCRIPT>
110             <TD VALIGN=TOP COLSPAN=2>
111             <BR><BR>
112             Stock Index Links <BR>
113             <SCRIPT LANGUAGE="JavaScript1.2">
114               document.writeln(genLinks(indexes));
115             </SCRIPT>
116             </TD>
117          </TR>
118          <TR>
119             <TD VALIGN=TOP COLSPAN=2>
120             <BR><BR>
121             [ <A HREF="prefs.html">Set Preferences</A> ]
122             </TD>
123          </TR>
124 </TABLE>
125 </BODY>
126 </HTML>
```

Parse That Cookie

Look at all those SCRIPT tags. From the looks of it, you can tell that this page is truly a shell that will be custom-designed on the fly. The first step is parsing that cookie. Function getAttributes() gets the call. To dynamically create a layout, we need this information quickly (before the page has loaded). That's why getAttributes() is called at line 35, a mere two lines after it is defined. Here are lines 13–33:

```
function getAttributes() {
  var htmlStr = GetCookie('htmlPrefs');
  if (htmlStr == null) {
    alert('Welcome. You must first set your user preferences.' +
    'Please choose OK to load the User Settings page.');
    self.location.href = 'prefs.html';
  }
  var htmlArray = htmlStr.split('-->');
  for (var i = 0; i < htmlArray.length; i++) {
    var tagInfo = htmlArray[i].split('=');
    if (tagInfo[0] != "") {
      if (tagInfo[0].indexOf('newsNames') == 0) {
```

```
      newsNames[newsNames.length] = tagInfo[1];
    }
    else if (tagInfo[0].indexOf('indexNames') == 0) {
      indexNames[indexNames.length] = tagInfo[1];
    }
  else { eval(tagInfo[0] + ' = "' + tagInfo[1] + '"'); }
    }
  }
}
```

Local variable *htmlStr* is set to the return of function `GetCookie()`. In *prefs.html*, the cookie named *prefStr* had the necessary form info, but *dive.html* needs the cookie named *htmlStr*. If it turns out that *htmlStr* is equal to null, that means the user hasn't yet set preferences, so he or she is made aware of this, and is then promptly redirected to *prefs.html* to make those changes.

Otherwise, *htmlStr* will be `split()` by every instance of `-->`, which returns an array assigned to local variable *htmlArray*. A *for* loop is used to iterate through each of the elements, assigning the values of each element along the way. By the way, this is almost identical to the logic in function `getPrefs()` of *prefs.html*. See lines 110-120 in the listing for *prefs.html*. Compare them with lines 20–32:

```
var htmlArray = htmlStr.split('-->');
for (var i = 0; i < htmlArray.length; i++) {
  var tagInfo = htmlArray[i].split('=');
  if (tagInfo[0] != "") {
    if (tagInfo[0].indexOf('news') == 0) {
      newsNames[newsNames.length] = tagInfo[1];
    }
    else if (tagInfo[0].indexOf('indexes') == 0) {
      indexes[indexNames.length] = tagInfo[1];
    }
  else { eval(tagInfo[0] + ' = "' + tagInfo[1] + '"'); }
  }
}
```

Dealing with the Unknown

Very interesting. `getPrefs()` in *prefs.html* knows it is going to work with the form represented in *formObj*, and assigns values, checks, and select options accordingly. `getAttributes()` doesn't have that luxury, though. It is necessary to have at least some idea of what to expect from the cookie. For example, we know that there will some link information about online news resources. The same goes for online stock indexes. Who knows how many of each there will be: 0, 10, maybe 50? Since this is unknown, we can put the link information of both in separate arrays. Here are lines 10–11:

```
var newsNames = new Array();
var indexNames = new Array();
```

Variable *newsNames* will hold the link information for news resources, and *indexNames* will hold the same for the stock indexes. Look at that sample cookie that you saw in the last section. Note the bolded text:

```
investor=Not Provided-->age=Not Provided-->strategy=Moderate-->
occupation=Not Provided-->newsNames0=Barron's Online,
http://www.barrons.com/-->newsNames1=CNN Interactive,
http://www.cnn.com/-->newsNames2=Fox News,
http://www.foxnews.com/-->newsNames4=The Wall Street Journal,
http://www.wsj.com/-->indexNames0=Dow Jones Indexes,
http://www.dowjones.com/-->indexNames2=The New York Stock Exchange,
http://www.nyse.com/-->background=images/fistthumb.gif-->
face=tahoma-->size=14-->
```

Those bolded names are markers for the link information headed for the new array variables declared above. Now, we also know that there will be some variables, but how do we name them? How many will there be? The code in *dive.html* certainly doesn't reveal any secrets. But the truth is, it doesn't matter. As long as *you* know what the variable names are, the logic in *dive.html* doesn't have to include explicit, hardcoded definitions. Here's what I mean. Take another look at the sample value of `GetCookies('htmlPrefs')`. Again, note the bolded text:

```
investor=Not Provided-->age=Not Provided-->strategy=Moderate-->
occupation=Not Provided-->newsNames0=Barron's Online,
http://www.barrons.com/-->newsNames1=CNN Interactive,
http://www.cnn.com/-->newsNames2=Fox News,http://www.foxnews.com/-->
newsNames4=The Wall Street Journal,http://www.wsj.com/-->
indexNames0=Dow Jones Indexes,http://www.dowjones.com/-->
indexNames2=The New York Stock Exchange,http://www.nyse.com/-->
background=images/fistthumb.gif-->face=tahoma-->size=14-->
```

The bolded text in this example represents the names of variables that will be defined shortly. That *for* loop in `getAttributes()` accommodates both the array elements' assignment and the "unknown" variable declaration. It's in lines 22–31:

```
var tagInfo = htmlArray[i].split('=');
  if (tagInfo[0] != "") {
    if (tagInfo[0].indexOf('newsNames') == 0) {
      newsNames[newsNames.length] = tagInfo[1];
    }
    else if (tagInfo[0].indexOf('indexNames') == 0) {
      indexNames[indexNames.length] = tagInfo[1];
    }
    else { eval(tagInfo[0] + ' = "' + tagInfo[1] + '"'); }
  }
```

Each element of *htmlArray* contains an equals sign (=) that separates the identifier from the value we really want. For each iteration of the *for* loop, `htmlArray[i]` is `split()` by =, and this two-element sub-array is assigned to local variable *tagInfo*.

If `tagInfo[0]` does not equal an empty string, we have a valid identifier-value pair. The empty string check is performed because of the way JScript returns the array from the `split()` method.

Each valid identifier-value pair falls into one of two categories: an array element or a regular variable. If the pair is an array element, it is also one of two types, one that contains a news link, or one that contains a stock index link. The following if-else statement determines the action to take under all circumstances:

```
if (tagInfo[0].indexOf('newsNames') == 0) {
  newsNames[newsNames.length] = tagInfo[1];
}
else if (tagInfo[0].indexOf('indexNames') == 0) {
  indexNames[indexNames.length] = tagInfo[1];
}
else { eval(tagInfo[0] + ' = "' + tagInfo[1] + '"'); }
```

Because of the naming convention used in *prefs.html*, if `tagInfo[0]` contains the string *newNames*, it must be associated with news links. Therefore, the value `tagInfo[1]` is assigned to the next available element in **newsNames**. If `tagInfo[0]` contains the string *indexNames*, it must be associated with stock indexes. Therefore, `tagInfo[1]` goes to the next element in **indexNames**. If `tagInfo[0]` contains neither string, then `tagInfo[0]` and `tagInfo[1]` must contain the name of a variable to be declared and a value to assign it. The code in line 30 knows just what to do:

```
eval(tagInfo[0] + ' = "' + tagInfo[1] + '"');
```

When this *for* loop has finished, here is the equivalent code generated:

```
newsNames[0] = 'Barron's Online,http://www.barrons.com/';
newsNames[1] = 'CNN Interactive,http://www.cnn.com/';
newsNames[2] = 'Fox News,http://www.foxnews.com/';
newsNames[3] = 'The Wall Street Journal,http://www.wsj.com/';
```

Those are the news links:

```
indexNames[0] = 'Dow Jones Indexes,http://www.dowjones.com/';
indexNames[1] = 'The New York Stock Exchange,http://www.nyse.com/';
```

Those are the stock index links:

```
var investor = 'Not Provided';
var age = 'Not Provided';
var strategy = 'Moderate';
var occupation = 'Not Provided';
var background = 'images/fistthumb.gif';
var face = 'tahoma';
var size = '14';
```

And those are the layout variables.

JavaScript Technique:
Naming Conventions Pay Off Again

I've preached about sound naming conventions before. I won't give you another sermon, but just consider how those news and stock index link elements and layout variables came to be. It began before any code was interpreted in *dive.html*. It began before any cookies were set in *prefs.html*. It began even before the user made his or her first change in the form in *prefs.html*. It started with the naming of the form fields.

Each of the news and stock index link variables has an identifier (e.g., *newsNames0* or *indexNames3*) that contains the name of a select list in *prefs. html*. Each of the layout variables has the name of one of the form elements, such as *background* or *size*. This name was included in the cookie strings, extracted and defined accordingly. Wisely planned naming conventions not only make things easier, they also make things possible. Stay on the lookout for opportunities to use them in your code.

Remember, nowhere in the file is any of this code listed. You can iterate through the elements of *newsNames* and *indexNames* to access their values, but you have to know the other variable names to access them.

We have all the information we need to set up the page the way the user wants it. Once we write the information to the page, it's done. We'll use `document.write()` to get everything we need on the page. There are eight calls to `document.write()`. Table 7-4 lists and describes each.

Table 7-4. Using document.write() to Create the HTML

Lines	Code	Description

50-51	`document.write('<STYLE type="text/css">`
	`TD { font-family: ' + face + '; font-`
	`size: ' + size + 'pt; } </STYLE>');`
		Creates a stylesheet on the fly

55-56	`document.write('<BODY BACKGROUND="' +` `background.replace(/thumb/, "") + '">');`	Defines a URL for background image
77	`document.write(investor);`	Adds the name of the investor
82	`document.write(age);`	Adds the age of the investor
91	`document.write(strategy);`	Adds the investor's strategy
99	`document.write(occupation);`	Adds the investor's occupation

Table 7-4. Using document.write( ) to Create the HTML (continued)

Lines	Code	Description
108	`document.write(genLinks(news));`	Adds the news links
114	`document.write(genLinks(indexes));`	Adds the stock index links

Though the 3rd through 6th calls are pretty much self-explanatory, the first two and last two are more involved. Let's start with lines 50–51:

```
document.write('<STYLE type="text/css"> TD { font-family: ' + face +
  '; font-size: ' + size + 'pt; } </STYLE>');
```

This call writes a style sheet to the page, but we'll insert layout variables *face* and *size* to dictate the type of font and the size.

JavaScript Technique: Dynamic DHTML

Dynamic DHTML is my from-the-hip definition of JavaScript writing DHTML on the fly. Consider that you can use `document.write()` to display HTML and even more JavaScript. If you combine that functionality with the added bonuses of style sheets, you have a lot of layout power in a little code. Here is how it's used in this application:

```
document.write('<STYLE TYPE="text/css"> TD { font-family: ' + face +
  '; font-size: ' + size + 'pt; } </STYLE>');
```

All I've done here is slip in variables *face* and *size*. Now the font face and size can be determined by changing the values of two variables. Not bad for a one-line style sheet. Think of the possibilities, though, if you have a lengthy definitive style sheet that controls styles for many more elements such as headers, form elements, and more. Style sheets give you fine-tuned control over document elements. Generating style sheets with JavaScript makes that same great control dynamic.

With the dynamically created style sheet in place, let's move on to getting the right background image in. Here are lines 55–56:

```
document.write('<BODY BACKGROUND="' +
  background.replace(/thumb/, "") + '">');
```

Remember that variable *background* contains the value *images/fistthumb.gif*. Great, except that's the thumbnail version of the background image. We want the real thing. No problem, each thumbnail image is named exactly as the full-blown version, except with the string *thumb* added. We can get the background image by removing "thumb" from *background*, which in this case is *images/fist.gif*. The `replace()` method makes the quick change.

The last two calls to document.write() use the only other function defined on the page—genLinks(). This function is similar to functions genBoxes() and genSelect() in *prefs.html* in that it loops through the elements of an array to create a custom string of HTML. The only difference is that this function returns a string of links, not checkboxes or OPTION tags. The "magic" happens in lines 37–45:

```
function genLinks(linkArr) {
  var linkStr = '';
  for (var i = 0; i < linkArr.length; i++) {
    var linkParts = linkArr[i].split(',')
    linkStr += '    - <A HREF="' + linkParts[1] + '"> ' +
      linkParts[0] + '</A><BR>'
    }
  return linkStr;
  }
```

genLinks() is designed to receive an array of delimited strings as its lone argument. The first element of each is a string to display as link text. The second element is the URL for the HREF attribute. Each of these is separated by a comma, so using the split() method by comma and assigning the array result to local variable *linkParts*, we can get at the separate parts. The *for* loop iterates as usual, creating a string of links to return when finished.

Potential Extensions

Even a little bit of creativity can take you places with this application. Here are a few of the possibilities that come to mind:

* Add fields to manipulate table cell background colors and font colors, and other elements for the layout look.

* Allow users to choose entire page themes.

* Add a couple of extra text fields so that the user can add his or her own favorite web site links (with names).

* Post banner ads according to the user's cookie preferences.

More Choices for the Layout Look

Users like lots of choices. Anything you can tweak on the user's page can be manipulated. This includes content and graphics in layers, other frames, and remote windows.

Adding Themes

This idea stems from Windows 95's desktop themes. Instead of letting users pick individual items, such as font face, size, and color, why not offer a couple of layout themes that make the choices all at once? Suppose you have a music-related web site. Consider the following select list:

```
<SELECT NAME="themes"onChange="swapImage('theImage',
   this.options[this.selectedIndex].value);">
<OPTION VALUE="none">None
<OPTION VALUE="bigband">Big Band
<OPTION VALUE="rocknroll">Rock 'n Roll
<OPTION VALUE="rap">Rap
<OPTION VALUE="country">Country
<OPTION VALUE="reggae">Reggae
<OPTION VALUE="grunge">Grunge
<OPTION VALUE="jazz">Jazz
<OPTION VALUE="club">Club Music
</SELECT>
```

Each of those OPTION values could relate to a thumbnail image of the potential theme. You can even use genSelect() and swapImage() in *prefs.html* to create the list and perform the rollovers. Keep in mind, however, that by selecting one of these themes, you'll have to somehow disable the individual layout features, such as background image and font specs. Notice the first OPTION displays "None." You'll probably want to include an OPTION tag for that so the user can make individual layout selections if desired.

Letting Users Create Their Own Links

The *Take-A-Dive* preferences form lets user pick from predetermined links. You could always add a couple of text fields for the user to enter his or her own favorite links. The following table should give you a good start:

```
<TABLE>
  <TR>
    <TD><B>Extra Links</B></TD>
    <TD>
      <INPUT TYPE=BUTTON VALUE="  Add  " onClick="addOpt(this.form);">
      <INPUT TYPE=BUTTON VALUE="Delete" onClick="deleteOpt(this.form);">
    </TD>
  </TR>
  <TR>
    <TD>Link Name</TD>
    <TD><INPUT TYPE=TEXT NAME="linkname" SIZE=20></TD>
  </TR>
  <TR>
    <TD>Link URL</TD>
    <TD><INPUT TYPE=TEXT NAME="linkURL" SIZE=20></TD>
  </TR>
</TABLE>
```

Users can add or delete links by typing in the link name and URL, and choosing "Add" or "Delete." You could then store these variables in an array, and add or remove the elements with functions such as addOpt() and delOpt() referenced in the code above. If you're ambitious, you could create a select list to display the links as you added or removed them.

Direct Banner Ad Marketing

Why not cater your advertising campaign to the user's interests? In the case of this pseudo-investment web site, I could code it so that users who consider themselves conservative investors would receive banner ads offering stable and lower-yielding investments, such as bonds. On the other hand, investors who were willing to "sell their mother" would receive banners offering opportunities in unstable, but higher yielding junk bonds and overseas investments.

8

Shopping Bag: The JavaScript Shopping Cart

Application Features

- Versatile Client-Side Shopping Cart
- User-Friendly Interface Makes Shopping Easy
- No Server-Side Processing Required (Until Check-out)
- Program Monitors All Selections and Keeps a Running Total
- Database Enables Accurate Product Searching

JavaScript Techniques

- Managing Multiple Windows and Document Content
- Maintaining Client State with Objects
- Adding Object Properties
- Reusing a JavaScript Database
- Number Rounding and String Conversion

If there is a single-most diverse and robust JavaScript application in this book, it is the one described here. With Shopping Bag, you need only the graphics and product details to quickly and easily add an online shopping cart to your site. You don't need to create extra files to display your products. Shopping Bag takes care of that on the fly. No need for a server to calculate tax and totals. Shopping Bag accurately computes them on the fly as well. Adding and removing products from a user's shopping bag takes only a click or two. Unlike server-based shopping bags, there's no waiting.

Shopping Bag Walk-Through

Something really easy and intuitive for the online consumer usually means some extra elbow grease for the programmer. Not to disappoint you, this is the case here. The fun and functionality you get in return, however, make the effort well worth it. The description of Shopping Bag's functionality and code are based on the following example.

Here is the four-step process:

1. The application loads.

2. A shopper browses products by category and product search, choosing several along the way.

3. Seemingly content, the shopper views the current selections and makes changes to quantity and contents.

4. Finally satisfied, the user decides to check out and pay.

This application also has several easy rules that users must follow to use Shopping Bag. You'll see these rules posted where applicable in each section. Let's help a user—call her Daisy Deep Pockets—part with some hard-earned money.

Step 1: Loading the Application

Opening *ch08\index.html* loads the screen shown in Figure 8-1. The opener is simply that, a kind of splash screen (without the splash). When Daisy clicks on the "Begin" link, she sees the screen shown in Figure 8-2.

Figure 8-1. A warm Shopping Bag welcome

What you have here is the opening (and help) screen loaded with the navigation links in a frame below. Have a good look before you move on.

Why two browser windows? There is no reason you couldn't pull it off with only the main window, but this method gives you the maximum amount of web real estate to market your wares. Besides, users won't be distracted by such browser buttons as "Bookmarks" and "Search." That means more attention will likely stay on your products. While you're at it, you could use the main window as a login page to distinguish between member and guest shoppers.

Step 2: Product Browsing and Selection

OK, Daisy is in. It's time for a look around. She chooses "Show All Categories" and generates a linked list of product categories.

Shopping Bag

Shopping Bag is designed to make your shopping and browsing experience easy. Use the links below to guide yourself. You can navigate to any point in the warehouse, adding or removing things from your shopping bag.

You can view your and change bag contents whenever you like. Here is a description of each Shopping Bag function:

Gimme One	Adds the product in view to your bag.
View/Change Bag	Displays an itemized, modifiable list of your current selected products.
Previous Category	Returns to the first product of the previous category. If you are currently viewing products in the first category, the program moves to the last category.
Previous Product	Returns to the previous product. If you are currently viewing the first product of a category, the program moves to the last product of the previous category.
Next Product	Advances to the next product. If you are currently viewing the last product of a category, the program moves to the first product of the next category.
Next Category	Advances to the first product of the next category. If you are currently viewing products in the last category, the program moves to the first product in the first category.
Show All Categories	Displays a linked list of all product categories.
Product Search	Enables you to search all products by name, description, and price.
Help	Loads this page.

Gimme One   View/Change Bag   Show All Categories   Product Search   Help

Previous Category   Previous Product   Next Product   Next Category

Figure 8-2. The Shopping Bag interface

Rule 1: When Shopping Bag initially loads, the user must choose "Show All Categories" or "Product Search" and choose a link from those sections in order to view products. Afterwards, choosing any of the "Category" or "Product" buttons in the navbar will work fine.

This displays a dazzling array of really cool product categories. Let's see, buildings, food, hardware—who wouldn't buy things like that online? After recovering from the astonishing wealth of choices, Ms. Pockets decides that she is running low on her collection of buildings and decides to see what Shopping Bag has to offer.

Following the "Buildings" links, she is stunned again to see the fire-sale prices on items such as the barn, castle, and tower. Overwhelmed, she settles for an igloo, as shown in Figure 8-3. Choosing "Gimme One," the igloo is added to her shopping bag, as the Alert box indicates.

Rule 2: Choosing "Gimme One" adds only one product to the shopping bag. Users can change quantities and remove selections by choosing "View/Change Bag."

Still hunting for a bargain, our relentless shopper decides to use the search feature to see if she can drum up any more hot items. She chooses "Product Search,"

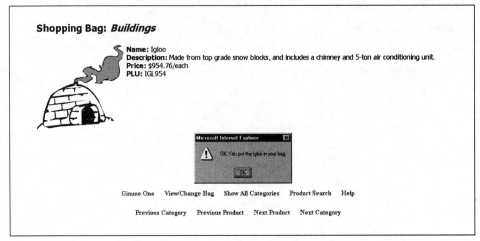

Figure 8-3. Putting the igloo in her bag

which brings up the simple search interface you see in Figure 8-4. Bargain hunting, she enters "1.15" to find products at that price. By sheer luck, her gamble pays
off. Five products come up with 1.15 in the price, as shown in Figure 8-5. A hairdryer, a necktie, and an order of fries each cost $1.15. She angles for the fries,
peeks at the details, and hastens to add them to her bag.

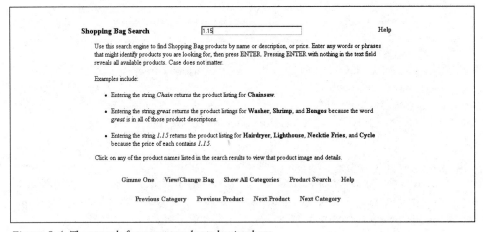

Figure 8-4. The search for great products begins here

Daisy heads back to the category listing by choosing "Show All Categories" once
again. This time, the clothing category piques her interest. Following the link, she
happens upon the necktie—the one in the list at an unbelievable $1.15. She
ignored it earlier, but it looks OK now. Add that one to the bag.

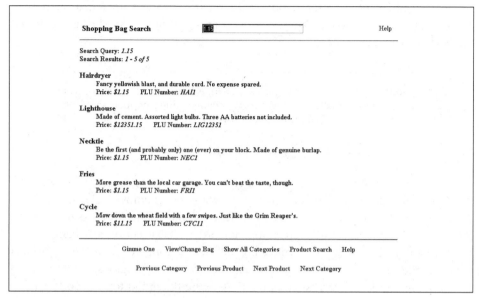

Figure 8-5. One search, multiple bargains

Step 3: Viewing and Changing the Order

Daisy decides she has seen enough for today and chooses "View/Change Bag." Shopping Bag generates her bag contents as shown in Figure 8-6. Notice that Shopping Bag has been keeping tabs on everything she has added to her own bag, right down to the tax, shipping, and total.

Index	Product	Category	PLU	Unit Price	Quantity	Product Total	Remove
	Your Shopping Bag!!!						
1	Igloo	Buildings	IGL954	$954.76	1	954.76	☐
2	Fries	Food	FRI1	$1.15	1	1.15	☐
3	Necktie	Clothing	NEC1	$1.15	1	1.15	☐
					SubTotal:	957.06	
					+ 6% Tax:	57.42	
					+ 2% Shipping:	19.14	
		Check Out	Reset Qtys	Change Bag	Total:	1033.62	

Gimme One   View/Change Bag   Show All Categories   Product Search   Help

Previous Category   Previous Product   Next Product   Next Category

Figure 8-6. Daisy's shopping bag contents, complete with pricing

Still excited about the igloos, Daisy changes the quantity of her igloo order to 6. She lives in a warm climate, so those things won't last. Better have at least that many. Those fries looked pretty good in the picture, so she bumps that quantity to 2. Unfortunately, her pockets aren't as deep as she thought, so she has to forfeit the necktie. There is always next time.

Rule 3: Shoppers must choose "Change Bag" to record changes to the shopping bag. In other words, changes don't happen simply by changing any "Quantity" select lists or checking "Remove" checkboxes and moving to another screen.

It's easy to see how Daisy can change her order. She changes quantities with the "Quantity" select list and deletes products with the "Remove" checkbox. Each product entry has a select list to change quantity and a checkbox to remove the product from the order. After changing her order, Daisy chooses "Change Bag," which displays her new bag, reflecting all her quantity changes and product removal. See Figure 8-7. Her bag now has her down for 6 igloos, two orders of fries, and one necktie. Tax and shipping costs bring the grand total to $6,190.57.

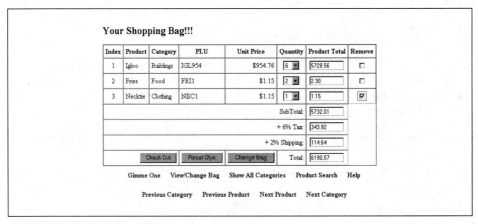

Your Shopping Bag!!!

Index	Product	Category	PLU	Unit Price	Quantity	Product Total	Remove
1	Igloo	Buildings	IGL954	$954.76	6 ▼	5728.56	☐
2	Fries	Food	FRI1	$1.15	2 ▼	2.30	☐
3	Necktie	Clothing	NEC1	$1.15	1 ▼	1.15	☑
					SubTotal:	5732.01	
					+ 6% Tax:	343.92	
					+ 2% Shipping:	114.64	
	Check Out	Reset Qtys	Change Bag		Total:	6190.57	

Gimme One   View/Change Bag   Show All Categories   Product Search   Help

Previous Category   Previous Product   Next Product   Next Category

Figure 8-7. Daisy's refined shopping bag

Rule 4: Submitting the Shopping Bag order form empties your shopping bag. If you want more stuff, you'll have to start filling a new, empty bag.

Step 4: Check Out

Content with her finishing touches, Daisy chooses "Check Out," which opens the form you see in Figure 8-8. Daisy can fill in her ordering information, submit it, and then anxiously await her shipment in the mail.

And so it goes . . . another satisfied customer. Let's move on to the next section to see how the Shopping Bag code keeps customers that way.

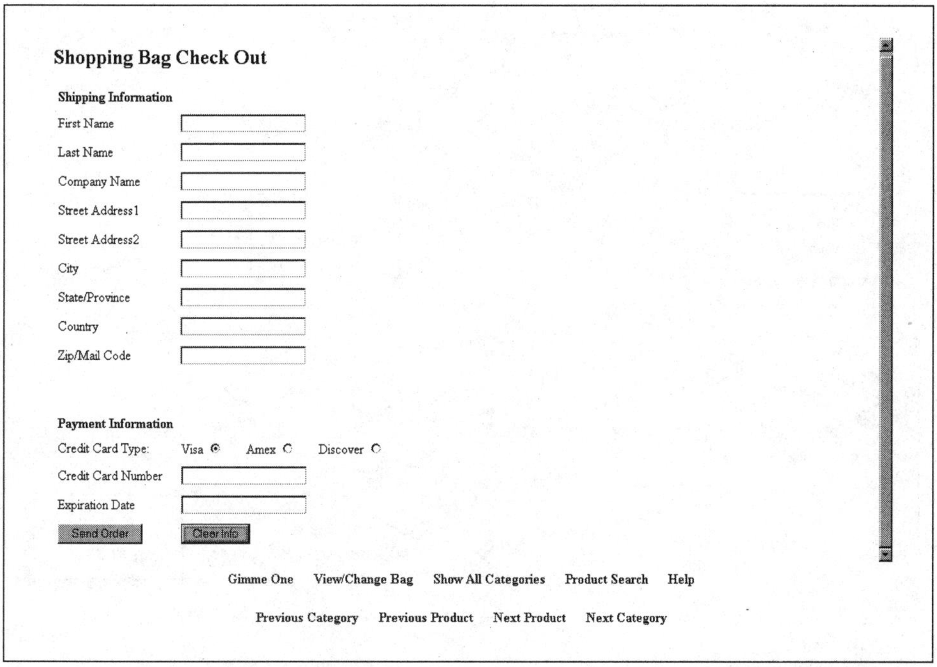

Figure 8-8. The order form

Execution Requirements

Shopping Bag utilizes JavaScript 1.2 and some CSS, so generation 3.x browsers need not apply. However, keep in mind that a significant number of users do shop, but don't keep the latest browser loaded. You can easily remove the CSS to make Shopping Bag compatible with MSIE and NN 3.x.

As far as scalability goes, you should conservatively be able to cram at least 500 items into the Shopping Bag warehouse. After all, adding a single product takes only one line of code. I stopped testing after reaching close to 700 items on my 120 MHz PC with 128 Meg of RAM. So unless you're competing with WalMart, Shopping Bag should work just fine.

Syntax Breakdown

Let's have a look at Shopping Bag's flow chart. Figure 8-9 shows how the user begins shopping, browses and chooses products, makes final changes at check out time, fills out payment and shipping info, and eventually submits the entire order to the server.

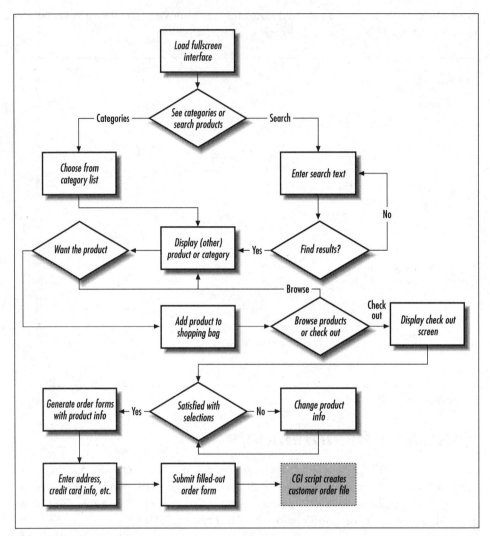

Figure 8-9. Shopping Bag overview

This application consists of eight files. This list describes each file and its purpose:

index.html

This opening page of Shopping Bag handles window management.

shopset.html

The frameset for the full-screen remote window. Contains both *intro.html* and *manager.html*.

intro.html

The default page for the largest of the frames and also the help document that lists the function of each navigation bar feature.

manager.html

> This is the Shopping Bag epicenter. All core functionality comes from code in this file, which will be the primary focus of the chapter.

inventory.js

> Contains functions, constructors, and arrays for building the Shopping Bag inventory. Much of its work occurs during loading.

search/index.html

> The frameset that loads the product search application. If you've even glanced at Chapter 1, you'll recognize this as a modified version of the search engine covered there.

search/main.html

> The help page for the search engine. Complete with examples.

search/nav.html

> The brains of the search engine application.

Because of the size of the application and the fact that you can find some of the JavaScript code used to manipulate layers in others chapters (3, 4, 6, 9, 10, and 11), it makes more sense to cover Shopping Bag differently.

As opposed to advancing through each of these files from top to bottom, let's cover the application in terms of its five basic operations:

1. Loading Shopping Bag: building the inventory and loading the display

2. Displaying products: moving from category to category and from product to product

3. Adding products to the shopping bag: keeping track of everything in the bag

4. Searching for products: running text searches against the products "in stock"

5. Changing shopping bag contents/checking out: making changes and paying

If you compare the earlier file descriptions with these descriptions, you can semi-extrapolate (i.e., guess) which files go with which operation. It isn't cut and dried, but operation 1 involves code from *index.html, shopset.html, inventory.js*; operations 2, 3, and 5 cover code in *manager.html*; and operation 4 is exclusive to the files in the *search* directory.

You'll still get the code on a file-by-file basis, but we'll be hopping around somewhat in order to cover the JavaScript functions of the operations. Each of these five sections is described mostly in terms of user actions, such as searching, changing product quantities, getting help, and so on. We'll also cover the relevant techniques along the way. Let's start with loading Shopping Bag.

Step 1: Loading Shopping Bag

JavaScript and the resident browser take care of most of the work here, although the user plays a small part. Consider the first page loaded—*index.html.* You can see what it looks like in Example 8-1.

Example 8-1. index.html

```
 1 <HTML>
 2 <HEAD>
 3 <TITLE>Shopping Bag</TITLE>
 4 <STYLE TYPE="text/css">
 5 <!--
 6 #welcome { text-align: center; margin-top: 150}
 7 //-->
 8 </STYLE>
 9 <SCRIPT LANGUAGE="JavaScript">
10 <!--
11 var shopWin = null;
12 var positionStr = '';
13 function whichBrowser() {
14   if(navigator.appVersion < 4) {
15     alert("You need MSIE 4.x or Netscape Navigator 4.x to use " +
16       "Shopping Bag.")
17     return false;
18     }
19   return true;
20   }
21
22 function launch() {
23   if(!whichBrowser()) { return; }
24   if(navigator.appName == "Netscape")
25     { positionStr = ",screenX=0,screenY=0"; }
26   else { positionStr = ",fullscreen=yes"; }
27   if(shopWin == null) {
28     shopWin = open("shopset.html", "", "width=" + screen.width +
29       ",height=" + screen.height + positionStr);
30     }
31   }
32 function closeUpShop() {
33   if (shopWin != null) {
34     if (typeof(shopWin) == "object") {
35       shopWin.close();
36       }
37     }
38   }
39 window.onunload = closeUpShop;
40 //-->
41 </SCRIPT>
42 </HEAD>
43 <BODY>
44 <DIV ID="welcome">
45   <H1>Welcome to Shopping Bag!!!</H1>
```

Example 8-1. index.html (continued)

```
46    <A HREF="javascript: launch();">Begin</A>
47  </DIV>
48  </BODY>
49  </HTML>
```

That might seem like a lot of JavaScript for a page that prints only five words on the screen; however, the additional code makes for a slightly better application. JavaScript defines and initializes a top-level member for multiple window management and identifies the browser type to provide cross-platform code when the remote window opens.

Top-Level Members

The variables and function in lines 11 and 32–38 exist to enforce one rule: if the main window closes, close the remote window too. Otherwise, Shopping Bag might experience a violent JavaScript-error death if the user decides, say, to reload the remote window.

Here's line 11:

```
    var shopWin = null;
```

And lines 32–38:

```
    function closeUpShop() {
      if (shopWin != null) {
        if (typeof(shopWin) == "object") {
          shopWin.close();
          }
        }
      }
    window.onunload = closeUpShop;
```

Variable *shopWin*, originally set to null, is later set to the remote window object (I'm jumping the gun, but see line 27). Function **closeUpShop()** is called when this window closes. This function determines whether the user still has the remote Shopping Bag open, and if so, closes it. If *shopWin* does not equal null and is of the type *object*, the remote window must be open. **closeUpShop()** closes the remote window just prior to unloading.

The only thing that concerns the user at this point is clicking the "Begin" link to open the remote window. That opens *shopset.html*, a frameset. You'll find the code in Example 8-2.

Example 8-2. shopset.html

```
1 <HTML>
2 <HEAD>
3 <TITLE>Shopping Bag Frameset</TITLE>
```

Example 8-2. shopset.html (continued)

```
 4 <SCRIPT LANGUAGE="JavaScript1.2">
 5 <!--
 6 function resetOpener() {
 7   opener.shopWin = null;
 8   }
 9 //-->
10 </SCRIPT>
11 </HEAD>
12 <FRAMESET ROWS="80%,20%" FRAMEBORDER=0 BORDER=0 onLoad="self.focus();"
13   onUnLoad="resetOpener();">
14 <FRAME SRC="intro.html" NORESIZE>
15 <FRAME SRC="manager.html" NORESIZE>
16 </FRAMESET>
17 </HTML>
```

This is your basic frameset with two rows. One is assigned a source of *intro.html*, the other gets *manager.html*. Not much JavaScript here, but let's see what there is:

```
function resetOpener() {
  opener.shopWin = null;
  }
```

Lines 6–8 have a function named `resetOpener()` called whenever the document in the parent window (in this case, the frameset) is unloaded. By setting `opener.shopWin` to null, `resetOpener()` allows the user to close the remote Shopping Bag window and reopen it again with the same "Begin" link.

That might seem trivial, even unnecessary. Notice, however, that in *index.html* (line 27), the extra window is opened only if *shopWin* equals null. Closing the window does not set *shopWin* equal to null, so `resetOpener()` steps in to help. Notice also that the *onLoad* event handler in the `FRAMESET` tag is set to `self.focus()`. This assures that the remote window doesn't open and load behind the main window, leaving the user wondering what happened.

That basically takes care of this frameset loading. There are still three pages that still need to load—*intro.html, manager.html*, and *inventory.js. intro.html* is a static help file. As *manager.html* loads, the embedded source file *inventory.js* comes with it. *manager.html* is worthy of a little bit of discussion later in this section, but *inventory.js* has the code we need to examine now. It's fairly long, but you'll get a good idea of the structure used to build the inventory.

inventory.js

inventory.js contains three functions. The first two are constructor functions. One defines a product; the other defines a product category. The last function creates arrays of objects created by those constructors. See for yourself in Example 8-3.

JavaScript Technique:
Multiple Window and Document Management

. While you're working with an application that utilizes only the main browser window, you don't have many window worries. However, once you spawn another window, you need a JavaScript window babysitter. Should the window always be on top or bottom? Is the parent window still open? What happens to the application when the parent or child window closes?

You probably won't have to deal with all of these for every multi-window application, but these issues do arise. You can stay ahead of the game by setting variables to values that always reflect the state of the windows. For example, the variable *shopWin* is equal to the remote window object when the remote Shopping Bag window is open and null when it is closed. Shopping Bag takes actions based on the value of *shopWin*. You can adopt a similar strategy for frames and framesets as well.

Variables *gimmeControl* and *browseControl* perform a similar function to monitor the document content. In other words, based on a document's current contents, you can adjust the behavior of your application.

Example 8-3. inventory.js

```
 1 function product(name, description, price, unit) {
 2    this.name = name;
 3    this.description = description;
 4    this.price = price;
 5    this.unit = unit;
 6    this.plu = name.substring(0, 3).toUpperCase() +
 7      parseInt(price).toString();
 8    this.icon = new Image();
 9    return this;
10    }
11 function category(name, description) {
12    this.name = name;
13    this.description = description;
14    this.prodLine = eval(name);
15    var imgDir = "images/" + name.toLowerCase() + "/";
16    for (var i = 0; i < this.prodLine.length; i++) {
17      this.prodLine[i].icon.src = imgDir +
18        this.prodLine[i].name.toLowerCase() + ".gif";
19      }
20    return this;
21    }
22 function makeProducts() {
23    Appliances = new Array(
24      new product("Dryer",
25        "Stylish pastel design, contemporary two-button engineering.",
26        263.37  ,
```

Example 8-3. inventory.js (continued)

```
27        "each"),
28      new product("Hairdryer",
29        "Fancy yellowish blast, and durable cord. No expense spared.",
30        1.15,
31        "pair"),
32      new product("Oven",
33        "Made in the 1850's, this coal-powered unit quickly blackens any" +
34           "favorite dish.",
35        865.78,
36        "each"),
37      new product("Radio",
38        "Revolutionary one-channel technology. White noise and static" +
39           "included.",
40          15.43,
41          "each"),
42      new product("Toaster",
43        "BBQ-style toaster. Only a moderate shock hazard.",
44        25.78,
45        "each"),
46      new product("Washer",
47        "Does a great job on partially everything.",
48        345.61,
49        "each")
50        );
51
52    Buildings = new Array(
53      new product("Barn",
54        "Complete with rusty silo and rotting doors. Pig sty sold" +
55        "separately.",
56        6350.57,
57        "each"),
58      new product("Lighthouse",
59        "Made of cement. Assorted light bulbs. Three AA batteries " +
60        "not included.",
61        12351.15,
62        "each"),
63      new product("Igloo",
64        "Made from top grade snow blocks, and includes a chimney and " +
65           "5-ton air conditioning unit.",
66        954.76,
67        "each"),
68      new product("City",
69        "Buildings, streets, lights, skyline. Excellent volume purchase.",
70        334165.95,
71        "each"),
72      new product("Castle",
73        "Sturdy medieval design, complete with alligators in moat, and " +
74           "remote control drawbridge.",
75        93245.59,
76        "each"),
77      new product("Tower",
78        "Really tall. Ideal for winning friends and spotting forest " +
```

Example 8-3. inventory.js (continued)

```
 79        "fires.",
 80        24345.87,
 81       "pair")
 82     );
 83
 84   Clothing = new Array(
 85     new product("Bowtie",
 86       "Swell red fabric. Doubles a bow for Christmas wreaths or " +
 87         "birthday gifts.",
 88       5.41,
 89       "five"),
 90     new product("Necktie",
 91       "Be the first (and probably only) one (ever) on your block. " +
 92         "Made of genuine burlap.",
 93       1.15,
 94       "each"),
 95     new product("Purse",
 96       "Attractive green material. Wards off most mammals.",
 97       18.97,
 98       "each"),
 99     new product("Jacket",
100       "Plush fake fur with fiberglass lining. Washer safe.",
101       180.72,
102       "each"),
103     new product("Glove",
104       "Covers all four fingers and one thumb. Fancy latex design.",
105       6.59,
106       "three"),
107     new product("Dress",
108       "Found at a garage sale. Also doubles as a picnic table cover.",
109       7.99,
110       "each"),
111     new product("Watch",
112       "Geuine replica. Doesn't tell time. You have to look at it.",
113       6.19,
114       "each")
115     );
116
117   Electronics = new Array(
118     new product("Camcorder",
119       "Solar-powered. Free microphone. Custom-built for blackmailing " +
120         "close relatives.",
121       60.45,
122       "each"),
123     new product("Stereo",
124       "Quadraphonic, pre 8-track sound. Leisure suit and roach killer " +
125         "shoes are optional",
126       54.91,
127       "each"),
128     new product("Speaker",
129       "Extra piece of hi-fi junk. Works best if discarded.",
130       1.90,
```

Example 8-3. inventory.js (continued)

```
131        "each"),
132      new product("Remote",
133        "Dozens of buttons. Controls everything- TV, VCR, stereo, " +
134          "pets, local government.",
135        465.51,
136        "each"),
137      new product("Cellphone",
138        "Product of tin can technology. 35-ft calling area. Dandy " +
139          "lavender plastic.",
140        64.33,
141        "each"),
142      new product("Camera",
143        "Takes brilliant one-color photos. Landfill safe.",
144        2.95,
145       "each"),
146      new product("Television",
147        "Two-channel UHF only model. Wow.",
148        22.57,
149        "each")
150      );
151
152  Food = new Array(
153      new product("Cheese",
154        "Wait 'til you get a wiff. Puts bleu cheese to shame.",
155        3.05,
156        "chunk"),
157      new product("Fries",
158        "More grease than the local car garage. You can't beat the " +
159          "taste, though.",
160        1.15,
161        "box"),
162      new product("Eggs",
163        "The standard breakfast staple.",
164        1.07,
165        "dozen"),
166      new product("Drumstick",
167        "This leg of pterodactyl is a sure crowd pleaser.",
168        100.00,
169        "half ton"),
170      new product("Chips",
171        "Opened-bag flavor. Guaranteed stale, or your money back.",
172        1.59,
173        "bag"),
174      new product("Shrimp",
175        "Great raw, served above room temperature.",
176        2.95,
177        "each")
178      );
179
180  Hardware = new Array(
181      new product("Chainsaw",
182        "Be your own eager beaver with this tree-cutting machine.",
```

Example 8-3. inventory.js (continued)

```
183        226.41,
184        "each"),
185      new product("Cycle",
186        "Mow down the wheat field with a few swipes. Just like the " +
187          "Grim Reaper's.",
188        11.15,
189        "each"),
190      new product("Hammer",
191        "Tempered steel head, fiberglass handle. Perfect for hitting " +
192          "things.",
193        9.87,
194        "each"),
195      new product("Lawnmower",
196        "Self-propelled (you propel it yourself).",
197        165.95,
198        "each"),
199      new product("Pliers",
200        "Perfect for eye brows and nose hairs.",
201        6.59,
202        "each"),
203      new product("Stake",
204        "This 2-in-1 miracle secures tents or gets rid of vampires.",
205        3.95,
206        "pair")
207      );
208
209   Music = new Array(
210      new product("Bongos",
211        "Great little noise makers for even the most sophisticated " +
212          "occasions.",
213        35.50,
214        "bongo"),
215      new product("Piano",
216        "It ain't grand, but this baby will make you sound like tavern " +
217          "material in no time.",
218        1001.40,
219        "each"),
220      new product("Notes",
221        "Choose from A, B, C, D, E, F, or G. Can be reused in any song.",
222        2.97,
223        "note"),
224      new product("Guitar",
225        "Strum, strum. This one is your fast track to fame and fortune.",
226        241.11,
227        "each"),
228      new product("Trumpet",
229        "Solid copper body, and not many dents. Extra spit valve " +
230          "included.",
231        683.59,
232        "each")
233      );
234
```

Example 8-3. inventory.js (continued)

```
235   categorySet = new Array(
236     new category("Appliances", "Kitchen machines to make life easier"),
237     new category("Buildings", "Architectural structures your can't " +
238       "resist"),
239     new category("Clothing", "Fashionably questionable apparel for " +
240       "the 21st century"),
241     new category("Electronics", "Nifty gizmos that drain your wallet"),
242     new category("Food", "The best product to order over the Net"),
243     new category("Hardware", "All kinds of general purpose " +
244       "construction tools"),
245     new category("Music", "The hottest new instruments from places " +
246       "you've never heard of")
247       );
248   }
```

Product properties

Remember the JavaScript objects we used in the earlier chapters? They're back with a vengeance. Each product is treated as an object with several properties; that is, each product has the following properties:

name
> The product name

description
> A basic description of the product

price
> The cost of the product

unit
> The unit by which the product is sold, e.g., by the dozen, the pair, per piece

plu
> The price lookup number: an arbitrary product number for inventory tracking and order processing

icon
> An image of each product

To achieve the desired result, the product constructor function is defined as follows in lines 1–10:

```
function product(name, description, price, unit) {
  this.name = name;
  this.description = description;
  this.price = price;
  this.unit = unit;
  this.plu = name.substring(0, 3).toUpperCase() +
    parseInt(price).toString();
  this.icon = new Image();
  return this;
  }
```

Notice that there are six properties created, but only four arguments expected. The number of properties and the number of expected arguments aren't correlated, but consider how each property receives its value. The first four are obvious. Properties *name, description, price,* and *unit* are all assigned the values of the matching argument names.

plu is a different story, though. It's actually a composite of the *name* and *price* properties. The uppercase of the first three characters of *name* plus the integer value of *price* make the PLU number. So a boat that cost $5501.00 has the *plu* property of BOA5501. Keep in mind that this is arbitrary. The products you sell probably have their own tracking numbers. I did it this way to keep things simple. The last property is *icon*, which for now is assigned a new *Image* object. There's no need for an argument to do that.

Product category properties

We know that each product is really a *product* object. Likewise, each product category is really a *category* object. Just as products have properties, so do categories. Have a look at the properties of the *category* object:

name
    The category name

description
    A basic description of the category

prodLine
    All the *products* within that category

A category constructor saves the day in lines 11–21:

```
function category(name, description) {
  this.name = name;
  this.description = description;
  this.prodLine = eval(name);
  var imgDir = "images/" + name.toLowerCase() + "/";
  for (var i = 0; i < this.prodLine.length; i++) {
    this.prodLine[i].icon.src = imgDir +
      this.prodLine[i].name.toLowerCase() + ".gif";
  }
  return this;
}
```

Each category has three properties—a string called *name*, another string called *description*, and an array called *prodLine*. Properties *name* and *description* seem straightforward, but where does the array come from, and how do you get it using eval()? The answers to both will be clearer in a moment, but this is the basic strategy: whatever you name the category, the product line will be an array of the same name. For example, if you name a category *stereos*, then the array containing all the stereo products will be called *stereos*. That is, *prodLine* would be a copy of the variable *stereo*, which is an array of different stereo products.

Remember that each product has a property called *icon*, which is an Image object that hasn't been assigned a source. Let's get some more mileage from the category name. Not only does every category keep its product line in an array of the same name, but all the images for the products in that category are stored in a directory of the same name.

All the products in the Music category are kept in the *music/* directory. The Hardware category has images in the *hardware/* directory, and so on. That sounds logical. If this type of directory structure is in place, then we can preload all the images for the category when the category is constructed. Lines 16–19 handle the job:

```
var imgDir = "images/" + name.toLowerCase() + "/";
for (var i = 0; i < this.prodLine.length; i++) {
  this.prodLine[i].icon.src = imgDir +
    this.prodLine[i].name.toLowerCase() + ".gif";
  }
```

If you examine the directory structure in *ch08*, you'll see this:

> *images/*
> > *appliances/*
> > *buildings/*
> > *clothing/*
> > *electronics/*
> > *food/*
> > *hardware/*
> > *music/*

Line 17 sets the SRC property of each icon (an Image) to *images/* + the product name in lowercase + / + ".*gif.*" This goes back to those naming conventions I've been talking about in several previous chapters. Each product has an image of the same name and is located in a folder with the same name as the category to which the product belongs. Here's the formula:

> *Each product image URL = images/category/product_name.gif*

If you browse *ch08\images*, you'll notice each image name corresponds with a Shopping Bag product located in a directory corresponding with a Shopping Bag category. This keeps things simple, and lets you add, remove, and keep track of products very easily.

If you have many large images, consider omitting image preloading. It sure is nice to have those images on the client machine so that the browsing experience has no delay. If you have lots of high-quality, large-sized images, though, the user might not be willing to wait until 500K of images load. Use your own discretion.

Creating products and categories

You've seen the constructor functions; now let's put them to work. The first thing to do is create the products, then the categories. Function **makeProducts()** does both. Here are lines 22–248. Since much of it is the same product constructor called repeatedly, this is the abbreviated version:

```
function makeProducts() {
  Appliances = new Array(
    new product("Dryer",
      "Stylish pastel design, contemporary two-button engineering.",
      263.37  ,
      "each"),
    new product("Hairdryer",
      "Fancy yellowish blast, and durable cord. No expense spared.",
      1.15,
      "pair"),
    new product("Oven",
      "Made in the 1850's, this coal-powered unit quickly blackens any" +
        "favorite dish.",
      865.78,
      "each"),
    new product("Radio",
      "Revolutionary one-channel technology. White noise and static" +
        "included.",
        15.43,
        "each"),
    new product("Toaster",
      "BBQ-style toaster. Only a moderate shock hazard.",
      25.78,
      "each"),
    new product("Washer",
      "Does a great job on partially everything.",
      345.61,
      "each")
    );
...
...  and so on ...
...
  categorySet = new Array(
    new category("Appliances", "Kitchen machines to make life easier"),
    new category("Buildings", "Architectural structures your can't " +
      "resist"),
```

```
        new category("Clothing", "Fashionably questionable apparel for " +
           "the 21st century"),
        new category("Electronics", "Nifty gizmos that drain your wallet"),
        new category("Food", "The best product to order over the Net"),
        new category("Hardware", "All kinds of general purpose " +
           "construction tools"),
        new category("Music", "The hottest new instruments from places " +
           "you've never heard of")
           );
    }
```

First come the products. Variable *Appliances* is set to an array. Each element in the array is a product object. Each call to *product* carries with it the expected arguments for building a product—a name, description, price, and unit. This happens for *Buildings, Clothing, Electronics, Food, Hardware,* and *Music.*

All that's left is coming up with the categories. Actually, the category names are already in place (Appliances, Buildings, Clothing, etc.); we just have to let Shopping Bag know that. Lines 235–248 make it happen:

```
categorySet = new Array(
    new category("Appliances", "Kitchen machines to make life easier"),
    new category("Buildings", "Architectural structures your can't " +
       "resist"),
    new category("Clothing", "Fashionably questionable apparel for " +
       "the 21st century"),
    new category("Electronics", "Nifty gizmos that drain your wallet"),
    new category("Food", "The best product to order over the Net"),
    new category("Hardware", "All kinds of general purpose " +
       "construction tools"),
    new category("Music", "The hottest new instruments from places " +
       "you've never heard of")
       );
```

Variable *categorySet* is also an array. Each element in the array is a category object constructed with two arguments, a name, and a description. The first argument is assigned to the *name* property, and the second is assigned to the *description* property. Take another look at line 14 of the category constructor:

```
this.prodLine = eval(name);
```

prodLine is set to the value of **eval(name)**. So the call to **category()** in line 249 means *prodLine* equals **eval("Appliances")**, which equals *Appliances*. Now the category named *Appliances* knows about all its products (there in the *prodLine* array). Each element in *categorySet* represents another Shopping Bag category. This makes adding and removing them a snap.

Creating the shopping bag

The products have all been created. The only thing left to create during load time is . . . well . . . a shopping bag. All this shopping bag needs is a few properties to handle the payment and an array to store all the products the user selects. The Bag() constructor in *manager.html* defines the one and only shopping bag. Here are lines 21–31 of *manager.html,* shown in Example 8-4 later in the chapter:

```
function Bag() {
    this.taxRate    = .06;
    this.taxTotal   = 0;
    this.shipRate   = .02;
    this.shipTotal  = 0;
    this.subTotal   = 0;
    this.bagTotal   = 0;
    this.things     = new Array();
    }
shoppingBag = new Bag();
```

There are two variables to hold arbitrary rates, *taxRate* and *shipRate*. One is a multiple for computing state sales tax. The other, also a multiple, is used to calculate shipping charges. Your tax structure will likely differ, but you can at least see the direction here. Three other variables, *taxTotal, subTotal,* and *shipTotal,* represent the sum of the tax, the sum of all the product selections and their quantities, and the grand sum that the user must pay, respectively. The last variable is an array. *things* will contain all the products, including quantities that the user selects. Variable *shoppingBag* is then set to the value a new Bag(). Let's shop around.

JavaScript Technique:
Maintaining Client State with JavaScript Objects

Notice that all of the user's products selections and shopping totals are stored in properties of shoppingBag(). This can be an effective way to organize information that grows and changes during the life cycle of an application. Generally speaking, the user can make any changes in quantity or product selection, and the properties of shoppingBag scale to fit. Keep this technique handy.

Step 2: Displaying Products

With the application loaded, one of the first things the user will want to do is view the inventory. The user can navigate from category to category with the "Previous Category" and "Next Category" links or from product to product with the "Previous Product" and "Next Product" links. Here's how it works. Recall lines 235–248 in *inventory.js:*

```
categorySet = new Array(
    new category("Appliances", "Kitchen machines to make life easier"),
```

```
       new category("Buildings", "Architectural structures your can't " +
          "resist"),
       new category("Clothing", "Fashionably questionable apparel for " +
          "the 21st century"),
       new category("Electronics", "Nifty gizmos that drain your wallet"),
       new category("Food", "The best product to order over the Net"),
       new category("Hardware", "All kinds of general purpose " +
          "construction tools"),
       new category("Music", "The hottest new instruments from places " +
          "you've never heard of")
       );
```

categorySet has seven category objects. The first one is referenced as `category-Set[0]`, the next `categorySet[1]`, and so forth. No matter what product a user is viewing, Shopping Bag knows the number (in this case, 0-6) of the category to which it belongs. If the user decides to move to the previous category, Shopping Bag subtracts 1 from the current category number, and shows the first product in that category. If Shopping Bag is in category 0 and the user wants to move to the previous category, Shopping Bag starts back at the top category number (in this case, 6).

If the user wants to view the next category, Shopping Bag simply adds 1 to the current category number. If the user is already in the last category, Shopping Bag starts at 0 again.

The same holds true for the products. Each category has a certain number of products. Shopping Bag knows the number to reference the current product in view, so choosing "Previous Product" or "Next Product" will cause the next or previous product to be displayed simply by subtracting or adding one, depending on what the user wants to do.

When the user reaches the last product in a category (going forwards), Shopping Bag realizes this and begins with product 0 of the next category. When the user reaches the first product in a category (going backwards), Shopping Bag realizes this as well, and begins with the last product of the previous category.

If I've confused you with that last explanation, the next diagram should help. Figure 8-10 shows how Shopping Bag takes the user through the categories. It works the same way with navigating through the products. When you reach the last product in one category, you move to the first product in the following category.

manager.html

All this functionality comes from the file *manager.html*. Example 8-4 shows the code.

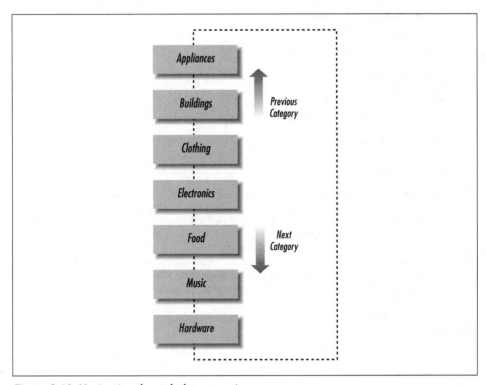

Figure 8-10. Navigating through the categories

Example 8-4. manager.html

```
 1 <HTML>
 2 <HEAD>
 3 <TITLE>Shopping Bag Manager</TITLE>
 4 <STYLE TYPE="text/css">
 5 <!--
 6 TD {font-weight: bold; margin-left: 20; margin-right: 20; padding: 10}
 7 //-->
 8 </STYLE>
 9 </HEAD>
10 <BODY onLoad="freshStart(); makeProducts();"
11    LINK=BLUE ALINK=BLUE VLINK=BLUE>
12 <SCRIPT LANGUAGE="JavaScript1.2" SRC="inventory.js"></SCRIPT>
13 <SCRIPT LANGUAGE="JavaScript1.2">
14 <!--
15 var gimmeControl = false;
16 var browseControl = false;
17 var curCLoc = -1;
18 var curPLoc = -1;
19 var infoStr = '';
20 var shoppingBag;
21 function Bag() {
22   this.taxRate   = .06;
```

Example 8-4. manager.html (continued)

```
23    this.taxTotal    = 0;
24    this.shipRate    = .02;
25    this.shipTotal   = 0;
26    this.subTotal    = 0;
27    this.bagTotal    = 0;
28    this.things    = new Array();
29    }
30
31 shoppingBag = new Bag();
32
33 function showStore() {
34    gimmeControl = false;
35    var header = '<HTML><TITLE>Category</TITLE><BODY BGCOLOR=FFFFFF>';
36    var intro = '<H2>Shopping Bag Product Categories</H2><B>';
37    var footer = '</DL></BLOCKQUOTE></BODY></HTML>';
38    var storeStr = '<BLOCKQUOTE><DL>';
39    for (var i = 0; i < categorySet.length; i++) {
40       storeStr += '<DT><A HREF="javascript: parent.frames[1].reCall(' +
41          i + ', 0);">' + categorySet[i].name + '</A><DD>' +
42          categorySet[i].description + '<BR><BR>';
43       }
44    infoStr = header + intro + storeStr + footer;
45    parent.frames[0].location.replace('javascript:
46 parent.frames[1].infoStr');
47    }
48
49 function portal() {
50    gimmeControl = false;
51    parent.frames[0].location.href = "search/index.html";
52    }
53 function display(cOffset, pOffset) {
54    if(!browseControl) {
55       alert("Start shopping by selecting a product category from " +
56          "Show All Categories or searching products from Product Search.");
57       return;
58       }
59    gimmeControl = true;
60    if (curPLoc + pOffset < 0 || curPLoc + pOffset ==
61       categorySet[curCLoc].prodLine.length) {
62       if (curPLoc + pOffset < 0) {
63          if (curCLoc - 1 < 0) { curCLoc = categorySet.length - 1; }
64          else { curCLoc--; }
65          curPLoc = categorySet[curCLoc].prodLine.length - 1;
66          }
67       else if (curPLoc + pOffset == categorySet[curCLoc].prodLine.length) {
68          if (curCLoc + 1 == categorySet.length) { curCLoc = 0; }
69          else { curCLoc++; }
70          curPLoc = 0;
71          }
72       }
73    else {
74       if (curCLoc + cOffset < 0 || curCLoc + cOffset ==
```

Example 8-4. manager.html (continued)

```
 75        categorySet.length) {
 76        curCLoc = (curCLoc + cOffset < 0 ? categorySet.length - 1 : 0);
 77        }
 78     else { curCLoc += cOffset; }
 79     if (cOffset == -1 || cOffset == 1) { curPLoc = 0; }
 80     else if (pOffset == 0) {
 81        curPLoc = (curPLoc >= categorySet[curCLoc].prodLine.length ? 0 :
 82           curPLoc)
 83        }
 84     else { curPLoc = curPLoc + pOffset; }
 85     }
 86  infoStr = '<HTML><HEAD><TITLE>Product Name</TITLE></HEAD>' +
 87     '<BODY><TABLE CELLPADDING=3><TR><TD VALIGN=TOP COLSPAN=2>' +
 88     '<FONT FACE=Tahoma><H2>Shopping Bag: <I>' +
 89     categorySet[curCLoc].name + '</I></H2><TR>' +
 90     '<TD VALIGN=TOP><IMG SRC="' +
 91     categorySet[curCLoc].prodLine[curPLoc].icon.src +
 92     '"></TD><TD VALIGN=TOP><FONT FACE=Tahoma>' +
 93     '<B>Name: </B>' +  categorySet[curCLoc].prodLine[curPLoc].name +
 94     '<BR><B>Description: </B>' +
 95     categorySet[curCLoc].prodLine[curPLoc].description + '<BR>' +
 96     '<B>Price: </B> $' +
 97     numberFormat(categorySet[curCLoc].prodLine[curPLoc].price) + '/' +
 98     categorySet[curCLoc].prodLine[curPLoc].unit + '<BR>' +
 99     '<B>PLU: </B>' + categorySet[curCLoc].prodLine[curPLoc].plu +
100     '</TD></TR></TABLE></BODY></HTML>';
101   parent.frames[0].location.href = 'javascript:
102 parent.frames[1].infoStr';
103   }
104
105 function reCall(cReset, pReset) {
106   browseControl = true;
107   curCLoc = cReset;
108   curPLoc = pReset;
109   display(0, 0);
110   }
111
112 function gimmeOne() {
113   if (!gimmeControl) {
114     alert("Nothing on this screen to give you.");
115     return;
116     }
117   for (var i = 0; i < shoppingBag.things.length; i++) {
118     if (categorySet[curCLoc].prodLine[curPLoc].plu ==
119       shoppingBag.things[i].plu) {
120       alert("That's already in your bag. You can change the quantity " +
121         "by choosing View/Change Bag.");
122       return;
123       }
124     }
125   shoppingBag.things[shoppingBag.things.length] =
126     categorySet[curCLoc].prodLine[curPLoc];
```

Example 8-4. manager.html (continued)

```
127   shoppingBag.things[shoppingBag.things.length - 1].itemQty = 1;
128   shoppingBag.things[shoppingBag.things.length - 1].category =
129     categorySet[curCLoc].name;
130   alert("OK. You put the " +
131     shoppingBag.things[shoppingBag.things.length - 1].name +
132     " in your bag.");
133   }
134
135 function showBag() {
136   if (shoppingBag.things.length == 0) {
137     alert("Your bag is currently empty. Put some stuff in.");
138     return;
139     }
140   gimmeControl = false;
141   var header = '<HTML><HEAD><TITLE>Your Shopping Bag</TITLE>' +
142     '</HEAD><BODY BGCOLOR=FFFFFF ' +
143     'onLoad="parent.frames[1].runningTab(document.forms[0]);">';
144   var intro = '<H2>Your Shopping Bag!!!</H2>' +
145     '<FORM onReset="' +
146     'setTimeout(\'parent.frames[1].runningTab(document.forms[0])\', ' +
147     '25);">';
148   var tableTop = '<TABLE BORDER=1 CELLSPACING=0 CELLPADDING=5>' +
149     '<TR><TH><B>Index' +
150     '<TH><B>Product<TH><B>Category' +
151     '<TH><B>PLU<TH><B>Unit Price' +
152     '<TH><B>Quantity<TH><B>Product Total' +
153     '<TH><B>Remove' +
154     '</TR>';
155   var itemStr = '';
156   for (var i = 0; i < shoppingBag.things.length; i++) {
157     itemStr += '<TR>' +
158       '<TD ALIGN=CENTER>' + (i + 1) + '</TD>' +
159       '<TD>' + shoppingBag.things[i].name + '</TD>' +
160       '<TD>' + shoppingBag.things[i].category + '</TD>' +
161       '<TD>' + shoppingBag.things[i].plu + '</TD>' +
162       '<TD ALIGN=RIGHT>$' +
163         parent.frames[1].numberFormat(shoppingBag.things[i].price) +
164       '</TD>' +
165       '<TD ALIGN=CENTER>' +
166       parent.frames[1].genSelect(shoppingBag.things[i].price,
167         shoppingBag.things[i].itemQty, i) + '</TD>' +
168       '<TD ALIGN=CENTER><INPUT TYPE=TEXT SIZE=10 VALUE="' +
169       parent.frames[1].numberFormat(shoppingBag.things[i].price *
170         shoppingBag.things[i].itemQty) +
171       '" onFocus="this.blur();"></TD>' +
172       '<TD ALIGN=CENTER><INPUT TYPE=CHECKBOX></TD>' +
173       '</TR>';
174     }
175   var tableBottom = '<TR>' +
176     '<TD ALIGN=RIGHT COLSPAN=6>SubTotal:</TD>' +
177     '<TD ALIGN=CENTER><INPUT TYPE=TEXT SIZE=10 NAME="subtotal" ' +
178     onFocus="this.blur();"></TD></TR>' +
```

Example 8-4. manager.html (continued)

```
179      '<TR><TD ALIGN=RIGHT COLSPAN=6> + 6% Tax:</TD>' +
180      '<TD ALIGN=CENTER><INPUT TYPE=TEXT SIZE=10 NAME="tax" ' +
181      'onFocus="this.blur();"></TD></TR><TR><TD ALIGN=RIGHT COLSPAN=6>' +
182      '2% Shipping:</TD><TD ALIGN=CENTER><INPUT TYPE=TEXT ' +
183      'SIZE=10 NAME="ship" onFocus="this.blur();"></TD></TR>' +
184      '<TR>' +
185      '<TD ALIGN=RIGHT COLSPAN=3><INPUT TYPE=BUTTON VALUE="Check Out" ' +
186      'onClick="parent.frames[1].checkOut(this.form);"></TD>' +
187      '<TD ALIGN=RIGHT><INPUT TYPE=RESET VALUE="Reset Qtys"></TD>' +
188      '<TD ALIGN=RIGHT><INPUT TYPE=BUTTON VALUE="Change Bag" ' +
189      'onClick="parent.frames[1].changeBag(this.form, true);"></TD>' +
190      '<TD ALIGN=RIGHT>Total:</TD><TD ALIGN=CENTER>' +
191      '<INPUT TYPE=TEXT NAME="total" SIZE=10 onFocus="this.blur();">' +
192      '</TD></TR>';
193
194      var footer = '</TABLE></FORM></BODY></HTML>';
195      infoStr = header + intro + tableTop + itemStr + tableBottom + footer;
196      parent.frames[0].location.replace('javascript:
197          parent.frames[1].infoStr');
198      }
199
200  function genSelect(priceAgr, qty, idx) {
201      var selStr = '<SELECT onChange="this.form.elements[' + (idx * 3 + 1) +
202          '].value = this.options[this.selectedIndex].value;
203      parent.frames[1].runningTab(this.form);">';
204      for (var i = 1; i <= 10; i++) {
205        selStr += '<OPTION VALUE="' + numberFormat(i * priceAgr) + '"' +
206          (i == qty ? ' SELECTED' : '') + '>' + i;
207        }
208      selStr += '</SELECT>';
209      return selStr;
210      }
211
212  function runningTab(formObj) {
213      var subTotal = 0;
214      for (var i = 0; i < shoppingBag.things.length; i++) {
215        subTotal += parseFloat(formObj.elements[(i * 3) + 1].value);
216        }
217      formObj.subtotal.value = numberFormat(subTotal);
218      formObj.tax.value = numberFormat(subTotal * shoppingBag.taxRate);
219      formObj.ship.value = numberFormat(subTotal * shoppingBag.shipRate);
220      formObj.total.value = numberFormat(subTotal +
221          round(subTotal * shoppingBag.taxRate) +
222          round(subTotal * shoppingBag.shipRate));
223      shoppingBag.subTotal = formObj.subtotal.value;
224      shoppingBag.taxTotal = formObj.tax.value;
225      shoppingBag.shipTotal = formObj.ship.value;
226      shoppingBag.bagTotal = formObj.total.value;
227      }
228
229  function numberFormat(amount) {
230      var rawNumStr = round(amount) + '';
```

Example 8-4. manager.html (continued)

```
231    rawNumStr = (rawNumStr.charAt(0) == '.' ? '0' + rawNumStr : rawNumStr);
232    if (rawNumStr.charAt(rawNumStr.length - 3) == '.') {
233      return rawNumStr
234      }
235    else if (rawNumStr.charAt(rawNumStr.length - 2) == '.') {
236      return rawNumStr + '0';
237      }
238    else { return rawNumStr + '.00'; }
239    }
240 function round(number,decPlace) {
241    decPlace = (!decPlace ? 2 : decPlace);
242    return Math.round(number * Math.pow(10,decPlace)) /
243      Math.pow(10,decPlace);
244    }
245
246 function changeBag(formObj, showAgain) {
247    var tempBagArray = new Array();
248    for (var i = 0; i < shoppingBag.things.length; i++) {
249      if (!formObj.elements[(i * 3) + 2].checked) {
250        tempBagArray[tempBagArray.length] = shoppingBag.things[i];
251        tempBagArray[tempBagArray.length - 1].itemQty =
252          formObj.elements[i * 3].selectedIndex + 1;
253        }
254      }
255    shoppingBag.things = tempBagArray;
256    if(shoppingBag.things.length == 0) {
257      alert("You've emptied your bag. Put some stuff in.");
258      parent.frames[1].showStore();
259      }
260    else { showBag(); }
261    }
262
263 function checkOut(formObj) {
264    gimmeControl = false;
265    if(!confirm("Do you have every product in the right quantity " +
266      "you need? Remember that you have to choose Change Bag to " +
267      "remove products or change quantities. If so, choose OK to check " +
268      "out.")) {
269      return;
270      }
271    if(shoppingBag.things.length == 0) {
272      showStore();
273      return;
274      }
275    var header = '<HTML><TITLE>Shopping Bag Check Out</TITLE>' +
276      '<BODY BGCOLOR=FFFFFF>';
277
278    var intro = '<H2>Shopping Bag Check Out</H2><FORM METHOD=POST ' +
279      'ACTION="http://your.webserver.com/cgi-bin/bag.cgi" ' +
280      'onSubmit="return parent.frames[1].cheapCheck(this);">';
281
282    var shipInfo = '<TABLE BORDER=0 CELLSPACING=0 CELLPADDING=5>' +
```

Example 8-4. manager.html (continued)

```
283     '<TR><TD><B>Shipping Information</TD></TR>'+
284     '<TR><TD>First Name</TD><TD><INPUT TYPE=TEXT NAME="fname"></TD>' +
285     '</TR><TR><TD>Last Name</TD><TD>' +
286     '<INPUT TYPE=TEXT NAME="lname"></TD></TR><TR><TD>Company Name</TD>' +
287     '<TD><INPUT TYPE=TEXT NAME="cname"></TD></TR><TR>' +
288     '<TD>Street Address1</TD><TD><INPUT TYPE=TEXT NAME="saddress1">' +
289     '</TD></TR><TR><TD>Street Address2</TD>' +
290     '<TD><INPUT TYPE=TEXT NAME="saddress2"></TD></TR><TR>' +
291     '<TD>City</TD><TD><INPUT TYPE=TEXT NAME="city"></TD></TR>' +
292     '<TR><TD>State/Province</TD>' +
293     '<TD><INPUT TYPE=TEXT NAME="stpro"></TD></TR><TR>' +
294     '<TD>Country</TD><TD><INPUT TYPE=TEXT NAME="country"></TD></TR>' +
295     '<TR><TD>Zip/Mail Code</TD><TD><INPUT TYPE=TEXT NAME="zip"></TD>' +
296     '</TR><TR><TD><BR><BR></TD></TR></TABLE>';
297
298  var payInfo = '<TABLE BORDER=0 CELLSPACING=0 CELLPADDING=5>' +
299     '<TR><TD><B>Payment Information</TD></TR>'+
300     '<TR><TD>Credit Card Type:       </TD>' +
301     '<TD>Visa <INPUT TYPE=RADIO NAME="ctype" VALUE="visa" CHECKED> ' +
302     '      ' +
303     'Amex <INPUT TYPE=RADIO NAME="ctype" VALUE="amex"> ' +
304     '      ' +
305     'Discover <INPUT TYPE=RADIO NAME="ctype" VALUE="disc"> ' +
306     '      </TD></TR>' +
307     '<TR><TD>Credit Card Number</TD>' +
308     '<TD><INPUT TYPE=TEXT NAME="cnumb"></TD></TR><TR>' +
309     '<TD>Expiration Date</TD><TD><INPUT TYPE=TEXT NAME="edate"></TD>' +
310     '</TR><TR><TD><INPUT TYPE=SUBMIT VALUE="Send Order"></TD>' +
311     '<TD><INPUT TYPE=RESET VALUE="Clear Info"></TD></TR>' +
312     '</TABLE>';
313
314  var itemInfo = '';
315  for (var i = 0; i < shoppingBag.things.length; i++) {
316     itemInfo += '<INPUT TYPE=HIDDEN NAME="prod' + i +
317        '" VALUE="' + shoppingBag.things[i].plu + '-' +
318        shoppingBag.things[i].itemQty + '">';
319     }
320  var totalInfo = '<INPUT TYPE=HIDDEN NAME="subtotal" VALUE="' +
321     shoppingBag.subTotal + '">' +
322     '<INPUT TYPE=HIDDEN NAME="taxtotal" VALUE="' +
323     shoppingBag.taxTotal + '">' +
324     '<INPUT TYPE=HIDDEN NAME="shiptotal" VALUE="' +
325     shoppingBag.shipTotal + '">' +
326     '<INPUT TYPE=HIDDEN NAME="bagtotal" VALUE="' +
327     shoppingBag.bagTotal + '">';
328
329  var footer = '</FORM></BODY></HTML>';
330
331  infoStr = header + intro + shipInfo + payInfo + itemInfo +
332     totalInfo + footer;
333     parent.frames[0].location.replace('javascript:
334        parent.frames[1].infoStr');
```

Example 8-4. manager.html (continued)

```
335    }
336
337 function cheapCheck(formObj) {
338    for (var i = 0; i < formObj.length; i++) {
339       if (formObj[i].type == "text" && formObj.elements[i].value == "") {
340         alert ("You must complete all fields.");
341         return false;
342         }
343       }
344    if(!confirm("If all your information is correct, " +
345       "choose OK to send your order, or choose Cancel to make changes.")) {
346       return false;
347       }
348    alert("Thank you. We'll be living off your hard-earned money soon.");
349    shoppingBag = new Bag();
350    showStore();
351    return true;
352    }
353
354 function help() {
355    gimmeControl = false;
356    parent.frames[0].location.href = "intro.html";
357    }
358
359 function freshStart() {
360    if(parent.frames[0].location.href != "intro.html") { help(); }
361    }
362
363 //-->
364 </SCRIPT>
365 <TABLE ALIGN=CENTER BORDER=0>
366    <TR>
367       <TD>
368       <A HREF="javascript: gimmeOne();">Gimme One<A>
369       </TD>
370       <TD>
371       <A HREF="javascript: showBag();">View/Change Bag<A>
372       </TD>
373       <TD>
374       <A HREF="javascript: showStore();">Show All Categories<A>
375       </TD>
376       <TD>
377       <A HREF="javascript: portal();">Product Search<A>
378       </TD>
379       <TD>
380       <A HREF="javascript: help();">Help<A>
381       </TD>
382    </TR>
383 </TABLE>
384 <TABLE ALIGN=CENTER BORDER=0>
385    <TR>
386       <TD>
```

Example 8-4. manager.html (continued)

```
387      <A HREF="javascript: display(-1,0);">Previous Category<A>
388      </TD>
389      <TD>
390      <A HREF="javascript: display(0,-1);">Previous Product<A>
391      </TD>
392      <TD>
393      <A HREF="javascript: display(0,1);">Next Product<A>
394      </TD>
395      <TD>
396      <A HREF="javascript: display(1,0);">Next Category<A>
397      </TD>
398   </TR>
399 </TABLE>
400 </BODY>
401 </HTML>
```

Just a quick note. Did you see that all the JavaScript is embedded after the BODY tag? Since there is a lot of image preloading and object creation at the beginning, Netscape Navigator will display that dull gray background in the window (or the frame in this case) until all that work is done. Only then will it parse the rest of the contents. As it stands, the browser will parse the BODY tag, and hence, the BGCOLOR attribute, *before* going about all the work.

Variables

Following is the code that makes the product display happen. Lines 15–18 set up four variables, and lines 53–103 define function display(). Variable *gimme-Control* indicates to Shopping Bag whether there is something on the screen (a product) that can be added to the shopping bag. Variable *browseControl* enforces the rule that the user must start browsing by clicking on "Show All Categories" or "Product Search." (See Rule 1.) You'll see both of these variables throughout the application, but display() deals with them first, so let's introduce them:

```
var gimmeControl = false;
var browseControl = false;
var curCLoc = -1;
var curPLoc = -1;
```

Variables *curCLoc* and *curPLoc* hold the respective index numbers of the category and product in view. These are the numbers I mentioned earlier in the section. Though both are set arbitrarily to –1, they change the moment the user chooses a category or a product. More on these two in a moment. Now let's see how it all happens. Here are lines 53–103:

```
function display(cOffset, pOffset) {
  if(!browseControl) {
    alert("Start shopping by selecting a product category from Show " +
      "All Categories or searching products from Product Search.");
    return;
    }
```

```
    gimmeControl = true;
    if (curPLoc + pOffset < 0 || curPLoc + pOffset ==
      categorySet[curCLoc].prodLine.length) {
      if (curPLoc + pOffset < 0) {
        if (curCLoc - 1 < 0) { curCLoc = categorySet.length - 1; }
        else { curCLoc--; }
        curPLoc = categorySet[curCLoc].prodLine.length - 1;
        }
      else if (curPLoc + pOffset == categorySet[curCLoc].prodLine.length) {
        if (curCLoc + 1 == categorySet.length) { curCLoc = 0; }
        else { curCLoc++; }
        curPLoc = 0;
        }
    }
    else {
      if (curCLoc + cOffset < 0 || curCLoc + cOffset ==
        categorySet.length) {
        curCLoc = (curCLoc + cOffset < 0 ? categorySet.length - 1 : 0);
        }
      else { curCLoc += cOffset; }
      if (cOffset == -1 || cOffset == 1) { curPLoc = 0; }
      else if (pOffset == 0) {
        curPLoc = (curPLoc >= categorySet[curCLoc].prodLine.length ? 0 :
          curPLoc)
        }
      else { curPLoc = curPLoc + pOffset; }
      }
    infoStr = '<HTML><HEAD><TITLE>Product Name</TITLE></HEAD>' +
      '<BODY><TABLE CELLPADDING=3><TR><TD VALIGN=TOP COLSPAN=2>' +
      '<FONT FACE=Tahoma><H2>Shopping Bag: <I>' +
        categorySet[curCLoc].name + '</I></H2><TR>' +
      '<TD VALIGN=TOP><IMG SRC="' +
      categorySet[curCLoc].prodLine[curPLoc].icon.src +
      '"></TD><TD VALIGN=TOP><FONT FACE=Tahoma>' +
      '<B>Name: </B>' +  categorySet[curCLoc].prodLine[curPLoc].name +
      '<BR><B>Description: </B>' +
      categorySet[curCLoc].prodLine[curPLoc].description + '<BR>' +
      '<B>Price: </B> $' +
      numberFormat(categorySet[curCLoc].prodLine[curPLoc].price) + '/' +
      categorySet[curCLoc].prodLine[curPLoc].unit + '<BR>' +
      '<B>PLU: </B>' + categorySet[curCLoc].prodLine[curPLoc].plu +
      '</TD></TR></TABLE></BODY></HTML>';

    parent.frames[0].location.href = 'javascript:parent.frames[1].infoStr';
    }
```

display()

display() has three jobs:

1. Determine whether it is allowed to display a product.

2. Determine which category/product the user wants to view.

3. Display that product.

Job 1 is pretty simple. If *browseControl* is `true`, the answer is yes. *browseControl* is originally set to `false`. Once the user chooses a product from "Product Search" or chooses a category from "Show All Categories," *browseControl* is set to true. Now `display()` can carry out jobs 2 and 3. Since a product will be displayed, *gimmeControl* is then set to true.

Notice that `display()` expects two arguments, *cOffset* and *pOffset*. One holds a value to determine how far to move from the current category number. The other does the same for the product number. *cOffset* and *pOffset* can be positive, negative, or zero. To make things simpler, let's assume that shopper Daisy Deep Pockets has already satisfied Rule 1 and can now use the "Next" and "Previous" links to navigate through the inventory. Look at the code for each of these links in lines 386–397:

```
<TD>
<A HREF="javascript: display(-1,0);">Previous Category<A>
</TD>
<TD>
<A HREF="javascript: display(0,-1);">Previous Product<A>
</TD>
<TD>
<A HREF="javascript: display(0,1);">Next Product<A>
</TD>
<TD>
<A HREF="javascript: display(1,0);">Next Category<A>
</TD>
```

Each of these links calls `display()` and passes in a pair of integers. Table 8-1 explains what each function call represents. Remember that *curCLoc* is the category number, and *curPLoc* is the product number.

Table 8-1. Determining the Value of curCLoc and curCPloc

Link	Arguments Passed	Explanation
Previous Category	-1, 0	Add -1 to *curCLoc*; add 0 to *curPLoc*.
Previous Product	0, –1	Add 0 to *curCLoc*; add –1 to *curPLoc*.
Next Product	0, 1	Add 0 to *curCLoc*; add 1 to *curPLoc*.
Next Category	1, 0	Add 1 to *curCLoc*; add 0 to *curPLoc*.

Exceptions to the Rule

This makes sense. If you want to go back one category, subtract 1 from the category number. If you want to view the next product, add 1 to the category number. There are three exceptions, however, that require additional logic:

1. There is no category or product with the number –1. If either the category number or product number is 0, and the user chooses "Previous Category" or "Previous Product," Shopping Bag is headed straight for an error.

2. There is no category with the number `categorySet[categorySet.length]`. Since there are only `categorySet.length` categories, the category number can never be higher than `categorySet.length` −1. If the category number is `categorySet.length` −1, and the user chooses "Next Product" or "Next Category," we get a JavaScript error. The same holds true for the products.

3. Navigating from category to category always displays the first product in the category no matter what the product number of the product the user is currently viewing.

Lines 60–85 provide the desired functionality and accommodate these three exceptions. This is a fairly extensive use of nested if-else statements, so you might want to review it for a while.

```
if (curPLoc + pOffset < 0 || curPLoc + pOffset ==
  categorySet[curCLoc].prodLine.length) {
  if (curPLoc + pOffset < 0) {
    if (curCLoc - 1 < 0) { curCLoc = categorySet.length - 1; }
    else { curCLoc--; }
    curPLoc = categorySet[curCLoc].prodLine.length - 1;
    }
  else if (curPLoc + pOffset == categorySet[curCLoc].prodLine.length) {
    if (curCLoc + 1 == categorySet.length) { curCLoc = 0; }
    else { curCLoc++; }
    curPLoc = 0;
    }
  }
else {
  if (curCLoc + cOffset < 0 || curCLoc + cOffset == categorySet.length) {
    curCLoc = (curCLoc + cOffset < 0 ? categorySet.length - 1 : 0);
    }
  else { curCLoc += cOffset; }
  if (cOffset == -1 || cOffset == 1) { curPLoc = 0; }
  else if (pOffset == 0) {
    curPLoc = (curPLoc >= categorySet[curCLoc].prodLine.length ? 0 :
      curPLoc)
    }
  else { curPLoc = curPLoc + pOffset; }
  }
```

The following pseudo-code rendition should clear up how this block works. The line numbers of the actual code follow each line of our translation:

```
1 IF the product number will be too small or too big THEN (73)
2     IF the product number will be too small THEN (74)
3         IF the category number will be too small THEN the category number
              equals the number of categories minus 1 (75)
4         ELSE The category number equals itself minus 1 (76)
5         The product number equals the number of products in the category
              number minus 1 (77)
6 ELSE IF the product number will be too big THEN (79)
7         IF the category number will be too big THEN the category number
              equals 0 (80)
```

```
 8              ELSE the category number equals itself plus 1 (81)
 9                  The product number equals 0 (82)
10 ELSE (85)
11      IF the category number will be too small OR too big THEN (86)
12              IF the category number is too small THEN category number equals
                    the number of categories minus 1 (87)
13              ELSE the category number equals 0 (88)
14      ELSE the category number equals itself plus the category offset (89)
15      IF the category offset equals -1 OR 1 THEN the product number
                equals 0 (90)
16      ELSE IF the product offset equals 0 THEN (91)
17              IF the product number is greater than or equal to the number of
                    products in the category number THEN the product number
                    equals 0 (92)
18      ELSE the product number equals itself plus the product offset (94)
```

The outermost *if* block handles the variables if the product number falls under either of the first two exceptions. The outermost *else* block handles the variables if the category number falls under either of the first two exceptions. To accommodate the third exception, line 80 sets the product number equal to 0 if the category offset moves up or down by 1.

Building the display page

Knowing the category and product number, Shopping Bag can now build the HTML to display the correct product. Nearly all of the remaining code in `display()` is dedicated to getting that product on the screen. Look at lines 86–102:

```
infoStr = '<HTML><HEAD><TITLE>Product Name</TITLE></HEAD>' +
    '<BODY><TABLE CELLPADDING=3><TR><TD VALIGN=TOP COLSPAN=2>' +
    '<FONT FACE=Tahoma><H2>Shopping Bag: <I>' + categorySet[curCLoc].name +
    '</I></H2><TR><TD VALIGN=TOP><IMG SRC="' +
    categorySet[curCLoc].prodLine[curPLoc].icon.src +
    '"></TD><TD VALIGN=TOP><FONT FACE=Tahoma><B>Name: </B>' +
    categorySet[curCLoc].prodLine[curPLoc].name + '<BR>' +
    '<B>Description: </B>' +
    categorySet[curCLoc].prodLine[curPLoc].description + '<BR>' +
    '<B>Price: </B> $' +
    numberFormat(categorySet[curCLoc].prodLine[curPLoc].price) + '/' +
    categorySet[curCLoc].prodLine[curPLoc].unit + '<BR>' +
    '<B>PLU: </B>' + categorySet[curCLoc].prodLine[curPLoc].plu +
    '</TD></TR></TABLE></BODY></HTML>';
parent.frames[0].location.href = 'javascript: parent.frames[1].infoStr';
```

As you can see, everything is based on one large concatenation of HTML to the initially empty string value of variable *infoStr*. Notice that the values of *curPLoc* and *curCLoc* are vital in referencing all the correct product information. `categorySet[curCLoc]` refers to the correct category, while `categorySet[curCLoc].prodLine[curPLoc]` refers to the correct product. Once the values of *curCLoc* and *curPLoc* have been determined, you can display the product information any way you like.

After *infoStr* has all the HTML it needs to display the product, the *href* property of the top frame is set to its value by way of a `javascript:` protocol. Remember that because of the scope of this protocol, you must provide an absolute reference to it (i.e., `parent.frames[1].infoStr` instead of just *infoStr*). See the JavaScript technique in Chapter 2, *The Online Test,* for the details.

Step 3: Showing All the Categories

Choosing "Show All Categories" is another way to navigate through the products. Function `showStore()` is readily equipped to handle this task, as lines 33–47 show:

```
function showStore() {
  gimmeControl = false;
  var header = '<HTML><TITLE>Category</TITLE><BODY BGCOLOR=FFFFFF>';
  var intro = '<H2>Shopping Bag Product Categories</H2><B>';
  var footer = '</DL></BLOCKQUOTE></BODY></HTML>';
  var storeStr = '<BLOCKQUOTE><DL>';
  for (var i = 0; i < categorySet.length; i++) {
    storeStr += '<DT><A HREF="javascript: parent.frames[1].reCall(' + i +
      ', 0);">' + categorySet[i].name + '</A><DD>' +
      categorySet[i].description + '<BR><BR>';
    }
  infoStr = header + intro + storeStr + footer;
  parent.frames[0].location.replace('javascript:
    parent.frames[1].infoStr');
  }
```

Displaying the First Product

Of course, Rule 1 imposes that the first (and only first) time the user displays a product must come from either "Show All Categories" or "Product Search." The "Product Search" feature is discussed shortly. Let's look at "Show All Categories" now. Showing all categories is fairly easy. `showStore()` simply iterates through all the elements in *categorySet*, generating a linked list with the name and description of each. After the last category, this linked list string (a.k.a., *infoStr*) is set as the *href* property of the top frame. Notice the code provided in each HREF tag is equal to:

```
javascript: parent.frames[1].reCall(' + i + ', 0)
```

Clicking any of the category links will call the function `reCall()` in *manager. html.* Here it is in lines 105–110:

```
function reCall(cReset, pReset) {
  browseControl = true;
  curCLoc = cReset;
  curPLoc = pReset;
  display(0, 0);
  }
```

reCall() expects two arguments, the category number represented by the value of *i* in line 42 and the number 0. The value of *i* is assigned to *curCLoc*. This determines, of course, the category that the user wants to view. The number 0 is assigned to *curPLoc*. Remember exception number 3? Viewing by category always starts the user at the first product in that category, which is prodLine[0].

After this happens, reCall() summons function display(), passing in two zeros as arguments. When we first examined the *if* statements in lines 60–85, we assumed that the user would always be viewing a product or category with a lower or higher value than *curCLoc* or *curPLoc*. The thing is, function reCall() has already set the values of these variables, so there is no need to "go anywhere." The user wants to see the product associated with the current values of *curCLoc* and *curPLoc*. That is what passing in the two zeros means, and the code in lines 60–85 accommodates that.

Where's the DHTML?

Notice that the product pages have no DHTML. No layers. Why shouldn't there be? Most browsers out there support JavaScript 1.2. I've even spent a couple of chapters incorporating cross-browser DHTML. Why back out now? When Shopping Cart initially loads, can't you just create a layer for each product, then hide and show the layer at will? Yes, you can, but . . .

Too much image preloading can hurt you. As mentioned earlier, if you have a lot of graphics, all that preloading might test the shopper's patience. Creating a layer for each product loads those images. Using plain HTML gets the job done with or without image preloading.

Now the user can navigate to and from products and categories at will. It's time to see what happens when the user sees something worth purchasing and decides to put one in the shopping bag.

Step 4: Adding Products to the Shopping Bag

Putting things in the shopping bag is easy. Users need only click the affectionately titled link "Gimme One." This calls the correspondingly named function gimmeOne(). Lines 112–133 have the details:

```
function gimmeOne() {
  if (!gimmeControl) {
    alert("Nothing on this screen to give you.");
    return;
    }
  for (var i = 0; i < shoppingBag.things.length; i++) {
```

```
    if (categorySet[curCLoc].prodLine[curPLoc].plu ==
      shoppingBag.things[i].plu) {
      alert("That's already in your bag. You can change the quantity " +
        "by choosing View/Change Bag.");
      return;
      }
    }
  shoppingBag.things[shoppingBag.things.length] =
    categorySet[curCLoc].prodLine[curPLoc];
  shoppingBag.things[shoppingBag.things.length - 1].itemQty = 1;
  shoppingBag.things[shoppingBag.things.length - 1].category =
    categorySet[curCLoc].name;
  alert("OK. You put the " +
    shoppingBag.things[shoppingBag.things.length - 1].name +
    " in your bag.");
  }
```

The first thing gimmeOne() does is to ensure that there is actually something on the screen to put in the shopping bag. Variable *gimmeControl* is set to true immediately before a product is displayed. Otherwise, any other functions displaying information on the screen set *gimmeControl* to `false`. Therefore, if *gimmeControl* is `false`, there is no product on the screen. The user is alerted, and gimmeOne() returns. Otherwise, gimmeOne() iterates through the elements of the *things* array, which is a property of the user's *shoppingBag* object to check whether the product currently in view is already in the user's bag.

gimmeOne() doesn't expect any arguments. It relies instead upon the current values of *curCLoc* and *curPLoc*. Assuming that each product has a unique PLU number, gimmeOne() looks for a match with any of the PLU numbers of the products currently in the bag. If it finds a match, the user is alerted that the product is already in the bag.

If the product isn't already in the bag, gimmeOne() puts it in. This poses an interesting situation, however. Answer this question: a product in the shopping bag is still a *product* object—true or false? If you answered true, you're right. However, any product in the user's shopping bag must be an extended, more complex *product*. Each product in the bag still has a name, description, PLU, and price, but each also needs a property to represent the quantity ordered and has to "know" to which category it belongs.

Each element in *things*, therefore, must have properties dynamically added to it. Lines 125–129 show how function gimmeOne() adds these specialized products to *things* and adds the properties to each object:

```
  shoppingBag.things[shoppingBag.things.length] =
    categorySet[curCLoc].prodLine[curPLoc];
  shoppingBag.things[shoppingBag.things.length - 1].itemQty = 1;
  shoppingBag.things[shoppingBag.things.length - 1].category =
    categorySet[curCLoc].name;
```

`shoppingBag.things[shoppingBag.things.length]` creates a reference to the *product* object currently at `categorySet[curCLoc].prodLine[curPLoc]`. This adds a "regular" *product* to the shopping bag. The next two lines add respective properties *itemQty*, initially set to 1, and *category* to the name of the category in which the current *product* object belongs.

JavaScript Technique: Adding Object Properties

There are a couple of ways to add properties to user-defined objects. The easiest is just to think of a property name and value, then add it to the object. Each element in things is a product, but these products are assigned two new values, `itemQty` and `category`. The following lines reflect that:

```
shoppingBag.things[shoppingBag.things.length - 1].itemQty = 1;
shoppingBag.things[shoppingBag.things.length - 1].category =
   categorySet[curCLoc].name;
```

Those objects have already been constructed, however, so properties must be added every time. If you want to add properties to all objects constructed in the future, use the *prototype* property. Suppose you want to add a sale price to any other products made:

```
product.prototype.salePrice = 0.00;
```

Any other objects constructed will now have a *salePrice* property with the default value of `0.00`.

The last thing `gimmeOne()` does is to advise the user that the product was successfully added to the shopping bag.

This process repeats itself for every product the user puts in the shopping bag until it is time to check out.

Searching for Products

You've probably noticed by now: the "Product Search" feature is a Chapter 1 transplant. The client-side search engine has been modified to suit the needs of Shopping Bag users. Everything is pretty much the same. The search capabilities, however, have been reduced to only a default Boolean OR search. In other words, if any of the text the user enters is found in the product information, that product is considered a match. There is no Boolean AND search and no search by URL. Still, the capability should be more than enough to fit the bill. There is one extra feature that the Chapter 1 engine doesn't have. Users can enter an empty string simply by pressing the Enter key. This performs a null search, which returns all the products in the database.

We won't get into the same level of detail as Chapter 1 does, but you should read over the next few paragraphs to see how easy it can be to extend organized Java-

Script applications. After all, like any other search engine, the user just wants to enter text to generate a list of linked results. To make this work for Shopping Bag without causing serious code changes to either application, the search engine needs to make the following accommodations:

- Display linked results that support the product/category navigation system explained in Step 2

- Be able to search the existing product database

- Return links to all the products in the database

Fortunately, these changes all can be made in one file—*search/nav.html.* So that you don't have to stare at another couple hundred lines of code, I'll show you only the relative code in *search/nav.html.*

Mapping the Products and Categories

We need to change things just a little for everything to operate smoothly. These changes come in the form of two new variables and a new function, as shown by:

```
var ref = top.frames[1];
var prodProfiles = new Array();
function genProfile() {
   for (var i = 0; i < ref.categorySet.length; i++) {
        for (var j = 0; j < ref.categorySet[i].prodLine.length; j++) {
          prodProfiles[prodProfiles.length] = new Array(i, j);
           }
      }
   }
```

Variable *ref* is used as an alias to `top.frames[1]`. Since most of the objects and variables referenced in this search engine application are located within *manager. html,* the object buried within objects will make for some pretty lengthy references with plenty of dot notation. Using *ref* instead of `top.frames[1]` shortens the writing somewhat. *prodProfiles* starts as an empty array but is soon filled with a call to function `genProfile()`.

`genProfile()` has one job and one job only—establish a system to reference any *product* object in any category by its category number and product number. The category number is paired with a product number.

For example, assume that *i*, the category number, is 1 and *j*, the product number, is 2. If you check *inventory.js*, you'll see that `categorySet[i].prodLine[j]` refers to the "Igloo" in the "Buildings" category. It's like plotting coordinates on a map.

The nested *for* loops in `genProfile()` iterate through each `category` (i) and `product` (j). `genProfile()` makes a mental note, if you will, of each products location in the category by storing the *i,j* integer pair in an array of its own. When all is finished, each element in *prodProfiles* represents a category/product number pair that references a unique product in a category.

You may ask: isn't that how the products are already referenced? The answer is yes. However, the search engine function now knows all of the possible combinations. Each pair is stored as an element in *prodProfiles*. This makes it very easy to refer to (and search and display) information about any product in the database.

Searching the Existing Database

The original version searched a web page name, description, and URL. Shopping Bag has similar items to search. The problem is that you have to do it according to the existing database. Fortunately, you can make a few changes to function `allowAny()`. Here it is in *search/nav.html*:

```
function allowAny(t) {
  var findings = new Array();
  for (var i = 0; i < prodProfiles.length; i++) {
    var compareElement  = ref.categorySet[prodProfiles[i][0]].
prodLine[prodProfiles[i][1]].name + ' ' +
      ref.categorySet[prodProfiles[i][0]].prodLine[prodProfiles[i][1]].
        description + ' ' +
      ref.categorySet[prodProfiles[i][0]].prodLine[prodProfiles[i][1]].
        price.toString() + ' ' +
      ref.categorySet[prodProfiles[i][0]].prodLine[prodProfiles[i][1]].
        plu;
    compareElement = compareElement.toUpperCase();
    for (var j = 0; j < t.length; j++) {
      var compareString = t[j].toUpperCase();
      if (compareElement.indexOf(compareString) != -1) {
        findings[findings.length] = new Array(prodProfiles[i][0],
          prodProfiles[i][1]);
        break;
      }
    }
  }
  verifyManage(findings);
}
```

Not much has really changed. The only thing we need to be concerned about is what to search. So the user can search product name, description, price, and PLU. `allowAny()` concatenates those four of each product in the database together. That makes one long string to compare against each of the words the user has entered. If a match occurs, the next available *findings* element is set to a new array with `prodProfiles[i][0]` and `prodProfiles[i][1]` as its elements. Remember that these two elements are integers that will be used to print out the results shortly.

Supporting Product/Category Navigation

Suppose you perform a search that returns a result set. Now you have to get it on the page. You would be a prime candidate for carpal tunnel syndrome if you decided to code it to display products from the search engine while ignoring the current product/category system. That is, whatever product links are displayed on the results page, users must be able to display the products as usual and then navigate freely with the "Next" and "Prev" buttons. Let's simply make changes to function `formatResults()`:

```
function formatResults(results, reference, offset) {
  docObj.open();
  docObj.writeln('<HTML>\n<HEAD>\n<TITLE>Search Results</TITLE></HEAD>' +
    '<BODY BGCOLOR=WHITE TEXT=BLACK>' +
    '<TABLE WIDTH=780 BORDER=0 ALIGN=CENTER CELLPADDING=3><TR><TD>' +
    '<HR NOSHADE WIDTH=100%></TD></TR><TR><TD VALIGN=TOP><B>' +
    'Search Query: <I>' +
    parent.frames[0].document.forms[0].query.value + '</I><BR>\n' +
    'Search Results: <I>' + (reference + 1) + ' - ' +
    (reference + offset > results.length ? results.length :
      reference + offset) +
    ' of ' + results.length + '</I><BR><BR>' + '<B>' +
    '\n\n<!- Begin result set //-->\n\n\t<DL>');
  var currentRecord = (results.length < reference + offset ?
    results.length : reference + offset);
  for (var i = reference; i < currentRecord; i++) {
    docObj.writeln('\n\n\t<DT>' + '<FONT SIZE=4>' +
      '<A HREF="javascript: top.frames[1].reCall(' + results[i][0] +
      ', ' + results[i][1] + ')">' +
      ref.categorySet[results[i][0]].prodLine[results[i][1]].name +
      '</A></FONT>\t<DD>' +
      ref.categorySet[results[i][0]].prodLine[results[i][1]].description +
      '\t<DD>' + 'Price: <I>$' +
      ref.numberFormat(ref.categorySet[results[i][0]].
        prodLine[results[i][1]].price) +
      '</I>       ' + 'PLU Number: <I>' +
      ref.categorySet[results[i][0]].prodLine[results[i][1]].plu +
      '</I><P>');
  }
  docObj.writeln('\n\t</DL>\n\n<!- End result set //-->\n\n');
  prevNextResults(results.length, reference, offset);
  docObj.writeln('<HR NOSHADE WIDTH=100%>' +
    '</TD>\n</TR>\n</TABLE>\n</BODY>\n</HTML>');
  docObj.close();
  document.forms[0].query.select();
}
```

Each result displays the product name, description, price, and PLU number. This function iterates through the elements of *results* and accesses the respective *prodLine* information using the integers in `results[i][0]` and `results[i][1]`. In other words, if results looks like this:

```
results = new Array(
  new Array(0, 1),    // Remember that the 0 element represents
  new Array(2, 2),    // the category number and the 1 element
  new Array(4, 1)     // represents the product number
  );
```

then the search results would contain the hairdryer (category 0, product 1), the purse (category 2, product 2), and the fries (category 4, product 1). Using these number pairs makes it easy to store a small amount of information and reference them later.

JavaScript Technique: Reusing a JavaScript Database

Happy is the coder who can use a bunch of data stored as JavaScript objects and arrays. Even happier is the coder who can access that information from a different application without re-inventing the wheel. That's what happens with Shopping Bag and the product search feature. Because of the relatively simple design, the database needs no changes when the search engine wants to search it.

A few lines of code changes in the search engine, and things are humming again like they always were. If you anticipate a situation like this, where your JavaScript database might be accessed from more than one application, keep it simple enough so that all apps can get at the data without extra coding.

All you have to do to get the product info on the screen is use the number pairs. The *for* loop in `formatResults()` prints the name, description, price, and PLU number by inserting the number pairs to the following variables:

```
ref.categorySet[results[i][0]].prodLine[results[i][1]].name
ref.categorySet[results[i][0]].prodLine[results[i][1]].description
ref.numberFormat(ref.categorySet[results[i][0]].prodLine[results[i][1]]
   price)
ref.categorySet[results[i][0]].prodLine[results[i][1]].plu
```

Each result is displayed with the above values contained in the string. A sample result would be:

Hairdryer

Fancy yellowish blast, and durable cord. No expense spared.
Price: $1.15 PLU Number: HAI1

The Code in the Link

The results have been displayed, but how can we code it so that the link utilizes the navigation system I've been preaching?

`formatResults()` offers the following solution:

```
'<A HREF="javascript: top.frames[1].reCall(' + results[i][0]+ ', ' +
   results[i][1] + ')">'
```

Each link uses a `javascript:` protocol to call function `reCall()`, which is the same function used to view products from the "Show All Categories" list. `reCall()` as you may "reCall" (sorry, I couldn't resist) expects two arguments—a category number and a product number. That's what we've been using in the search engine. All we have to do is to include each of the elements of the number pairs in the call, and we're set. So the hairdryer, for example would have the following link:

```
<A HREF="javascript: top.frames[1].reCall(0, 1)">Hairdryer</A>
```

Look what happens to the 0 and 1 when they show up at `reCall()`:

```
function reCall(cReset, pReset) {
   browseControl = true;
   curCLoc = cReset;
   curPLoc = pReset;
   display(0, 0);
   }
```

Variable *curCLoc* is set to the value of the category number in *cReset*; likewise, with *curPLoc* and *pReset*. The search engine coexists with the rest of Shopping Bag, and there were very few adjustments needed.

Step 5: Changing the Order/ Checking Out

When the user is either out of cash or doesn't see anything else desirable, it's time to head for the door. Clicking the "View/Change Bag" link opens the screen, similar to that in Figure 8-8. The user's shopping bag has to do more than just display his or her selections. Consider all the requirements:

- Display each product and its category, PLU number, and price per unit.

- Provide an interactive form to change product quantities, delete product selections, and recalculate product costs.

- Display running totals including the total for each product and quantity, the subtotal, and any applicable taxes.

It probably doesn't surprise you to know, then, that there are also several functions ready and waiting to accommodate these Shopping Bag needs. They are as follows:

`showBag()`

Display the contents of the shopping bag.

`genSelect()`

Generate dynamic select lists to change product quantities.

`runningTab()`

Manage the calculation and display of any prices or costs.

`numberFormat()`

Ensure accurate calculations and consistent displays in 0.00 format.

`round()`

Ensure accurate calculations.

`changeBag()`

Remove product selections from and change product quantities of the user's shopping bag.

Function `showBag()` gets the call as soon as the user follows the link. Look at lines 135–198:

```
function showBag() {
  if (shoppingBag.things.length == 0) {
    alert("Your bag is currently empty. Put some stuff in.");
    return;
    }
  gimmeControl = false;

  var header = '<HTML><HEAD><TITLE>Your Shopping Bag</TITLE>' +
    '</HEAD><BODY BGCOLOR=FFFFFF ' +
      'onLoad="parent.frames[1].runningTab(document.forms[0]);">';

  var intro = '<H2>Your Shopping Bag!!!</H2><FORM onReset="' +
    'setTimeout(\'parent.frames[1].runningTab(document.forms[0])\', ' +
    '25);">';

  var tableTop = '<TABLE BORDER=1 CELLSPACING=0 CELLPADDING=5>' +
    '<TR><TH><B>Index' +
    '<TH><B>Product<TH><B>Category' +
    '<TH><B>PLU<TH><B>Unit Price' +
    '<TH><B>Quantity<TH><B>Product Total' +
    '<TH><B>Remove' +
    '</TR>';

  var itemStr = '';
  for (var i = 0; i < shoppingBag.things.length; i++) {
    itemStr += '<TR>' +
      '<TD ALIGN=CENTER>' + (i + 1) + '</TD>' +
      '<TD>' + shoppingBag.things[i].name + '</TD>' +
      '<TD>' + shoppingBag.things[i].category + '</TD>' +
      '<TD>' + shoppingBag.things[i].plu + '</TD>' +
      '<TD ALIGN=RIGHT>$' +
```

```
          parent.frames[1].round(shoppingBag.things[i].price) + '</TD>' +
          '<TD ALIGN=CENTER>' +
          parent.frames[1].genSelect(shoppingBag.things[i].price,
          shoppingBag.things[i].itemQty, i) + '</TD>' +
          '<TD ALIGN=CENTER><INPUT TYPE=TEXT SIZE=10 VALUE="' +
          parent.frames[1].numberFormat(shoppingBag.things[i].price *
          shoppingBag.things[i].itemQty) + '" onFocus="this.blur();"></TD>' +
          '<TD ALIGN=CENTER><INPUT TYPE=CHECKBOX></TD></TR>';
      }

   var tableBottom = '<TR>' +
     '<TD ALIGN=RIGHT COLSPAN=6>SubTotal:</TD>' +
     '<TD ALIGN=CENTER><INPUT TYPE=TEXT SIZE=10 NAME="subtotal" ' +
     'onFocus="this.blur();"></TD></TR><TR>' +
     '<TD ALIGN=RIGHT COLSPAN=6> + 6% Tax:</TD>' +
     '<TD ALIGN=CENTER><INPUT TYPE=TEXT SIZE=10 NAME="tax" ' +
     'onFocus="this.blur();"></TD></TR><TR>' +
     '<TD ALIGN=RIGHT COLSPAN=6> + 2% Shipping:</TD>' +
     '<TD ALIGN=CENTER><INPUT TYPE=TEXT SIZE=10 NAME="ship" ' +
     'onFocus="this.blur();"></TD></TR>' +
     '<TR><TD ALIGN=RIGHT COLSPAN=3>' +
     '<INPUT TYPE=BUTTON VALUE="Check Out" ' +
     'onClick="parent.frames[1].checkOut(this.form);"></TD>' +
     '<TD ALIGN=RIGHT><INPUT TYPE=RESET VALUE="Reset Qtys"></TD>' +
     '<TD ALIGN=RIGHT><INPUT TYPE=BUTTON VALUE="Change Bag" ' +
     'onClick="parent.frames[1].changeBag(this.form, true);"></TD>' +
     '<TD ALIGN=RIGHT>Total:</TD><TD ALIGN=CENTER>' +
     '<INPUT TYPE=TEXT NAME="total" SIZE=10 onFocus="this.blur();">' +
     '</TD></TR>';

   var footer = '</TABLE></FORM></BODY></HTML>';
   infoStr = header + intro + tableTop + itemStr + tableBottom + footer;
   parent.frames[0].location.replace('javascript:
      parent.frames[1].infoStr');
   }
```

You'll see that **showBag()** does nothing more than generate the table and form you see in Figure 8-8. However, **showBag()** must first verify that there is something in the shopping bag to display:

```
if (shoppingBag.things.length == 0) {
  alert("Your bag is currently empty. Put some stuff in.");
  return;
  }
```

If **things.length** equals 0, then the user hasn't put anything in the bag. There is no use continuing. If the user's bag contains at least one thing, the process continues. Lines 140–154 set variables *header, intro,* and *tableTop* to the top of the table with the headings and necessary columns. You can see that **showBag()** calls several other functions:

```
gimmeControl = false;
var header = '<HTML><HEAD><TITLE>Your Shopping Bag</TITLE>' +
```

```
'</HEAD><BODY BGCOLOR=FFFFFF ' +
'onLoad="parent.frames[1].runningTab(document.forms[0]);">';

var intro = '<H2>Your Shopping Bag!!!</H2><FORM onReset=' +
'"setTimeout(\'parent.frames[1].runningTab(document.forms[0])\', ' +
'25);">';

var tableTop = '<TABLE BORDER=1 CELLSPACING=0 CELLPADDING=5>' +
'<TR><TH><B>Index' +
'<TH><B>Product<TH><B>Category' +
'<TH><B>PLU<TH><B>Unit Price' +
'<TH><B>Quantity<TH><B>Product Total' +
'<TH><B>Remove' +
'</TR>';
```

Everything generated is pretty static, except for the *onLoad* event handler call to `parent.frames[1].runningTab()`. We'll see how that works in a moment. When the table header info has been established, it's time to iterate through all the products in the user's shopping bag. As you might have guessed, that `showBag()` makes `things.length` iterations, and constructs a table row full of data for each. Here is the code again in lines 155–174:

```
var itemStr = '';
for (var i = 0; i < shoppingBag.things.length; i++) {
  itemStr += '<TR>' +
    '<TD ALIGN=CENTER>' + (i + 1) + '</TD>' +
    '<TD>' + shoppingBag.things[i].name + '</TD>' +
    '<TD>' + shoppingBag.things[i].category + '</TD>' +
    '<TD>' + shoppingBag.things[i].plu + '</TD>' +
    '<TD ALIGN=RIGHT>$' +
    parent.frames[1].round(shoppingBag.things[i].price) + '</TD>' +
    '<TD ALIGN=CENTER>' +
    parent.frames[1].genSelect(shoppingBag.things[i].price,
    shoppingBag.things[i].itemQty, i) + '</TD>' +
    '<TD ALIGN=CENTER><INPUT TYPE=TEXT SIZE=10 VALUE="' +
    parent.frames[1].numberFormat(shoppingBag.things[i].price *
    shoppingBag.things[i].itemQty) + '" onFocus="this.blur();"></TD>' +
    '<TD ALIGN=CENTER><INPUT TYPE=CHECKBOX></TD>' +
    '</TR>';
}
```

Making Select Lists

To match the table headers just created, the *for* loop creates a product index column (so that you can count the products one by one), a name, the category, the PLU, the price per unit, a quantity select list, a total cost for the quantity, and even a checkbox to remove the product. Each of these is contained in its own **TD** tag. The creation of the quantity select list is more involved than usual, and worth a closer look. The list is created by function `genSelect()`. There are other versions

in this book that you're probably familiar with. Here is yet another take in lines
200–210:

```
function genSelect(priceAgr, qty, idx) {
    var selStr = '<SELECT onChange="this.form.elements[' + (idx * 3 + 1) +
        '].value = this.options[this.selectedIndex].value; ' +
        'parent.frames[1].runningTab(this.form);">';
    for (var i = 1; i <= 10; i++) {
        selStr += '<OPTION VALUE="' + numberFormat(i * priceAgr) + '"' +
            (i == qty ? ' SELECTED' : '') + '>' + i;
    }
    selStr += '</SELECT>';
    return selStr;
}
```

This function accepts three arguments—the product price, the current quantity,
and the number (which is the value of *i* in the current *for* loop of showBag()) to
access the text field that will be printed next to the select list. I have preset the
maximum quantity of products that a user can order as 10. You can increase that
number as high as you like. To create this list, genSelect() iterates from 1–10
inclusive, and creates an OPTION tag out of the following syntax, which is assigned
cumulatively to *selStr*:

```
selStr += '<OPTION VALUE="' + numberFormat(i * priceAgr) + '"' +
    (i == qty ? ' SELECTED' : '') + '>' + i;
```

Each OPTION tag created is pretty simple. Its VALUE attribute is set to the per-unit
price of the product multiplied by *i*, which is the quantity associated with that
option. For example, a product valued at $1.00 per unit would generate the fol-
lowing OPTION tags:

```
<OPTION VALUE="1.00" SELECTED>1
<OPTION VALUE="2.00">2
<OPTION VALUE="3.00">3
<OPTION VALUE="4.00">4
<OPTION VALUE="5.00">5
<OPTION VALUE="6.00">6
<OPTION VALUE="7.00">7
<OPTION VALUE="8.00">8
<OPTION VALUE="9.00">9
<OPTION VALUE="10.00">10
```

Another thing: if *i* is equal to the current quantity (*qty*) of the product, the OPTION
tag of the same quantity is marked as SELECTED. Since the default value of every
item initially put in the shopping bag is 1, the OPTION tag with the text 1 is always
selected. This comes in very handy when the user wants to make changes in
quantity. We'll get there shortly.

I skipped the original value of *selStr*. Allow me to backtrack:

```
var selStr = '<SELECT onChange="this.form.elements[" + (idx * 3 + 1) +
    '].value = this.options[this.selectedIndex].value; ' +
    'parent.frames[1].runningTab(this.form);">';
```

Each select list has associated with it an *onChange* event handler that changes the value of `elements[(idx * 3 )+ 1]` to the value of the current selected option. Remember that each `OPTION` value is the product of the product's unit price times 1-10. Using the $1.00 example from above, if the user chooses 4 from the select list, the value of `elements[(idx * 3) + 1]` will change to 4.00. That's a little tricky. Which form element is that? To help answer that, review the code in `showBag()` at lines 166–167:

```
parent.frames[1].genSelect(shoppingBag.things[i].price,
    shoppingBag.things[i].itemQty, i)
```

Now look at the arguments that `genSelect()` expects in line 200:

```
function genSelect(priceAgr, qty, idx) {
```

From both of these, you can see that the value of *idx* is always the current value of *i*, which is initialized and incremented by 1 in line 156. If the user has 10 products in the shopping bag, *idx* will range from 1–10. Therefore, the select tags that `showBag()` will create will look as follows:

```
<!-- For the 1st Product //-->
<SELECT onChange='this.form.elements[1].value =
    this.options[this.selectedIndex].value;
    parent.frames[1].runningTab(this.form);'>
<!--For the 2nd Product //-->
<SELECT onChange='this.form.elements[4].value =
    this.options[this.selectedIndex].value;
    parent.frames[1].runningTab(this.form);'>
<!--For the 3rd Product //-->
<SELECT onChange='this.form.elements[10].value =
    this.options[this.selectedIndex].value;
    parent.frames[1].runningTab(this.form);'>
```

. . . and so on. Think about it. `form.elements[1]` is the text field immediately following the first select list. Or at least it will be: at the time *onChange* event handler was created, that field didn't exist. `form.elements[4]` refers to the text field immediately following the select list in the next row. Referencing the text field is a matter of calculating which element index it will have after the form has been created. Here is how I came up with `(idx * 3) + 1`.

Each product selected is displayed in one table row. Each table row has the three form elements in the same order:

* A select list for the quantity

* A text field to display the product total

* A checkbox for removing the product

That means the first text field is `elements[1]`; the next is `elements[4]`. The text field, therefore, is the second element in each group of three. `genSelect()` creates the correct code by continually multiplying by 3 and adding 1.

Keeping Track of the Bill

How about the rest of the code in the **onChange** event handler? Not only does this event handler populate the respective product total field with the correct total, but it calls **runningTab()** to recalculate the total cost of the purchase. Here is **runningTab()** in lines 212–227:

```
function runningTab(formObj) {
  var subTotal = 0;
  for (var i = 0; i < shoppingBag.things.length; i++) {
    subTotal += parseFloat(formObj.elements[(i * 3) + 1].value);
  }
  formObj.subtotal.value = numberFormat(subTotal);
  formObj.tax.value = numberFormat(subTotal * shoppingBag.taxRate);
  formObj.ship.value = numberFormat(subTotal * shoppingBag.shipRate);
  formObj.total.value = numberFormat(subTotal +
  round(subTotal * shoppingBag.taxRate) + round(subTotal *
    shoppingBag.shipRate));
  shoppingBag.subTotal = formObj.subtotal.value;
  shoppingBag.taxTotal = formObj.tax.value;
  shoppingBag.shipTotal = formObj.ship.value;
  shoppingBag.bagTotal = formObj.total.value;
  }
```

This function is pretty easy. It performs three basic operations:

1. Calculate and display the subtotal, which is the sum of all the product totals (lines 213–217).

2. Calculate and display the sales tax, shipping charges, and grand total (lines 218–222).

3. Store those totals in the *shoppingBag* object properties (lines 223–226).

Functions **numberFormat()** and **round()** ensure that all the math is done correctly and displayed in 0.00 or .00 format. Here they are in lines 229–239:

```
function numberFormat(amount) {
  var rawNumStr = round(amount) + '';
  rawNumStr = (rawNumStr.charAt(0) == '.' ? '0' + rawNumStr : rawNumStr);
  if (rawNumStr.charAt(rawNumStr.length - 3) == '.') {
    return rawNumStr
    }
  else if (rawNumStr.charAt(rawNumStr.length - 2) == '.') {
    return rawNumStr + '0';
    }
  else { return rawNumStr + '.00'; }
  }
```

numberFormat() simply returns a rounded-off version of **amount** in 0.00 format. This is accomplished by calling **round()** and passing **amount** as an argument. Function **round()** rounds the number to the default two decimal places, as shown here:

```
function round(number,decPlace) {
  decPlace = (!decPlace ? 2 : decPlace);
  return Math.round(number *
    Math.pow(10,decPlace)) / Math.pow(10,decPlace);
  }
```

JavaScript Technique: Number Rounding and String Conversion

You'd think that asking JavaScript to `alert()` the product of 1.15 * 3, the price per unit of fries times a quantity of 3, would not be a big deal. We all know it is going to be 3.45, right? Try it, though. You'll get 3.4499999999999997. Where did that come from? JavaScript represents floating numbers with signed 64-bit IEEE-754 floating-point values. The bits of precision from floating-point values can cause the result. If you'd like to know more, check out the following URLs:

http://help.netscape.com/kb/client/970930-1.html

http://www.psc.edu/general/software/packages/ieee/ieee.html

Whatever the cause, we need a workaround. How about asking JavaScript to alert the product of 115 * 3? Notice this is 100 times the amount of the previous multiplication, which is 345. That's the same answer JavaScript reports, too. Arithmetic works fine for integers. The workaround here is to perform arithmetic on integers, then convert the JavaScript *Number* to a JavaScript *String*, inserting the decimal point where it needs to go. That is exactly what functions `numberFormat()` and `round()` do together. If you need to perform more calculations, you can change the *String* back to a number, remove the decimal point, and you're back in business.

If the argument named *amount*, which is a number, equals itself rounded off with `Math.round()`, then *amount* is an integer, so it needs .00 added on the end to have the correct format. If `amount * 10` equals `Math.round(amount *10)`, that means *amount* is in 0.0 format and needs 0 concatenated to it to conform. Otherwise, the amount has a value that extends at least to the hundredths place (.00). No string manipulation is necessary.

Wrapping Up showBag(): Displaying the Totals and More

Now each selected product has its own table row with widgets for computing quantities and for removing them from the shopping bag. It's time to add the last couple of rows. These rows contain form fields to display the subtotal, tax totals, and grand total. They also contain user action buttons "Check Out," "Reset Qtys," and "Change Bag." Here are lines 175–194:

```
var tableBottom = '<TR>' +
  '<TD ALIGN=RIGHT COLSPAN=6>SubTotal:</TD>' +
  '<TD ALIGN=CENTER><INPUT TYPE=TEXT SIZE=10 NAME="subtotal" ' +
  'onFocus="this.blur();"></TD></TR><TR>' +
  '<TD ALIGN=RIGHT COLSPAN=6> + 6% Tax:</TD><TD ALIGN=CENTER>' +
  '<INPUT TYPE=TEXT SIZE=10 NAME="tax" onFocus="this.blur();">' +
  '</TD></TR><TR><TD ALIGN=RIGHT COLSPAN=6> + 2% Shipping:</TD>' +
  '<TD ALIGN=CENTER><INPUT TYPE=TEXT SIZE=10 NAME="ship" ' +
  'onFocus="this.blur();"></TD></TR><TR>' +
  '<TD ALIGN=RIGHT COLSPAN=3><INPUT TYPE=BUTTON VALUE="Check Out" ' +
  'onClick="parent.frames[1].checkOut(this.form);"></TD>' +
  '<TD ALIGN=RIGHT><INPUT TYPE=RESET VALUE="Reset Qtys"></TD>' +
  '<TD ALIGN=RIGHT><INPUT TYPE=BUTTON VALUE="Change Bag" ' +
  'onClick="parent.frames[1].changeBag(this.form, true);"></TD>' +
  '<TD ALIGN=RIGHT>Total:</TD><TD ALIGN=CENTER>' +
  '<INPUT TYPE=TEXT NAME="total" SIZE=10 onFocus="this.blur();">' +
  '</TD></TR>';
var footer = '</TABLE></FORM></BODY></HTML>';
```

Upon reviewing this HTML, you can see that the fields to display the totals are initially empty. The call to **runningTab()** in the *onLoad* event of this document will populate those fields with the required values shortly. Also notice that each field has the following code:

```
onFocus='this.blur();'
```

Since there is no need for the user to modify these fields, clicking the mouse in the text field immediately blurs the field. This code keeps people from changing the text, and is also in the product total input fields.

There are three buttons: "Check Out," "Reset Qtys," and "Change Bag." Here is a look at each.

The "Check Out" button

When the user has had enough, he or she just needs to enter payment information and send off the order. Clicking this button calls function **checkOut()**. This function does two things:

- Generates an order form to enter payment information

- Generates additional **HIDDEN** fields that represent all of the selected products

The function is long, so let's take it in two parts. Here are lines 263–312:

```
function checkOut(formObj) {
  gimmeControl = false;
  if(!confirm("Do you have every product in the right quantity " +
    "you need? Remember that you have to choose Change Bag to remove " +
    "products or change quantities. If so, choose OK to check out.")) {
```

```
    return;
    }
  if(shoppingBag.things.length == 0) {
    showStore();
    return;
    }
  var header = '<HTML><TITLE>Shopping Bag Check Out</TITLE>' +
    '<BODY BGCOLOR=FFFFFF>';
  var intro = '<H2>Shopping Bag Check Out</H2><FORM METHOD=POST " +
    'ACTION="http://your_web_server/cgi-bin/bag.cgi" ' +
    'onSubmit="return parent.frames[1].cheapCheck(this);">';

  var shipInfo = '<TABLE BORDER=0 CELLSPACING=0 CELLPADDING=5>' +
    '<TR><TD><B>Shipping Information</TD></TR><TR>' +
    '<TD>First Name</TD><TD><INPUT TYPE=TEXT NAME="fname"></TD></TR>' +
    '<TR><TD>Last Name</TD><TD><INPUT TYPE=TEXT NAME="lname">' +
    '</TD></TR><TR><TD>Company Name</TD>' +
    '<TD><INPUT TYPE=TEXT NAME="cname"></TD></TR><TR>' +
    '<TD>Street Address1</TD><TD><INPUT TYPE=TEXT NAME="saddress1">' +
    '</TD></TR><TR><TD>Street Address2</TD><TD>' +
    '<INPUT TYPE=TEXT NAME="saddress2"></TD></TR><TR>' +
    '<TD>City</TD><TD><INPUT TYPE=TEXT NAME="city"></TD></TR>' +
    '<TR><TD>State/Province</TD><TD><INPUT TYPE=TEXT NAME="stpro">' +
    '</TD></TR><TR><TD>Country</TD><TD>' +
    '<INPUT TYPE=TEXT NAME="country"></TD></TR><TR>' +
    '<TD>Zip/Mail Code</TD><TD><INPUT TYPE=TEXT NAME="zip"></TD>' +
    '</TR><TR><TD><BR><BR></TD></TR></TABLE>';

  var payInfo = '<TABLE BORDER=0 CELLSPACING=0 CELLPADDING=5><TR>' +
    '<TD><B>Payment Information</TD></TR><TR>' +
    '<TD>Credit Card Type:       </TD>' +
    '<TD>Visa <INPUT TYPE=RADIO NAME="ctype" VALUE="visa" CHECKED> ' +
    '      ' +
    'Amex <INPUT TYPE=RADIO NAME='ctype' VALUE="amex"> ' +
    '      ' +
    'Discover <INPUT TYPE=RADIO NAME="ctype" VALUE="disc"> ' +
    '      </TD></TR><TR>' +
    '<TD>Credit Card Number</TD><TD><INPUT TYPE=TEXT NAME="cnumb">' +
    '</TD></TR><TR><TD>Expiration Date</TD>' +
    '<TD><INPUT TYPE=TEXT NAME="edate"></TD></TR><TR>' +
    '<TD><INPUT TYPE=SUBMIT VALUE="Send Order"></TD>' +
    '<TD><INPUT TYPE=RESET VALUE="Clear Info"></TD></TR></TABLE>';
```

It is pretty long, but all of it is 100% static. The code here provides the check-out form as shown in Figure 8-8. The form contains fields for the user to enter basic payment information. Each field is uniquely named so that the server-side processing script can correctly identify each piece of info.

The last part of function **checkOut()** prepares the **HIDDEN** fields to record all the user product selections. Here are lines 314–319:

```
  for (var i = 0; i < shoppingBag.things.length; i++) {
    itemInfo += '<INPUT TYPE=HIDDEN NAME="prod' + i +
      '" VALUE="' + shoppingBag.things[i].plu + '-' +
      shoppingBag.things[i].itemQty + '">';
```

This generates a HIDDEN field named *prod* + the value of *i*. The value is set to the syntax of *PLU-quantity*. So if the user requests two orders of fries, the value attribute for this HIDDEN field would be VALUE="FRI1-2". After a HIDDEN field for each selected product and quantity is created, checkOut() concatenates all the totals as the value of a HIDDEN field.

Lines 320–327 show how:

```
var totalInfo = '<INPUT TYPE=HIDDEN NAME="subtotal" VALUE="' +
  shoppingBag.subTotal + '">' +
  '<INPUT TYPE=HIDDEN NAME="taxtotal" VALUE="' +
  shoppingBag.taxTotal + '">' +
  '<INPUT TYPE=HIDDEN NAME="shiptotal" VALUE="' +
  shoppingBag.shipTotal + '">' +
  '<INPUT TYPE=HIDDEN NAME="bagtotal" VALUE="' +
  shoppingBag.bagTotal + '">';
```

Add a "Send Order" button to submit the information and a "Clear Info" button to clear the form, and that accounts for the entire check-out form. Before we move on, notice that the *onSubmit* event handler of this on-the-fly form calls function cheapCheck(). This function does nothing more than check to make sure that when the form is submitted none of the fields in which the user has to enter information is left empty.

Here are lines 337–352:

```
function cheapCheck(formObj) {
  for (var i = 0; i < formObj.length; i++) {
    if (formObj[i].type == "text" && formObj.elements[i].value == "") {
      alert ("You must complete all fields.");
      return false;
      }
    }
  if(!confirm("If all your information is correct, choose OK to send " +
    "your order, or choose Cancel to make changes.")) {
    return false;
    }
  alert("Thank you. We'll be living off your hard-earned money soon.");
  shoppingBag = new Bag();
  showStore();
  return true;
  }
```

If any of the fields is blank, cheapCheck() alerts the user, and returns false to prevent submitting the form. You'll probably want to custom-design a form validation function to suit your own needs, but at least this gives you a starting point. Notice, too, that if the user has filled out the form correctly, that variable *shoppingBag* is set to a fresh new Bag(), and the user is redirected to the display of all Shopping Bag categories, performed by calling showStore().

Finishing the Display

Now that showBag() has set variables *header, intro, tableTop, itemStr, totalInfo, tableBottom,* and *footer* to all the values needed to create a cohesive display, the function puts all that information on the screen. Check out lines 195–197:

```
infoStr = header + intro + tableTop + itemStr + tableBottom + footer;
parent.frames[0].location.replace('javascript:parent.frames[1].infoStr');
```

What About the Server Side?

The shopping experience has come to an end on the client side. So how does the user actually pay for and receive the goods? You will ultimately need some type of server-side processing to log the orders into, say, a database for processing. I've included a bare-bones CGI script written in Perl that creates a unique ASCII file on the server for each transaction that occurs and writes all of the product and payment information to that file. You can find it in *ch08\bag.cgi.* The following procedure shows you how to get it working for Shopping Bag. It assumes that your web server has Perl installed and that the directory in which *bag.pl* resides has write and execute permissions enabled.

1. Copy *bag.cgi* to the folder (say, *cgi-bin*) where you can run CGI scripts.

2. In line 279, change the ACTION attribute to the URL of wherever you put *bag. cgi* on your web server.

When shoppers choose "Check Out," *bag.cgi* will be called to process the information and return a basic confirmation of receipt. By the way, for secure transactions, you'll also want to use an SSL (Secure Socket Layer) server or some type of encryption to exchange sensitive credit card and ordering information between the server and the client.

"Reset Qtys"

This is simply a "Reset" button that clears the form of any changes. If you choose "Change Bag," however, you change the contents and quantities of the bag permanently.

"Change Bag"

Suppose the user has made several changes to product quantities and also checked the "Remove" checkbox in a couple of other products. Choosing "Change Bag" registers those changes, then displays the bag again, reflecting the new contents and quantities. Here is function changeBag() in lines 246–261:

```
function changeBag(formObj, showAgain) {
  var tempBagArray = new Array();
  for (var i = 0; i < shoppingBag.things.length; i++) {
```

```
    if (!formObj.elements[(i * 3) + 2].checked) {
      tempBagArray[tempBagArray.length] = shoppingBag.things[i];
      tempBagArray[tempBagArray.length - 1].itemQty =
        formObj.elements[i * 3].selectedIndex + 1;
      }
    }
  shoppingBag.things = tempBagArray;
  if(shoppingBag.things.length == 0) {
    alert("You've emptied your bag. Put some stuff in.");
    parent.frames[1].showStore();
    }
  else { showBag(); }
  }
```

The technique is fairly simple:

1. Create an empty array called *tempBagArray.*

2. Iterate through each element (a *product*) of the *things* array.

3. If the associated checkbox is not checked, add it as the next element of *tempBagArray.*

4. Set the quantity of the most recently added product of *tempBagArray* to the quantity selected by the user in the associated select list.

5. Set *things* equal to *tempBagArray,* and redisplay the bag contents.

Referencing the respective checkbox is done the same way that function `runningTab()` set the value of each product total. Each following checkbox is accessed by the element of index `(i * 3) + 2`. If there are no elements in *tempBagArray* after all the iterations, then the user has deleted all the products from the bag. The user is reminded of this and told to load up once again.

The Forgotten Functions

We've gone through almost everything, except for three functions that have not yet been covered. They play a fairly small role, but are worth noting. They are `portal()`, `help()`, `freshStart()`. Here is `portal()` at lines 49–52:

```
function portal() {
  gimmeControl = false;
  parent.frames[0].location.href = "search/index.html";
  }
```

Since displaying the product search engine interface won't display any products, variable *gimmeControl* is set to `false` before loading the *search/index.html.* It's the same routine for `help()` in lines 354–357:

```
function help() {
  gimmeControl = false;
  parent.frames[0].location.href = "intro.html";
  }
```

The only difference is, `parent.frames[0]` loads *intro.html* instead. Finally, there's `freshStart()`:

```
function freshStart() {
  if(parent.frames[0].location.href != "intro.html") { help(); }
  }
```

Function `freshStart()` makes certain that every time the user loads (more specifically, reloads) *shopset.html*, `parent.frames[0]` always begins with *intro.html*. You can find this in the *onLoad* event handler in line 10.

Potential Extensions

Even a little bit of creativity can take you places with this application. Here are a few of the possibilities that come to mind:

- Make "smarter" products.
- Add refined search capabilities.
- Add cookie features for frequent shoppers.

Making Smarter Products

It's not as though each product has its own IQ. Suppose, however, you added a property, an array, to the *product* constructor that held the names and category/product number pairs of those products related to the one currently in view. The *product* constructor might then look like so:

```
function product(name, description, price, unit, related) {
  this.name = name;
  this.description = description;
  this.price = price;
  this.unit = unit;
  this.related = related;
  this.plu = name.substring(0, 3).toUpperCase() +
    parseInt(price).toString();
  this.icon = new Image();
  return this;
  }
```

The argument *related* represents an array that you can assign to the *related* property. Whenever the user views a product, you could then iterate through the *related* elements, generating links to them. This is a way to cross-market your products.

If this sounds a little new to you, visit amazon.com. Search for a book on one of your favorite topics. When you click on one of the links from the results list, the page profiling your book will also provide links to other books purchased by those who bought the book you're viewing.

Add Refined Search Capabilities

This goes back to extending the search engine capabilities, but there are several ways you can modify it for Shopping Bag. First, consider adding the Boolean AND search capability. It won't be that difficult. Just copy function `requireAll()` from the original application in Chapter 1, then modify it as described earlier for `allowAny()`. You'll also have to make an adjustment in `validate()` to indicate which of the search functions to use.

Instead of searching the entire product database, the user might want to search only one or more categories. Consider adding a multiple select list in *nav.html*:

```
<SELECT MULTIPLE SIZE=5>
<OPTION VALUE="Appliances">Appliances
<OPTION VALUE="Building">Building
<OPTION VALUE="Clothing">Clothing
<OPTION VALUE="Electronics">Electronics
<OPTION VALUE="Food">Food
<OPTION VALUE="Hardware">Hardware
<OPTION VALUE="Music">Music
</SELECT>
```

Though it's hard-coded here, you could employ the logic similar to that in `genSelect()` to achieve a more dynamic result. When the search is performed, you can search only those products in the categories that the user has selected, thereby narrowing the search.

Another feature you could add is to be able to search by price range. If a shopper is looking for products less than $50, more than $100, or perhaps between $50 and $100, you could allow flags such as >, <, >=, and <=. You will have to make changes in `validate()` and `formatResults()` in order to accommodate.

Adding Cookies

Suppose your site has products that change rapidly. Maybe it's common for shoppers to return frequently. It sure would be convenient if they didn't have to fill out their payment information every time they checked out. Why not add the cookie functions from Chapter 7, *Cookie-Based User Preferences?* That way, the user's information is kept on the client browser and can be accessed and used to populate the payment form. This extra functionality is somewhat challenging, but you'll feel like a JavaScript hero when you finish. Though functions `GetCookie()` and `SetCookie()` enable you to write to and extract from the cookie, you'll need a function to assemble the form field data (probably as a single string) and a function to populate the form fields once the data has been extracted.

Ciphers in JavaScript

If you just finished the previous chapter, this one will give your brain a little breather. This chapter is lighter and deals with an application based on pure, simple fun—ciphering techniques with JavaScript. The application jumbles text messages into what seems like a bunch of junk, meaningful only to those who possess the key to reveal its secret.

This interface displayed in Figure 9-1 is fairly simple. With the Caesar cipher selected, it's just a paragraph describing the cipher, a select list used to choose a number key, and a text area to enter text to encipher and decipher.

The text "JavaScript is the scripting language of choice across the planet, don't you agree?" is entered in the text area. Selecting 6 from the Shift list, then choosing the "Encipher" button yields the scrambled text you see in Figure 9-2. Here it is again:

```
pg1gyixovz oy znk yixovzotm rgtm0gmk ul inuoik jutz 4u0 gmxkk
```

Choosing "Decipher" returns the text to its original form. Notice that the text is returned in all lowercase. The Vigenere cipher works about the same way. Choose "Vigenere Cipher" from the cipher list at the top, and Figure 9-3 is what you'll see.

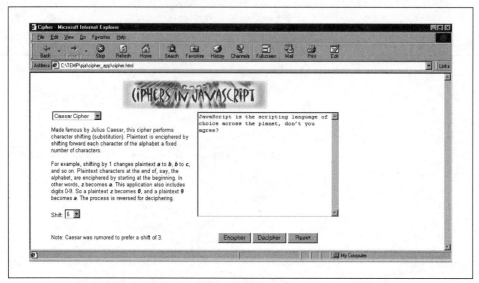

Figure 9-1. The cipher interface

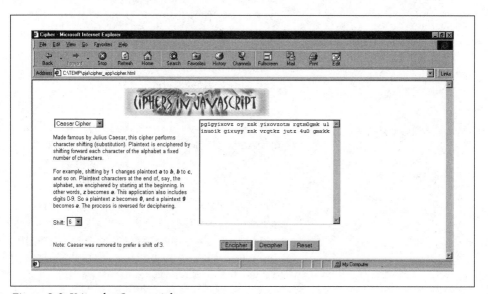

Figure 9-2. Using the Caesar cipher

With this cipher, there is no select list to choose a number key. This time, there is a field to enter a word or phrase as the key. Check out how the term "code junky" ciphers the original text. It's listed here and also shown in Figure 9-4:

```
loye1w4sdv 1w duo uqumydvx4 zdrpenq2 2i 111s0g dg0852 vvh y5nx2v gswd 8cw
dk0yr
```

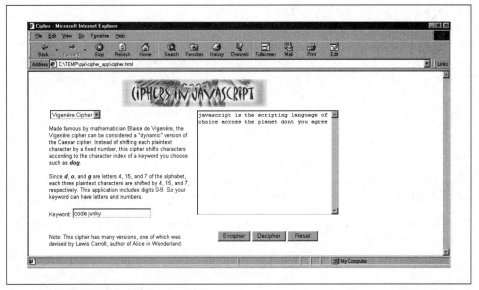

Figure 9-3. The Vigenere cipher interface

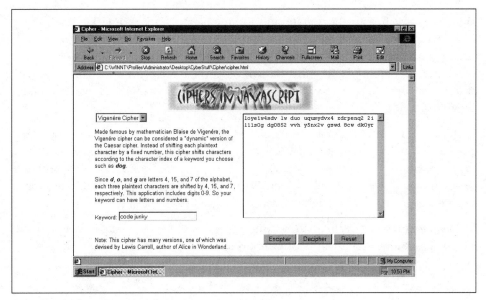

Figure 9-4. The Vigenere cipher in action

Of course, choosing "Decipher" using "code junky" as the key returns the text to meaningful form. Since you might be new to the concept of ciphers, here's a crash course on the subject. It explains cipher basics and offers details about the two ciphers used in the application—the Caesar cipher and the Vigenére cipher.

How Ciphers Work

So, what is a cipher anyway? A cipher is an algorithm or set of algorithms that systematically convert a sender's intended message text to what appears to be meaningless text, which can be converted back to the sender's original message only by authorized recipients. The following terms and definitions will help you understand ciphering and deciphering in general and the code behind them.

The term *plaintext* refers the sender's original message. The meaning in plaintext is what the sender wants to convey to the recipient(s).

The term *ciphertext* refers to plaintext whose appearance has been encrypted, or algorithmically changed. Ciphertext becomes plaintext once it has been decrypted.

Many ciphers use one or more keys. A *key* is string of text or bits used to encrypt or decrypt data. RSA Data Security, Inc. (*http://www.rsa.com/*), a leading encryption technology firm, states that a key determines the mapping of the plaintext to the ciphertext. A key could be just about anything, such as the word "cleveland," the phrase "winners never quit, quitters never win," the binary number 10011011, or even some wild string, such as %_-.;,(<<*&^.

Ciphers in which both the sender and the recipient use the same key to encrypt and decrypt the message are said to be part of a *symmetric-key cryptosystem.* Ciphers in which data is encrypted and decrypted with a pair of keys—one freely distributed to the public, the other known only to the recipient—are said to be part of a *public-key cryptosystem.* Ciphers in this application employ a symmetric-key cryptosystem.

There are hundreds of documented ciphers. Some date back thousands of years, devised by great leaders or scientists of the past; others date back to only last week, devised by some geeky teenager who experienced epiphany after setting a personal high score on Tomb Raider. Whatever the source, ciphers fall into three general categories: concealment, transposition, and substitution.

Concealment ciphers include the plaintext within the ciphertext. It is up to the recipient to know which letters or symbols to exclude from the ciphertext in order to yield the plaintext. Here is an example of a concealment cipher:

```
i2132i5321k34e1245ch456oc12o1234at567e
```

Remove all the numbers, and you'll have *i like chocolate.* How about this one?

```
Larry even appears very excited. No one worries.
```

The first letter from each word reveals the message *leave now.* Both are easy, indeed, but many people have crafted more ingenious ways of concealing the messages. By the way, this type of cipher doesn't even need ciphertext, such as that in the above examples. Consider the invisible drying ink that kids use to send secret messages. In a more extreme example, a man named Histiaeus, during 5th century B.C., shaved the head of a trusted slave, then tattooed the message onto his bald head. When the slave's hair grew back, Histiaeus sent the slave to the message's intended recipient, Aristagoros, who shaved the slave's head and read the message instructing him to revolt.

Transposition ciphers also retain the characters of the plaintext within the cipher-text. Ciphertext is created simply by changing the order of the existing plaintext characters. Try this one:

```
uo yn os dn ep ed yx al ag eh tf oy te fa se ht
```

Bunch those letters together, then reverse their order. You'll get the message "the safety of the galaxy depends on you."

Substitution ciphers replace each character of plaintext with another character or symbol. Consider this:

```
9-15-14-12-25-20-8-9-14-11-9-14-14-21-13-2-5-18-19
```

If you substitute each number with the associated letter of the alphabet, you'll reveal the phrase "I only think in numbers." (For example, "I" is the 9th letter of the alphabet, "o" is the 15th, etc.) Substitution ciphers can utilize just about any character set for encryption and decryption. Both ciphers in this application are substitution ciphers.

A Few Words on Cracking the Code

The ciphertext that this application generates can, at first glance, look remarkably complex. In reality, any decent cryptanalyst could break the cipher in a matter of minutes with only a pencil and paper. Fortunately, security is *much* more ensured by using such algorithms as the RSA, IDEA, and triple DES. I can't show you how to crack those, but I'll give you a hint about why simple substitution and transposi-tion ciphers are so vulnerable.

The primary weapon against these types of ciphers is letter-frequency distribution. That is, some letters show up more than others in everyday conversation in the English language. The most common letters in the English language, from most to least frequent, are E-T-N-R-O-A-I-S. The least common are J, K, Q, X, and Z.[*]

Another way to compromise a simple cipher is to analyze digraphs and trigraphs. A *digraph* is a two-character string, such as *ab* or *cd*. A trigraph is a three-letter string, such as *abc* or *bcd*. Digraphs and trigraphs also have high and low frequen-cies in the English language. The U.S. Army considers the following digraphs most frequent: *en, er, re, nt, th, on,* and *in*. The least frequent are *df, hu, ia, lt,* and *mp*.

---

[*] From the *U.S. Army Field Manual* 34-40-2.

For trigraphs, the most common are *ent, ion, and, ing, ive, tho,* and *for.* The least common are *eri, hir, iet, der,* and *dre.*

The most frequent letters, digraphs, and trigraphs not only hint at what many letters might be, but also indicate what they and surrounding letters probably are not. Consider how many digraphs and trigraphs you use in everyday conversation: *is, be, am, or, not, are, yes, the.* The list goes on. Even though the ciphers used in this application aren't top quality, they're still a lot of fun, and a great way to keep out the casual nosey intruder.

The Caesar Cipher

Used by Julius Caesar to communicate with his army general, this cipher is one of the first known to be used for securing messages. The algorithm here is simply to shift the letters of the alphabet between 1 and 25 places (from b-z) so that a shift of 3 causes a plaintext letter *a* to become a ciphertext *d*, and vice versa. Letters that are shifted past *z* resume at the beginning. In other words, a shift of 3 converts a plaintext *z* to a ciphertext *c*. The number is the key that both sending and receiving parties use to encipher and decipher the message.

Notice that once a key is chosen, each character always has the same corresponding plaintext or ciphertext character associated with it. For example, a shift of 3 means that the plaintext *a* is always a ciphertext *d*. That is, there is only one cipher alphabet. The Caesar cipher is said to be *monoalphabetic.*

The Vigenere Cipher

This cipher was proposed by mathematician Blaise de Vigenere in the 16th century. It is a *polyalphabetic* cipher because it uses more than one cipher alphabet. In other words, a plaintext *a* does not always equal a ciphertext *d*, as the Caesar cipher does with a shift of 3.

Instead of a number, this cipher utilizes a keyword. Suppose you want to cipher the plaintext *meet at midnight*, and you choose the keyword *vinegar.* The letters of the keyword are then lined up in succession with the letters of the plaintext, like so:

> *vine ga rvinegar*
> *meet at midnight*

OK. *V* is the 22nd letter in the alphabet. *I* is 9th. Letters *n, e, g, a,* and *r* are 14th, 5th, 7th, 1st, and 18th, respectively. So plaintext letter *m* is shifted 22, the first *e* is shifted 9, the second *e* is shifted 14, and so on. Here's what you get:

> *hmrx gt ddlammhk*

If you think about it, this cipher is like the Caesar cipher on the fly. A new Caesar is performed on every character.

If you want to learn more about ciphers, you can download a multitude of the once "classified" U.S. Army documents in PDF format at *http://www.und.nodak.edu/org/crypto/crypto/army.field.manual/separate.chaps/*.

This copy is stored on the web site of the Crypto Drop Box. Check out the home page at *http://www.und.nodak.edu/org/crypto/crypto/*. You'll find enough resources there to keep you busy for days.

Execution Requirements

This application uses JavaScript 1.2 and DHTML, so only browsers 4.x and higher are allowed to play. There is a lot of string matching and replacement, which makes JavaScript 1.2 really shine.

The Syntax Breakdown

Fortunately, this application requires only two files. Better yet, we'll only be looking at the code in one of them. The two files are *index.html* and *dhtml.js* (*dhtml.js* is covered in Chapter 6, *Implementing JavaScript Source Files*). Before we look at any code, let's consider a few abstract concepts about how this application might "look." This application is constructed from a very basic object-oriented perspective. The shopping cart in Chapter 8, *Shopping Bag: The JavaScript Shopping Cart*, covers another application that utilizes object orientation, but the cipher app takes that approach a little further.

There are two ciphers in this application. Each cipher has certain things in common with all other ciphers, no matter what kind of cipher each may be. Remember that there are three basic types of ciphers—concealment, transposition, and substitution. This application contains two substitution ciphers: the Caesar cipher and the Vigenére cipher. Figure 9-5 shows a basic structure of the hierarchy just described.

The figure shows that the *ConcealmentCipher*, *TranspositionCipher*, and *SubstitutionCipher* objects inherit everything from the *Cipher* object, somewhat like a subclass. Therefore, the Vigenére cipher and the Caesar cipher are instances of the *SubstitutionCipher* object and contain all its properties and methods.

For the sake of intellectual curiosity, let's see how this model can be extended. Figure 9-6 shows how other cipher types can easily be added to the hierarchy

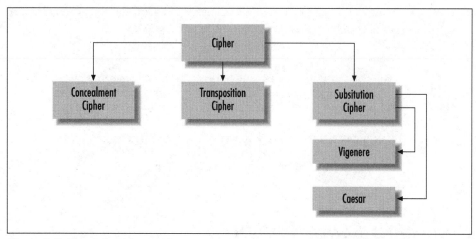

Figure 9-5. The cipher structure

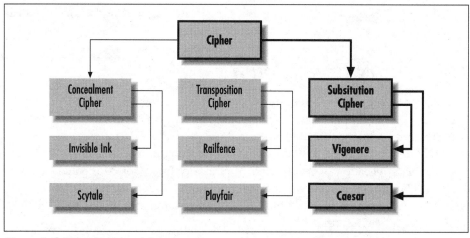

Figure 9-6. Extending the cipher structure

without redesigning anything. The bold portion of the structure identifies the part of the hierarchy used in the application.

As you can see, the number of cipher types and individual ciphers can be added to this structure, ad infinitum, without changing any of the existing code of the ciphers currently in place. You can also "subclass" the subclasses. Object-oriented design proves beneficial once again. Keep this in mind as we go through the supporting code in the next few pages. You'll see how easy it is to add more ciphers to the application without having to retool.

Let's take a look at *index.html* in Example 9-1.

Example 9-1. index.html

```
1 <HTML>
2 <HEAD>
3   <TITLE>Cipher</TITLE>
4 <STYLE TYPE="text/css">
5 <!--
6 BODY { margin-left: 50 px; font-family: arial; }
7 I { font-weight: bold; }
8 //-->
9 </STYLE>
10 <SCRIPT LANGUAGE="JavaScript1.2" SRC="dhtml.js"></SCRIPT>
11 <SCRIPT LANGUAGE="JavaScript1.2">
12 <!--
13
14 var caesar = '<FONT SIZE=2>Made famous by Julius Caesar, this cipher ' +
15   'performs character shifting (substitution). Plaintext is ' +
16   'enciphered by shifting forward each character of the alphabet a ' +
17   'fixed number of characters.<BR><BR>For example, shifting by 1 ' +
18   'changes plaintext <I>a</I> to <I>b</I>, <I>b</I> to <I>c</I>, ' +
19   'and so on. Plaintext characters at the end of, say, the alphabet, ' +
20   'are enciphered by starting at the beginning. In other words, ' +
21   '<I>z</I> becomes <I>a</I>. This application also includes digits ' +
22   '0-9. So a plaintext <I>z</I> becomes <I>0</I>, and a plaintext ' +
23   '<I>9</I> becomes <I>a</I>. The process is reversed for deciphering.' +
24   '<BR><FORM>Shift: ' +
25   genSelect('Shift', 35, 0, 0) +
26   '</FORM><BR>Note: Caesar was rumored to prefer a shift of 3.';
27
28 var vigenere = '<FONT SIZE=2>Made famous by mathematician Blaise de ' +
29   'Vigenere, the Vigenere cipher can be considered a "dynamic" ' +
30   'version of the Caesar cipher. Instead of shifting each plaintext ' +
31   'character by a fixed number, this cipher shifts characters ' +
32   'according to the character index of a keyword you choose such as ' +
33   '<I>dog</I>.<BR><BR>Since <I>d</I>, <I>o</I>, and <I>g</I> are ' +
34   'letters 4, 15, and 7 of the alphabet, each three plaintext ' +
35   'characters are shifted by 4, 15, and 7, respectively. This ' +
36   'application includes digits 0-9. So your keyword can have letters ' +
37   'and numbers.<BR><BR><FORM>Keyword: <INPUT TYPE=TEXT NAME="KeyWord" ' +
38   'SIZE=25></FORM><BR>Note: This cipher has many versions, one of ' +
39   'which was devised by Lewis Carroll, author of Alice in Wonderland.';
40
41 var curCipher = "caesar";
42
43 function Cipher() {
44   this.purify = purify;
45   this.chars = 'abcdefghijklmnopqrstuvwxyz0123456789';
46   }
47
48 function purify(rawText) {
49   if (!rawText) { return false; }
50   var cleanText = rawText.toLowerCase();
```

Example 9-1. index.html (continued)

```
51   cleanText = cleanText.replace(/\s+/g,' ');
52   cleanText = cleanText.replace(/[^a-z0-9\s]/g,'');
53   if(cleanText.length == 0 || cleanText.match(/^\s+$/) != null) {
54     return false;
55     }
56   return cleanText
57   }
58
59 function SubstitutionCipher(name, description, algorithm) {
60   this.name = name;
61   this.description = description;
62   this.substitute = substitute;
63   this.algorithm = algorithm;
64   }
65 SubstitutionCipher.prototype = new Cipher;
66
67 function substitute(baseChar, shiftIdx, action) {
68   if (baseChar == ' ') { return baseChar; }
69   if(action) {
70     var shiftSum = shiftIdx + this.chars.indexOf(baseChar);
71     return (this.chars.charAt((shiftSum < this.chars.length) ?
72       shiftSum : (shiftSum % this.chars.length)));
73       }
74     else {
75       var shiftDiff = this.chars.indexOf(baseChar) - shiftIdx;
76       return (this.chars.charAt((shiftDiff < 0) ?
77         shiftDiff + this.chars.length : shiftDiff));
78       }
79     }
80
81 function caesarAlgorithm (data, action) {
82   data = this.purify(data);
83   if(!data) {
84     alert('No valid text to ' + (action ? 'cipher.' : 'decipher.'));
85     return false;
86     }
87   var shiftIdx =
88     (NN ? refSlide("caesar").document.forms[0].Shift.selectedIndex :
   document.forms[1].Shift.selectedIndex);
89   var cipherData = '';
90   for (var i = 0; i < data.length; i++) {
91     cipherData += this.substitute(data.charAt(i), shiftIdx, action);
92     }
93   return cipherData;
94   }
95
96 function vigenereAlgorithm (data, action) {
97   data = this.purify(data);
98   if(!data) {
99     alert('No valid text to ' + (action ? 'cipher.' : 'decipher.'));
100    return false;
101    }
```

Example 9-1. index.html (continued)

```
102    var keyword = this.purify((NN ?
103      refSlide("vigenere").document.forms[0].KeyWord.value :
104      document.forms[2].KeyWord.value));
105    if(!keyword || keyword.match(/\^s+$/) != null) {
106      alert('No valid keyword for ' + (action ? 'ciphering.' :
107        'deciphering.'));
108      return false;
109      }
110    keyword = keyword.replace(/\s+/g, '');
111    var keywordIdx = 0;
112    var cipherData = '';
113    for (var i = 0; i < data.length; i++) {
114      shiftIdx = this.chars.indexOf(keyword.charAt(keywordIdx));
115      cipherData += this.substitute(data.charAt(i), shiftIdx, action);
116      keywordIdx = (keywordIdx == keyword.length - 1 ? 0 : keywordIdx + 1);
117      }
118    return cipherData;
119    }
120
121 var cipherArray = [
122    new SubstitutionCipher("caesar", caesar, caesarAlgorithm),
123    new SubstitutionCipher("vigenere", vigenere, vigenereAlgorithm)
124    ];
125
126 function showCipher(name) {
127    hideSlide(curCipher);
128    showSlide(name);
129    curCipher = name;
130    }
131
132 function routeCipher(cipherIdx, data, action) {
133    var response = cipherArray[cipherIdx].algorithm(data, action);
134    if(response) {
135      document.forms[0].Data.value = response;
136      }
137    }
138
139 //-->
140 </SCRIPT>
141 </HEAD>
142 <BODY BGCOLOR=#FFFFFF>
143
144 <DIV>
145    <TABLE BORDER=0>
146      <TR>
147        <TD ALIGN=CENTER COLSPAN=3>
148        <IMG SRC="images/cipher.jpg">
149        </TD>
150      </TR>
151      <TR>
152        <TD VALIGN=TOP WIDTH=350>
153        <FORM>
```

Example 9-1. index.html (continued)

```
154        <SELECT NAME="Ciphers"
155          onChange="showCipher(this.options[this.selectedIndex].value);">
156        <OPTION VALUE="caesar">Caesar Cipher
157        <OPTION VALUE="vigenere">Vigenére Cipher
158        </SELECT>
159        </TD>
160        <TD ALIGN=CENTER>
161        <TEXTAREA NAME="Data" ROWS="15" COLS="40" WRAP="PHYSICAL"></TEXTAREA>
162        <BR><BR>
163        <INPUT TYPE=BUTTON VALUE="Encipher"
164          onClick="routeCipher(this.form.Ciphers.selectedIndex,
165             this.form.Data.value, true);">
166        <INPUT TYPE=BUTTON VALUE="Decipher"
167          onClick="routeCipher(this.form.Ciphers.selectedIndex,
168             this.form.Data.value, false);">
169        <INPUT TYPE=BUTTON VALUE="  Reset   "
170          onClick="this.form.Data.value='';">
171        </FORM>
172        </TD>
173      </TR>
174    </TABLE>
175 </DIV>
176
177 <SCRIPT LANGUAGE="JavaScript1.2">
178 <!--
179 document.forms[0].Ciphers.selectedIndex = 0;
180 genLayer("caesar", 50, 125, 350, 200, showName, caesar);
181 genLayer("vigenere", 50, 125, 350, 200, hideName, vigenere);
182 //-->
183 </SCRIPT>
184 </BODY>
185 </HTML>
```

The JavaScript source file *dhtml.js* is the first code interpreted. The code in that file utilizes DHTML to set up the layers and generate select lists on the fly. We'll get to that shortly. The next code of interest comes in lines 14–39. Variables *caesar* and *vigenere* are designed and set to the value of HTML strings. Each of these, as you might have guessed, defines an interface layer of a cipher. Everything is static, expect for the call to function `genSelect()` in the value of *caesar*. Here it is:

```
genSelect('Shift', 35, 0, 0)
```

This creates a select list named *Shift*, which starts at 0, ends at 35, and has Option 0 selected. The **VALUE** and **TEXT** attributes are set to the number used for counting. This code comes straight from Chapter 5, *ImageMachine*. If you made the JavaScript library that I had suggested in Chapter 6, you should definitely have included this code in it. You'll find this function defined at the bottom of *dhtml.js*.

Defining a Cipher

The next lines of code define all ciphers that are and will be. Lines 43–46 contain the `Cipher()` constructor:

```
function Cipher() {
  this.purify = purify;
  this.chars = 'abcdefghijklmnopqrstuvwxyz0123456789';
  }
```

That's a pretty small constructor. If you expected some huge complex definition with all sorts of differential equations and spherical geometry designed to split the fourth dimension, sorry to let you down. `Cipher()` defines ciphers at a really high level. The only two assumptions made about all ciphers in this application is that:

- They *all* know how to format user data (using its only method), be it plaintext or ciphertext.

- Each cipher knows which characters it will include for ciphering (using its only property).

JavaScript Technique:
Assigning Methods to Your Objects

As small as it is, the `Cipher()` constructor introduces a new concept. That is, objects we've created in other chapters contained only properties. The `Cipher()` constructor has a property called *chars*, but also has a method named `purify()`.

Properties are easy to assign. Just assign the value you want to a variable using the `this.variable_name` syntax. Assigning methods is a little different. You first define a function, then use the same `this.variable_name` syntax to *refer* to the function. That's exactly what happens in the `Cipher()` constructor. The script has function `purify()` defined. `Cipher()` has a variable named *this. purify* referencing the `purify` method. Notice that there are no parentheses. This identifies a reference. Had *this.purify* been set to `purify()`, the `purify()` function would have been called, and *this.purify* would be set to whatever the function returned.

Referring to a function within a constructor assigns a `purify()` method to any variable set to `new Cipher()`. That's what happens with the elements in `cipherArray`, as you'll soon see.

No matter if the data will be enciphered or deciphered, it must conform to certain rules. Here are those rules:

- Each character must be a–z or 0–9. All others will be omitted. Case does not matter.

- Whitespaces will be neither enciphered, or deciphered. Multiple adjacent whitespaces will be reduced to single whitespaces.

- One or more newline characters are converted to single whitespaces.

Nice rules. Simple, too. All we need is something to enforce them. Enter function `purify()` in lines 48–57:

```
function purify(rawText) {
  if (!rawText) { return false; }
  var cleanText = rawText.toLowerCase();
  cleanText = cleanText.replace(/\s+/g,' ');
  cleanText = cleanText.replace(/[^a-z0-9\s]/g,'');
  if(cleanText.length == 0 || cleanText.match(/^\s+$/) != null) {
    return false;
  }
  return cleanText
}
```

This function returns one of two values: `false` or formatted text ready for cipher action. Returning `false` will cancel any cipher operation. If *rawText* contains anything to format, `purify()` first converts all letters to lowercase. Here's how:

```
cleanText = cleanText.replace(/\s+/g,' ');
```

Using regular expression matching, the `replace()` method of the *String* object searches for all the whitespaces in the entire string, which are replaced by a single whitespace, no matter how many adjacent ones there are. After that, `purify()` replaces all other characters that are not a–z or 0–9 or single whitespaces with an empty character. This removes all non-qualifying characters. Here is the workhorse `replace()` method at work again:

```
cleanText = cleanText.replace(/[^a-z0-9\s]/g,'');
```

The formatting is now complete. The time has come to check whether there is anything useful remaining to cipher. As long as the formatted string contains at least one character that is a–z or 0–9, everything is fine. However, there are two cases where this is untrue:

- After all the non-qualifying characters have been removed, there are no characters left.

- After all the non-qualifying characters have been removed, only whitespaces are left.

JavaScript Technique: More String Matching and Replacing

You just have to love JavaScript 1.2's regular expression matching. This application makes more use of it than previous applications. Let's have another look at the regular expression in line 52.

```
/[^a-z0-9\s]/g
```

Although it isn't long, the syntax might be a little confusing. This regular expression is known as a *negated character set*. In other words, anything *not* contained within the definition constitutes a match. You can utilize square brackets in a regular expression to specify a range of characters to include (or in this case, exclude). Consider this:

```
/[a-z]/g
```

This expression matches any of the lowercase letters of the alphabet. The g indicates that the search matches all characters in this range, not just the first one encountered You can include as many ranges as you like.

```
/[a-z0-9\s]/g
```

This expression matches any of the lowercase letters of the alphabet or any digit or whitespace. However, the cipher application in this case is interested in anything that does not match these. The circumflex (^) inside square brackets negates any special characters after it, which yields our original syntax.

```
/[^a-z0-9\s]/g
```

This is the tip of the string-matching iceberg. You can use these regular expressions to validate and format social security numbers, email addresses, URLs, phone numbers, zip codes, dates, times, and more. If you're new to regular expressions, you can get the full reference of regular expression definitions and special character meanings at "What's New In JavaScript 1.2" at *http:// developer1.netscape.com:80/docs/manuals/communicator/jsguide/regexp.htm.*

If either is the case, it's time to call off the operation and hold out for better data. Lines 53–55 perform the check. This causes **purify()** to return **false** if either occurs:

```
if(cleanText.length == 0 || cleanText.match(/^\s+$/) != null) {
   return false;
}
```

As far as knowing which characters qualify, **Cipher** uses the following string:

```
this.chars = 'abcdefghijklmnopqrstuvwxyz0123456789';
```

Defining a Substitution Cipher

Now that the mother of all *Cipher* objects—`Cipher()`—has been defined, let's create a more specific version. That's right—the spec for all substitution ciphers: `SubstitutionCipher()`. Study lines 59–65:

```
function SubstitutionCipher(name, description, algorithm) {
   this.name = name;
   this.description = description;
   this.substitute = substitute;
   this.algorithm = algorithm;
   }
SubstitutionCipher.prototype = new Cipher;
```

The assumption for every *Cipher* object is that each one knows how to format any user data. Substitution ciphers contain further assumptions. Here they are:

1. Each has a name and description.

2. Each uses a general method for substituting characters for both enciphering and deciphering.

3. Each has a specific implementation of the general substitution method. This is what makes one substitution cipher different from other substitution ciphers.

4. Each *SubstitutionCipher* object is also a *Cipher* object.

Assigning a name and description to each is pretty simple. Any two strings you pass in when you call **new** `SubstitutionCipher()` will work just fine. Incidentally, the variables *caesar* and *vigenere* instantiated earlier with all that HTML will be the description of each. That takes care of the first assumption. Now, what about defining a general substitution method? This method can substitute one character for another. That's it. Each call to this method returns one character, which is a substitute for another.

Performing Basic Substitution

Each `SubstitutionCipher` uses the same method to replace one character in the *chars* string with another. The `substitute()` function, shown below, is defined as a method for each instantiation of `SubstitutionCipher`:

```
function substitute(baseChar, shiftIdx, action) {
   if (baseChar == ' ') { return baseChar; }
   if(action) {
     var shiftSum = shiftIdx + this.chars.indexOf(baseChar);
     return (this.chars.charAt((shiftSum < this.chars.length) ?
       shiftSum : (shiftSum % this.chars.length)));
     }
   else {
     var shiftDiff = this.chars.indexOf(baseChar) - shiftIdx;
     return (this.chars.charAt((shiftDiff < 0) ?
```

```
        shiftDiff + this.chars.length : shiftDiff));
    }
  }
```

This method expects three arguments. *baseChar* is the character that will be replaced by another. *shiftIdx* is an integer that determines "how much" shift to apply in order to find the correct substitution. *action* is a Boolean value that specifies whether *baseChar* should be treated as plaintext or ciphertext. To leave whitespace unchanged, the first line returns *baseChar* as is if *baseChar* is indeed a whitespace. Otherwise, this method uses *action* to determine how to calculate the amount of shift. If *action* is `true`, the enciphering algorithm is used. If *action* is `false`, the deciphering algorithm is used.

Remember that *chars* contains a string of all the qualifying characters. The enciphering algorithm simply determines the index of *baseChar* within *chars*, then chooses the character of *chars* at that index plus the value of *shiftIdx*.

Here's an example. Suppose that *baseChar* is d, *shiftIdx* is 8, and `chars.indexOf('d')` is 3. That brings us to line 70:

```
var shiftSum = shiftIdx + this.chars.indexOf(baseChar);
```

Variable *shiftSum* equals 11 (8 + 3). So `chars.charAt(11)` is the letter l. That is what `substitute()` would return in this case. That seems straightforward. It is, but suppose *baseChar* is letter o, and *shiftIdx* is 30. Check the math. *shiftSum* now equals 45. The problem is, *chars* has only 36 characters (a–z and 0–9). Therefore, `chars.charAt(45)` doesn't exist.

When the algorithm reaches the last character of *chars*, it must "wrap" around and start over with 0, and begin adding again from there. You can use the modulus operator to get the desired effect. Think about it: the modulus operator returns the integer remainder of two operands. Here are several examples:

4 % 3 = 1. Dividing 4 by 3 leaves a remainder of 1.
5 % 3 = 2. Dividing 5 by 3 leaves a remainder of 2.
6 % 3 = 0. Dividing 6 by 3 leaves no remainder.

All you need to do is use the return of the modulus operation. So instead of using a `shiftSum` of 45, you would use `shiftSum % chars.length`, which equals 9. `chars.charAt(9)` is the letter j. This explains the ensuing code for the enciphering algorithm:

```
return (this.chars.charAt((shiftSum < this.chars.length) ? shiftSum :
    (shiftSum % this.chars.length)));
```

In this case, `substitute()` returns `chars.charAt(shiftSum)` or `chars.charAt(shiftSum % this.chars.length)`, depending on the size of *shiftSum* and the length of *chars*. How about the keyword *this*? You may be wondering what it is doing there. Keep in mind that `substitute()` is not a function; it is a method of whatever variable is instantiated as a `SubstitutionCipher`. Using *this*, within this method will refer to any property of the instantiated variable. Since `SubstitutionCipher` inherits all the properties of `Cipher`, the instantiated variable "owns" a property called *chars*.

The procedure isn't much different for the deciphering algorithm. The only change is that it subtracts *shiftIdx* to reach the correct character in *chars*. In this case, variable *shiftDiff* is set to the difference of the index of *baseChar* and *shiftIdx*, which is as follows.

```
var shiftDiff = this.chars.indexOf(baseChar) - shiftIdx;
```

Again, this is fairly simple. If *shiftDiff* is less than 0, however, you run into the same problem as when *shiftSum* was more than `chars.length` – 1. The solution is to add *shiftDiff* to `chars.length`. That's right . . . add. *shiftDiff* is negative, which means adding the two together yields a number *shiftDiff* less than `chars.length`, which is the desired index for deciphering. The code below reflects whether `substitute()` uses *shiftDiff* or *shiftDiff* + `chars.length` as the index for deciphering:

```
return (this.chars.charAt((shiftDiff < 0) ?
  shiftDiff + this.chars.length : shiftDiff));
```

Different Substitutions for Different Ciphers

We just examined what all of the *SubstitutionCiphers* have in common—the `substitute()` method. Now let's take a look at what sets them apart. The *SubstitutionCipher* constructor expects an argument named *algorithm*. This argument is not a string, a Boolean, a number, or even an object. This argument is a reference to a function that will implement (call) the `substitute()` method in a unique way.

For the Caesar cipher, the argument passed in is a reference to function `caesarAlgorithm()`. The Vigenere cipher, not surprisingly, receives a reference to function `vigenereAlgorithm()`. Let's look at the functions of each.

Caesar algorithm

The Caesar algorithm is the easier of the two. Lines 81–94 contain the code:

```
function caesarAlgorithm (data, action) {
  data = this.purify(data);
  if(!data) {
    alert('No valid text to ' + (action ? 'cipher.' : 'decipher.'));
    return false;
    }
  var shiftIdx =
  (NN ? refSlide("caesar").document.forms[0].Shift.selectedIndex :
    document.forms[1].Shift.selectedIndex);
```

```
var cipherData = '';
for (var i = 0; i < data.length; i++) {
  cipherData += this.substitute(data.charAt(i), shiftIdx, action);
  }
return cipherData;
}
```

The first few lines format the data, then check to see whether there is any qualifying character left over. The string in argument *data* is formatted by calling `purify()` and passing in *data* as the argument. As long as the call to `purify()` doesn't return `false`, the cipher continues. See the earlier section on the `purify()` method for details about the method's return.

The next thing to do is determine the number of characters by which the user wants to shift the text. That's pretty easy. It comes from the select list in the form on the layer named *caesar*. I haven't mentioned anything about that yet, but you can jump ahead to lines 180-181 if you want to see the call to create both layers. However, the Navigator DOM differs from the Internet Explorer DOM when it comes to accessing form elements in different layers. The select list has the name *Shift*.

In Navigator, it looks like this:

```
document.layers['caesar'].document.forms[0].Shift.selectedIndex
```

In MSIE, though, it looks like this:

```
document.forms[1].Shift.selectedIndex
```

As you just saw, accessing forms and form elements in layers requires different syntax. The document object model in NN differs from the one in MSIE. This isn't the first time we've seen it in this book. In fact, the majority of code in *dhtml.js* exists only for creating and manipulating layers in both browsers. Do yourself a favor. Make sure you know when you'll have to accommodate both and when you won't. Until we see a unified DOM, keep the following resources handy.

Microsoft's DHTML Objects:

http://www.microsoft.com/workshop/author/dhtml/reference/ objects.asp
Netscape's Style Sheet Reference and Client-Side JavaScript Reference:

http://developer1.netscape.com:80/docs/manuals/communicator/ dynhtml/jss34.htm and *http://developer.netscape.com/docs/manuals/ js/client/jsref/index.htm*

Variable *shiftIdx* accounts for that difference by using the *NN* variable to determine which of the two to access. The call to `refSlide()` in line 88 is a convenient way to refer to **document.layers["caesar"]**. Now that *shiftIdx* has been assigned, **caesarAlgorithm()** iterates **data.length** times, calling **substitute()** each time and concatenating its return to the once-empty local variable *cipherData*. Argument **action** is passed in each time to properly indicate to **substitute()** whether to encipher or decipher. After the last iteration, **caesarAlgorithm()** returns *cipherData,* which now contains the properly ciphered string.

Vigenere Algorithm

That is the simpler of the two cipher algorithms explained. Let's look at **vigenereAlgorithm()**. The primary difference here is that the argument *shiftIdx* passed to **substitute()** in **caesarAlgorithm()** remains constant. With this function, *shiftIdx* can (and usually does) change with every call to **substitute()**. The other difference is that the user chooses a keyword instead of a number. Here are lines 96–119:

```
function vigenereAlgorithm (data, action) {
  data = this.purify(data);
  if(!data) {
    alert('No valid text to ' + (action ? 'cipher.' : 'decipher.'));
    return false;
    }
  var keyword =
    this.purify((NN ?
      refSlide("vigenere").document.forms[0].KeyWord.value :
      document.forms[2].KeyWord.value));
  if(!keyword || keyword.match(/\^s+$/) != null) {
    alert('No valid keyword for ' +
    (action ? 'ciphering.' : 'deciphering.'));
    return false;
    }
  keyword = keyword.replace(/\s+/g, '');
  var keywordIdx = 0;
  var cipherData = '';
  for (var i = 0; i < data.length; i++) {
    shiftIdx = this.chars.indexOf(keyword.charAt(keywordIdx));
    cipherData += this.substitute(data.charAt(i), shiftIdx, action);
    keywordIdx = (keywordIdx == keyword.length - 1 ? 0 : keywordIdx + 1);
    }
  return cipherData;
  }
```

The first five lines are the same as in **caesarAlgorithm()**. They do the same formatting and validating. The next few lines perform similar work on the keyword. The keyword comes from the form field located on the layer named *vigenere*. Remember that we have to accommodate both Navigator and MSIE DOMs.

In Navigator, it looks like this:

```
document.layers['vigenere'].document.forms[0].KeyWord.value
```

In MSIE, though, it looks like this:

```
document.forms[2].KeyWord.value
```

Variable *keyword* then is assigned as follows:

```
var keyword = this.purify((NN ?
  refSlide("vigenere").document.forms[0].KeyWord.value :
  document.forms[2].KeyWord.value));
```

Notice that the `purify()` method is used again. It is designed for plaintext and ciphertext, but the demands for the keyword are very similar. Since the `substitute()` method can substitute only characters in *chars*, the keyword must contain characters from `chars` as well. Acceptable keywords include *people*, *machines*, *init2wnit*, and *1or2or3*. However, using characters not in *chars* can still be acceptable. Remember that `purify()` removes all characters that aren't a–z or 0–9, and replaces all newline and carriage return characters and multiple whitespaces with single whitespaces. While the user might enter `1@@#derft` as a keyword, `purify()` formats that string and returns *1derft*, and that contains qualifying characters. Now consider a keyword with whitespaces, say all the spaces in between. This contains qualifying characters, except for those whitespaces. Line 110 removes them:

```
keyword = keyword.replace(/\s+/g, '');
```

The bottom line is: as long as there is at least one qualifying character in the keyword, that is what will be used in `vigenereAlgorithm()`.

How shiftIdx Changes

The plaintext (or ciphertext) and the keyword have been formatted. All that remains is to substitute each of the characters accordingly. By definition of the Vigenére cipher, each character of text is enciphered or deciphered according to the index of the next character in the keyword. This brings us to lines 111–118:

```
var keywordIdx = 0;
var cipherData = '';
for (var i = 0; i < data.length; i++) {
  shiftIdx = this.chars.indexOf(keyword.charAt(keywordIdx));
  cipherData += this.substitute(data.charAt(i), shiftIdx, action);
  keywordIdx = (keywordIdx == keyword.length - 1 ? 0 : keywordIdx + 1);
  }
return cipherData;
```

Using variable *keywordIdx* starting at 0, we can get the index of each keyword character as follows:

```
keyword.charAt(keywordIdx)
```

For each character of *data* (the plaintext or ciphertext), *shiftIdx* is set to the index of *chars* at `keyword.charAt(keywordIdx)`. Variable *cipherData* is then set equal to itself plus the return of the `substitute()` method, which receives a fresh copy of `data.charAt(i)` and *shiftIdx*, along with `action`. Incrementing *keywordIdx* by 1 afterwards sets things up for the next iteration.

Each SubstitutionCipher Is Also a Cipher

Since all ciphers, no matter what kind they are, must have the same basic characteristics, the *SubstitutionCipher* constructor must inherit all the properties of *Cipher*. That takes place in one line:

```
SubstitutionCipher.prototype = new Cipher;
```

Now each instantiated *SubstitutionCipher* object has a property called *chars* and a method called `purify()`. Every *SubstitutionCipher* then, is a more specific version of a *Cipher*.

JavaScript Technique: Tapping into JavaScript Object Inheritance

As mentioned in the last chapter, JavaScript employs prototype-based inheritance, not class-based inheritance common to languages such as Java. Chapter 8's 'The JavaScript Technique: Adding Object Properties" shows you how to add properties such as strings or numbers to existing objects. You can also utilize the *prototype* property of constructor functions to create inheritance hierarchy. That's what happens in line 65. *SubstitutionCipher* inherits all the properties of *Cipher*. This lets you leverage the true power of object-oriented programming (as far as JavaScript is concerned). You can get more information about JavaScript inheritance at Netscape's DevEdge Online at:

http://developer1.netscape.com:80/docs/manuals/communicator/jsobj/contents.htm#1030750

Creating Each Instance of SubstitutionCipher

Up to this point, we've seen how the two ciphers work. Now it's time to examine how to create the objects that represent the two ciphers and how to construct the interface for using them. Creating the objects takes only four lines. Here they are, lines 121–124:

```
var cipherArray = [
    new SubstitutionCipher("caesar", caesar, caesarAlgorithm),
    new SubstitutionCipher("vigenere", vigenere, vigenereAlgorithm)
    ];
```

Variable *cipherArray* is set to an array. Each of the elements is a *SubstitutionCipher*. Why put them in an array? The reason is that the application knows which cipher to use according to the OPTION selected in the first select list on the page. We'll cover that in a moment.

JavaScript Technique: Using Alternate Syntax

As of JavaScript 1.2, you can replace code such as:

```
var myArray = new Array(1,2,3);
```

with a shortened version like this:

```
var myArray = [1,2,3];
```

You can also create objects on the fly as follows. Instead of this:

```
function myObj() {
  this.name="A New Object";
  this.description = "Old School Object";
  }

var objOne = new myObj();
```

try this:

```
var myObj = {name: "A New Object", description: "New School Object"};
```

Notice that the property and method name-value pairs are separated by a comma. Both 4.x versions of MSIE and Navigator support these. Take your pick.

For now, notice that each call to the `SubstitutionCipher()` constructor passes with it the expected strings, a name and a description, and a reference to a function, which will be assigned to the `algorithm` property of each *SubstitutionCipher* object created. That creates the objects. Let's look at the interface. This happens between the BODY tags:

```
<DIV>
  <TABLE BORDER=0>
    <TR>
      <TD ALIGN=CENTER COLSPAN=3>
      <IMG SRC="images/cipher.jpg">
      </TD>
    </TR>
    <TR>
      <TD VALIGN=TOP WIDTH=350>
      <FORM>
      <SELECT NAME="Ciphers"
        onChange="showCipher(this.options[this.selectedIndex].value);">
      <OPTION VALUE="caesar">Caesar Cipher
      <OPTION VALUE="vigenere">Vigenére Cipher
      </SELECT>
      </TD>
      <TD ALIGN=CENTER>
      <TEXTAREA NAME="Data" ROWS="15" COLS="40"
        WRAP="PHYSICAL"></TEXTAREA>
      <BR><BR>
```

```
<INPUT TYPE=BUTTON VALUE="Encipher"
  onClick="routeCipher(this.form.Ciphers.selectedIndex,
  this.form.Data.value, true);">
<INPUT TYPE=BUTTON VALUE="Decipher"
  onClick="routeCipher(this.form.Ciphers.selectedIndex,
  this.form.Data.value, false);">
<INPUT TYPE=BUTTON VALUE="  Reset  "
  onClick="this.form.Data.value='';">
</FORM>
</TD>
</TR>
</TABLE>
</DIV>
```

This code creates a two-row table. The top row houses the graphic in a TD with COLSPAN set to 2. The bottom row contains two data cells. The one at the left contains a single select list, and looks like this:

```
<SELECT NAME="Ciphers"
  onChange="showCipher(this.options[this.selectedIndex].value);">
<OPTION VALUE="caesar">Caesar Cipher
<OPTION VALUE="vigenere">Vigenére Cipher
</SELECT>
```

This list determines which cipher interface is currently displayed. Since there are only two, it's either one or the other. The *onChange* event handler calls the showCipher() function, passing in the value of the option currently selected. This function is pretty short. You'll find it in lines 126–130:

```
function showCipher(name) {
  hideSlide(curCipher);
  showSlide(name);
  curCipher = name;
  }
```

The code inside might look familiar. It hails from previous chapters like Chapter 3, *The Interactive Slideshow*, or Chapter 6. You'll find functions hideSlide() and showSlide() in *dhtml.js*. Refer to Chapter 3 for detailed coverage.

Notice that the data cell is set to a width of 350 pixels. Other than a select list, that data cell is pretty empty. Fortunately, two layers will fill in that available browser real estate. You can see the calls to create them in lines 180–181. Function genLayer() creates the cipher layers and is also in *dhtml.js*. This, too, is a function from the past and won't be covered here:

```
genLayer("caesar", 50, 125, 350, 200, showName, caesar);
genLayer("vigenere", 50, 125, 350, 200, hideName, vigenere);
```

This creates the text displays for each cipher, along with the additional select list for the Caesar cipher and the text field for the Vigenere cipher. As just mentioned, you can change the option between Caesar cipher and Vigenére cipher in the top select list, which then displays the proper cipher layer.

As for the other data cell in the bottom table row, it contains a text area and three buttons. Here they are again in lines 161–170:

```
<TEXTAREA NAME="Data" ROWS="15" COLS="40" WRAP="PHYSICAL"></TEXTAREA>
<BR><BR>
<INPUT TYPE=BUTTON VALUE="Encipher"
  onClick="routeCipher(this.form.Ciphers.selectedIndex,
  this.form.Data.value, true);">
<INPUT TYPE=BUTTON VALUE="Decipher"
  onClick="routeCipher(this.form.Ciphers.selectedIndex,
  this.form.Data.value, false);">
<INPUT TYPE=BUTTON VALUE="  Reset  " onClick="this.form.Data.value='';">
```

The textarea field holds the plain text (or ciphertext). The "Encipher" button causes the text contained within it to be enciphered. It's the reverse for the "Decipher" button. Both call the same function, `routeCipher()`. Both pass in the value of the textarea field. The difference is that the last argument is true for one and false for the other.

Choosing the Right Cipher

Choosing the right cipher is easy. The correct cipher always corresponds with the index of the top select list in the form and the index of `cipherArray`. You can see this in `routeCipher()` shown here:

```
function routeCipher(cipherIdx, data, action) {
  var response = cipherArray[cipherIdx].algorithm(data, action);
  if(response) {
    document.forms[0].Data.value = response;
    }
  }
```

This function accepts three arguments. We've already discussed the last two. *data* is the text in the textarea, and *action* is either `true` or `false`. The first one, *cipherIdx*, comes from `document.forms[0].Ciphers.selectedIndex`. It has to be 0 or 1. Whichever it is, the `algorithm()` method of the corresponding *SubstitutionCipher* object in `cipherArray` gets the call. If `algorithm()` returns a non-false value, it must be qualified enciphered (or deciphered) text.

A Final Thought

You've probably realized by now, but the code in line 179:

```
document.forms[0].Ciphers.selectedIndex = 0;
```

simply resets the selected OPTION in the top select list to the first one. This forces the OPTION selected to match the cipher layer in view, even if the user reloads the page.

Potential Extensions

While this application is cool to play with as is, the next level is to send it in email. You can do that in three easy steps. First, copy the following function, and paste it between your SCRIPT tags:

```
function sendText(data) {
  paraWidth = 70;
  var iterate = parseInt(data.length / paraWidth);
  var border = '\n-------\n';
  var breakData = '';
  for (var i = 1; i <= iterate; i++) {
    breakData += data.substring((i - 1) * paraWidth, i * paraWidth) +
      '\r';
    }
  breakData += data.substring((i - 1) * paraWidth, data.length);
  document.CipherMail.Message.value = border + breakData + border;
  document.CipherMail.action =
    "mailto:someone@somewhere.com\?subject=The Secret Message";
  return true;
  }
```

This performs some last millisecond formatting before sending the email. The formatting inserts carriage returns every *paraWidth* characters. This ensures that the email message that the recipient receives isn't one line of text 40 miles long. The next thing to do is add the second form required. Insert this code after the closing FORM tag in the current document:

```
FORM NAME="CipherMail" ACTION="" METHOD="POST" ENCTYPE="text/plain"
  onSubmit="return sendText(document.forms[0].Data.value);">
<INPUT TYPE=HIDDEN NAME="Message">
<INPUT TYPE=SUBMIT VALUE="   Send   ">
</FORM>
```

This form, named CipherMail, contains a lone HIDDEN field. The last thing to do is change the form references in the cipher algorithm functions.

Change lines 87–89:

```
var shiftIdx = (NN ?
  refSlide("caesar").document.forms[0].Shift.selectedIndex :
  document.forms[1].Shift.selectedIndex);
```

to this:

```
var shiftIdx = (NN ?
  refSlide("caesar").document.forms[0].Shift.selectedIndex :
  document.forms[2].Shift.selectedIndex);
```

Then lines 102-104 from this:

```
var keyword = this.purify((NN ?
  refSlide("vigenere").document.forms[0].KeyWord.value :
  document.forms[2].KeyWord.value));
```

to this:

```
var keyword = this.purify((NN ?
  refSlide("vigenere").document.forms[0].KeyWord.value :
  document.forms[3].KeyWord.value));
```

You need to make these changes because you added another form to the hierarchy in the previous step. `sendText()` sets the value of this hidden field to the value of whatever text is entered in the textarea. `sendText()` then submits this form, which has the `ACTION` attribute set to `mailto:your_e-mail@your_mail_server.com`. Figure 9-7 shows what the message looks like when it arrives. That's the view from my Hotmail account. Upon receipt, the user can cut and paste the text between the dashed lines, then decipher the message with the previously agreed-upon cipher and key. Now your visitors are using encrypted mail, and you're the genius behind it!

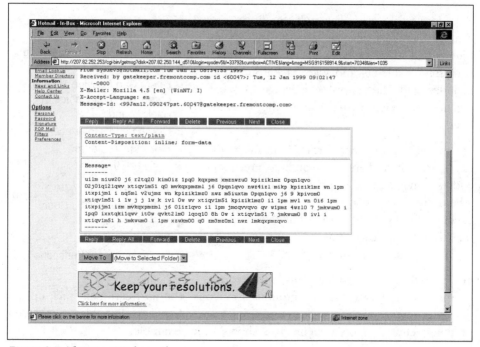

Figure 9-7. The encrypted email

P.S. This will work only if the user has the NN or MSIE email client correctly configured, which is most likely the case.

P.P.S. \ch09\cipher2.html has the email functionality added.

10

Cyber Greetings:
Drag-and-Drop Email

This application is built simply for fun. Users can kill plenty of time at your site by sending friends and loved ones custom-made greetings with silly characters and wild backgrounds, all included with the snappiest message they can conjure up. Figure 10-1 shows the opening interface.

On the left is an entry form. Users fill in the necessary ingredients, including recipient address, message, and greeting. This is also where users can choose the background, by clicking "Backgrounds -->" until they see the one they want. The same goes for the icons. "Icons -->" has the same effect.

To the right is the display. This is where the user can see the available backgrounds and icons. The user can then "pick up" an icon and drag it onto the background display area. Any icons like this are included on the greeting as shown. Figure 10-2 shows a nice example.

Application Features

- Ships Custom Greetings You Design
- Users Can Position Multiple Logos on Their Choice of Background
- User-Friendly Interface
- Message Tester for Previewing

JavaScript Techniques

- Differentiating Web Code
- Cross-Frame Communication
- Optimizing Your Functions

When the greeting is done, users can preview the work in progress by choosing "Test." This opens a remote window that shows what the greeting will look like when the recipient views it. See Figure 10-3.

Once satisfied, the user simply chooses "Send." That submits all the form info to a ready-and-willing server-side script that creates the greeting and returns a final confirmation page containing a "Send" button (Figure 10-4). When the button is pressed, the script sends email to the recipient, providing the URL of the card.

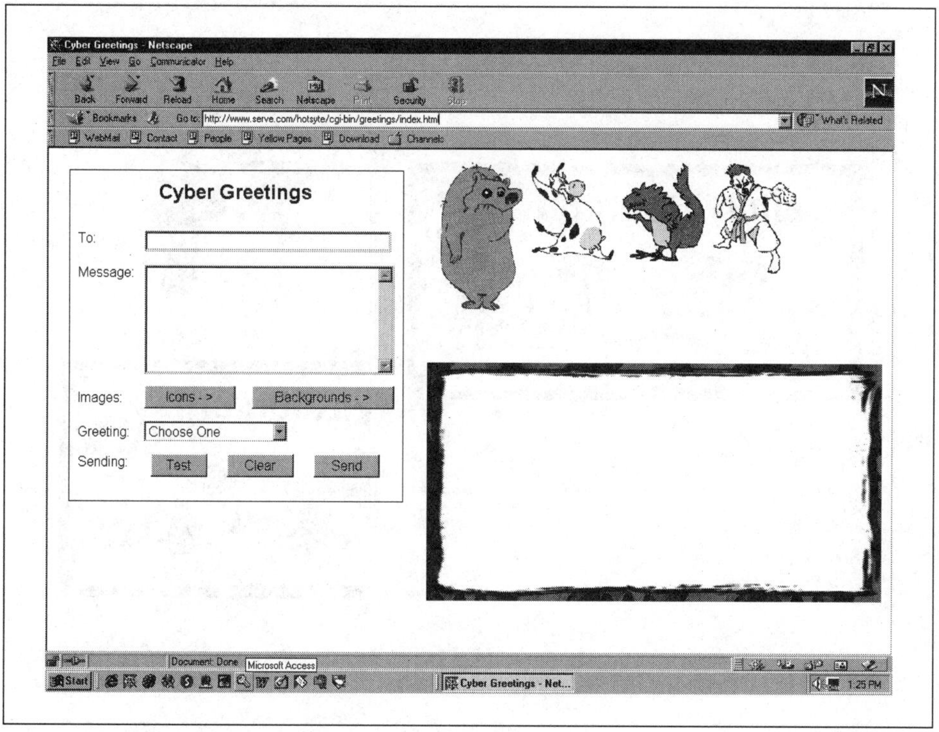

Figure 10-1. The Cyber Greetings default screen

Figure 10-2. Recognize anyone in this group photo?

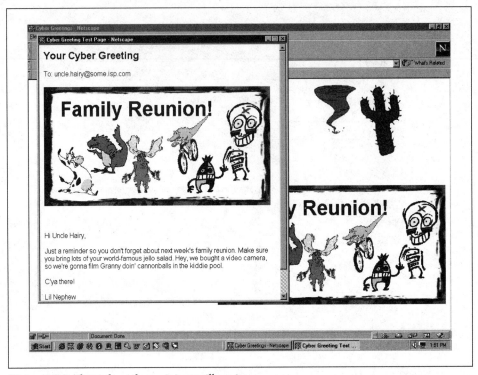

Figure 10-3. This is how the recipient will see it

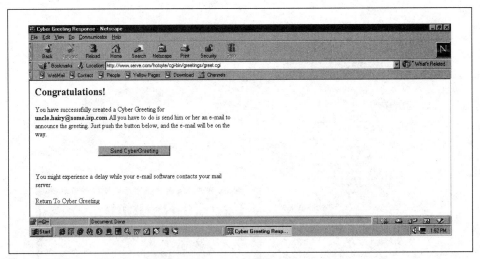

Figure 10-4. Success: just submit this form, and off the message goes

Now it's up to the user to read the mail. (I don't have an Uncle Hairy, so I sent this one to my Hotmail account.) Figure 10-5 shows what a greeting announcement looks like. Not much to it, just a simple message and a link. Once the recipient follows the link in the email message, the document that loads is exactly what the sender created. Figure 10-6 proves it.

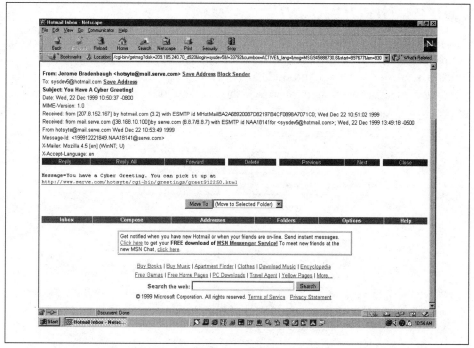

Figure 10-5. The Cyber Greeting announcement

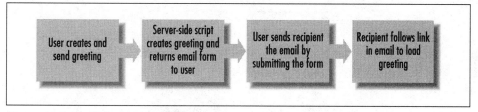

Figure 10-6. The CyberGreetings flow

Execution Requirements

You'll need MSIE or Navigator 4.x or higher because of the DHTML and massive stylesheet positioning. The program is designed for a monitor with a resolution of at least 1024×768, though you can modify it to accommodate 800×600. I wouldn't go any lower.

This program also requires a web server with a server-side scripting environment. Don't let that scare you if you aren't familiar with server-side scripting. I've provided a script that is fairly easy to install on just about every web server on Earth. It is written in Perl. You just have to copy to the correct directory and set up some permissions. You can get those details in Appendix C, *Using Perl Scripts.*

Syntax Breakdown

This is another application that warrants a flowchart before we look at any code. Figure 10-7 shows how the user enters the recipient's email address and message, chooses a greeting and background, then positions desired icons "on top" of the greeting card. The user then previews the work. Once satisfied, it's off to the server, and so on.

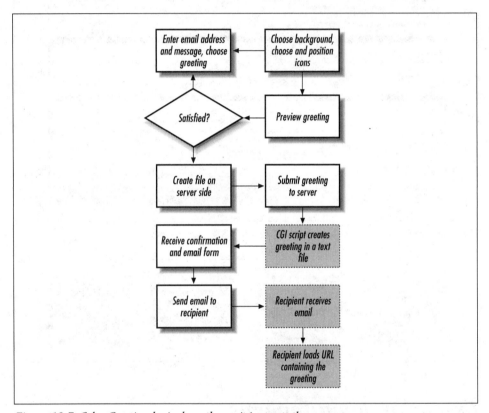

Figure 10-7. CyberGreeting logic: how the recipient gets the message

This application works on two levels—in the client browser and on the web server. The browser is obviously where the user creates the entire greeting—background, icon graphics, and message. When the user submits the HTML form, the information is sent back to a web server, where a file is created to match the greeting. The web server returns an HTML form so the greeting sender can send an email message to the recipient. This message contains nothing more than an announcement of the cyber greeting and a link that the recipient must follow to "pick it up." The recipient follows the link to load the awaiting Cyber Greeting.

Let's go over this app first in terms of the client and then the server. There are four files. The following list gives a quick rundown:

index.html
> Top level; holds the frameset

back.html
> Contains the workspace for choosing the greeting, background, and icons

front.html
> Contains the interface for creating and sending the message

greet.pl
> The server-side script used to create and store each greeting in a file, then create an HTML form to send email to the recipient

As you can see from the screen captures, there are two sides to this interface. The back (*back.html*) is the greeting display where the user can see what he or she has after choosing the greeting and positioning any graphics. The front (*front. html*) contains the entry form and is responsible for entering email address and a message, choosing backgrounds, and producing the available graphics, referred to as icons. Both documents are referenced in *index.html*. Example 10-1 has the details.

Example 10-1. index.html

```
 1 <HTML>
 2 <HEAD>
 3    <TITLE>Cyber Greetings</TITLE>
 4 <SCRIPT LANGUAGE="JavaScript1.2">
 5 <!--
 6
 7 var greetings = [
 8    'Choose One', 'Family Reunion!',
 9    'Get Well Soon','Thinking Of You',
10    'Big Party!', 'Psst... You\'re Invited.',
11    'Happy Birthday!', 'Congratulations!',
12    'We\'re Gonna Miss U', 'Just A Reminder',
13    'Don\'t Forget'
14    ];
15
16 var baseURL = ".";
17
18 //-->
19 </SCRIPT>
20 </HEAD>
21 <FRAMESET COLS="450,*" FRAMEBORDER="2" BORDER="0">
22    <FRAME SRC="front.html" NAME="Front" NORESIZE>
23    <FRAME SRC="back.html" NAME="Back" NORESIZE SCROLLING="NO">
24 </FRAMESET>
25 </HTML>
```

index.html contains an array called *greetings* in lines 7–14. These are the greetings that users can choose from. *baseURL* contains the base directory on the web server of this application. Everything is contained within it: all four files, all the images, and the directory that will contain each user-created greeting. *baseURL* is even included in the greeting itself. When you change this value, you change it for the entire application—client and server.

So why declare a variable and an array in this file? Both files defined in the frames of *index.html* need those greetings to create the respective pages *as they load*. If *greetings* were defined in one of the other two files, it might not have loaded by the time the JavaScript code in the other file tried to access it. The same goes for *baseURL*. This helps avoid load-time errors.

The Other Two Documents

The concept of front and back sides are analogous to a traditional postcard. The front (I think) has the address and message on it, and the back has the pretty picture of picknickers on the beach. In this case, *back.html* contains the background display area and the icons for you to drag. This file is responsible for much of the initial setup during the document loading. *front.html* facilitates things after the document loads, such as entering a message and choosing and sending a greeting. It makes sense, then, to cover *back.html* first. Fortunately, you've probably seen much of it in earlier chapters. Take a look at Example 10-2.

Example 10-2. back.html

```
 1 <HTML>
 2 <HEAD>
 3   <TITLE>Cyber Greetings</TITLE>
 4 <STYLE TYPE="text/css">
 5 <!--
 6
 7 .Greeting
 8   {
 9     font-family: Arial;
10     font-size: 48px;
11     font-weight: bold;
12   }
13
14 //-->
15 </STYLE>
16 <SCRIPT LANGUAGE="JavaScript1.2">
17 <!--
18
19 var NN       = (document.layers ? true : false);
20 var hideName = (NN ? 'hide' : 'hidden');
21 var showName = (NN ? 'show' : 'visible');
22 var zIdx     = -1;
23
```

Example 10-2. back.html (continued)

```
24 var iconNum  = 4;
25 var startWdh = 25;
26 var imgIdx   = 0;
27 var activate = false;
28 var activeLayer = null;
29
30 var backImgs = [];
31 var icons = [
32    'bear', 'cowprod', 'dragon', 'judo',
33    'robot', 'seniorexec', 'dude', 'juicemoose',
34    'logo1', 'logo2', 'logo3','tree',
35    'sun', 'gator', 'tornado', 'cactus'
36    ];
37
38 function genLayout() {
39
40   for (var i = 0; i <= 7; i++) {
41     backImgs[i] = new Image();
42     backImgs[i].src = top.baseURL + '/images/background' + i +
43       '.jpg';
44     }
45
46   genLayer("Back", 10, 250, backImgs[1].width, backImgs[1].height,
47     showName, '<IMG NAME="background" SRC="' + top.baseURL +
48     '/images/background0.jpg">');
49
50   for (var j = 0; j < parent.greetings.length; j++) {
51     genLayer("greeting" + j, 50, 275, 500, 100, hideName,
52       '<SPAN CLASS="Greeting">' + parent.greetings[j] + '</SPAN>');
53     }
54
55   for (var i = 0; i < icons.length; i++) {
56     if (i % iconNum == 0) { startWdh = 25; }
57     else { startWdh += 110; }
58     genLayer(icons[i], startWdh, 15, 100, 100, (i < iconNum ? showName :
59       hideName), '<A HREF="javascript: changeAction(\'' + icons[i] +
60       '\',' + (i + 1) + ');"><IMG SRC="' + top.baseURL +
61       '/images/' + icons[i] + '.gif" BORDER="0"></A>');
62     }
63   startWdh = 25;
64   }
65
66 function genLayer(sName, sLeft, sTop, sWdh, sHgt, sVis, copy) {
67   if (NN) {
68     document.writeln('<LAYER NAME="' + sName + '" LEFT=' + sLeft +
69       ' TOP=' + sTop + ' WIDTH=' + sWdh + ' HEIGHT=' + sHgt +
70       ' VISIBILITY="' + sVis + '" z-Index=' + (++zIdx) + '>' + copy +
71       '</LAYER>');
72     }
73   else {
74     document.writeln('<DIV ID="' + sName +
75       '" STYLE="position:absolute; overflow:none; left:' +
```

Example 10-2. back.html (continued)

```
 76        sLeft + 'px; top:' + sTop + 'px; width:' + sWdh + 'px; height:' +
 77        sHgt + 'px; visibility:' + sVis + '; z-Index=' + (++zIdx) + '">' +
 78        copy + '</DIV>'
 79        );
 80     }
 81   }
 82
 83 function hideSlide(name) {
 84   refSlide(name).visibility = hideName;
 85   }
 86
 87 function showSlide(name) {
 88   refSlide(name).visibility = showName;
 89   }
 90
 91 function refSlide(name) {
 92   if (NN) { return document.layers[name]; }
 93   else { return eval('document.all.' + name + '.style'); }
 94   }
 95
 96 function motionListener() {
 97   if (NN) {
 98     window.captureEvents(Event.MOUSEMOVE);
 99     window.onmousemove = grabXY;
100     }
101   else {
102     document.onmousemove = grabXY;
103     }
104   }
105
106 function grabXY(ev) {
107   if (activate) {
108     if(NN) {
109       var itemWdh = refSlide(activeLayer).document.images[0].width;
110       var itemHgt = refSlide(activeLayer).document.images[0].height;
111       refSlide(activeLayer).left = ev.pageX - parseInt(itemWdh / 2);
112       refSlide(activeLayer).top = ev.pageY - parseInt(itemHgt / 2);
113       }
114     else {
115       var itemWdh = document.images[imgIdx].width;
116       var itemHgt = document.images[imgIdx].height;
117       refSlide(activeLayer).left = event.x - parseInt(itemWdh / 2);
118       refSlide(activeLayer).top = event.y - parseInt(itemHgt / 2);
119       }
120     }
121   }
122
123 function changeAction(name, MSIERef) {
124   activate = !activate;
125   activeLayer = name;
126   imgIdx = MSIERef;
127   }
```

Example 10-2. back.html (continued)

```
128
129 //-->
130 </SCRIPT>
131 </HEAD>
132 <BODY onLoad="motionListener();">
133
134 <SCRIPT LANGUAGE="JavaScript1.2">
135 <!--
136
137 genLayout();
138
139 //-->
140 </SCRIPT>
141
142 </BODY>
143 </HTML>
```

Before the sender can create a greeting, several functions have to generate a lot of
layers and determine the location of the mouse-pointer arrow relative to the document. There is very similar functionality discussed in Chapter 3, *The Interactive
Slideshow,* and Chapter 8, *Shopping Bag: The JavaScript Shopping Cart.* In fact, several of the functions came directly from those chapters. I'll mention them as we go
along. For now, look at the onslaught of variables declared at the top in lines 19–36:

```
var NN     = (document.layers ? true : false);
var hideName = (NN ? 'hide' : 'hidden');
var showName = (NN ? 'show' : 'visible');
var zIdx    = -1;

var iconNum  = 4;
var startWdh = 25;
var imgIdx   = 0;
var activate = false;
var activeLayer = null;

var backImgs = [];
var icons = [
    'bear', 'cowprod', 'dragon', 'judo',
    'robot', 'seniorexec', 'dude', 'juicemoose',
    'logo1', 'logo2', 'logo3','tree',
    'sun', 'gator', 'tornado', 'cactus'
    ];
```

The first four variables were brought in from earlier scripts. *NN* helps determine
which browser is being used. *showName* and *hideName* are different strings for
showing and hiding layers, depending on the browser, and *zIdx* represents an
integer that will be used to set the z-index of each layer created. Variable
iconNum is an integer that determines how many icons to display on the screen at
a time. We start with 4. *startWdh* is used to initially position all the icons. You'll
see that shortly in function genLayout().

imgIdx tracks images. *activate* is a Boolean variable that determines whether a layer should be dragged or dropped. *activeLayer* determines which layer the user currently has the mouse pointer over after clicking.

If that isn't enough, there are also two array variables. *backImgs* is originally set to an empty array. It will soon be populated with *Image* objects, each containing a background image. The background images are named *background0.jpg*, *background1.jpg*, *background2.jpg*, and so forth.

icons is an array of strings that identifies the name of each icon. That means that each icon will be created on a layer of the *icon* element's name. The image used for the icon is also the same name. The layer named *bear*, for example, will contain the image *bear.gif*. By the way, all the icon images are transparent GIFs. White is the transparent color. Since the background images are primarily white, you can place icons on top of one another and still see "all the way" to the background without one icon covering a portion of the other.

Walking on Familiar Ground

If you have been working with other chapters in this book, you'll be glad to know that some of your hard work will be rewarded. A few functions used here have been used throughout, so you can breeze through them. This happens in other chapters, too, but even more so here.

Table 10-1 will help identify which functions you have probably seen.

Table 10-1. Functions for Layer Manipulation

Function	Purpose	Chapter(s)
genLayer()	Create the layers in NN or MSIE	3, 4, 6, 9, 11
hideSlide()	Hide layers by name	3, 4, 6, 9, 11
showSlide()	Show layers by name	3, 4, 6, 9, 11
refSlide()	Refer to layers by name	3, 4, 6, 9, 11
motionListener()	Track mouse movement	11
grabXY()	Obtain x and y positions of element	11

The first four functions in the table are exactly the same as in other chapters. If you aren't familiar with these functions, see the discussion in Chapter 3. motionListener(), however, has been altered slightly, making it worthy of discussion. Function grabXY() can be found in Chapter 11, *Context-Sensitive Help*. It, too, has undergone significant changes. Here are the rest of the functions that make things happen.

Places Everyone!

While the application loads, *back.html* is working diligently to preload all the images, create and position all the layers, then show or hide them as needed. Function genLayout() coordinates every bit of this. Watch how things unfold in lines 38–64:

```
function genLayout() {

  for (var i = 0; i <= 7; i++) {
    backImgs[i] = new Image();
    backImgs[i].src = top.baseURL + '/images/background' + i +
    '.jpg';
  }

  genLayer("Back", 10, 250, backImgs[1].width, backImgs[1].height,
    showName, '<IMG NAME="background" SRC="' + top.baseURL +
    '/images/background0.jpg">');

  for (var j = 0; j < parent.greetings.length; j++) {
    genLayer("greeting" + j, 50, 275, 500, 100, hideName,
      '<SPAN CLASS="Greeting">' + parent.greetings[j] + '</SPAN>');
  }

  for (var i = 0; i < icons.length; i++) {
    if (i % iconNum == 0) { startWdh = 25; }
    else { startWdh += 110; }
    genLayer(icons[i], startWdh, 15, 100, 100, (i < iconNum ? showName :
      hideName), '<A HREF="javascript: changeAction(\'' + icons[i] +
      '\',' + (i + 1) + ');"><IMG SRC="' + top.baseURL +
      '/images/' + icons[i] + '.gif" BORDER="0"></A>');
  }
  startWdh = 25;
  }
```

The first thing genLayout() handles is preloading the background images. The user will likely want to see all the images before choosing one, so preloading is a good idea. Using *backImgs*, the function creates an *Image* object for each element and assigns its source accordingly using top.baseURL (declared earlier in *index. html*, remember?), the string *background*, the value of *i*, and the string *.jpg*:

```
for (var i = 0; i <= 7; i++) {
  backImgs[i] = new Image();
  backImgs[i].src = top.baseURL + '/images/background' + i + '.jpg';  }
```

After loading all the images, the first thing to set up is the default background. You can choose any of them, but for simplicity, I chose *background0.jpg*, and put it in a layer named *Back*. The layer width and height are set to those of the background image. This becomes important when positioning the icons later:

```
genLayer("Back", 10, 250, backImgs[1].width, backImgs[1].height,
  showName, '<IMG NAME="background" SRC="' + top.baseURL +
  '/images/background0.jpg">');
```

Now the background layer and default image are in place. The next thing to do is set up the greetings. These are simply layers with large text, such as "Family Reunion" or "Thinking Of You." These greetings come from the *greetings* array in *index.html.* Let's apply them in lines 50–53:

```
for (var j = 0; j < parent.greetings.length; j++) {
  genLayer("greeting" + j, 50, 275, 500, 100, hideName,
    '<SPAN CLASS="Greeting">' + parent.greetings[j] + '</SPAN>');
  }
```

This means there will be **parent.greetings.length** greetings, all of which have the same left and top positions of 50 and 275, respectively. The user can't move these, but they are nicely positioned at the upper left of the background display area. Each greeting is contained within its own layer. The layer contains a set of **SPAN** tags to make use of the stylesheet class definition named *Greeting,* defined at the top of the document.

With the background and greetings in place, all that is left is the icon placement. See lines 55–62:

```
for (var i = 0; i < icons.length; i++) {
  if (i % iconNum == 0) { startWdh = 25; }
  else { startWdh += 110; }
  genLayer(icons[i], startWdh, 15, 100, 100, (i < iconNum ? showName :
    hideName), '<A HREF="javascript: changeAction(\'' + icons[i] +
    '\',' + (i + 1) + ');"><IMG SRC="' + top.baseURL +
    '/images/' + icons[i] + '.gif" BORDER="0"></A>');
  }
```

Each element in *icons* will represent an icon layer. Variable *iconNum* dictates that four icons be shown at a time. Also, each of the images is 100 pixels wide. The heights vary. Variable *startWdh* starts at 25. Its value will determine the left pixel position of each layer created. I chose an arbitrary width of 10 pixels between each of the four icons. In other words, starting at 25 pixels to the right of the left margin, a new icon is positioned every 110 pixels (100 pixels of width for the layer and 10 pixels between). After *iconNum* of icons has been created and positioned, the process starts over with the same 25-pixel reference point. Two programming features enable this process. One is an if-else statement executed before each layer is created with **genLayer()**; the other is the use of the modulus (**%**) operator. Take a closer look at both:

```
if (i % iconNum == 0) { startWdh = 25; }
else { startWdh += 110; }
```

As the *for* loop executes, *i* becomes larger and larger. Every time *i* is a multiple of *iconNum* (4, in this case), it's time to start a new group of icons with the first one in the group again being left-positioned at 25 pixels. *startWdh* is set to a value of 25. For example, it is time to start over when *i* reaches 4, 8, 12, 16, and 20. If *i* is any other value, this indicates that the next icon should be left-positioned 110 pixels from that of the last icon. That's why 110 is added to the current value of *startWdh*. The modulus operator returns an integer indicating the remainder of a quotient. If the remainder is 0, *i* is a multiple of *iconNum*.

Knowing where to left-position the layer is the hard part. Now `genLayout()` finishes its duties by creating a layer for each icon with a custom call to `genLayer()` each time:

```
genLayer(icons[i], startWdh, 15, 100, 100, (i < iconNum ? showName :
    hideName), '<A HREF="javascript: changeAction(\'' + icons[i] + '\',' +
    (i + 1) + ');"><IMG SRC="' + top.baseURL + '/images/' +
    icons[i] + '.gif" BORDER="0"></A>');
```

Each icon layer contains a lone `IMG` tag surrounded by an anchor tag. Note that the second and third arguments passed to `genLayer()` are values for the left and top properties of the layer. *startWdh* always represents the left; the top is fixed at 15 pixels. The sixth argument passed determines whether the icon should be visible or hidden. The default is to show only the first set of icons created. In this case, that's the first four layers. Therefore, the conditional operator in the sixth argument is such that if *i* is less than *iconNum* (e.g., 0, 1, 2, or 3), the layer should be visible. All others should be hidden. If the icon should be visible, variable *showName* is passed in. Otherwise, *hideName* gets the call.

The last thing to consider before moving on is the nature of the anchor tag. What does it do? Consider this. Whenever the user passes the mouse over the icon and clicks for the first time, he or she obviously wants to "pick up" that icon and drag it somewhere. To make that happen, a `javascript:` protocol in the `HREF` attribute makes a call to function `changeAction()`, discussed shortly. All `HREF` attributes make the same call to this function, but each icon link must pass to `changeAction()` information specific to itself.

First, `changeAction()` needs to know the name of the icon it will be dealing with. That's easy. Pass in `icons[i]`, which holds the correct string. Next, we have to pass in an integer that represents the icon in the MSIE document object model. That is, in order for this drag-and-drop functionality to work, MSIE will need to know to which image it is referring. Remember that the first image created on the page was the background image, so it is `document.images[0]`. The first icon is `document.images[1]`. All other icons represent `document.images[i + 1]`. That's why the value of `(i + 1)` is passed. This will become more apparent when we look at `changeAction()` and `grabXY()`.

That's a lot of explaining for a 27-line function. Let's set *startWdh* to 25 and move on.

Tracking the Mouse Location

`motionListener()` enables JavaScript to capture the mouse activities with the *onmousemove* event handler. It is very easy to set up. The only difference between the two browsers is that Navigator needs the `captureEvents()` method called, and that it implements the *mousemove* event from the window. MSIE does so from the document. Here are lines 96–104:

```
function motionListener() {
  if (NN) {
    window.captureEvents(Event.MOUSEMOVE);
    window.onmousemove = grabXY;
    }
  else {
    document.onmousemove = grabXY;
    }
  }
```

Whenever the user moves the mouse, function `grabXY()` is called. Remember that there are no parentheses needed to call the function. *onmousemove* is referring to `grabXY`, not calling it. The *onLoad* event calls `motionListener()` function in line 132. It is called only once, so mouse tracking occurs for the duration of the application.

Calling All Icons

When the user clicks an icon, the call to `changeAction()` essentially brings the icon to life, making it available for transport. Lines 123–127 have the details:

```
function changeAction(name, MSIERef) {
  activate = !activate;
  activeLayer = name;
  imgIdx = MSIERef;
  }
```

Remember variables *activate* and *activeLayer?* They were declared long ago at the top of the document. *activate* starts out as false, which means—as we'll soon see in `grabXY()`—not to reposition any layers according to mouse movement. The first time `changeAction()` is called, *activate* becomes true, putting `grabXY()` in action. The layer will follow wherever the mouse pointer may go. The only way to stop this is to click again. This time global variable *activate* is changed to its opposite, which is false. The dragging stops.

Remember how `changeaction()` is designed to pass in two arguments? One is the name of the layer on which to perform the action, assigned to *name*. The other is the image index to properly reference the image in the `document.images` array for MSIE. This value is assigned to *MSIERef*. *activeLayer* is set to the value of *name*, and *imgIdx* is set to the value of *MSIERef.* That's just what we need to drag these icons around, whichever browser is being used.

Moving the Icons

`motionListener()` has it so `grabXY()` is called every time the user moves the mouse. You can see what happens in lines 106–121:

```
function grabXY(ev) {
  if (activate) {
    if(NN) {
      var itemWdh = refSlide(activeLayer).document.images[0].width;
      var itemHgt = refSlide(activeLayer).document.images[0].height;
      refSlide(activeLayer).left = ev.pageX - parseInt(itemWdh / 2);
      refSlide(activeLayer).top = ev.pageY - parseInt(itemHgt / 2);
    }
    else {
      var itemWdh = document.images[imgIdx].width;
      var itemHgt = document.images[imgIdx].height;
      refSlide(activeLayer).left = event.x - parseInt(itemWdh / 2);
      refSlide(activeLayer).top = event.y - parseInt(itemHgt / 2);
    }
  }
}
```

`grabXY()` is called, but the only way any of the code in the function runs is if variable *activate* is true. The first time the user clicks one of the icon links, *activate* becomes true. The nested *if-else* statement runs. If the user has Navigator, the *if* statement block is executed. Otherwise, the *else* block is executed. Both perform the same function, but for a particular browser.

Both code blocks declare local variables *itemWdh* and *itemHgt*. These will determine the left and top positions of the icon clicked. So why not just set them to the coordinates of the mouse pointer's current location? After all, that is by nature what we are using to track the mouse movement.

You could, but there's a catch. If you do, that means the mouse-pointer arrow will be at the upper-left corner of the icon for the duration of the drag. That looks a little odd, but even worse, the user might be able to move the mouse fast enough to escape the dragging motion and click while not over the icon. The user might have to click a couple of times to "release" the icon.

The solution is to position the icon so that the mouse-pointer arrow is always located in the center of the icon. Regardless of browser, *itemWdh* and *itemHgt* represent the respective width and height of the icon image that the user clicked. You have to get these values differently, depending on the browser. Notice the difference. Navigator wants it like this:

```
var itemWdh = refSlide(activeLayer).document.images[0].width;
var itemHgt = refSlide(activeLayer).document.images[0].height;
```

To get at the image, you have to reference the appropriate layer, then the document, then `images[0]` (it's the only image in the layer). It's not the same in MSIE:

```
var itemWdh = document.images[imgIdx].width;
var itemHgt = document.images[imgIdx].height;
```

MSIE has no layer array. You can access the images straight from the *images* array. However, you need to know the correct image, which is referenced by *imgIdx*. Remember, we set that with every call to `changeAction()`. Review that function if this doesn't make sense.

We now have a handle on the correct image width and height. All we need is some quick math to center the mouse pointer over the icons.

Let's tackle this by example. Suppose the user clicks on an icon to begin dragging. At the time of the click, the mouse-pointer arrow was at 100 pixels right of the document's left border and 100 pixels below the document's top border (not the screen). Let's suppose that the icon image is 100 pixels in width and 150 pixels in height. If we set the left and top properties of the icon to 100, 100, that puts the icon's upper-left corner directly "underneath" the pointer arrow. Nice, but we want the pointer arrow in the middle of the icon.

You can get to the middle of the icon by subtracting half the image width from the left position and half the image height from the top position. We know that *itemWdh* is 100, and *itemHgt* is 150. Here's how the new positions break down:

```
Icon left = pointer arrow horizontal (x) location-(100/2)=100-(50)=50
Icon top = pointer arrow vertical (y) location-(150/2)=100-(75)=25
```

Instead of setting *left* and *top* to 100, 100, they are set to 50, 25. This puts the pointer arrow smack in the center of the icon. To be sure that the division by two comes out with an integer, we'll use `parseInt()` to return the integer portion. Look once again at the code in `grabXY()`. Here's how this is implemented in Navigator:

```
refSlide(activeLayer).left = ev.pageX - parseInt(itemWdh / 2);
refSlide(activeLayer).top = ev.pageY - parseInt(itemHgt / 2);
```

The event model in Navigator utilizes an event object created on the fly, reflected here in the local variable *ev*. The *pageX* and *pageY* properties of that event object contain the values for the *x,y* coordinates of the active layer. MSIE, on the other hand, has a global event object from which the coordinates can be accessed:

```
refSlide(activeLayer).left = event.x - parseInt(itemWdh / 2);
refSlide(activeLayer).top = event.y - parseInt(itemHgt / 2);
```

Properties *x* and *y* contain the equivalent values. Now the icon can be dragged and dropped at will.

After the Documents Load

The real action begins in *front.html*. Example 10-3 shows the code. The first dozen lines or so contain style sheet properties. The next couple hundred lines define the JavaScript variables and functions responsible for capturing all the information for creating, testing, and finally sending the greeting.

Example 10-3. front.html

```
 1 <HTML>
 2 <HEAD>
 3 <TITLE></TITLE>
 4 <STYLE TYPE="text/css">
 5 <!--
 6
 7 TD
 8   {
 9     font-family: Arial;
10   }
11
12 .Front
13   {
14     position: absolute;
15     left: 25;
16     top: 25;
17     width: 325;
18     border: 1px solid;
19     background: #ffffee;
20   }
21
22 //-->
23 </STYLE>
24 <SCRIPT LANGUAGE="JavaScript1.2">
25 <!--
26
27
28 var curGreet = iconIdx = 0;
29 var backgroundIdx = 0;
30 var bRef = parent.Back
31
32 function showGreeting(selIdx) {
33   if (selIdx > 0) {
34     bRef.hideSlide("greeting" + curGreet);
35     bRef.showSlide("greeting" + selIdx);
36     curGreet = selIdx;
37     }
38   }
39
40 function nextBackground() {
41   backgroundIdx = (backgroundIdx == bRef.backImgs.length - 1 ?
42     backgroundIdx = 0 : backgroundIdx + 1);
43   if(document.all) {
44     bRef.document.background.src = bRef.backImgs[backgroundIdx].src;
```

Example 10-3. front.html (continued)

```
45      }
46    else {
47      bRef.document.layers["Back"].document.images[0].src =
48        bRef.backImgs[backgroundIdx].src;
49      }
50    }
51
52  function nextIcons() {
53    for (var i = bRef.iconNum * iconIdx; i < (bRef.iconNum * iconIdx) +
54      bRef.iconNum; i++) {
55      if (i < bRef.icons.length && !onCard(i)) {
56        bRef.hideSlide(bRef.icons[i]);
57        }
58      }
59    iconIdx = (iconIdx >= (bRef.icons.length / bRef.iconNum)  - 1 ? 0 :
60      iconIdx + 1);
61    for (var i = bRef.iconNum * iconIdx; i < (bRef.iconNum * iconIdx) +
62      bRef.iconNum; i++) {
63      if (i < bRef.icons.length) {
64        bRef.showSlide(bRef.icons[i]);
65        }
66      else { break; }
67      }
68    }
69
70  function resetForm() {
71    if (document.all) {
72      bRef.hideSlide("greeting" +
73        document.EntryForm.Greetings.selectedIndex);
74      document.EntryForm.reset();
75      }
76    else {
77      bRef.hideSlide("greeting" +
78      document.layers["SetupForm"].document.EntryForm.Greetings.selectedIndex);
79      document.layers["SetupForm"].document.EntryForm.reset();
80      }
81    }
82
83  function onCard(iconRef) {
84    var ref   = bRef.refSlide(bRef.icons[iconRef]);
85    var ref2 = bRef.refSlide("Back");
86    if(document.all) {
87      if((parseInt(ref.left) >= parseInt(ref2.left)) &&
88        (parseInt(ref.top) >= parseInt(ref2.top)) &&
89        (parseInt(ref.left) + parseInt(ref.width) <= parseInt(ref2.left) +
90          parseInt(ref2.width)) &&
91        (parseInt(ref.top) + parseInt(ref.height) <= parseInt(ref2.top) +
92        parseInt(ref2.height))) {
93        return true;
94        }
95      }
96    else {
```

Example 10-3. front.html (continued)

```
97    if((ref.left >= ref2.left) &&
98      (ref.top >= ref2.top) &&
99      (ref.left + ref.document.images[0].width <=  ref2.left +
100     ref2.document.images[0].width) &&
101     (ref.top + ref.document.images[0].height <= ref2.top +
102     ref2.document.images[0].height)) {
103       return true;
104       }
105     }
106   ref.left = ((iconRef % bRef.iconNum) * 110) + bRef.startWdh;
107   ref.top = 15;
108   return false;
109   }
110
111 function shipGreeting(fObj) {
112 if (fObj.Recipient.value == "") {
113     alert('You need an email address in the To: field');
114     return false;
115     }
116   else if (fObj.Message.value == "") {
117     alert("You need to type a Message.");
118     return false;
119     }
120   else if (fObj.Greetings.selectedIndex == 0) {
121     alert('You need to choose a Greeting.');
122     return false;
123     }
124
125   fObj.EntireMessage.value = genGreeting(fObj);
126
127   fObj.BaseURL.value = top.baseURL;
128   return true;
129   }
130
131 function testGreeting(fObj) {
132   var msgStr = '<HTML><TITLE>Cyber Greeting Test Page</TITLE>' +
133     genGreeting(fObj) + '<TABLE ALIGN="CENTER"><TR><TD><FORM>' +
134     '<INPUT TYPE=BUTTON VALUE="     OK     " onClick="self.close();">' +
135     '</FORM></TD></TR></TABLE></HTML>';
136   newWin = open('', '', 'width=' + (
137     bRef.backImgs[backgroundIdx].width + 50) +
138     ',height=600,scrollbars=yes');
139   with(newWin.document) {
140     open();
141     writeln(msgStr);
142     close();
143     }
144   newWin.focus();
145   }
146
147 function genGreeting(fObj) {
148   var greetingIdx = fObj.Greetings.selectedIndex;
```

Example 10-3. front.html (continued)

```
149    var msg = fObj.Message.value;
150
151    msg = msg.replace(/\r+/g, "");
152    msg = msg.replace(/\n+/g, "<BR><BR>");
153
154    var msgStr = '<TABLE BORDER=0><TR><TD COLSPAN=2><FONT FACE=Arial>' +
155      '<H2>Your Cyber Greeting</H2>To: ' + fObj.Recipient.value +
156      '<BR><BR></TD></TR><TR><TD VALIGN=TOP><IMG SRC="' +
157      top.baseURL + '/images/background' + backgroundIdx + '.jpg">' +
158      '<DIV STYLE="position:relative;left:40;top:-255;font-family:Arial;' +
159      'font-size:48px;font-weight:bold;">' + parent.greetings[greetingIdx] +
160      '</DIV>';
161
162    var iconStr = '';
163    for (var i = 0; i < bRef.icons.length; i++) {
164      if(onCard(i)) {
165        iconStr += '<DIV STYLE="position:absolute;left:' +
166        bRef.refSlide(bRef.icons[i]).left + ';top:' +
167        (parseInt(bRef.refSlide(bRef.icons[i]).top) -
168        (document.all ? 140 : 150)) + ';"><IMG SRC="' +
169        top.baseURL + '/images/' + bRef.icons[i] + '.gif"></DIV>';
170        }
171      }
172
173    msgStr += iconStr + '</TD></TR><TR><TD WIDTH=' +
174      bRef.backImgs[backgroundIdx].width + '><FONT FACE=Arial>' + msg +
175      '</TD></TR></TABLE>';
176    return msgStr;
177    }
178
179 //-->
180 </SCRIPT>
181
182 </HEAD>
183 <BODY onLoad="resetForm();">
184 <DIV ID="SetupForm" CLASS="Front">
185 <FORM NAME="EntryForm"
186   ACTION="http://www.your_domain.com/cgi-bin/greetings/greet.pl"
187   METHOD="POST" TARGET="_top" OnSubmit="return shipGreeting(this);">
188 <INPUT TYPE=HIDDEN NAME="EntireMessage">
189
190 <INPUT TYPE=HIDDEN NAME="BaseURL">
191   <TABLE CELLSPACING="0" CELLPADDING="5" WIDTH="375">
192     <TR>
193       <TD COLSPAN="3"><CENTER><H2>Cyber Greetings</H2></CENTER></TD>
194     </TR>
195     <TR>
196       <TD HEIGHT="40" VALIGN="TOP">
197       To:
198       </TD>
199       <TD COLSPAN="2" VALIGN="TOP">
200         <INPUT TYPE=TEXT NAME="Recipient" SIZE="25">
```

Example 10-3. front.html (continued)

```
201       </TD>
202     </TR>
203     <TR>
204       <TD HEIGHT="80" VALIGN="TOP">Message: </TD>
205       <TD COLSPAN="2" VALIGN="TOP">
206       <TEXTAREA ROWS="7" COLS="25" NAME="Message" WRAP="PHYSICAL">
207         </TEXTAREA>
208       </TD>
209     </TR>
210     <TR>
211       <TD>Images:</TD>
212       <TD HEIGHT="40" COLSPAN="2">
213       <INPUT TYPE=BUTTON VALUE="  Icons - >  " onClick="nextIcons();">
214          
215       <INPUT TYPE=BUTTON VALUE="Backgrounds - >"
216         onClick="nextBackground();">
217       </TD>
218     </TR>
219     <TR>
220       <TD>Greeting:</TD>
221       <TD HEIGHT="40" COLSPAN="2">
222       <SCRIPT LANGUAGE="JavaScript1.2">
223       <!--
224
225       var sel = '<SELECT NAME="Greetings"
226         onChange="showGreeting(this.selectedIndex);">';
227       for (var i = 0; i < parent.greetings.length; i++) {
228         sel += '<OPTION>' + parent.greetings[i];
229         }
230       sel += '</SELECT>';
231       document.writeln(sel);
232
233       //-->
234       </SCRIPT>
235       </TD>
236     </TR>
237     <TR>
238       <TD VALIGN=TOP>Sending: </TD>
239       <TD HEIGHT="40" ALIGN="CENTER">
240       <INPUT TYPE=BUTTON VALUE="  Test  "
241         onClick="testGreeting(this.form);">
242           
243       <INPUT TYPE=BUTTON VALUE="  Clear  " onClick="resetForm();">
244           
245       <INPUT TYPE=SUBMIT VALUE="  Send  ">
246       </FORM>
247       </TD>
248     </TR>
249   </TABLE>
250 </FORM>
251 </DIV>
252 </BODY>
253 </HTML>
```

Meet the Variables

Though *front.html* doesn't contain nearly as many variables as *back.html*, here are the players in lines 28–30:

```
var curGreet = iconIdx = 0;
var backgroundIdx = 0;
var bRef = parent.Back;
```

Variable *curGreet* represents the index of the select list of greetings. It is originally set to 0. *iconIdx* is a variable used for tracking the icons by index. It, too, is initially set to zero. The last variable in the list is *bRef,* which is simply a reference to the script and window object in the frame named *Back.* This will make life much easier.

JavaScript Technique: Differentiating Web Code

The application in this chapter, unlike most of the other chapters, actually has a decent amount of hardcoded HTML. I suggest you make different codes look different. For example, in all client-side programming, my HTML is always uppercase. I don't use many uppercase letters in JavaScript. Anyone who has even glanced at these two languages could tell the difference, but this makes it stand out even more.

This might not sound like a big deal. However, I picked up the habit from a programmer who uses a lot of Cold Fusion Markup Language (CFML), a popular server-side scripting language. All his code contains HTML, CFML, JavaScript, and SQL (Structured Query Language) for database queries. That's four languages in the same script. Suppose you are using Active Server Pages. That opens the door for HTML, VBScript, JavaScript, JScript, and SQL. How many more acronyms do you need?

Needless to say, I developed my own strategy, posthaste.

Displaying the Greetings

Now that the select list of greetings is all set, the user can display the greeting of choice by highlighting the corresponding option. The *onChange* event handler in the select list calls **showGreeting()**, as follows:

```
function showGreeting(selIdx) {
  if (selIdx > 0) {
    bRef.hideSlide("greeting" + curGreet);
    bRef.showSlide("greeting" + selIdx);
    curGreet = selIdx;
    }
  }
```

JavaScript Technique: Cross-Frame Communication

You might remember from Chapter 1, *The Client-Side Search Engine*, that we used a variable named *docObj* to refer easily to the document object in (`parent.frames[1]`). It's the same here, but we're referring instead to the window *Back*. There are variables declared in *back.html* that are used in *front. html* as well. Using a variable to refer to `parent.Back` makes writing your code a little easier on the eyes (writing only *bRef* instead of `parent.Back`), and lets you easily reference data from other frames. You'll be doing yourself a favor by creating such a variable and using it in your code. Consider the following function `onCard()` which is defined in *front.html*. This function not only uses *bRef*, but also creates two other "alias" variables named *ref* and *ref2* to refer to specific layers. This is what the function looks like:

```
function onCard(iconRef) {
  var ref = bRef.refSlide(bRef.icons[iconRef]);
  var ref2 = bRef.refSlide("Back");
  if(document.all) {
    var ref = bRef.refSlide(bRef.icons[iconRef]);
    var ref2 = bRef.refSlide("Back");
    if((parseInt(ref.left) >= parseInt(ref2.left)) &&
      (parseInt(ref.top) >= parseInt(ref2.top)) &&
      (parseInt(ref.left) + parseInt(ref.width) <= parseInt(ref2.left) +
      parseInt(ref2.width)) &&
      (parseInt(ref.top) + parseInt(ref.height) <= parseInt(ref2.top) +
      parseInt(ref2.height))) {
      return true;
      }
    }
  else {
    if((ref.left >= ref2.left) &&
      (ref.top >= ref2.top) &&
      (ref.left + ref.document.images[0].width <=  ref2.left +
      ref2.document.images[0].width) &&
      (ref.top + ref.document.images[0].height <= ref2.top +
      ref2.document.images[0].height)) {
      return true;
      }
    }
  ref.left = ((iconRef % bRef.iconNum) * 110) + bRef.startWdh;
  ref.top = 15;
  return false;
  }
```

Certainly not the longest function I've ever written, but consider the same function without *bRef*, *ref*, and *ref2*. It's quite a bit longer and more unwieldy:

```
function onCard(iconRef) {
  if(document.all) {
```

—Continued—

```
        if((parseInt(parent.Back.refSlide(parent.Back.icons[iconRef]).left) >=
            parseInt(parent.Back.refSlide("Back").left)) &&
            (parseInt(parent.Back.refSlide(parent.Back.icons[iconRef]).top) >=
            parseInt(parent.Back.refSlide("Back").top)) &&
            (parseInt(parent.Back.refSlide(parent.Back.icons[iconRef]).left) +
            parseInt(parent.Back.refSlide(parent.Back.icons[iconRef]).width) <=
            parseInt(parent.Back.refSlide("Back").left) +
            parseInt(parent.Back.refSlide("Back").width)) &&
            -parseInt(parent.Back.refSlide(parent.Back.icons[iconRef]).top) +
          parseInt(parent.Back.refSlide(parent.Back.icons[iconRef]).height) <=
            parseInt(parent.Back.refSlide("Back").top) +
            parseInt(parent.Back.refSlide("Back").height))) {
            return true;
              }
            }
        else {
          if((parent.Back.refSlide(parent.Back.icons[iconRef]).left >=
            parent.Back.refSlide("Back").left) &&
            (parent.Back.refSlide(parent.Back.icons[iconRef]).top >=
            parent.Back.refSlide("Back").top) &&
            (parent.Back.refSlide(parent.Back.icons[iconRef]).left +
            parent.Back.refSlide(parent.Back.icons[iconRef]).document.
    images[0].width <=
            parent.Back.refSlide("Back").left +
            parent.Back.refSlide("Back").document.images[0].width) &&
            (parent.Back.refSlide(parent.Back.icons[iconRef]).top +
            parent.Back.refSlide(parent.Back.icons[iconRef]).document.
    images[0].height <= parent.Back.refSlide("Back").top +
            parent.Back.refSlide("Back").document.images[0].height)) {
            return true;
              }
            }
        parent.Back.refSlide(parent.Back.icons[iconRef]).left =
            ((iconRef % parent.Back.iconNum) * 110) + parent.Back.startWdh;
        parent.Back.refSlide(parent.Back.icons[iconRef]).top = 15;
        return false;
            }
```

The next block of logic worth review appears in lines 225-231. As the browser parses
the HTML, the JavaScript executed here creates a select list using the *greetings* array
defined in *index.html*. Have a closer look:

```
var sel = '<SELECT NAME="Greetings" ' +
   'onChange="showGreeting(this.selectedIndex);">';
for (var i = 0; i < parent.greetings.length; i++) {
  sel += '<OPTION>' + parent.greetings[i];
   }
sel += '</SELECT>';
document.writeln(sel);
```

showGreeting() expects one argument—the *selectedIndex* of the *Greetings* select list. As long as *selIdx* is not 0 (the greeting would read "Choose One"), showGreeting() hides the currently visible greeting layer and displays the greeting layer associated with the option selected. The value of *selIdx* then becomes the current value of the visible layer, which sets things up for the next time.

Moving Through All the Images

To look through the available background images, the user simply clicks the "Backgrounds -->" button until he or she finds the one that is most suitable. Clicking this button calls function **nextBackground()**, listed in lines 40–50:

```
function nextBackground() {
  backgroundIdx = (backgroundIdx == bRef.backImgs.length - 1 ?
    backgroundIdx = 0 : backgroundIdx + 1);
  if(document.all) {
    bRef.document.background.src = bRef.backImgs[backgroundIdx].src;
    }
  else {
    bRef.document.layers["Back"].document.images[0].src =
      bRef.backImgs[backgroundIdx].src;
    }
  }
```

The background images are preloaded in lines 40–44 of file *back.html*. Since each is named according to the *background0.jpg, background1.jpg, background2.jpg,* etc., convention, we can use an integer, *backgroundIdx,* along with string concatenation to iterate through the images. When the document loads, *backgroundIdx* is set to 0. Each time the user clicks "Background -->," that value is increased by 1 until there are no more images to reference. In other words, when *backgroundIdx* reaches **top.Back.backImgs.length - 1**, it is reset to 0 to start again from the beginning.

We can use this newly determined value to change the *src* property of the correct *Image* object. Since the background image was placed in a layer for more accurate positioning, we have to resort to accessing the disparate DOMs of NN and MSIE in different ways.

For MSIE, the image is considered a property of the document object, like so:

```
top.Back.document.background.src
```

For Navigator, you have to go to the document object within the layer. Since the layer is named *Back*, reaching the desired *Image* looks like this:

```
top.Back.document.layers["Back"].document.images[0].src
```

Once the syntax has been determined, you just set the path to the *src* property of the *backImgs* Image using *backgroundIdx*. By the way, this is not the first time

I've used this method of iteration. You can find similar examples in Chapter 3 and Chapter 8. Now the user can cycle through the backgrounds. We need something similar for the icons. That's where `nextIcons()` comes in, lines 52–68:

```
function nextIcons() {
  for (var i = bRef.iconNum * iconIdx; i < (bRef.iconNum * iconIdx) +
    bRef.iconNum; i++) {
    if (i < bRef.icons.length && !onCard(i)) {
      bRef.hideSlide(bRef.icons[i]);
      }
    }
  iconIdx = (iconIdx >= (bRef.icons.length / bRef.iconNum)  - 1 ? 0 :
    iconIdx + 1);
  for (var i = bRef.iconNum * iconIdx; i < (bRef.iconNum * iconIdx) +
    bRef.iconNum; i++) {
    if (i < bRef.icons.length) {
      bRef.showSlide(bRef.icons[i]);
      }
    else { break; }
    }
  }
```

The user iterates through these as with the backgrounds, but there is more to it than changing the *src* property of a single image. Instead, each icon is an image in its own layer. So clicking the "Icons -->" button is a little more involved. Not only do we have to hide each layer currently showing, but we have to decide which layer to show, and we need to do this in groups.

It doesn't make much sense for the user to click 20 times to see the 20 available icons. That can be monotonous and a waste of browser real estate. You can see from the earlier graphics that I've chosen to display the icons in groups of four. Whatever number you choose, it is represented by the value of variable *iconNum* set at line 24 of *back.html*. Since this is *front.html*, the script refers to it as `top.Back.iconNum`. The idea is to display *iconNum* icons each time the user clicks "Icons -->." If you have 20 icons, the user can expect to see five groups of icons. Of course, we also want to make it easy to add and subtract icons at will. If you remove one icon, the user will see four groups each of four icons and one group of three. Meanwhile, you don't have to make any changes in `nextIcons()`.

It's fairly easy. Start with the first four, then hide them and display the next four, and so on until you run out of icons. Then you start over. So the English translation is: hide four old ones, then show four new ones. Let's take a closer look at the JavaScript version. To identify each group, we'll use variable *iconIdx*, originally set to 0. The first group is associated with 0; the second is associated with 1, and so on.

As soon as the user chooses "Icons -->," we have to hide whatever icons are in the group associated with *iconIdx*:

```
for (var i = bRef.iconNum * iconIdx; i < (bRef.iconNum * iconIdx) +
  bRef.iconNum; i++) {
  if (i < bRef.icons.length && !onCard(i)) {
    bRef.hideSlide(bRef.icons[i]);
  }
}
```

Variable *i* is set to `iconNum * iconIdx`. *i* will be incremented by 1 as long as it is less than (`iconNum * iconIdx`) + `iconNum`. If that seems confusing, think about what happens when the document finishes loading. *iconNum* is 4 and *iconIdx* is 0. That means that when this function is first called, *i* will be 0, 1, 2, and 3. The next time, *iconIdx* will be 1 (that happens later in the function), so *i* will be 4, 5, 6, and 7. And so it goes.

Variable *i* holds an integer that will be used to access an element in the *icons* array. Why? Each icon is its own layer, correct? The code in *back.html* names each layer according to the elements in the *icons* array. `icons[0]` refers to the *bear* layer, for example.

All we need to do is hide the layers associated with 0, 1, 2, and 3, except if the user has dragged one of those icons on to the background display area. Function `onCard()` handles that, which we'll cover shortly. For now, let's assume that none of the icons has been moved so we can get through the function more easily. With that in mind, we just call *hideSlide* from *back.html* and pass in the right layer name, accessed using *i*, no less:

```
bRef.hideSlide(bRef.icons[i]);
```

The old icons are out, and we need to make way for the next group. Before we do though, we have to make sure that we aren't already at the last group of the icons. If so, we have to set *iconIdx* to 0 again. Otherwise, *iconIdx* will be incremented by one. Lines 59–60 do the trick:

```
iconIdx = (iconIdx >= (bRef.icons.length / bRef.iconNum)  - 1 ? 0 :
  iconIdx + 1);
```

One more iteration and the new group will be visible. Lines 61–67 contain a *for* loop that takes care of that:

```
for (var i = bRef.iconNum * iconIdx; i < (bRef.iconNum * iconIdx) +
  bRef.iconNum; i++) {
  if (i < bRef.icons.length) {
    bRef.showSlide(bRef.icons[i]);
  }
  else { break; }
}
```

The plan is to make *iconNum* iterations and reveal the next group of icons. We previously incremented or reset *iconIdx* in line 59–60, so all that's left is to make almost the exact same *for* loop as we did to hide the old group. This time, though, we'll use showSlide() instead. There's a catch, however. Remember that the plan is to make *iconNum* iterations, but what if this is the last group before starting over again and there aren't *iconNum* icons left? If you have 20 icons, and you want to show four at a time, there will be five groups of four. However, if you have 19 icons *and* you want to display four at a time, there are still five groups, but the last group will contain only three icons. That's why we need the extra *if-else* statement to test if it is less than the number of total icons. If so, nextIcons() makes the icon visible. Otherwise, there aren't any more icons in that group, the loop is broken with *break*.

Keeping Dragged Icons in Place

As you just read, iterating through the icons involves hiding some old ones and showing some new ones. That works pretty well except when the user has dragged one of the icons over to the background display area. We want to leave it where it is no matter what. Function onCard() works hard to determine whether each icon it examines should be left alone or hidden and returned to its rightful position. Here are lines 83–109. onCard() doesn't do any hiding or showing. It returns true or false so that other functions can take action accordingly:

```
function onCard(iconRef) {
  var ref = bRef.refSlide(bRef.icons[iconRef]);
  var ref2 = bRef.refSlide("Back");
  if(document.all) {
    if((parseInt(ref.left) >= parseInt(ref2.left)) &&
      (parseInt(ref.top) >= parseInt(ref2.top)) &&
      (parseInt(ref.left) + parseInt(ref.width) <= parseInt(ref2.left) +
      parseInt(ref2.width)) &&
      (parseInt(ref.top) + parseInt(ref.height) <= parseInt(ref2.top) +
      parseInt(ref2.height))) {
      return true;
      }
    }
  else {
    if((ref.left >= ref2.left) &&
      (ref.top >= ref2.top) &&
      (ref.left + ref.document.images[0].width <=  ref2.left +
      ref2.document.images[0].width) &&
      (ref.top + ref.document.images[0].height <= ref2.top +
      ref2.document.images[0].height)) {
      return true;
      }
    }
  ref.left = ((iconRef % bRef.iconNum) * 110) + bRef.startWdh;
  ref.top = 15;
  return false;
  }
```

Before looking more closely at onCard(), we need to know what qualifies an icon as being over the background display area. In the simplest case, all edges of the icon (even if the edge is transparent) must be on or inside *all* the boundaries of the background image. Figure 10-8 demonstrates what stays and what goes.

Figure 10-8. Out of bounds: only the judo kid stays

Assuming that the whitespace is the background display area, the little guy to the right is way off. The cactus is close, but a couple of its edges go outside the border of the background image. The cactus, too, must be returned. Only the judo kid will stay in view. Here's how it all works.

Everything is done according to pixel position. Since the background is contained within a layer, we can use DHTML to determine its left and top positions in relation to the document's left and top borders. Since the layer contains only one image, we can use the *width* and *height* properties of that *Image* object to accurately determine the width and height of the layer. The same holds true for the icons. We'll use the *left* and *top* properties of the layer and the *width* and *height* properties of the *Image*. This function has a couple of nested *if* statements, but the outermost if and else clauses basically perform the same action—one for MSIE; one for Navigator. Here is the first half of onCard(), the part that works for IE:

```
if(document.all) {
    if((parseInt(ref.left) >= parseInt(ref2.left)) &&
        (parseInt(ref.top) >= parseInt(ref2.top)) &&
        (parseInt(ref.left) + parseInt(ref.width) <= parseInt(ref2.left) +
        parseInt(ref2.width)) &&
```

```
(parseInt(ref.top) + parseInt(ref.height) <= parseInt(ref2.top) +
parseInt(ref2.height))) {
return true;
     }
  }
```

The background image has four edges. So does each icon. Therefore, we need four tests to make sure no icon edge exceeds a background edge. Here is the English version of the hefty *if* statement in lines 87–94:

> IF the left edge of the icon is touching or farther right than the left edge of the background,
> AND the top edge of the icon is touching or below the top edge of the background,
> AND the right edge of the icon is touching or farther left than the right edge of the background,
> AND the bottom edge of the icon is touching or above the bottom edge of the background, then
> RETURN TRUE.

Determining the left and top edge positions of each layer is fairly simple. Just use the *left* and *top* properties of each layer. Determining the right and bottom edge positions of each layer isn't much more difficult. The right edge is simply the left position plus the width of the layer. The bottom is just the top position plus the height.

By now, you have probably noticed two things. First, variables *ref* and *ref2* have been set to the layers of the icon and background, respectively. I did that only to make the code a little easier to read. Second, the function `parseInt()` is everywhere. MSIE returns the left and top properties as strings such as 250px instead of 250. `parseInt()` converts the string value to a number, so we can do the math.

The outermost else clause does the same thing for NN. You don't really need the calls to `parseInt()` because Navigator returns the top and left properties as a number.

```
else {
  if((ref.left >= ref2.left) &&
    (ref.top >= ref2.top) &&
    (ref.left + ref.document.images[0].width <=  ref2.left +
    ref2.document.images[0].width) &&
    (ref.top + ref.document.images[0].height <= ref2.top +
    ref2.document.images[0].height)) {
    return true;
    }
  }
```

So, if the icon in question passes all four tests, both browsers return true. If not, see what happens:

```
ref.left = ((iconRef % bRef.iconNum) * 110) + bRef.startWdh;
ref.top = 15;
return false;
```

onCard() realizes that the icons are not on the background display and returns them to their original position. All icons have the same top position of 15 pixels. The left position of each, however, depends on the order in which it comes in the group. No problem. A quick calculation with variables *iconRef* and *iconNum* can determine where the original position of the icon was. As it turns out, each icon image is 100 pixels wide. There are 10 pixels of horizontal space between each, so the positioning is fairly easy. Last of all, the function returns false.

Testing the Work

It would be nice if the sender could preview what the recipient was going to get. Choosing "Test" opens a remote browser window to do this. Lines 131–145 lead the way:

```
function testGreeting(fObj) {
  var msgStr = '<HTML><TITLE>Cyber Greeting Test Page</TITLE>' +
    genGreeting(fObj) + '<TABLE ALIGN="CENTER"><TR><TD><FORM>' +
    '<INPUT TYPE=BUTTON VALUE="      OK      " onClick="self.close();">' +
    '</FORM></TD></TR></TABLE></HTML>';
  newWin =  open('', '', 'width=' + (bRef.backImgs[backgroundIdx].width +
    50) + ',height=600,scrollbars=yes');
  with(newWin.document) {
    open();
    writeln(msgStr);
    close();
    }
  newWin.focus();
  }
```

testGreeting() has only two responsibilities: open a window wide enough to display the message, then write whatever content it is passed to that new window's document stream. The content is stored in local variable *msgStr*. It consists of a little bit of static HTML, and the rest is the dynamic greeting content, which comes from function genGreeting(), which, in turn, is on deck. *msgStr* also contains at the end of it a form with a button to close the remote window. Call it a nice touch. Once *msgStr* is loaded with goodies, testGreeting() opens a window that is 50 pixels wider than the width of the background image and arbitrarily 600 pixels high. The function writes the contents to the document stream, applies focus to the newly opened window, and this one's history.

Creating the Actual Greeting

testGreeting() provides a window for the greeting preview; however, gen-Greeting() creates the work that goes inside.

Here are all 31 lines, 147–177:

```
function genGreeting(fObj) {
  var greetingIdx = fObj.Greetings.selectedIndex;
  var msg = fObj.Message.value;

  msg = msg.replace(/\r+/g, "");
  msg = msg.replace(/\n+/g, "<BR><BR>");

  var msgStr = '<TABLE BORDER=0><TR><TD COLSPAN=2><FONT FACE=Arial>' +
    '<H2>Your Cyber Greeting</H2>To: ' + fObj.Recipient.value +
    '<BR><BR></TD></TR><TR><TD VALIGN=TOP><IMG SRC="' + top.baseURL +
    '/images/background' + backgroundIdx + '.jpg">' +
    '<DIV STYLE="position:relative;left:40;top:-255;font-family:Arial;' +
    'font-size:48px;font-weight:bold;">' +
    parent.greetings[greetingIdx] + '</DIV>';

  var iconStr = '';
  for (var i = 0; i < bRef.icons.length; i++) {
    if(onCard(i)) {
      iconStr += '<DIV STYLE="position:absolute;left:' +
        bRef.refSlide(bRef.icons[i]).left + ';top:' +
        (parseInt(bRef.refSlide(bRef.icons[i]).top) -
        (document.all ? 140 : 150)) + ';"><IMG SRC="' + top.baseURL +
        '/images/' + bRef.icons[i] + '.gif"></DIV>';
    }
  }

  msgStr += iconStr + '</TD></TR><TR><TD WIDTH=' +
    bRef.backImgs[backgroundIdx].width + '><FONT FACE=Arial>' + msg +
    '</TD></TR></TABLE>';
  return msgStr;
}
```

This function is a little thorny, but we can makes things much easier by examining the function in terms of the items it is required to provide. Think about it. genGreeting() only needs to return HTML to represent the following:

- Text that displays the email of the recipient

- The background image

- The correctly positioned greeting

- The correctly positioned icons

- The sender's text message

That isn't very much, but before creating the content, we have to do a little housekeeping. See lines 148–152:

```
var greetingIdx = fObj.Greetings.selectedIndex;
var msg = fObj.Message.value;
msg = msg.replace(/\r+/g, "");
msg = msg.replace(/\n+/g, "<BR><BR>");
```

We declare two local variables, *greetingIdx* and *msg*. *greetingIdx* is the *selectedIndex* of the "Greetings" select list. *msg* represents the message the user enters in the Message field. Since the greeting will be displayed as HTML, newline characters aren't interpreted. That means any breaks must be replaced with <BR> tags. Now we can start creating the greeting. Let's begin from the top of the greeting and work down. Lines 154–160 get things going:

```
var msgStr = '<TABLE BORDER=0><TR><TD COLSPAN=2><FONT FACE=Arial>' +
  '<H2>Your Cyber Greeting</H2>To: ' + fObj.Recipient.value +
  '<BR><BR></TD></TR><TR><TD VALIGN=TOP><IMG SRC="' + top.baseURL +
  '/images/background' + backgroundIdx + '.jpg">' +
  '<DIV STYLE="position:relative;left:40;top:-255;font-family:Arial;' +
  'font-size:48px;font-weight:bold;">' + parent.greetings[greetingIdx] +
  '</DIV>';
```

Everything is contained within a table, which makes life easier. So local variable *msgStr* is set to the beginning of a table. The first row contains a header followed by the first of the four items required—the recipient's email address. That is located in the value of the Recipient field of the form named *EntryForm*. The background image comes in the next row. Using variables *baseURL* and *backgroundIdx*, it isn't hard to create a string that represents the path to the appropriate background image. Remember that if the Greetings select list has a *selectedIndex* of 4, then *background4.jpg* is currently in view.

Notice that there is no DHTML to position the background image on the page. Since the header and the greeting will likely only be one line apiece, this really wasn't needed. We know that the image will wind up somewhere near the top of the page with a left alignment. In the last few lines of this code, the greeting chosen by the sender is positioned relative to the background image placed just before it. The left is set to 40 pixels. The top is set to –255. Those are custom settings that compensate for the position of the background image as shown in *back. html* and the actual placement of the background image in the greeting. When you add your backgrounds, you'll probably have to eyeball this between the look on *back.html* and the preview document, adjusting the left and top positions until they match. After that, you won't have to worry about it until you make any significant changes, such as modifying the background image size.

Three required items down, two to go. The next "item" is the icons that the user dragged into the display area. Lines 162–171 accommodate:

```
var iconStr = '';
for (var i = 0; i < bRef.icons.length; i++) {
  if(onCard(i)) {
    iconStr += '<DIV STYLE="position:absolute;left:' +
    bRef.refSlide(bRef.icons[i]).left +
    ';top:' + (parseInt(bRef.refSlide(bRef.icons[i]).top) -
```

```
          (document.all ? 140 : 150)) + ';"><IMG SRC="' +
          top.baseURL + '/images/' + bRef.icons[i] + '.gif"></DIV>';
      }
    }
```

Local variable *iconStr*, initially set to an empty string, will hold the URLs and positions of all icons within the background display area. The procedure is fairly easy: iterate through all the icons. For each one that is within the display area, create the HTML required to duplicate that icon (the image) on another page in the same location relative to the background image (the left and top positions). Remember that function `onCard()` determines the icon placement and hence, its eligibility.

The code generated for each is an `IMG` tag surrounded by `DIV` tags. The `DIV` tag is assigned a `STYLE` attribute and assigned an absolute left position of the current icon's left position and an absolute top position of the current icon's top position, minus 140 or 150 pixels, depending on whether the browser is Internet Explorer or Navigator. Two questions, right?

1. Why can I use the left position of the icon as it has yet to offset the top position by 100 or so pixels?

2. Why are the pixel offsets different for each browser?

Good questions.

First think of the whereabouts of the background image on the greetings interface. It's about halfway down the page, depending on your monitor resolution. Now consider the background image in the test greeting. It's near the top of the page, just under the heading and the recipient's email address. The pixel offset compensates for the difference. Had the background image appeared in the same position in both the interface and the test greeting (which is accurate for the real greeting as well), this extra positioning wouldn't be necessary. As for the difference in pixel offsets between browsers, each appears to position its layers slightly differently. The 10-pixel difference corrects that.

After creating a layer for each positioned icon, *iconStr* is concatenated to *msgStr*, along with some closing HTML and *msg*, to make a complete Cyber Greeting embedded within a table:

```
    msgStr += iconStr + '</TD></TR><TR><TD WIDTH=' +
      bRef.backImgs[backgroundIdx].width + '><FONT FACE=Arial>' + msg +
      '</TD></TR></TABLE>';
    return msgStr;
```

msg is inserted to a data cell the same width as the background image for nicer formatting. This entire string is then returned.

Sending It Off

The user has crafted a snappy greeting, tested it several times, and is finally satisfied. Choosing "Send" is all that remains. Doing so calls the function ship-Greeting(). Here it is in lines 111–129:

```
function shipGreeting(fObj) {
if (fObj.Recipient.value == "") {
    alert('You need an email address in the From: field');
    return false;
    }
  else if (fObj.Message.value == "") {
    alert("You need to type a Message.");
    return false;
    }
  else if (fObj.Greetings.selectedIndex == 0) {
    alert('You need to choose a Greeting.');
    return false;
    }
  fObj.EntireMessage.value = genGreeting(fObj);
  fObj.BaseURL.value = top.baseURL;
  return true;
  }
```

This function is fairly short and is called via the *onSubmit* event handler in line 187. Not only does shipGreeting() prepare the form for submission to the web server, it also performs quick validation. As long as the sender has followed some simple instructions, things will go smoothly. The only rules I've imposed are that the sender must enter something both for an email address and for a message, and choose a greeting from the select list. You might consider being stricter, but these will do for now.

If the entered information passes all three "rigorous" tests, shipGreeting() changes the value of three hidden fields located at lines 188–190. Originally set as empty strings, fields *EntireMessage* and *BaseURL* are set to information that the server-side script will need. To keep the server-side script from having to create the HTML for the greeting, EntireMessage.value is set to the output of genGreeting().

The other piece of information that the script will need on the other side is the base URL that will help point to all the greetings, background images, and icons. So BaseURL.value is set to the value of top.baseURL. After that happens, the form is submitted to the URL assigned in the ACTION attribute *greet.pl*. You can see that in line 186.

JavaScript Technique: Optimizing Your Functions

How do you know how much code to put in one function before it gets too large? When do you say to yourself, "OK. I'll stop here and create the rest of this in another function"? I've never been able to devise a set of guidelines for that, but I always try to get the most use from the least amount of code. Here is what I mean. Consider function `genGreeting()`. It helps generate the code for both the greeting preview and the actual submission. How about `onCard()`? This is integral to determining the icon position when the user is clicking through all the available icons. It also plays a part in creating code for the preview and the submission. In most cases, you can gain this advantage by making the function smaller. That isn't always possible or efficient, but it's a great asset when it is.

Note

A final note before we move on to the server-side script. `resetForm()` in lines 70–81 just keeps the entry form clean every time the FORM is loaded for the first time or refreshed. It is called with the `onLoad` event handler in the `BODY` tag. With that in mind, let's see what happens when our app hits the web server.

The Server Side

Like the Shopping Cart application in Chapter 8, this application requires some type of server-side mechanism. The greetings the user creates are generated using JavaScript on the client side. This information is then sent back to the web server to a script in an application-serving environment, such as Active Server Pages, Server-side JavaScript, or Cold Fusion.

This script environment will read the information that the user submitted, then create a unique file and write the greeting code inside it. The unique filename is the same one sent in the email message to the recipient. The file will be ready and waiting when the recipient follows the link in his or her email message.

After that, the script will print a response to the greeting sender to confirm that all is well, and more importantly, to prepare a ready-made HTML form that the creator submits to send email to the recipient.

Now, I realize you picked up this book for JavaScript, but the script I've provided is written in Perl and is short and sweet. Besides, Perl is a relatively easy and powerful language and is quickly becoming the WinNT scripting language of choice. See Appendix C, *Using Perl Scripts*, for more information on setting up Perl to run the scripts and an explanation of how the two Perl scripts for the applications of this book work.

Potential Extensions

Let's look at a few ways to take this application further.

Add a Link Back to Cyber Greetings

Why not add a link back to the Cyber Greetings site? You can do so by adding the following code to function `genGreeting()` in *front.html*:

```
+ ' <A HREF="' + top.baseURL + '/index.html">Go To Cyber Greeting</A>';
```

This assumes that *index.html*, *front.html*, and *back.html* are all located in the directory referred to in *baseURL*. If not, replace `top.baseURL` in the above statement with the hardcoded URL you want to use.

Add Image Themes

This application is begging for image themes. Christmas, Valentine's Day, St. Patrick's Day, Halloween, just about anything you can think of. No need to focus on holidays. You can use seasonal backgrounds and matching icons, get well or happy birthday themes, or just about any other topic you want to include.

Banner Ad Campaigns

If you're going to let people use this service for free, why not generate a little revenue? In your `shipGreeting()` function, you could use some logic to choose a banner and embed the `IMG` tag code at the bottom of the greeting. If you use themes as mentioned previously, you could assign banners that correspond to the theme chosen.

Make the Greetings More Interactive

This application uses JavaScript events to create custom greetings. Custom, yes, but not very interactive. Try sending people greetings with image rollovers or things to click or move around. If you have a cool Java applet or two, you could offer those as greetings as well. People love useless stuff to play with; that accounts for thousands of web sites.

11

Context-Sensitive Help

No matter how easy you think you've made a program to use, someone will inevitably get stuck or have a question. Some user questions have obvious answers. Others can trip *you* up, and you're the one who wrote the thing! Depending on the quality, online documentation can either get users back on track quickly or derail them even further. The help files have to be easy to use, too. That's what this application is all about.

Not just easy for the user to navigate, but easy for you to set up and maintain. This is another one of those applications that, in and of itself,

serves little purpose. Yet just like the application in Chapter 7, *Cookie-Based User Preferences*, the code within it can be dropped into one of your applications to work for you.

I named the application Select List JavaScript; it demonstrates some of the visually unimpressive but useful things you can do with JavaScript and select lists. Figure 11-1 shows the opening interface.

This application shows how select lists can change background color, load documents, and populate other select lists, all with a little JavaScript. While this serves little more than academic value, choosing the bottom link, labeled "Help," opens a remote window with documentation pertaining to changing the document background color. Look at Figure 11-2.

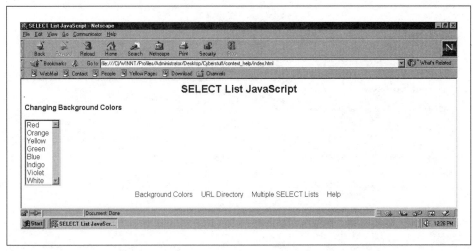

Figure 11-1. Select List JavaScript

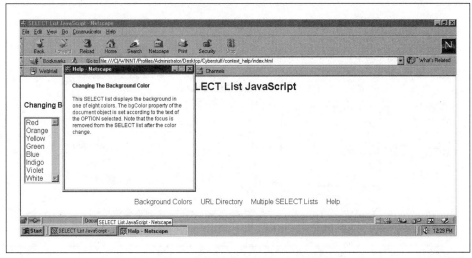

Figure 11-2. Explaining the process of changing the background color

Not exciting, I'll grant. However, clicking the "URL Directory" link (which loads the URL Directory page), then clicking "Help" loads the documentation for the URL loading procedure. See Figure 11-3. Pretty cool. Now users don't have to search for the right help file. Chances are, they have a question about what is currently in view. The help files are now context-sensitive.

It's as if the application has some extra intelligence. It always "knows" where the user "is." As an added touch, some of the documentation text is hyperlinked to other information for follow-up. However, the user doesn't have to click on the link to load another document. Simply passing the mouse-pointer arrow over any link reveals the information in a highlighted layer. See Figure 11-4.

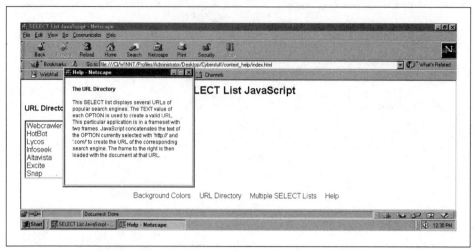

Figure 11-3. Same link, different documentation

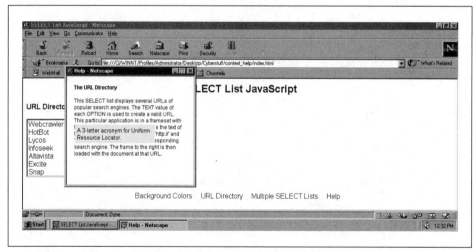

Figure 11-4. Extra info, no waiting

Now the user doesn't have to go back to the original document after following the link. Removing the mouse-pointer arrow from the link hides the layer again. This functionality can be applied to almost any application for which users need help.

Execution Requirements

You'll need MSIE or Navigator 4.x or higher because of the DHTML and use of the new event model. Make sure that you have a monitor with a resolution of at least 1024 × 768. It's not mandatory, but otherwise the help window will cover much of the main window content.

Syntax Breakdown

This application is contained in a frameset with a number of files. Here is a quick rundown:

index.html
> Top level; holds the frameset and top-level variables

top.html
> Displays Select List JavaScript header

nav.html
> Displays the page links

background.html
> Changes background colors

multiselect.html
> Populates one select list based on selections in two others

urldirectory.html
> Loads search engines based on select list option

help/background.html
> Help document associated with *background.html*

help/multiselect.html
> Help document associated with *multiselect.html*

help/urldirectory.html
> Help document associated with *urldirectory.html*

help/help.js
> JavaScript source file.

It's not likely that you'll want to get neck-deep into the logic behind all that that select list functionality in *background.html, multiselect.html,* and *urldirectory.html.* It's really easy to pick up, and that isn't what this chapter is about. Make sure you at least take a look at repopulating select lists in *multiselect.html,* though. It is handy. Instead, let's make our way through this in two steps:

1. Context-sensitive help: loading the right document in the help window (in *nav.html*)

2. Showing and hiding the extra information: getting the mouseovers running (in *help/help.js*)

Context-Sensitive Help

This one is pretty easy. It all happens in *nav.html.* Example 11-1 shows the code.

Example 11-1. nav.html

```
 1 <HTML>
 2 <HEAD>
 3   <TITLE>top.html</TITLE>
 4 </HEAD>
 5 <STYLE TYPE="text/css">
 6 <!--
 7
 8 A
 9   {
10     text-decoration: none;
11   }
12
13 BODY
14   {
15     font-family: Arial;
16     text-align: center;
17   }
18
19 //-->
20 </STYLE>
21 <SCRIPT>
22 <!--
23 var helpWin;
24
25 function inContext(currFile) {
26   var start = currFile.lastIndexOf('/') + 1;
27   var stop  = currFile.lastIndexOf('.');
28   var helpName = currFile.substring(start, stop);
29   if(helpWin == null || helpWin.closed) {
30     helpWin = open('help/' + helpName + '.html', 'helpFile',
31       'width=' + top.wdh + ',height=' + top.hgt +
32       ',left=100,top=100,scrollbars=no');
33     }
34   else {
35     helpWin.location.href = 'help/' + helpName + '.html';
36     }
37   helpWin.focus();
38   }
39
40 //-->
41 </SCRIPT>
42 <BODY>
43
44 <A HREF="background.html" TARGET="WorkArea">Background Colors</A>
45    
46 <A HREF="urldirectory.html" TARGET="WorkArea">URL Directory</A>
47    
48 <A HREF="multiselect.html" TARGET="WorkArea">Multiple SELECT Lists</A>
49    
50 <A HREF="javascript: inContext(parent.WorkArea.location.href);">Help</A>
51
52 </BODY>
53 </HTML>
```

Function `inContext()` works on one premise: for each document for which you want to display help, create the help documentation in a file of the same name with an *.html* extension. That is, *background.html,* the file that changes background colors, has a corresponding file in the *help/* directory named *background. html.* Lines 25–38 have the details:

```
function inContext(currFile) {
  var start = currFile.lastIndexOf('/') + 1;
  var stop  = currFile.lastIndexOf('.');
  var helpName = currFile.substring(start, stop);
  if(helpWin == null || helpWin.closed) {
    helpWin = open('help/' + helpName + '.html', 'helpFile', 'width=' +
      top.wdh + ',height=' + top.hgt +
      ',left=100,top=100,scrollbars=no');
    }
  else {
    helpWin.location.href = 'help/' + helpName + '.html';
    }
  helpWin.focus();
  }
```

This function expects a URL as an argument. *currFile* could be an absolute URL such as *http://some.place.com/some/document.html. currFile* could also be a relative URL with a query, such as *document.cgi?search=all.* From each URL, we need only the filename, not the host and domain or upper-level directories before it, and not the file extension or query string after it. In other words, we need everything after the last slash (/), if there is one, and up to but not including the last period in the URL (assuming that every filename has an extension, there will always be one).

Therefore, variable *start* gives us the index of the last forward slash + 1. Suppose there isn't a forward slash in the URL. No problem. The return from `lastIndexOf()` if no forward slash is encountered is -1. Add 1 to that, and you have 0. That's where we need to start. Variable *stop* is set to the index of the last instance of a period in the URL. Now the `substring()` method in line 28 gently plucks the desired substring from the URL and assigns it to `helpName`. Have a closer look:

```
var helpName = currFile.substring(start, stop);
```

The next few lines open a window using *helpName* in accordance with the help file document convention. The first parameter of the `open()` method in lines 30–32 dynamically points to the correct help file:

```
helpWin = open('help/' + helpName + '.html', 'helpFile', 'width=' +
  top.wdh + ',height=' + top.hgt + ',left=100,top=100,scrollbars=no');
```

Notice that the width and height of the remote window is determined on the fly using variables *top.wdh* and *top.hgt,* both set to 300. These two variables are located in *index.html.* Since the application refers to these variables in other parts of the app, I put them there to capitalize on the easy *top* reference. You'll see why we use the variables to determine the window dimensions a little later. The only thing you need now is a good link to call the function. Here it is in line 50:

```
<A HREF="javascript: inContext(parent.WorkArea.location.href);">Help</A>
```

Following this link calls `inContext()`, and passes the URL of the document currently loaded in the frame named *WorkArea*. As long as you have a like-named document in the *help/* directory, your new pop-up help system can expand or contract to accommodate just about any program.

JavaScript Technique: Controlling Remote Windows

How many help windows does the user really need open at a time? One is a pretty good guess. Here's how to keep it that way. Did you notice that global variable *helpWin* is set to the remote window object after it is declared without being initialized? In other words, *helpWin* is declared but set to nothing, giving it a value of null. Then the help window is opened by setting the return equal to previously null *helpWin*.

The first time the user clicks for help, the following code "decides" whether to open a new one or set the location of the existing open window:

```
if(helpWin == null || helpWin.closed) {
  helpWin = open('help/' + helpName + '.html', 'helpFile',
    'width=' + top.wdh + ',height=' + top.hgt +
    ',left=100,top=100,scrollbars=no');
  }
else {
  helpWin.location.href = 'help/' + helpName + '.html';
  }
```

If *helpWin* is null, then it has not been instantiated with the return of the `open()` method. `inContext()` then opens a fresh new remote window. If *helpWin* is already an object, then as a window object, *helpWin* contains the *closed* property, which is true if the window is closed and false otherwise. Therefore, if *helpWin.closed* is true the user has already opened and closed the remote window. That means we'll need another.

If *helpWin.closed* is false, the remote window is still open, so line 35 simply loads the appropriate document without calling `open()`. So what's the big hoohah? If the user clicks "Help" again before closing the window he or she just opened, and another pops up. Click it again, and there will be three. Who needs that? Checking for the null value and the *closed* property can prevent this. It doesn't matter if the user has the window open.

This method of yielding the filename by way of / and . is not fool-proof. For example, URLs that point to default filenames will break the system, such as *http://web.net.com/* or *../.* What kind of file name are you going to reference with that? Make sure you modify your code for these URLs if you plan on using them.

Showing and Hiding Extra Information

The pop-up technique we just reviewed loads the help documents we need. Using links and mouseovers to display extra help info requires the wizardry of DHTML— some we've used earlier and some new stuff. Fortunately, most of it lies in the JavaScript source file *help/help.js*. Example 11-2 shows the code.

Example 11-2. help/help.js

```
1 var NN    = (document.layers ? true : false);
2 var hideName = (NN ? 'hide' : 'hidden');
3 var showName = (NN ? 'show' : 'visible');
4 var zIdx    = -1;
5 var helpWdh  = 200;
6 var helpHgt  = 200;
7 var x, y, totalWidth, totalHeight;
8
9 function genLayer(sName, sLeft, sTop, sWdh, sHgt, sVis, copy) {
10   if (NN) {
11     document.writeln('<LAYER NAME="' + sName + '" LEFT=' + sLeft +
12       ' TOP=' + sTop + ' WIDTH=' + sWdh + ' HEIGHT=' + sHgt +
13       ' VISIBILITY="' + sVis + '" z-Index=' + (++zIdx) + '>' + copy +
14       '</LAYER>');
15     }
16   else {
17     document.writeln('<DIV ID="' + sName +
18       '" STYLE="position:absolute; overflow:none; left:' +
19       sLeft + 'px; top:' + sTop + 'px; width:' + sWdh + 'px; height:' +
20       sHgt + 'px; visibility:' + sVis + '; z-Index=' + (++zIdx) + '">' +
21       copy + '</DIV>'
22       );
23     }
24   }
25
26 function hideSlide(name) {
27   refSlide(name).visibility = hideName;
28   }
29
30 function showSlide(name) {
31   refSlide(name).visibility = showName;
32   }
33
34 function refSlide(name) {
```

Example 11-2. help/help.js (continued)

```
35   if (NN) { return document.layers[name]; }
36   else { return eval('document.all.' + name + '.style'); }
37   }
38
39 function motionListener() {
40   if (NN) {
41     window.captureEvents(Event.MOUSEMOVE);
42     window.onmousemove = grabXY;
43     }
44   else {
45     document.onmousemove = grabXY;
46     }
47   }
48
49 function grabXY(ev) {
50   if(NN) {
51     x = ev.pageX;
52     y = ev.pageY;
53     }
54   else {
55     x = event.x;
56     y = event.y;
57     }
58   }
59
60 function helpDisplay(name, action) {
61   if(action) {
62     totalWidth = x + helpWdh;
63     totalHeight = y + helpHgt;
64     x = (totalWidth > opener.top.wdh ? x -
65       (totalWidth - opener.top.wdh + 75) : x);
66     y = (totalHeight > opener.top.hgt ? y -
67       (totalHeight - opener.top.hgt) : y);
68     refSlide(name).left = x - 10;
69     refSlide(name).top = y + 8;
70     showSlide(name);
71     }
72   else { hideSlide(name); }
73   }
74
75 motionListener();
```

Let's examine this functionality in two steps. First we'll talk about creating the layers that contain the extra information. Then, we'll look at what goes into showing and hiding those layers.

Creating the Layers

If you've seen any of Chapters 3, 4, 6, 7, or 9, the first two dozen lines will seem very familiar. If you haven't, take a look at Chapter 3 for the details of functions genLayer(), hideSlide(), showSlide(), and refSlide(). We'll create the layers just as we did in the other chapters. We need to add an additional step, though. Variables *helpWdh* and *helpHgt* are set to 200 pixels each. They define the "default" width and height of each layer. That's important because we'll need these variables, along with *top.wdh* and *top.hgt*, for positioning in a moment.

Those functions are the tools we need to create the layers. All we need to do is call **genLayer()**, and pass in the content, among other variables. You'll find the call to this function in each of the help files. All things being much the same in other help documents, let's look at the code in *help/background.html*:

```
var helpOne = '<SPAN CLASS="helpSet">This property is a string that ' +
   'reflects the current background color of the document.</SPAN>';
var helpTwo = '<SPAN CLASS="helpSet">This property of the ' +
   '<TT>window</TT> object contains the object hierachy of the current ' +
   'Web page.</SPAN>';

genLayer("bgColor", 0, 0, helpWdh, helpHgt, hideName, helpOne);
genLayer("document", 0, 0, helpWdh, helpHgt, hideName, helpTwo);
```

Variable *helpOne* contains the string that will display the first extra link (**"bgColor"**), and *helpTwo* performs likewise for the document link. This isn't just text, though. Both strings contain a pair of **SPAN** tags assigned to the cascading stylesheet class definition *.helpSet*. The *.helpSet* class is defined in the **STYLE** tags. Here is a peek. This isn't the most elaborate style sheet class definition you'll ever see, but it does a good job of defining the layers.

```
.helpSet
  {
    background-color: #CCFFCC;
    padding: 5px;
    border: 2px;
    width: 200px;
    font: normal 10pt Arial;
    text-align: left;
  }
```

The script contains two calls to **genLayer()**. Notice that instead of passing in numbers for the width and height of each layer, variables *helpWdh* and *helpHgt* are passed in instead. This will set us up for better positioning later on. Each of the layers is originally set as hidden with the help of variable *hideName*.

The layers have now been created. All the user needs to do is effectively display them on demand. That functionality comes from functions **motionListener()**, **grabXY()**, and **helpDisplay()**. First **motionListener()** from lines 39–47:

```
function motionListener() {
  if (NN) {
    window.captureEvents(Event.MOUSEMOVE);
    window.onmousemove = grabXY;
    }
```

```
      else {
        document.onmousemove = grabXY;
        }
      }
```

We should display the layer wherever the link to each layer winds up on the page. To do that, we have to track the location of the mouse on the screen when it passes over the link. Function `motionListener()` assigns the *onMouseMove* event handler to call function `grabXY()` every time the user moves the mouse. Both Navigator and MSIE implement *onMouseMove*, but Navigator does so in the *window* object and MSIE in the *document* object. Navigator also needs a call to the `captureEvents()` method to specify the *mousemove* event.

Function `grabXY()` assigns variables x and y to the horizontal and vertical pixel coordinates of the pointer arrow every time the user moves the mouse. Here are lines 49-58:

```
    function grabXY(ev) {
      if(NN) {
        x = ev.pageX;
        y = ev.pageY;
        }
      else {
        x = event.screenX;
        y = event.screenY;
        }
      }
```

These coordinates are implemented differently in MSIE and NN. Navigator 4.x creates an event object on the fly for each call to the event handler. The object is reflected in parameter *ev*. Internet Explorer, on the other hand, has a built-in event object. Calling `grabXY()` every time the user moves the mouse keeps variables x and y constantly updated. When the user moves over a link, x and y will contain values that make a good reference point for positioning the extra help layers.

Showing the Info

When the user passes the mouse over the link, that calls function `helpDisplay()`. Here first is the HTML (from *background.html*) that calls the function, then the function itself:

```
    <A HREF="javascript: void(0);"
      onMouseOver="helpDisplay('bgColor', true);"
      onMouseOut="helpDisplay('bgColor', false);">
      bgColor
      </A>
```

The *onMouseOver* event handler is responsible for revealing the layer; *onMouse-Out* is responsible for hiding it again. Both are taken care of with `help-Display()`. See lines 60–73:

```
function helpDisplay(name, action) {
  if(action) {
    totalWidth = x + helpWdh;
    totalHeight = y + helpHgt;
    x = (totalWidth > opener.top.wdh ? x -
      (totalWidth - opener.top.wdh + 75) : x);
    y = (totalHeight > opener.top.hgt ? y -
      (totalHeight - opener.top.hgt) : y);
    refSlide(name).left = x - 10;
    refSlide(name).top = y + 8;
    showSlide(name);
    }
  else { hideSlide(name); }
  }
```

`helpDisplay()` expects two arguments. One is the name of the layer to show or hide, the other is a Boolean value that determines whether to show or hide the layer. That's the first decision to make—decide whether to show or hide the layer. If *action* is `false`, the procedure is easy. Just call `hideSlide()`, and be done with it. If *action* is `true`, that means it's time to show the layer. Just call `showSlide()`, right? Not quite. It's a little more complicated.

JavaScript Technique: Using Links Without the Click

Sometimes you'll want links to do something only when you pass the mouse over or away from them instead of clicking. Here are two ways to prevent undesired effects from clicking:

Use `javascript: void(0)` in the `HREF` attribute
  The `void` operator ignores the return of any action, including the *click* event. You don't have to use 0, but it is an easy operand. You can see an example just before this sidebar.

Use `onClick="return false;"`
  Returning `false` will cancel loading of any document specified in the `HREF` attribute. Try it like this:

  ```
  <A HREF="" onMouseOver="doSomething();" onClick="return false;">Do
  Something</A>
  ```

  No matter what might be in the `HREF` attribute, the document won't load.

Managing the Link Location

Calling `showSlide()` would get the job done, but you might get more than you bargained for. Remember lines 30–32 of *nav.html?*

```
helpWin = open('help/' + helpName + '.html', 'helpFile', 'width=' +
  top.wdh + ',height=' + top.hgt + ',left=100,top=100,scrollbars=no');
```

The width of the window is 300 pixels. So is the height. Now check back to lines 5 and 6 of *help.js*:

```
var helpWdh  = 200;
var helpHgt  = 200;
```

The width and height of each layer is set to 200 pixels. Actually, the layer height grows dynamically according to the amount of content within, much like data cells in a table. However, we still need a reference. It doesn't take a math whiz to see that if the link winds up on the page further to the right than 100 pixels (actually less, since those 300 pixels represent the outer width of the window, not the inner width, where the document is actually displayed), at least a portion of the layer will be displayed out of view. To prevent this, we'll do some math of our own before we position and show the layer.

It works like this: if the horizontal coordinate of the mouse pointer plus the width of the layer to display is greater than the viewable width of the remote window, display the layer back to the left by an offsetting number of pixels. Consider line 62:

```
totalWidth = x + helpWdh;
```

Variable *totalWidth* is equal to the horizontal coordinate plus the width of the layer. Now you can see why we use variables to set the dimensions with variables *helpWdh* and *helpHgt* instead of numbers such as 200. Now consider line 64–65.

```
x = (totalWidth > opener.top.wdh ? x -
    (totalWidth - opener.top.wdh + 75) : x);
```

If *totalWidth* is greater than the width of the remote window (less the border), the horizontal coordinate needs to be adjusted. We simply adjust it to the left by subtracting the difference between `totalWidth` and the width of the remote window. This ensures that all the layers are displayed horizontally. The same goes for the height. You can see this in lines 63 and 66–67. This might not work if you set the value for *helpHgt* relatively low and then create the layer with a lot of text.

Potential Extensions

The help application presented here would probably work for most small- to medium-sized applications. As applications scale upwards, however, so can the need for more help features. Consider the following suggestions for beefing up your online help.

Table of Contents

Sometimes users are looking for documentation about something unrelated to the current screen content. One of the easiest ways to lets users browse is to offer a table of contents page that neatly lists links to all help documents. You can do this

JavaScript Technique: Layers Without the LAYER Tags

All this time, you've seen DHTML layers as DIV tags for MSIE and LAYER tags for Navigator. Actually, the LAYER tag works fine, but it won't become a standard. All indications from the World Wide Web Consortium point to a standardized document object model very similar to that supported by MSIE. Consider the following code:

```
<HTML>
<HEAD>
  <TITLE>DHTML Layer</TITLE>
  <SCRIPT LANGUAGE="JavaScript1.2">
<!--
var action = true;
function display(name) {
  if (document.all) {
    var layerObj = eval("document.all." + name + ".style");
    var hide = "hidden";
    var show = "visible";
    }
  else {
    var layerObj = eval("document." + name);
    var hide = "hide";
    var show = "show";
    }
  layerObj.visibility = (action ?  hide : show);
  action = !action;
  }

//-->
</SCRIPT>
</HEAD>
<BODY>
<DIV ID="dhtml"
  STYLE="position:relative;background-color:#FFACEE;width:200;">
  This is a DHTML layer.
</DIV>
<BR>
<A HREF="javascript:display('dhtml');">Show/Hide</A>
</BODY>
</HTML>
```

This is file *\ch11\layer.html.* As you can see, there are no LAYER tags, yet both NN and MSIE respond to this code (which hides and shows the layer upon clicking). Though Navigator won't currently allow access to most elements of the document object model, it does allow access to positioning properties.

So which is best? Why didn't I use this method in the first place in the other chapters? Both work well, but I personally prefer the genLayer() method of dynamically creating LAYER tags in Navigator and DIVs in MSIE. What's important is that you have another option. Try both. See what works best for you.

with a static HTML page, or you can use JavaScript to generate the list dynamically using an array:

```
function showContents() {
  var helpDocs = ['background', 'multiselect', 'urldirectory'];
  var helpLinks = '<UL>';
  for (var i = 0; i < helpDocs.length; i++) {
    helpLinks += '<LI><A HREF="' + helpDocs[i] + '.html">' +
      helpDocs[i] + '</A>';
    }
  helpLinks = '</UL>';
  document.writeln(helpLinks);
  }
```

Searchable Help Files

If you need a few help documents, why not make use of the search app in Chapter 1, *The Client-Side Search Engine*? That's always a classy way to spruce up user interactivity.

Ask a Pro

Sometimes users just can't find what they want. If you have the personnel, consider adding a forms-based email page so that users can answer a few questions and send them to qualified personnel.

Phone Directory

If you really want customer service, provide a list of phone numbers and email addresses so that users can actually contact a human. Like the forms-based email option, this is resource-intensive. Make sure you have people to field calls before you post the phone numbers. People will call. I've had people call me after visiting my site, and my number was hard to get.

Epilogue

This is another reason I wanted my own book. After clawing your way to the last page of the last chapter of one of those other Web publications whose page count is rivaled perhaps only by the *Holy Bible* and *War and Peace*, what do you usually get? A few appendixes and an index. That's great, but that's like climbing to the top of a mountain and having nothing to look down upon. Where's the sense of accomplishment?

If you made it to this side of the book, you've come a long way, and not just by the number of pages you turned. Think about how good a JavaScript coder you were when you first thumbed through these pages at the store and decided to buy it. Think of what you know now. It's a good feeling to witness your own development and take a few steps closer to the top.

Of course, we can enjoy our success, but we shouldn't get too comfortable. Technology is changing at the speed of competition. As soon as this book hits the shelves, developers will likely have whipped up another batch of JavaScript extensions and techniques. I'm going to check them out ASAP. Let me know if you run into any good ones. C'ya on the Net.

—Jerry Bradenbaugh
hotsyte@mail.serve.com

JavaScript Reference

This appendix contains JavaScript syntax reference in the following areas:

- Objects, methods, and properties
- Top-level functions and properties
- Event handlers

In general, JavaScript has a three-pronged structure: core, client-side, and server-side. Core JavaScript refers to those features that can be used on both the client and server sides. Client- and server-side JavaScript includes core JavaScript plus extensions of each particular environment. For example, client-side JavaScript contains the *window* and the *document* objects, something the server would have no use for. Similarly, server-side JavaScript contains the *File* object.

The material here is current as of client-side JavaScript 1.3 and core JavaScript 1.4. Everything in the following pages comes straight from the Netscape sites:

> *http://developer1.netscape.com:80/docs/manuals/js/core/jsref/index.htm*
> *http://developer1.netscape.com:80/docs/manuals/js/client/jsref/index.htm*

You can find Microsoft Jscript resources at:

> *http://msdn.microsoft.com/scripting/default.htm?/scripting/jscript/default.htm*

Keep this as a handy quick reference, but always refer back to the Netscape and Microsoft material for the latest material.

Browser Compatibility

Table A-1 shows which JavaScript version is supported in the various versions of Navigator and Internet Explorer.

Table A-1. JavaScript Compatibility

JavaScript Version	Navigator Version	MSIE Version
JavaScript 1.0	Navigator 2.0	MSIE 3.x
JavaScript 1.1	Navigator 3.0	
JavaScript 1.2	Navigator 4.0-4.05	MSIE 4.x – 5.0
JavaScript 1.3	Navigator 4.06-4.5	
JavaScript 1.4		

Objects, Methods, and Properties

This section itemizes JavaScript objects by description, compatibility, properties, and methods.

Anchor

A place in a document that is the target of a hypertext link. Using the HTML **A** tag or calling the **String.anchor** method, the JavaScript runtime engine creates an *Anchor* object corresponding to each **A** tag in your document that supplies the NAME attribute. It puts these objects in an array in the *document.anchors* property. You access an *Anchor* object by indexing this array.

Compatability
> JavaScript 1.0 / client

Method summary
> This object inherits the **watch** and **unwatch** methods from **Object**.

Applet

The HTML **<APPLET>** tag. The JavaScript runtime engine creates an *Applet* object corresponding to each applet in your document. It puts these objects in an array in the *document.applets* property. You access an *Applet* object by indexing this array.

Compatability
> JavaScript 1.1 / client

Property summary
> The *Applet* object inherits all public properties of the Java applet. Properties are detailed in Table A-2.

Method summary
> The *Applet* object inherits all public methods of the Java applet. Methods are detailed in Table A-3.

Table A-2. Applet Properties

Property	Description	Version
constructor	Specifies the function that creates an object's prototype.	1.1
index	For an array created by a regular expression match, the zero-based index of the match in the string.	1.2
input	For an array created by a regular expression match, reflects the original string against which the regular expression was matched.	1.2
length	Reflects the number of elements in an array.	1.1
prototype	Allows the addition of properties to all objects.	1.1

Table A-3. Applet Methods

Method	Description	Version
concat	Specifies the function that creates an object's prototype.	1.2
join	Joins all elements of an array into a string.	1.1
pop	Removes the last element from an array and returns that element.	1.2
push	Adds one or more elements to the end of an array and returns the new length of the array.	1.2
reverse	Transposes the elements of an array: the first array element becomes the last and the last becomes the first.	1.2
shift	Removes the first element from an array and returns that element.	1.2
slice	Extracts a section of an array and returns a new array.	1.2
sort	Sorts the elements of an array.	1.1
splice	Adds and/or removes elements from an array.	1.2
toSource	Returns an array literal representing the specified array; you can use this value to create a new array. Overrides the `Object.toSource` method.	1.3
toString	Returns a string representing the array and its elements. Overrides the `Object.toString` method.	1.1
unshift	Adds one or more elements to the front of an array and returns the new length of the array.	1.2
valueOf	Returns the primitive value of the array. Overrides the `Object.valueOf` method.	1.1

Area

Defines an area of an image as an image map. When the user clicks the area, the area's hypertext reference is loaded into its target window. *Area* objects are a type of *Link* object.

Compatability
> JavaScript 1.1 / client

Array

Lets you work with arrays.

Compatability
> JavaScript 1.1 / core

Boolean

The *Boolean* object is an object wrapper for a boolean value.

Compatability
> JavaScript 1.1 / core

Property summary
> Boolean properties are detailed in Table A-4.

Method summary
> Boolean methods are detailed in Table A-5.

Table A-4. Boolean Properties

Property	Description	Version
constructor	Specifies the function that creates an object's prototype.	1.1
prototype	Defines a property that is shared by all *Boolean* objects.	1.1

Table A-5. Boolean Methods

Method	Description	Version
toSource	Returns an object literal representing the specified *Boolean* object; you can use this value to create a new object. Overrides the `Object.toSource` method.	1.3
toString	Returns a string representing the specified object. Overrides the `Object.toString` method.	1.1

Table A-5. Boolean Methods (continued)

Method	Description	Version
valueOf	Returns the primitive value of a *Boolean* object. Overrides the `Object.valueOf` method.	1.1

Button

A push button on an HTML form.

Compatibility
> JavaScript 1.0 / client

Event handlers
> onBlur, onClick, onFocus, onMouseDown, onMouseUp

Property summary
> Properties are detailed in Table A-6.

Method summary
> Methods are detailed in Table A-7. In addition, this object inherits the watch and unwatch methods from Object.

Table A-6. Button Properties

Property	Description	Version
form	Specifies the form containing the *Button* object.	1.0
name	Reflects the NAME attribute.	1.0
type	Reflects the TYPE attribute.	1.1
value	Reflects the VALUE attribute.	1.0

Table A-7. Button Methods

Method	Description	Version
blur	Removes focus from the button.	1.0
click	Simulates a mouse-click on the button.	1.0
focus	Gives focus to the button.	1.0
handleEvent	Invokes the handler for the specified event.	1.2

Checkbox

A checkbox on an HTML form. A checkbox is a toggle switch that lets the user set a value on or off.

Compatability
> JavaScript 1.0 / client

Event handlers

    `onBlur`, `onClick`, `onFocus`

Property summary

    Properties are detailed in Table A-8.

Method summary

    Methods are detailed in Table A-9. In addition, this object inherits the `watch` and `unwatch` methods from `Object`.

Table A-8. Checkbox Properties

Property	Description	Version
checked	Boolean property that reflects the current state of the checkbox.	
defaultChecked	Boolean property that reflects the CHECKED attribute.	
form	Specifies the form containing the *Checkbox* object.	1.0
name	Reflects the NAME attribute.	1.0
type	Reflects the TYPE attribute.	1.1
value	Reflects the VALUE attribute.	1.0

Table A-9. Checkbox Methods

Method	Description	Version
blur	Removes focus from the checkbox.	1.0
click	Simulates a mouse-click on the checkbox.	1.0
focus	Gives focus to the checkbox.	1.0
handleEvent	Invokes the handler for the specified event.	1.2

Date

Lets you work with dates and times.

Compatability

    JavaScript 1.0 / core

Property summary

    Properties are detailed in Table A-10.

Method summary

    Methods are detailed in Table A-11.

Table A-10. Date Properties

Property	Description	Version
constructor	Specifies the function that creates an object's prototype.	1.1
prototype	Allows the addition of properties to a *Date* object.	1.1

Table A-11. Date Methods

Method	Description	Version
getDate	Returns the day of the month for the specified date according to local time.	1.0
getDay	Returns the day of the week for the specified date according to local time.	1.0
getFullYear	Returns the year of the specified date according to local time.	1.3
getHours	Returns the hour in the specified date according to local time.	1.0
getMilliseconds	Returns the milliseconds in the specified date according to local time.	1.3
getMinutes	Returns the minutes in the specified date according to local time.	1.0
getMonth	Returns the month in the specified date according to local time.	1.0
getSeconds	Returns the seconds in the specified date according to local time.	1.0
getTime	Returns the numeric value corresponding to the time for the specified date according to local time.	1.0
getTimezoneOffset	Returns the time-zone offset in minutes for the current locale.	1.0
getUTCDate	Returns the day (date) of the month in the specified date according to universal time.	1.3
getUTCDay	Returns the day of the week in the specified date according to universal time.	1.3
getUTCFullYear	Returns the year in the specified date according to universal time.	1.3
getUTCHours	Returns the hours in the specified date according to universal time.	1.3
getUTCMilliseconds	Returns the milliseconds in the specified date according to universal time.	1.3
getUTCMinutes	Returns the minutes in the specified date according to universal time.	1.3
getUTCMonth	Returns the month in the specified date according to universal time.	1.3

Table A-11. Date Methods (continued)

Method	Description	Version
getUTCSeconds	Returns the seconds in the specified date according to universal time.	1.3
getYear	Returns the year in the specified date according to local time.	1.0
parse	Returns the number of milliseconds in a date string since January 1, 1970, 00:00:00, local time.	1.0
setDate	Sets the day of the month for a specified date according to local time	1.0
setFullYear	Sets the full year for a specified date according to local time.	1.3
setHours	Sets the hours for a specified date according to local time.	1.0
setMilliseconds	Sets the milliseconds for a specified date according to local time.	1.3
setMinutes	Sets the minutes for a specified date according to local time.	1.0
setMonth	Sets the month for a specified date according to local time.	1.0
setSeconds	Sets the seconds for a specified date according to local time.	1.0
setTime	Sets the value of a *Date* object according to local time.	1.0
setUTCDate	Sets the day of the month for a specified date according to universal time.	1.3
setUTCFullYear	Sets the full year for a specified date according to universal time.	1.3
setUTCHours	Sets the hour for a specified date according to universal time.	1.3
setUTCMilliseconds	Sets the milliseconds for a specified date according to universal time.	1.3
setUTCMinutes	Sets the minutes for a specified date according to universal time.	1.3
setUTCMonth	Sets the month for a specified date according to universal time.	1.3
setUTCSeconds	Sets the seconds for a specified date according to universal time.	1.3
setYear	Sets the year for a specified date according to local time.	1.0
toGMTString	Converts a date to a string, using the Internet GMT conventions.	1.0
toLocaleString	Converts a date to a string, using the current locale's conventions.	1.0

Table A-11. Date Methods (continued)

Method	Description	Version
toSource	Returns an object literal representing the specified *Date* object; you can use this value to create a new object. Overrides the `Object.toSource` method.	1.3
toString	Returns a string representing the specified *Date* object. Overrides the `Object.toString` method.	1.1
toUTCString	Converts a date to a string, using the universal time convention.	1.3
UTC	Returns the number of milliseconds in a *Date* object since January 1, 1970, 00:00:00, universal time.	1.0
valueOf	Returns the primitive value of a *Date* object. Overrides the `Object.valueOf` method.	1.1

Document

Contains information about the current document, and provides methods for displaying HTML output to the user.

Compatability

JavaScript 1.0 / client

Event handlers

onClick, onDblClick, onKeyDown, onKeyPress, onKeyUp, onMouseDown, onMouseUp

Property summary

Properties are detailed in Table A-12.

Method summary

Methods are detailed in Table A-13. In addition, this object inherits the **watch** and **unwatch** methods from **Object**.

Table A-12. Document Properties

Property	Description	Version
alinkColor	A string that specifies the ALINK attribute.	1.0
anchors	An array containing an entry for each anchor in the document.	1.0
applets	An array containing an entry for each applet in the document.	1.1
bgColor	A string that specifies the BGCOLOR attribute.	1.0
cookie	Specifies a cookie.	1.0

Table A-12. Document Properties (continued)

Property	Description	Version
domain	Specifies the domain name of the server that served a document.	1.1
embeds	An array containing an entry for each plug-in in the document.	1.1
fgColor	A string that specifies the TEXT attribute.	1.0
formName	A separate property for each named form in the document.	1.1
forms	An array a containing an entry for each form in the document.	1.1
images	An array containing an entry for each image in the document.	1.1
lastModified	A string that specifies the date the document was last modified.	1.0
layers	Array containing an entry for each layer within the document.	1.2
linkColor	A string that specifies the LINK attribute.	1.0
links	An array containing an entry for each link in the document.	1.0
plugins	An array containing an entry for each plug-in in the document.	1.0
referrer	A string that specifies the URL of the calling document.	1.1
title	A string that specifies the contents of the TITLE tag.	1.0
URL	A string that specifies the complete URL of a document.	1.0
vlinkColor	A string that specifies the VLINK attribute.	1.0

Table A-13. Document Methods

Method	Description	Version
captureEvents	Sets the document to capture all events of the specified type.	1.2
close	Closes an output stream and forces data to display.	1.0
getSelection	Returns a string containing the text of the current selection.	1.2
handleEvent	Invokes the handler for the specified event.	1.2
open	Opens a stream to collect the output of **write** or **writeln** methods.	1.0

Table A-13. Document Methods (continued)

Method	Description	Version
releaseEvents	Sets the window or document to release captured events of the specified type, sending the event to objects further along the event hierarchy.	1.2
routeEvent	Passes a captured event along the normal event hierarchy.	1.2
write	Writes one or more HTML expressions to a document in the specified window.	1.0
writeln	Writes one or more HTML expressions to a document in the specified window and follows them with a newline character.	1.0

Event

The event object contains properties that describe a JavaScript event and is passed as an argument to an event handler when the event occurs.

Compatability

 JavaScript 1.2 / client

Property summary

 Properties are detailed in Table A-14. Not all of these properties are relevant to each event type.

Table A-14. Event Properties

Property	Description	Version
data	Returns an array of strings containing the URLs of the dropped objects. Passed with the *DragDrop* event.	1.2
height	Represents the height of the window or frame.	1.2
layerX	Number specifying either the object width when passed with the resize event or the cursor's horizontal position in pixels relative to the layer in which the event occurred. Note that layerX is synonymous with x.	1.2
layerY	Number specifying either the object height when passed with the resize event, or the cursor's vertical position in pixels relative to the layer in which the event occurred. Note that layerY is synonymous with y.	1.2
modifiers	String specifying the modifier keys associated with a mouse or key event. Modifier key values are: ALT_MASK, CONTROL_MASK, SHIFT_MASK, and META_MASK.	1.2

Table A-14. Event Properties (continued)

Property	Description	Version
pageX	Number specifying the cursor's horizontal position in pixels, relative to the page.	1.2
pageY	Number specifying the cursor's vertical position in pixels relative to the page.	1.2
screenX	Number specifying the cursor's horizontal position in pixels, relative to the screen.	1.2
screenY	Number specifying the cursor's vertical position in pixels, relative to the screen.	1.2
target	String representing the object to which the event was originally sent (all events).	1.2
type	String representing the event type. (All events)	1.2
which	Number specifying either the mouse button that was pressed or the ASCII value of a pressed key. For a mouse, 1 is the left button, 2 is the middle button, and 3 is the right button.	1.2
width	Represents the width of the window or frame.	1.2
x	Synonym for layerX.	1.2
y	Synonym for layerY.	1.2

FileUpload

Compatability

JavaScript 1.0 / client

Refers to a file upload element on an HTML form. A file upload element lets the user supply a file as input.

Event handlers

onBlur, onChange, onFocus

Property summary

Properties are detailed in Table A-15.

Method summary

Methods are detailed in Table A-16. In addition, this object inherits the watch and unwatch methods from Object.

Table A-15. FileUpload Properties

Property	Description	Version
form	Specifies the form containing the *FileUpload* object.	1.0
name	Reflects the NAME attribute.	1.0
type	Reflects the TYPE attribute.	1.1

Table A-15. FileUpload Properties (continued)

Property	Description	Version
value	Reflects the current value of the file upload element's field; this corresponds to the name of the file to upload.	1.0

Table A-16. FileUpload Methods

Method	Description	Version
blur	Removes focus from the object.	1.0
focus	Gives focus to the object.	1.0
handleEvent	Invokes the handler for the specified event.	1.2
select	Selects the input area of the file upload field.	1.0

Form

Lets users input text and make choices from Form elements such as checkboxes, radio buttons, and selection lists. You can also use a form to post data to a server.

Compatability
> JavaScript 1.0 / client

Event handlers
> onReset, onSubmit

Property summary
> Properties are detailed in Table A-17.

Method summary
> Methods are detailed in Table A-18.

Table A-17. Form Properties

Property	Description	Version
action	Reflects the ACTION attribute.	1.0
elements	An array reflecting all the elements in a form.	1.0
encoding	Reflects the ENCTYPE attribute.	1.0
length	Reflects the number of elements on a form.	1.0
method	Reflects the METHOD attribute.	1.0
name	Reflects the NAME attribute.	1.0
target	Reflects the TARGET attribute.	1.0

Table A-18. Form Methods

Method	Description	Version
handleEvent	Invokes the handler for the specified event.	1.2
reset	Simulates a mouseclick on a reset button for the calling form.	1.1
submit	Submits a form.	1.0

Frame

A window can display multiple, independently scrollable frames on a single screen, each with its own distinct URL. These frames are created using the FRAME tag inside a <FRAMESET> tag. Frames can point to different URLs and be targeted by other URLs, all within the same screen. A series of frames makes up a page. The *Frame* object is a convenience for thinking about the objects that constitute these frames. However, JavaScript actually represents a frame using a *window* object. Every *Frame* object is a *window* object and has all the methods and properties of a *window* object. There are a few minor differences between a window that is a frame, and a top-level window. See **window** for complete information on frames.

Compatability
> JavaScript 1.0 / client

Function

Specifies a string of JavaScript code to be compiled as a function.

Compatability
> JavaScript 1.1 / core

Property summary
> Properties are detailed in Table A-19.

Method summary
> Methods are detailed in Table A-20.

Table A-19. Function Properties

Property	Description	Version
arguments	An array corresponding to the arguments passed to a function.	1.1
arguments.callee	Specifies the function body of the currently executing function.	1.2
arguments.caller	Specifies the name of the function that invoked the currently executing function.	1.1
arguments.length	Specifies the number of arguments passed to the function.	1.1

Table A-19. Function Properties (continued)

Property	Description	Version
arity	Specifies the number of arguments expected by the function.	1.2
constructor	Specifies the function that creates an object's prototype.	1.1
length	Specifies the number of arguments expected by the function.	1.1
prototype	Allows the addition of properties to a *Function* object.	1.1

Table A-20. Function Methods

Method	Description	Version
apply	Allows you to apply a method of another object in the context of a different object (the calling object).	1.3
call	Allows you to call (execute) a method of another object in the context of a different object (the calling object).	1.3
toSource	Returns a string representing the source code of the function. Overrides the `Object.toSource` method.	1.3
toString	Returns a string representing the source code of the function. Overrides the `Object.toString` method.	1.1
valueOf	Returns a string representing the source code of the function. Overrides the `Object.valueOf` method.	1.1

Hidden

A *Text* object that is suppressed from form display on an HTML form. A *Hidden* object is used for passing name/value pairs when a form submits.

Compatability
> JavaScript 1.0 / client

Property summary
> Properties are detailed in Table A-21.

Method summary
> This object inherits the **watch** and **unwatch** methods from **Object**.

Table A-21. Hidden Properties

Property	Description	Version
form	Specifies the form containing *Hidden* object.	1.0
name	Reflects the NAME attribute.	1.0
type	Reflects the TYPE attribute.	1.1
value	Reflects the current value of *Hidden* object.	1.0

History

Contains an array of information on the URLs that the client has visited within a window. This information is stored in a history list and is accessible through the browser's Go menu.

Compatability
    JavaScript 1.0 / client

Property summary
    Properties are detailed in Table A-22.

Method summary
    Methods are detailed in Table A-23. This object inherits the **watch** and **unwatch** methods from **Object**.

Table A-22. History Properties

Property	Description	Version
current	Specifies the URL of the current history entry.	1.1
length	Reflects the number of entries in the history list.	1.0
next	Specifies the URL of the next history entry.	1.1
previous	Specifies the URL of the previous history entry.	1.1

Table A-23. History Methods

Method	Description	Version
back	Loads the previous URL in the history list.	1.0
forward	Loads the next URL in the history list.	1.0
go	Loads a URL from the history list.	1.0

Image

Refers to an image on an HTML form.

Compatability
    JavaScript 1.1 / client

Event handlers

onAbort, onError, onKeyDown, onKeyPress, onKeyUp, onLoad

Property summary

Properties are detailed in Table A-24.

Method summary

Methods are detailed in Table A-25. This object inherits the `watch` and `unwatch` methods from `Object`.

Table A-24. Image Properties

Property	Description	Version
border	Reflects the BORDER attribute.	1.1
complete	Boolean value indicating whether the web browser has completed its attempt to load the image.	1.1
height	Reflects the HEIGHT attribute.	1.1
hspace	Reflects the HSPACE attribute.	1.1
lowsrc	Reflects the LOWSRC attribute.	1.1
name	Reflects the NAME attribute.	1.1
src	Reflects the SRC attribute.	1.1
vspace	Reflects the VSPACE attribute.	1.1
width	Reflects the WIDTH attribute.	1.1

Table A-25. Image Methods

Method	Description	Version
handleEvent	Invokes the handler for the specified event.	1.2

Java

A top-level object used to access any Java class in the package *java.**. The *java* object is a convenience synonym for the property *Packages.java*.

Compatability

JavaScript 1.1

JavaArray

A wrapped Java array accessed from within JavaScript code is a member of the type `JavaArray`.

Compatability

JavaScript 1.1 / core

Property summary

Properties are detailed in Table A-26.

Method summary

Methods are detailed in Table A-27.

Table A-26. JavaArray Property

Property	Description	Version
length	The number of elements in the Java array represented by JavaArray.	1.1

Table A-27. JavaArray Method

Method	Description	Version
toString	In JavaScript 1.4, this method is overridden by the inherited method java.lang.Object. toString. In JavaScript 1.3 and earlier, this method returns a string identifying the object as a *JavaArray*.	1.1

JavaClass

A JavaScript reference to a Java class. A *JavaClass* object is a reference to one of the classes in a Java package, such as netscape.javascript.JSObject. A *JavaPackage* object is a reference to a Java package, such as netscape. javascript. In JavaScript, the JavaPackage and JavaClass hierarchy reflect the Java package and class hierarchy.

Compatability

JavaScript 1.1 / core

Property summary

The properties of a *JavaClass* object are the static fields of the Java class.

Method summary

The methods of a *JavaClass* object are the static methods of the Java class.

JavaObject

The type of a wrapped Java object accessed from within JavaScript code. The *JavaObject* object is an instance of a Java class that is created in or passed to Java-Script. JavaObject is a wrapper for the instance; all references to the class instance are made through the JavaObject. Any Java data brought into JavaScript is converted to JavaScript data types. When the *JavaObject* is passed back to Java, it is unwrapped and can be used by Java code.

Compatability
   JavaScript 1.1 / core

Property summary
   The properties of a `JavaPackage` are the *JavaClass* objects and any other *JavaPackage* objects it contains.

JavaPackage

In Java, a package is a collection of Java classes or other Java packages. For example, the `netscape` package contains the package `netscape.javascript`; the `netscape.javascript` package contains the `JSObject` and `JSException` classes.

In JavaScript, a `JavaPackage` is a reference to a Java package. For example, a reference to `netscape` is a `JavaPackage`. `netscape.javascript` is both a `JavaPackage` and a property of the `netscape JavaPackage`. A *JavaClass* object is a reference to one of the classes in a package, such as `netscape.javascript.JSObject`. The `JavaPackage` and `JavaClass` hierarchy reflect the Java package and class hierarchy. Although the packages and classes contained in a `JavaPackage` are its properties, you cannot use a `for...in` statement to enumerate them as you can enumerate the properties of other objects.

Compatability
   JavaScript 1.1 / core

Property summary
   The properties of a `JavaPackage` are the *JavaClass* objects and any other *JavaPackage* objects it contains.

Layer

Corresponds to a layer in an HTML page and provides a means for manipulating that layer.

Compatability
   JavaScript 1.2 / client

Property summary
   Properties are detailed in Table A-28.

Method summary
   Methods are detailed in Table A-29. This object inherits the `watch` and `unwatch` methods from `Object`.

Table A-28. Layer Properties

Property	Description	Version
above	The layer object above this one in z-order, among all layers in the document or the enclosing window object if this layer is top-most.	1.2
background	The image to use as the background for the layer's canvas.	1.2
bgColor	The color to use as a solid background color for the layer's canvas.	1.2
below	The layer object below this one in z-order, among all layers in the document or null if this layer is at the bottom.	1.2
clip.bottom	The bottom edge of the clipping rectangle (the part of the layer that is visible).	1.2
clip.height	The height of the clipping rectangle (the part of the layer that is visible).	1.2
clip.left	The left edge of the clipping rectangle (the part of the layer that is visible).	1.2
clip.right	The right edge of the clipping rectangle (the part of the layer that is visible).	1.2
clip.top	The top edge of the clipping rectangle (the part of the layer that is visible).	1.2
clip.width	The width of the clipping rectangle (the part of the layer that is visible).	1.2
document	The layer's associated document.	1.2
left	The horizontal position of the layer's left edge, in pixels, relative to the origin of its parent layer.	1.2
name	A string specifying the name assigned to the layer through the ID attribute in the LAYER tag.	1.2
pageX	The horizontal position of the layer, in pixels, relative to the page.	1.2
pageY	The vertical position of the layer, in pixels, relative to the page.	1.2
parentLayer	The layer object that contains this layer, or the enclosing window object if this layer is not nested in another layer.	1.2
siblingAbove	The layer object above this one in z-order, among all layers that share the same parent layer, or null if the layer has no sibling above.	1.2
siblingBelow	The layer object below this one in z-order, among all layers that share the same parent layer, or null if layer is at the bottom.	1.2

Table A-28. Layer Properties (continued)

Property	Description	Version
src	A string specifying the URL of the layer's content.	1.2
top	The vertical position of the layer's top edge, in pixels, relative to the origin of its parent layer.	1.2
visibility	Whether or not the layer is visible.	1.2
zIndex	The relative z-order of this layer with respect to its siblings.	1.2

Table A-29. Layer Methods

Method	Description	Version
captureEvents	Sets the window or document to capture all events of the specified type.	1.2
handleEvent	Invokes the handler for the specified event.	1.2
load	Changes the source of a layer to the contents of the specified file, and simultaneously changes the width at which the layer's HTML contents will be wrapped.	1.2
moveAbove	Stacks this layer above the layer specified in the argument, without changing either layer's horizontal or vertical position.	1.2
moveBelow	Stacks this layer below the specified layer, without changing either layer's horizontal or vertical position.	1.2
moveBy	Changes the layer position by applying the specified deltas, measured in pixels.	1.2
moveTo	Moves the top-left corner of the window to the specified screen coordinates.	1.2
moveToAbsolute	Changes the layer position to the specified pixel coordinates within the page (instead of the containing layer).	1.2
releaseEvents	Sets the layer to release captured events of the specified type, sending the event to objects further along the event hierarchy.	1.2
resizeBy	Resizes the layer by the specified height and width values (in pixels).	1.2
resizeTo	Resizes the layer to have the specified height and width values (in pixels).	1.2
routeEvent	Passes a captured event along the normal event hierarchy.	1.2

Link

By using the HTML **A** or **AREA** tag or by a call to the **String.link** method. The JavaScript runtime engine creates a *Link* object corresponding to each **A** and **AREA** tag in your document that supplies the HREF attribute. It puts these objects as an array in the *document.links* property. You access a *Link* object by indexing this array.

Compatability

    JavaScript 1.0 / client

Event handlers

    Area objects have the following event handlers: onDblClick, onMouseOut, onMouseOver

    Link objects have the following event handlers: onClick, onDblClick, onKeyDown, onKeyPress, onKeyUp, onMouseDown, onMouseOut, onMouseUp, onMouseOver

Property summary

    Properties are detailed in Table A-30.

Method summary

    Methods are detailed in Table A-31. This object inherits the **watch** and **unwatch** methods from **Object**.

Table A-30. Link Properties

Property	Description	Version
hash	Specifies an anchor name in the URL.	1.0
host	Specifies the host and domain name, or IP address, of a network host.	1.0
hostname	Specifies the host:port portion of the URL.	1.0
href	Specifies the entire URL.	1.0
pathname	Specifies the URL-path portion of the URL.	1.0
port	Specifies the communications port that the server uses.	1.0
protocol	Specifies the beginning of the URL, including the colon.	1.0
search	Specifies a query string.	1.0
target	Reflects the TARGET attribute.	1.0
text	A string containing the content of the corresponding A tag.	1.0

Table A-31. Link Methods

Method	Description	Version
`handleEvent`	Invokes the handler for the specified event.	1.2

Location

Contains information on the current URL.

Compatability
> JavaScript 1.0 / client

Property summary
> Properties are detailed in Table A-32.

Method summary
> Methods are detailed in Table A-33. This object inherits the `watch` and `unwatch` methods from `Object`.

Table A-32. Location Properties

Property	Description	Version
`hash`	Specifies an anchor name in the URL.	1.0
`host`	Specifies the host and domain name, or IP address, of a network host.	1.0
`hostname`	Specifies the `host:port` portion of the URL.	1.0
`href`	Specifies the entire URL.	1.0
`pathname`	Specifies the URL-path portion of the URL.	1.0
`port`	Specifies the communications port that the server uses.	1.0
`protocol`	Specifies the beginning of the URL, including the colon.	1.0
`search`	Specifies a query string.	1.0

Table A-33. Location Methods

Method	Description	Version
`reload`	Loads the specified URL over the current history entry.	1.1
`replace`	Forces a reload of the window's current document.	1.1

Math

A built-in object that has properties and methods for mathematical constants and functions. For example, the *Math* object's *PI* property has the value of *pi*.

Compatability

JavaScript 1.0 / core

Property summary

Properties are detailed in Table A-34.

Method summary

Methods are detailed in Table A-35.

Table A-34. Math Properties

Property	Description	Version
E	Euler's constant and the base of natural logarithms, approximately 2.718.	1.0
LN10	Natural logarithm of 10, approximately 2.302.	1.0
LN2	Natural logarithm of 2, approximately 0.693.	1.0
LOG10E	Base 10 logarithm of E, approximately 0.434.	1.0
LOG2E	Base 2 logarithm of E, approximately 1.442.	1.0
PI	Ratio of the circumference of a circle to its diameter, approximately 3.14159.	1.0
SQRT1_2	Square root of 1/2; equivalently, 1 over the square root of 2, approximately 0.707.	1.0
SQRT2	Square root of 2, approximately 1.414.	1.0

Table A-35. Math Methods

Method	Description	Version
abs	Returns the absolute value of a number.	1.0
acos	Returns the arc cosine (in radians) of a number.	1.0
asin	Returns the arc sine (in radians) of a number.	1.0
atan	Returns the arc tangent (in radians) of a number.	1.0
atan2	Returns the arc tangent of the quotient of its arguments.	1.0
ceil	Returns the smallest integer greater than or equal to a number.	1.0
cos	Returns the cosine of a number.	1.0
exp	Returns E to the number power, where number is the argument, and E is Euler's constant, the base of the natural logarithms.	1.0
floor	Returns the largest integer less than or equal to a number.	1.0
log	Returns the natural logarithm (base E) of a number.	1.0
max	Returns the greater of two numbers.	1.0

Table A-35. Math Methods (continued)

Method	Description	Version
min	Returns the lesser of two numbers.	1.0
pow	Returns base to the exponent power, that is, base to the exponent power.	1.0
random	Returns a pseudo-random number between 0 and 1.	1.0
round	Returns the value of a number rounded to the nearest integer.	1.0
sin	Returns the sine of a number.	1.0
sqrt	Returns the square root of a number.	1.0
tan	Returns the tangent of a number.	1.0

MimeType

A MIME type (Multipart Internet Mail Extension) supported by the client.

Compatability
> JavaScript 1.1 / client

Property summary
> Properties are detailed in Table A-36.

Method summary
> This object inherits the watch and unwatch methods from Object.

Table A-36. MimeType Properties

Property	Description	Version
description	A description of the MIME type.	1.0
enabledPlugin	Reference to the *Plugin* object configured for the MIME type.	1.0
suffixes	A string listing possible filename extensions for the MIME type, for example, "mpeg, mpg, mpe, mpv, vbs, mpegv".	1.0
type	The name of the MIME type, for example, "video/mpeg" or "audio/x-wav".	1.0

Navigator

Lets you work with numeric values. The *Number* object is an object wrapper for primitive numeric values.

Compatability
> JavaScript 1.0 / client

Property summary

Properties are detailed in Table A-37

Method summary

Methods are detailed in Table A-38. This object inherits the `watch` and `unwatch` methods from `Object`.

Table A-37. Navigator Properties

Property	Description	Version
appCodeName	Specifies the code name of the browser.	1.0
appName	Specifies the name of the browser.	1.0
appVersion	Specifies version information for the Navigator.	1.0
language	Indicates the translation of the Navigator being used.	1.2
mimeTypes	An array of all MIME types supported by the client.	1.1
platform	Indicates the machine type for which the Navigator was compiled.	1.2
plugins	An array of all plug-ins currently installed on the client.	1.1
userAgent	Specifies the user-agent header.	1.1

Table A-38. Navigator Methods

Method	Description	Version
javaEnabled	Tests whether Java is enabled.	1.1
plugins.refresh	Makes newly installed plug-ins available and optionally reloads open documents that contain plug-ins.	1.1
preference	Allows a signed script to get and set certain Navigator preferences.	1.2
taintEnabled	Specifies whether data tainting is enabled.	1.1

Netscape

A top-level object used to access any Java class in the package `netscape.*`. The *netscape* object is a top-level, predefined JavaScript object. You can automatically access it without using a constructor or calling a method.

Compatability

JavaScript 1.1 / core

Number

Lets you work with numeric values. The *Number* object is an object wrapper for primitive numeric values.

Compatability
    JavaScript 1.1 / core

Property summary
    Properties are detailed in Table A-39.

Method summary
    Methods are detailed in Table A-40.

Table A-39. Number Properties

Property	Description	Version
constructor	Specifies the function that creates an object's prototype.	1.1
MAX_VALUE	The largest representable number.	1.1
MIN_VALUE	The smallest representable number.	1.1
NaN	Special "not a number" value.	1.1
NEGATIVE_INFINITY	Special value representing negative infinity; returned on overflow.	1.1
POSITIVE_INFINITY	Special value representing infinity; returned on overflow.	1.1
prototype	Allows the addition of properties to a *Number* object.	1.1

Table A-40. Number Methods

Method	Description	Version
toSource	Returns an object literal representing the specified *Number* object; you can use this value to create a new object. Overrides the `Object.toSource` method.	1.3
toString	Returns a string representing the specified object. Overrides the `Object.toString` method.	1.1
valueOf	Returns the primitive value of the specified object. Overrides the `Object.valueOf` method.	1.1

Object

`Object` is the primitive JavaScript object type. All *JavaScript* objects are descended from `Object`. That is, all JavaScript objects have the methods defined for `Object`.

Compatability

> JavaScript 1.0 / core

Property summary

> Properties are detailed in Table A-41.

Method summary

> Methods are detailed in Table A-42.

Table A-41. Object Properties

Property	Description	Version
constructor	Specifies the function that creates an object's prototype.	1.1
prototype	Allows the addition of properties to all objects.	1.1

Table A-42. Object Methods

Method	Description	Version
eval	Deprecated. Evaluates a string of JavaScript code in the context of the specified object.	1.1
toSource	Returns an object literal representing the specified object; you can use this value to create a new object.	1.3
toString	Returns a string representing the specified object.	1.0
unwatch	Removes a watchpoint from a property of the object.	1.2
valueOf	Returns the primitive value of the specified object.	1.1
watch	Adds a watchpoint to a property of the object.	1.2

Option

Corresponds to an option in a SELECT list.

Compatability

> JavaScript 1.1 / client

Property summary

> Properties are detailed in Table A-43.

Method summary

> Methods are detailed in Table A-44. This object inherits the **watch** and **unwatch** methods from **Object**.

Table A-43. Option Properties

Property	Description	Version
defaultSelected	Specifies the initial selection state of the option.	1.1
selected	Specifies the current selection state of the option.	1.1
text	Specifies the text for the option.	1.1
value	Specifies the value that is returned to the server when the option is selected and the form is submitted.	1.1

Table A-44. Option Methods

Method	Description	Version
reload	Loads the specified URL over the current history entry.	1.1
replace	Forces a reload of the window's current document.	1.1

Packages

A top-level object used to access Java classes from within JavaScript code.

Compatability
> JavaScript 1.1 / core

Property summary
> Properties are detailed in Table A-45.

Table A-45. Packages Properties

Property	Description	Version
className	The fully qualified name of a Java class in a package other than netscape, java, or sun that is available to JavaScript.	1.1
java	Any class in the Java package java.*.	1.1
netscape	Any class in the Java package netscape.*.	1.1
sun	Any class in the Java package sun.*.	1.1

Password

A text field on an HTML form that conceals its value by displaying asterisks (*). When the user enters text into the field, asterisks (*) hide entries from view.

Compatability
> JavaScript 1.0 / client

Event handlers
> onBlur, onFocus

Property summary
> Properties are detailed in Table A-46.

Method summary
> Methods are detailed in Table A-47. This object inherits the **watch** and **unwatch** methods from **Object**.

Table A-46. Password Properties

Property	Description	Version
defaultValue	Reflects the VALUE attribute.	1.0
form	Specifies the form containing the *Password* object.	1.0
name	Reflects the NAME attribute.	1.0
type	Reflects the TYPE attribute.	1.1
value	Reflects the current value of the *Password* object's field.	1.0

Table A-47. Password Methods

Method	Description	Version
blur	Removes focus from the object.	1.0
focus	Gives focus to the object.	1.0
handleEvent	Invokes the handler for the specified event.	1.2
select	Selects the input area of the object.	1.0

Plugin

A plug-in module installed on the client. *Plugin* objects are predefined *JavaScript* objects that you access through the *navigator.plugins* array. A *Plugin* object is a plug-in installed on the client. A plug-in is a software module that the browser can invoke to display specialized types of embedded data within the browser.

Compatability
> JavaScript 1.1 / client

Property summary
> Properties are detailed in Table A-48.

Table A-48. Plugin Properties

Property	Description	Version
description	A description of the plug-in.	1.1
filename	Name of the plug-in file on disk.	1.1

Table A-48. Plugin Properties (continued)

Property	Description	Version
length	Number of elements in the plug-in's array of *MimeType* objects.	1.1
name	Name of the plug-in.	1.1

This object inherits the `watch` and `unwatch` methods from `Object`.

Radio

An individual radio button in a set of radio buttons on an HTML form. The user can use a set of radio buttons to choose one item from a list.

Compatability
    JavaScript 1.0 / client

Property summary
    Properties are detailed in Table A-49.

Method summary
    Methods are detailed in Table A-50. This object inherits the `watch` and `unwatch` methods from `Object`.

Table A-49. Radio Properties

Property	Description	Version
checked	Lets you programmatically select a radio button	1.0
defaultChecked	Reflects the CHECKED attribute.	1.0
form	Specifies the form containing the *Radio* object.	1.0
name	Reflects the NAME attribute.	1.0
type	Reflects the TYPE attribute.	1.1
value	Reflects the VALUE attribute.	1.0

Table A-50. Radio Methods

Method	Description	Version
blur	Removes focus from the radio button.	1.1
click	Simulates a mouse-click on the radio button.	1.0
focus	Gives focus to the radio button.	1.1
handleEvent	Invokes the handler for the specified event.	1.2

RegExp

A regular expression object contains the pattern of a regular expression. It has properties and methods for using that regular expression to find and replace matches in strings. In addition to the properties of an individual regular expression object that you create using the `RegExp` constructor function, the predefined *RegExp* object has static properties that are set whenever any regular expression is used.

Compatability

  JavaScript 1.2 / core

Property summary

  Properties are detailed in Table A-51.

Method summary

  .Methods are detailed in Table A-52 .

Table A-51. RegExp Properties

Property	Description	Version
`$1, ..., $9`	Parenthesized substring matches, if any.	1.2
`$_`	Same as input.	1.2
`$*`	Same as `multiline`.	1.2
`$&`	Same as `lastMatch`.	1.2
`$+`	Same as `lastParen`.	1.2
`` $` ``	Same as `leftContext`.	1.2
`$'`	Same as `rightContext`.	1.2
`constructor`	Specifies the function that creates an object's prototype.	1.2
`global`	Whether or not to test the regular expression against all possible matches in a string, or only against the first.	1.2
`ignoreCase`	Whether or not to ignore case while attempting a match in a string.	1.2
`input`	The string against which a regular expression is matched.	1.2
`lastIndex`	The index at which to start the next match.	1.2
`lastMatch`	The last matched characters.	1.2
`lastParen`	The last parenthesized substring match, if any.	1.2
`leftContext`	The substring preceding the most recent match.	1.2
`multiline`	Whether or not to search in strings across multiple lines.	1.2
`prototype`	Allows the addition of properties to all objects.	1.1
`rightContext`	The substring following the most recent match.	1.2
`source`	The text of the pattern.	1.2

Table A-52. RegExp Methods

Method	Description	Version
compile	Compiles a regular expression object.	1.2
exec	Executes a search for a match in its string parameter.	1.2
test	Tests for a match in its string parameter.	1.2
toSource	Returns an object literal representing the specified object; you can use this value to create a new object. Overrides the Object.toSource method.	1.3
toString	Returns a string representing the specified object. Overrides the Object.toString method.	1.1
valueOf	Returns the primitive value of the specified object. Overrides the Object.valueOf method.	1.1

Reset

A reset button on an HTML form. A reset button returns all elements in a form back to their defaults.

Compatability

JavaScript 1.0 / client

Event handlers

onBlur, onClick, onFocus

Property summary

Properties are detailed in Table A-53.

Method summary

Methods are detailed in Table A-54. This object inherits the watch and unwatch methods from Object.

Table A-53. Reset Properties

Property	Description	Version
form	Specifies the form containing the *Reset* object.	1.0
name	Reflects the NAME attribute.	1.0
type	Reflects the TYPE attribute.	1.1
value	Reflects the VALUE attribute.	1.0

Table A-54. Reset Methods

Method	Description	Version
blur	Removes focus from the reset button.	1.0
click	Simulates a mouse-click on the reset button.	1.0
focus	Gives focus to the reset button.	1.0
handleEvent	Invokes the handler for the specified event.	1.2

Screen

Compatability
    JavaScript 1.0 / client

Property summary
    Properties are detailed in Table A-55.

Table A-55. Screen Properties

Property	Description	Version
availHeight	Specifies the height of the screen, in pixels, minus permanent or semi-permanent user interface features displayed by the operating system, such as the taskbar on Microsoft Windows.	1.2
availWidth	Specifies the width of the screen, in pixels, minus permanent or semi-permanent user interface features displayed by the operating system, such as the taskbar on Microsoft Windows.	1.2
colorDepth	The bit depth of the color palette, if one is in use; otherwise, the value is derived from `screen.pixelDepth`.	1.2
height	Display screen height.	1.2
pixelDepth	Display screen color resolution (bits per pixel).	1.2
width	Display screen width.	1.2

Select

A selection list on an HTML form. The user can choose one or more items from a selection list, depending on how the list was created.

Compatability
    JavaScript 1.0 / client

Event handlers
    onBlur, onChange, onFocus

Property summary

Properties are detailed in Table A-56.

Method summary

Methods are detailed in Table A-57. This object inherits the `watch` and `unwatch` methods from `Object`.

Table A-56. Select Properties

Property	Description	Version
form	Specifies the form containing the selection list.	1.0
length	Reflects the number of options in the selection list.	1.0
name	Reflects the NAME attribute.	1.0
options	Reflects the OPTION tags.	1.0
selectedIndex	Reflects the index of the selected option (or the first selected option, if multiple options are selected).	1.0
type	Specifies that the object represents a selection list and whether it can have one or more selected options.	1.1

Table A-57. Select Methods

Method	Description	Version
blur	Removes focus from the selection list.	1.0
focus	Gives focus to the selection list.	1.0
handleEvent	Invokes the handler for the specified event	1.2

String

An object representing a series of characters in a string.

Compatability

JavaScript 1.0 / core

Property summary

Properties are detailed in Table A-58.

Method summary

Methods are detailed in Table A-59. This object inherits the `watch` and `unwatch` methods from `Object`.

Table A-58. String Properties

Property	Description	Version
constructor	Specifies the function that creates an object's prototype.	1.1
length	Reflects the length of the string.	1.0
prototype	Allows the addition of properties to a *String* object.	1.1

Table A-59. String Methods

Method	Description	Version
anchor	Creates an HTML anchor that is used as a hypertext target.	1.0
big	Causes a string to be displayed in a big font as if it were in a <BIG> tag.	1.0
blink	Causes a string to blink as if it were in a <BLINK> tag.	1.0
bold	Causes a string to be displayed as if it were in a <B> tag.	1.0
charAt	Returns the character at the specified index.	1.0
charCodeAt	Returns a number indicating the Unicode value of the character at the given index.	1.2
concat	Combines the text of two strings and returns a new string.	1.2
fixed	Causes a string to be displayed in fixed-pitch font as if it were in a <TT> tag.	1.0
fontcolor	Causes a string to be displayed in the specified color as if it were in a <FONT COLOR=color> tag.	1.0
fontsize	Causes a string to be displayed in the specified font size as if it were in a <FONT SIZE=size> tag.	1.0
fromCharCode	Returns a string created by using the specified sequence of Unicode values.	1.2
indexof	Returns the index within the calling *String* object of the first occurrence of the specified value, or -1 if not found.	1.0
italics	Causes a string to be italic, as if it were in an <I> tag.	1.0
lastindexOf	Returns the index within the calling *String* object of the last occurrence of the specified value, or -1 if not found.	1.0
link	Creates an HTML hypertext link that requests another URL.	1.0
match	Used to match a regular expression against a string.	1.2

Table A-59. String Methods (continued)

Method	Description	Version
replace	Used to find a match between a regular expression and a string, and to replace the matched substring with a new substring.	1.2
search	Executes the search for a match between a regular expression and a specified string.	1.2
slice	Extracts a section of a string and returns a new string.	1.0
small	Causes a string to be displayed in a small font, as if it were in a \<SMALL> tag.	1.0
split	Splits a *String* object into an array of strings by separating the string into substrings.	1.0
strike	Causes a string to be displayed as struck-out text, as if it were in a \<STRIKE> tag.	1.0
sub	Causes a string to be displayed as a subscript, as if it were in a \<SUB> tag.	1.0
substr	Returns the characters in a string beginning at the specified location through the specified number of characters.	1.0
substring	Returns the characters in a string between two indexes into the string.	1.0
sup	Causes a string to be displayed as a super-script, as if it were in a \<SUP> tag.	1.0
toLowerCase	Returns the calling string value converted to lowercase.	1.0
toSource	Returns an object literal representing the spec-ified object; you can use this value to create a new object. Overrides the `Object.toSource` method.	1.3
toString	Returns a string representing the specified object. Overrides the `Object.toString` method.	1.1
toUpperCase	Returns the calling string value converted to uppercase.	1.0
valueOf	Returns the primitive value of the specified object. Overrides the `Object.valueOf` method.	1.1

Submit

Corresponds to a "submit" button on an HTML form. A submit button causes a form to be sent to a server.

Compatability
    JavaScript 1.0 / client

Event handlers
    onBlur, onClick, onFocus

Property summary
    Properties are detailed in Table A-60.

Method summary
    Methods are detailed in Table A-61. This object inherits the watch and unwatch methMds from Object.

Table A-60. Submit Properties

Property	Description	Version
form	Specifies the form containing the *Submit* object.	1.0
name	Reflects the NAME attribute.	1.0
type	Reflects the TYPE attribute.	1.1
value	Reflects the VALUE attribute.	1.0

Table A-61. Submit Methods

Method	Description	Version
blur	Removes focus from the submit button.	1.0
click	Simulates a mouseclick on the submit button.	1.0
focus	Gives focus to the submit button.	1.0
handleEvent	Invokes the handler for the specified event.	1.2

sun

A top-level object used to access any Java class in the package sun.*. The *sun* object is a top-level, predefined *JavaScript* object. You can automatically access it without using a constructor or calling a method. The *sun* object is a convenience synonym for the property Packages.sun.

Compatability
    JavaScript 1.1 / core

Text

A text input field on an HTML form. The user can enter a word, phrase, or series of numbers in a text field.

Compatability
    JavaScript 1.0 / client

Event handlers
    onBlur, onChange, onFocus, onSelect

Property summary

Property summary

Properties are detailed in Table A-62.

Method summary

Methods are detailed in Table A-63. This object inherits the `watch` and `unwatch` methods from `Object`.

Table A-62. Text Properties

Property	Description	Version
defaultValue	Reflects the VALUE attribute.	1.0
form	Specifies the form containing the *Text* object.	1.0
name	Reflects the NAME attribute.	1.0
type	Reflects the TYPE attribute.	1.1
value	Reflects the current value of the *Text* object's field.	1.0

Table A-63. Text Methods

Method	Description	Version
blur	Removes focus from the object.	1.0
focus	Gives focus to the object.	1.0
handleEvent	Invokes the handler for the specified event.	1.2
select	Selects the input area of the object.	1.0

Textarea

A multiline input field on an HTML form. The user can use a text area field to enter words, phrases, or numbers.

Compatability

JavaScript 1.1 / client

Event handlers

onBlur, onChange, onFocus, onKeyDown, onKeyPress, onKeyUp, onSelect

Property summary

Properties are detailed in Table A-64.

Method summary

Methods are detailed in Table A-65. This object inherits the `watch` and `unwatch` methods from `Object`.

Table A-64. Textarea Properties

Property	Description	Version
defaultValue	Reflects the VALUE attribute.	1.0
form	Specifies the form containing the *Textarea* object.	1.0

Table A-64. Textarea Properties (continued)

Property	Description	Version
name	Reflects the NAME attribute.	1.0
type	Specifies that the object is a *Textarea* object.	1.1
value	Reflects the current value of the *Textarea* object.	1.0

Table A-65. Textarea Methods

Method	Description	Version
blur	Removes focus from the object.	1.0
focus	Gives focus to the object.	1.0
handleEvent	Invokes the handler for the specified event.	1.2
select	Selects the input area of the object.	1.0

Window

Represents a browser window or frame. This is the top-level object for each *document, Location,* and *History* object group.

Compatability

JavaScript 1.0 / client

Event handlers

onBlur, onDragDrop, onError, onFocus, onLoad, onMove, onResize, onUnload

Property summary

Properties are detailed in Table A-66.

Method summary

Methods are detailed in Table A-67. This object inherits the watch and unwatch methods from Object.

Table A-66. Window Properties

Property	Description	Version
closed	Specifies whether a window has been closed.	1.1
defaultStatus	Reflects the default message displayed in the window's status bar.	1.0
document	Contains information on the current document and provides methods for displaying HTML output to the user.	1.0
frames	An array reflecting all the frames in a window.	1.0
history	Contains information on the URLs that the client has visited within a window.	1.1

Table A-66. Window Properties (continued)

Property	Description	Version
innerHeight	Specifies the vertical dimension, in pixels, of the window's content area.	1.2
innerWidth	Specifies the horizontal dimension, in pixels, of the window's content area.	1.2
length	The number of frames in the window.	1.0
location	Contains information on the current URL.	1.0
locationbar	Represents the browser window's location bar.	1.2
menubar	Represents the browser window's menu bar.	1.2
name	A unique name used to refer to this window.	1.0
opener	Specifies the window name of the calling document when a window is opened using the open method.	1.1
outerHeight	Specifies the vertical dimension, in pixels, of the window's outside boundary.	1.2
outerWidth	Specifies the horizontal dimension, in pixels, of the window's outside boundary.	1.2
pageXOffset	Provides the current x position, in pixels, of a window's viewed page.	1.2
pageYOffset	Provides the current y position, in pixels, of a window's viewed page.	1.2
parent	A synonym for a window or frame whose frameset contains the current frame.	1.0
personalbar	Represents the browser window's personal bar (also called the directories bar).	1.2
scrollbars	Represents the browser window's scroll bars.	1.2
self	A synonym for the current window.	1.0
status	Specifies a priority or transient message in the window's status bar.	1.0
statusbar	Represents the browser window's status bar.	1.2
toolbar	Represents the browser window's tool bar.	1.2
top	A synonym for the topmost browser window.	1.0
window	A synonym for the current window.	1.0

Table A-67. Window Methods

Method	Description	Version
alert	Displays an Alert dialog box with a message and an "OK" button.	1.0
back	Undoes the last history step in any frame within the top-level window.	1.2

Table A-67. Window Methods (continued)

Method	Description	Version
blur	Removes focus from the specified object.	1.0
captureEvents	Sets the window or document to capture all events of the specified type.	1.2
clearInterval	Cancels a timeout that was set with the setInterval method.	1.2
clearTimeout	Cancels a timeout that was set with the setTimeout method.	1.0
close	Closes the specified window.	1.0
confirm	Displays a Confirm dialog box with the specified message and "OK" and "Cancel" buttons.	1.0
disableExternalCapture	Disables external event capturing set by the enableExternalCapture method.	1.2
enableExternalCapture	Allows a window with frames to capture events in pages loaded from different locations (servers).	1.2
find	Finds the specified text string in the contents of the specified window.	1.2
focus	Gives focus to the specified object.	1.1
forward	Loads the next URL in the history list.	1.2
handleEvent	Invokes the handler for the specified event.	1.2
home	Points the browser to the URL specified in preferences as the user's home page.	1.2
moveBy	Moves the window by the specified amounts.	1.2
moveTo	Moves the top-left corner of the window to the specified screen coordinates.	1.2
open	Opens a new web browser window.	1.0
print	Prints the contents of the window or frame.	1.2
prompt	Displays a Prompt dialog box with a message and an input field.	1.0
releaseEvents	Sets the window to release captured events of the specified type, sending the event to objects further along the event hierarchy.	1.2
resizeBy	Resizes an entire window by moving the window's bottom-right corner by the specified amount.	1.2
resizeTo	Resizes an entire window to the specified outer height and width.	1.2
routeEvent	Passes a captured event along the normal event hierarchy.	1.2
scroll	Scrolls a window to a specified coordinate.	1.1

Table A-67. Window Methods (continued)

Method	Description	Version
scrollBy	Scrolls the viewing area of a window by the specified amount.	1.2
scrollTo	Scrolls the viewing area of the window to the specified coordinates, such that the specified point becomes the top-left corner.	1.2
setInterval	Evaluates an expression or calls a function every time a specified number of milliseconds elapses.	1.2
setTimeout	Evaluates an expression or calls a function one time after a specified number of milliseconds has elapsed.	1.0
stop	Stops the current download.	1.2

Top-Level Properties and Functions

Top-level properties and functions are not associated with any object. Table A-68 details the top-level properties. Table A-69 details the top-level functions.

Table A-68. Top-Level Properties

Property	Description	Version
infinity	A numeric value representing infinity.	1.3
NaN	A value representing Not-A-Number.	1.3
undefined	The value undefined.	1.3

Table A-69. Top-Level Functions

Function	Description	Version
escape	Returns the hexadecimal encoding of an argument in the ISO Latin-1 character set; used to create strings to add to a URL.	1.0
eval	Evaluates a string of JavaScript code without reference to a particular object.	1.0
isFinite	Evaluates an argument to determine whether it is not a number.	1.3
isNaN	Returns a string representing the specified object. Overrides the Object.toString method.	1.0
Number	Converts an object to a number.	1.2
parseFloat	Parses a string argument and returns a floating-point number.	1.0
parseInt	Parses a string argument and returns an integer.	1.0

Table A-69. Top-Level Functions (continued)

Function	Description	Version
string	Converts an object to a string.	1.2
unescape	Returns the ASCII string for the specified hexadecimal encoding value.	1.0

Event Handlers

This section contains syntax for JavaScript's 23 event handlers.

onAbort

Event handler for **Image**. Executes JavaScript code when an *abort* event occurs; that is, when the user aborts the loading of an image (for example, by clicking a link or by clicking the "Stop" button).

Compatability
    JavaScript 1.1

Event properties
    onAbort has the following event properties:

    Type
        Indicates the type of event

    Target
        Indicates the object to which the event was originally sent

onBlur

Event handler for **Button**, **Checkbox**, **FileUpload**, **Layer**, **Password**, **Radio**, **Reset**, **Select**, **Submit**, **Text**, **Textarea**, and **Window**. Executes JavaScript code when a blur event occurs; that is, when a form element loses focus or when a window or frame loses focus.

Compatability
    JavaScript 1.0

Event properties
    onBlur has the following event properties:

    Type
        Indicates the type of event

    Target
        Indicates the object to which the event was originally sent

onChange

Executes JavaScript code when a change event occurs; that is, when a `Select`, `Text`, or `Textarea` field loses focus and its value has been modified. Event handler for `FileUpload`, `Select`, `Text`, and `Textarea`.

Compatability
JavaScript 1.0

Event properties
onChange has the following event properties:

Type
Indicates the type of event

Target
Indicates the object to which the event was originally sent

onClick

Event handler for `Button`, `Document`, `Checkbox`, `Link`, `Radio`, `Reset`, and `Submit`. Executes JavaScript code when a click event occurs; that is, when an object on a form is clicked. (A click event is a combination of the *MouseDown* and *MouseUp* events.)

Compatibility
JavaScript 1.0

Event properties
onClick has the following event properties:

Type
Indicates the type of event

Target
Indicates the object to which the event was originally sent

LayerX, layerY, pageX, pageY, screenX, screenY
Represent the cursor location at the time the event occurred

Which
Represents 1 for a left mouseclick and 3 for a right mouseclick

Modifiers
Contains the list of modifier keys held down while the event occurred

onDblClick

Event handler for `Document` and `Link`. Executes JavaScript code when a *DblClick* event occurs; that is, when the user double-clicks a form element or a link.

Compatability
> JavaScript 1.2

Event properties
> onDblClick has the following properties:

Type
> Indicates the type of event

Target
> Indicates the object to which the event was originally sent

LayerX, layerY, pageX, pageY, screenX, screenY
> Represent the cursor location at the time the event occurred

Which
> Represents 1 for a left mouseclick and 3 for a right mouseclick

Modifiers
> Contains the list of modifier keys held down while the event occurred

onDragDrop

Event handler for **Document** and **Link**. Executes JavaScript code when a *DragDrop* event occurs; that is, when the user drops an object onto the browser window, such as dropping a file.

Compatability
> JavaScript 1.2

Event properties
> onDragDrop has the following event properties:

Type
> Indicates the type of event

Target
> Indicates the object to which the event was originally sent

lvt
> Returns an *Array* of *Strings* containing the URLs of the dropped objects

Modifiers
> Contains the list of modifier keys held down while the event occurred

ScreenX, screenY
> Represent the cursor location at the time the event occurred

onError

Executes JavaScript code when an error event occurs; that is, when the loading of a document or image causes an error.

Compatability

JavaScript 1.1

Event properties

onDragDrop has the following event properties:

Type

Indicates the type of event

Target

Indicates the object to which the event was originally sent

onFocus

Event handler for `Button`, `Checkbox`, `FileUpload`, `Frame`, `Layer`, `Password`, `Radio`, `Reset`, `Select`, `Submit`, `Text`, `Textarea`, and `Window`. Executes JavaScript code when a focus event occurs; that is, when a window, frame, or frameset receives focus or when a form element receives input focus.

Compatability

JavaScript 1.0

Event properties

onFocus has the following event properties:

Type

Indicates the type of event

Target

Indicates the object to which the event was originally sent

onKeyDown

Event handler for `Document`, `Image`, `Link`, and `Textarea`. Executes JavaScript code when a *KeyDown* event occurs; that is, when the user depresses a key.

Compatability

JavaScript 1.2

Event properties

onKeyDown has the following event properties:

Type

Indicates the type of event.

Target

Indicates the object to which the event was originally sent.

LayerX, layerY, pageX, pageY, screenX, screenY
> For an event over a window, these represent the cursor location at the time the event occurred. For an event over a form, they represent the position of the form element.

Which
> Represents the ASCII value of the key pressed. To get the actual letter, number, or symbol of the pressed key, use the `String.fromCharCode` method. To set this property when the ASCII value is unknown, use the `String.charCodeAt` method.

Modifiers
> Contains the list of modifier keys held down when the event occurred.

onKeyPress

Event handler for `Document`, `Image`, `Link`, and `Textarea`. Executes JavaScript code when a *KeyPress* event occurs; that is, when the user presses or holds down a key.

Compatability
> JavaScript 1.2

Event properties
> onKeyPress has the following event properties:

Type
> Indicates the type of event.

Target
> Indicates the object to which the event was originally sent.

LayerX, layerY, pageX, pageY, screenX, screenY
> For an event over a window, these represent the cursor location at the time the event occurred. For an event over a form, they represent the position of the form element.

Which
> Represents the ASCII value of the key pressed. To get the actual letter, number, or symbol of the pressed key, use the `String.fromCharCode` method. To set this property when the ASCII value is unknown, use the `String.charCodeAt` method.

Modifiers
> Contains the list of modifier keys held down when the event occurred.

onKeyUp

Event handler for Document, Image, Link, and Textarea. Executes JavaScript code when a KeyUp event occurs; that is, when the user releases a key.

Compatability

JavaScript 1.2

Event properties

onKeyUp has the following event properties:

Type

Indicates the type of event.

Target

Indicates the object to which the event was originally sent.

LayerX, layerY, pageX, pageY, screenX, screenY

For an event over a window, these represent the cursor location at the time the event occurred. For an event over a form, they represent the position of the form element.

Which

Represents the ASCII value of the key pressed. To get the actual letter, number, or symbol of the pressed key, use the String.fromCharCode method. To set this property when the ASCII value is unknown, use the String.charCodeAt method.

Modifiers

Contains the list of modifier keys held down when the event occurred.

onLoad

Event handler for Image, Layer, and Window. Executes JavaScript code when a load event occurs; that is, when the browser finishes loading a window or all frames within a <FRAMESET> tag.

Compatability

JavaScript 1.0

Event properties

onLoad has the following event properties:

Type

Indicates the type of event

Target

Indicates the object to which the event was originally sent

Width, height

> For an event over a window, but not over a layer, these represent the width and height of the window

onMouseDown

Event handler for `Button`, `Document`, and `Link`. Executes JavaScript code when a `MouseDown` event occurs; that is, when the user depresses a mouse button.

Compatability

> JavaScript 1.2

Event properties

> onMouseDown has the following event properties:

Type

> Indicates the type of event

Target

> Indicates the object to which the event was originally sent

LayerX, layerY, pageX, pageY, screenX, screenY

> Represent the cursor location at the time the `MouseDown` event occurred

Which

> Represents 1 for a left-mouse-button down and 3 for a right-mouse-button down

Modifiers

> Contains the list of modifier keys held down while the event occurred

onMouseMove

Because mouse movement happens so frequently, by default, **onMouseMove** is not an event of any object. You must explicitly set it to be associated with a particular object. Executes JavaScript code when a *MouseMove* event occurs; that is, when the user moves the cursor.

Compatability

> JavaScript 1.2

Event properties

> onMouseMove has the following event properties:

Type

> Indicates the type of event

Target

> Indicates the object to which the event was originally sent

LayerX, layerY, pageX, pageY, screenX, screenY
> Represent the cursor location at the time the **MouseMove** event occurred

onMouseOut

Event handler for **Layer** and **Link**. Executes JavaScript code when a *MouseOut* event occurs; that is, each time the mouse pointer leaves an area (client-side image map) or link from inside that area or link.

Compatability
> JavaScript 1.2

Event properties
> onMouseOut has the following event properties:

> *Type*
>> Indicates the type of event

> *Target*
>> Indicates the object to which the event was originally sent

> *LayerX, layerY, pageX, pageY, screenX, screenY*
>> Represent the cursor location at the time the **MouseOut** event occurred

onMouseOver

Event handler for **Layer** and **Link**. Executes JavaScript code when a *MouseOver* event occurs; that is, once each time the mouse pointer moves over an object or area from outside that object or area.

Compatability
> JavaScript 1.2

Event properties
> onMouseOver has the following event properties:

> *Type*
>> Indicates the type of event

> *Target*
>> Indicates the object to which the event was originally sent

> *LayerX, layerY, pageX, pageY, screenX, screenY*
>> Represent the cursor location at the time the **MouseOver** event occurred

onMouseUp

Event handler for **Button**, **Document**, and **Link**. Executes JavaScript code when a **MouseUp** event occurs; that is, when the user releases a mouse button.

Compatability
  JavaScript 1.2

Event properties
  onMouseUp has the following event properties:

  Type
      Indicates the type of event.

  Target
      Indicates the object to which the event was originally sent

  LayerX, layerY, pageX, pageY, screenX, screenY
      Represent the cursor location at the time the `MouseUp` event occurred

  Which
      Represents 1 for a left-mouse-button down and 3 for a right-mouse-button down

  W
      Contains the list of modifier keys held down when the *MouseUp* event occurred

onMove

Event handler for `Window`. Executes JavaScript code when a move event occurs; that is, when the user or script moves a window or frame.

Compatability
  JavaScript 1.2

Event properties
  onMove has the following event properties:

  Type
      Indicates the type of event

  Target
      Indicates the object to which the event was originally sent

  ScreenX, screenY
      Represent the position of the top-left corner of the window or frame

onReset

Event handler for `Form`. Executes JavaScript code when a reset event occurs; that is, when a user resets a form (clicks a "Reset" button).

Compatability
  JavaScript 1.1

Event properties

onReset has the following event properties:

Type

Indicates the type of event

Target

Indicates the object to which the event was originally sent

onResize

Event handler for `Window`. Executes JavaScript code when a resize event occurs; that is, when a user or script resizes a window or frame.

Compatability

JavaScript 1.2

Event properties

onResize has the following event properties:

Type

Indicates the type of event

Target

Indicates the object to which the event was originally sent

Width, height

Represent the width and height of the window or frame

onSelect

Event handler for `Text` and `Textarea`. Executes JavaScript code when a select event occurs; that is, when a user selects some of the text within a text or textarea field.

Compatability

JavaScript 1.0

Event properties

onSelect has the following event properties:

Type

Indicates the type of event

Target

Indicates the object to which the event was originally sent

onSubmit

Event handler for `Form`. Executes JavaScript code when a submit event occurs; that is, when a user submits a form.

Compatability
> JavaScript 1.0

Event properties
> onSubmit has the following event properties:

> *Type*
>> Indicates the type of event

> *Target*
>> Indicates the object to which the event was originally sent

onUnload

Event handler for `Window`. Executes JavaScript code when a submit event occurs; that is, when a user submits a form.

Compatability
> JavaScript 1.0

Event properties
> onUnload has the following event properties:

> *Type*
>> Indicates the type of event

> *Target*
>> Indicates the object to which the event was originally sent

B

Web Resources

This appendix provides links to JavaScript- and web-related resources. Sections include JavaScript, Perl, and CGI references and graphics resources. The last section, "Similar Applications," points to other web sites that have applications similar to the ones in this book. It's a good idea to see how other coders solve similar problems.

Cool JavaScript Sites

These are a few sites that use JavaScript to make things happen. Most of the code is pure JavaScript and DHTML. One site requires the Macromedia Flash 3 plug-in, but any recent 4.x or 5.x version of MSIE and NN will have it. Talk about eye candy.

GaboCorp:
> *http://www.gabocorp.com/*

Doc Ozone:
> *http://www.ozones.com/blueprint.html*

Scrutinizer by Vivatrix:
> *http://vivatrix.com/demos/en/scrutinizer*

Honda Automobiles:
> *http://www.honda1999.com/*

Haznet's Fallout Shelter:
> *http://www.budziak.com/haznet/javascript.html*

JavaScript Reference

These URLs helped me big time over the last few months. They'll do they same for you. You'll find JavaScript reference material, tutorials, scripts, articles, and plenty more.

Core JavaScript Reference:
  http://developer1.netscape.com/docs/manuals/js/core/jsref/contents.htm

Doc JavaScript:
  http://www.webreference.com/js/

HotSyte—The JavaScript Resource:
  http://www.serve.com/hotsyte/

Microsoft Scripting Technologies (JScript):
  http://msdn.microsoft.com/scripting/default.htm?/scripting/jscript/default.htm

Microsoft Developer Network (JScript):
  http://msdn.microsoft.com/developer/default.htm

The JavaScript Source:
  http://javascript.internet.com/

Cut-n-Paste JavaScript:
  http://www.infohiway.com/javascript/indexf.htm

JavaScriptWorld:
  http://www.jsworld.com/

webmonkey/JavaScript:
  http://www.hotwired.com/webmonkey/javascript/?tw=javascript

CNET Builder.com:
  http://builder.cnet.com/Programming/

JavaScripts.com:
  http://www.javascripts.com/

eScriptZone.com:
  http://www.escriptzone.com/

JavaScript FAQs

You have questions. They have answers. These FAQs, particularly the one at IRT. org, cover issues from very basic to complex.

IRT.org:
  http://www.irt.org/script/faq.htm

JS Beginners:
http://www.geol.uni-erlangen.de/geojs/JS_tutorial/JS_beginners.html

DevEdge NewsGroup FAQ:
http://developer.netscape.com/support/faqs/champions/javascript.html

JavaScript Beginner's FAQ:
http://www.it97.de/JavaScript/JS_tutorial/3rdless.html

The JavaScript Mini-FAQ:
http://www.dannyg.com/javascript/jsminifaq.html

DHTML Reference

This is a good grab bag to keep you up to date on the latest DHTML info. Many of the articles at these sites cover cross-browser topics or thorough discussion of IE- or NN-specific topics.

DevHead dHTML:
http://www.zdnet.com/devhead/filters/dhtml/

Dynamic HTML Zone:
http://www.dhtmlzone.com/index.html

Dynamic Drive:
http://www.dynamicdrive.com/

Inside DHTML:
http://www.insidedhtml.com/

The Dynamic Duo:
http://www.dansteinman.com/dynduo/

Dynamic HTML Guru Resource:
http://www.htmlguru.com/

webmonkey/dynamic_html:
http://www.hotwired.com/webmonkey/dynamic_html/

Frequently Asked Questions About Dynamic HTML:
http://www.microsoft.com/workshop/author/dhtml/dhtmlqa.asp

Document Object Model Reference

These resources provide information about the Document Object Models standard by the World Wide Web Consortium.

Document Object Model:
http://www.w3.org/DOM/

Document Object Model FAQ:
  http://www.w3.org/DOM/faq.html

Perl/CGI Reference

If you want to further explore the Common Gateway Interface and Perl, start here. Perl resources are as vast as the language. Make sure you download and install plenty of modules for extra functionality.

Perl.com:
  http://www.perl.com/pace/pub

Perl Reference Page:
  http://reference.perl.com/query.cgi?section=tutorials

An Introduction to The Common Gateway Interface:
  http://www.utoronto.ca/webdocs/CGI/cgi1.html

Graphics Resources

Since graphics and JavaScript ultimately cross paths, the URLs here give you a few resources to articles and free graphics.

Cooltype.com:
  http://cooltype.webpedia.com/

AndyArt:
  http://www.andyart.com/

Site Builder Workshop—Image Gallery:
  http://www.microsoft.com/workshop/c-frame.htm#/gallery/images/default.asp

Similar Applications

This section provides links to sites with applications similar (or in the ballpark, at least) to the ones discussed in this book.

Client-Side Search Engines

Most JavaScript search engines I've found on the web are designed to pass queries to multiple search engines such as Yahoo!, Infoseek, and AltaVista. Here are a few sites with client-side JavaScript search apps. All seem to work well, but don't have the functionality of the app in Chapter 1. Either way, check them out. You might pick up some pointers if you study the source code.

The Computer Crap Search Engine:

http://www.geocities.com/SiliconValley/Horizon/2188/search.html

I've seen more creative titles, but author Nathan Wiegand uses similar coding to the one discussed here.

JavaScript Search Functions:

http://www.serve.com/hotsyte/wildman/web_search/site_search.html

You can find this app by Tim Hobbs on *hotsyte.com.*

Online Tests

You have to look hard, but you can find JavaScript tests out there. Here are a few that I found.

D2 Test:

http://inetpubl.com/psy/psy.htm

This concentration test by Inet Publishing uses JavaScript to pit your concentration and counting skills against the clock.

Hardware Fundamentals Practice Test:

http://www.cit.ac.nz/smac/hf100/test1s.htm

This test is pretty neat. It's a practice test about disk formatting, drive partitioning, storage capacity, and more. The cool thing is that the application lets you know if you are correct as soon as you answer. It is actually a series of practice tests. Try the same path with *test2s.htm* through *test9.htm* (nothing at *test6.htm*). You can find more of the same on the subject of C programming at *http://www.cit.ac.nz/smac/cprogram/c_054s.htm.* These tests are provided by the Central Institute of Technology in New Zealand.

Norm's Multiple Choice Test:

http://lisa.unomaha.edu/2.0/test.html

You might not be crazy about the yellow background, but this test, too, gets the job done using JavaScript. Instead of rewriting the page every time, this test inserts questions and answer choices in form fields. It also tracks your cumulative score.

Test 2000:

http://www.jchelp.com/test2000/drvframe.htm

This multiple-choice test is designed to help drivers prepare for the written portion of the California driver's test. It allows you to view all results at the end rather than one by one. You can also view the correct answers and explanations.

Slideshows

Here are a few interesting slideshow apps.

Project Management—A Slide Show:

> *http://www.geocities.com/~mohan_iyer/slideshow.htm*

This DHTML application has animated slides. The graphics take a while to download, but it's worth the wait. You can find the JavaScript in the hard-to-find *slideshow.js* file.

web blazonry:

> *http://blazonry.com/javascript/slideshow/*

This cool slideshow displays the evolution of the *mkaz* web site, presumably from its inception. Pure image rollovers.

Apartment Home Animated Virtual Tour:

> *http://www.mark-taylor.com/virtualtour/index.htm*

This automated slideshow gives users a tour of an apartment home complex. The image download is fairly lengthy, but the developer realizes this and tries to entertain you so that you don't click elsewhere.

Multiple Search Engine Interfaces

There is no shortage of JavaScript search engines on the Net. Here are some of the dozens I encountered.

Ultimate Universal Interface for Search Engines (UUISE):

> *http://www.cris.com/~anathema/UUISE/index.html*

This slick program utilizes cookies to let users customize their multi-engine search. Users can select up to 10 search engines out of several dozen choices. The rest of the program is displayed in a simple remote window with a text field and image links to the 10 engines of choice.

WebSight:

> *http://rampages.onramp.net/~jnardo/websight/website1.htm*

This application is similar to mine, but allows you to perform extra Boolean filtering. Complete with a help file.

Virtual Meta Search 2:

> *http://WebcastLinks.com/vmsearch/vmsearch.html*

This application lets you choose up to 6 out of 31 search engines and returns results from each of the engines in separate frames.

Computer ESP Bargain Agent:

> *http://www.shopper.com/shop/*

> Rather than querying search engine databases, this application searches online computer store databases so you can find the gear you need.

Rollover Generators

There are a number of rollover apps on the Net. Why not visit these sites and see what they're made of?

The Mighty Mouseover Machine:

> *http://builder.cnet.com/Programming/Kahn/012898/index.html*

> Charity Khan's site probably gets more hits than Builder.com knows what to do with. Her app utilizes a remote window to create an image template and eventually create the code.

OnMouseOver Whipper:

> *http://wsabstract.com/mousewhipper/index.htm*

> This web abstraction application allows only one image pair at a time. However, it's quite cool because the coder added a slick auto-detect feature that accesses the width and height of the images. The app finds them for you. It's a matter of creating an *Image()* object and grabbing properties from there. Nice work.

JavaScript Rollover Generator:

> *http://webreview.com/wr/pub/98/03/13/coder/rollover.html*

> Like the Whipper, you can do only one pair at a time. However, you control lots of settings. You can also preview the rollover before you keep the code.

Libraries

I certainly don't have the market cornered on JavaScript libraries. The ones listed here contain some heavy-duty code for cranking out DHTML. When you have a few extra hours, download these libraries and try to figure out the code. You might lose a few neurons, but your investment will pay big programming dividends.

DHTMLLib Version 2:

> *http://www.insidedhtml.com/dhtmllib/page1.asp*

> This library from InsideDHTML.com is the hookup for cross-browser application building. Based on MSIE's document object model, this library enables you to write code supported in both object models (NN and MSIE).

FreeDOM:

> *http://www.builder.com/Programming/FreeDOM/*

This library available on C|Net allows you to better create and manipulate JavaScript objects outside the context of the DOMs.

The JavaScript Menu Component:

> *http://developer.netscape.com/viewsource/smith_menu/smith_menu.html*

The Netscape library files (*menu.js*) allow you to easily add floating menus with child menus. Did I mention cross-browser? Check this one out.

JavaScript DHTML Collapsible Lists:

> *http://developer.netscape.com/docs/technote/dynhtml/collapse/index.*
> *html#xbrowser*

The code documented here allows you to make Windows Explorer-like collapsing structures to organize and link your content. You'll even find a link to a code generator that helps you make the DHTML.

ScriptBuilder.com:

> *http://www.scriptbuilder.com/netobjects/library.nsf/By+Language*

This NetObjects script repository has plenty of cut-and-paste code. Not all the code is in *.js* files, but you and your text editor can change all that.

Cookies

The following two links point to a number of cookie apps. They range from simple to advanced, enough to keep you busy for awhile.

Cookie Demos:

> *http://www.cookiecentral.com/demomain.htm*

This page contains a list of links to cookie demos from Cookie Central. Applications feature setting user preferences, individual visitor hit counting, and browser detection

Shopping Cart Using Cookies:

> *http://www.ozemail.com.au/~dcrombie/cartdemo/index.html*

Here you can see how cookies can be used in shopping carts apps. You can rework it and add it to the shopping cart app in Chapter 8.

Shopping Carts

JavaScript shopping carts aren't new to the Net. Check out the ones below. All but the first two are free.

Shop@ssitant:

http://www.floyd.co.uk/

This commercial application has many features and benefits for the web shopper. This was developed by a skilled team of JavaScript gurus, so don't feel intimidated.

Shopmaster:

http://www.shopmaster.net/shopmaster/shop.htm

The app at this site demos a fairly robust shopping cart, complete with thumbnail images for group displays, product info display with mouseovers, and more.

A Simple Shopping Cart Program:

http://lymdenlodge.hypermart.net/ShoppingCart.htm

Simple indeed, but it might be all you need if you're hustling only a few well-known products. Product selection, cost calculation, and payment info are all on one page.

JShop JavaScript Shopping Cart:

http://javaboutique.internet.com/JShop/

This application from JavaBoutique is a good basic shopping cart. It has potential, but you'll likely need to add significant code to make it work for you.

Wildman's Shopping Cart:

http://www.serve.com/hotsyte/wildman/shopping_cart/shop_cart._intro.html

Creator Timothy Hobbs left this application on HotSyte. It uses cookies to store user selections.

Shopping Cart Using Cookies:

http://www.ozemail.com.au/~dcrombie/cartdemo/index.html

A good place to see how cookies can be used in shopping carts apps. Then you can rework it and add it to the shopping cart app in Chapter 8.

Ciphers

You can find hordes of sites with great cipher information. However, those using JavaScript to demonstrate them seem sparse. If you find others, please let me know.

Ciphers by Gordon McComb:

http://gmccomb.com/commerce/frame.html

This site comes from one of the first authors ever to write about JavaScript. Check out the JavaScript cipher and JavaScript password-protect examples.

RSA Algorithm JavaScript Page:

http://www.orst.edu/dept/honors/makmur/

This multi-page introduction to RSA encryption shows you how to implement a very basic form of RSA with JavaScript. Bring a healthy knowledge of factoring prime numbers if you're going to examine the code.

Ciphers in JavaScript:

http//www.serve.com/hotsyte/ciphers/

Of course, there is always my site. This application covers substitution and transposition ciphers.

Drag-and-Drop Concepts

This links point to a few resources that leverage browser event models and JavaScript.

DHTMLLib Demos/ Drag and Drop:

http://www.insidedhtml.com/dhtmllib/demos/dragdrop.asp

This demo is part of the SiteExperts DHTMLLib library mentioned earlier. This incorporates cross-browser DHTML that allows smooth dragging and dropping.

Dynamic Duo—Drag and Drop Concepts:

http://www.dansteinman.com/dynduo/dragconcepts/dragconcepts.html

Dan Steinman takes you through a JavaScript/DHTML tutorial for mouse events. Plenty of code and examples.

Netscape's Visual DHTML:

http://developer.netscape.com/docs/examples/dynhtml/visual/index.htm

I'm not real big on sticking with browser-dependent technology, but this Netscape-only Drag-and-Drop DHTML editor is great. This application uses JavaScript 1.2 to the fullest extent to give the user a web-based GUI. Even if you don't plan on using the app, run the demo to see how it all works.

Drag and Drop:

http://www.dpunkt.de/javascript/bsp/script2/dragdrop/index.html

This quickie example page (written in German, I believe) gives you another perspective on drag and drop.

Coolnerds Dynamic HTML Examples:

http://www.milliscrip.com/webauth/dhtml/dragdrop.htm

I'd call this the online equivalent of Mr. Potato Head. Build your own face by dragging and dropping your choice of hair, eyes mouth, nose, and more. This is actually a VBScript example, but you can see how the DOM goes to work anyway.

Context-Sensitive Help

I have yet to run into an online help application on the Net such as the one described in Chapter 11. However, you'll find the code at the following links more than worth your while. Each uses similar code to produce cool, yet slightly different effects.

The Microsoft Home Page:

http://www.microsoft.com/ms.htm

Right off the home page, Microsoft developers have embedded expandable lists in the nav bar. Each list offers links to other pages, or even other lists.

The JavaScript Menu Component:

http://developer.netscape.com/viewsource/smith_menu/smith_menu.html

This article steps you through the process of creating cross-browser DHTML menus similar to the ones on the Microsoft home page. Author Gary Smith takes a worthwhile object-oriented approach.

The Menu Toolkit:

http://www.insidedhtml.com/constsets/menus/menubar.asp

This demo comes from one of the many inside DHTML toolkits. Absorb this code.

C

Using Perl Scripts

This appendix contains four sections:

1. A Perl/CGI Overview

2. Getting Perl

3. The Shopping Bag Script—*bag.pl*

4. The CyberGreeting Script—*greet.pl*

The first section contains a little background on Perl and mentions some of its advantages. The next section tells you where to download Perl, giving you several choices depending on your operating system. The last two sections explain how the Perl scripts in Chapter 8, *Shopping Bag: The JavaScript Shopping Cart*, and Chapter 10, *Cyber Greetings: Drag-and-Drop Email*, work.

A Perl/CGI Overview

The acronym stands for Practical Extraction and Report Language. It was originally designed for text and file manipulation, but also does well for managing system tasks and creating dynamic content for the Web. Perl has its roots in programming languages, such as C, sed, awk, and sh.

What's So Good About Perl?

Perl is popular for a number of reasons. As far as languages go, Perl is pretty easy to learn. It is extremely powerful. It is used in just about every kind of programming scenario imaginable. Here are some of the many ways Perl is used:

- For dynamic web page content

- In CGI scripts for countless web apps

- To access databases

- For building search engines and web robots

- For password protection and other encryption

- For system administration, site logging, and scheduled tasks

- For networking tasks and other scripting

- For chat servers and message boards

Perl is quickly finding its way into many other arenas. You can use Perl:

- To extend Java, C, VisualBasic, Delphi, and other code

- In XML (Extensible Markup Language) applications

- As PerlScript, an ActiveX scripting engine

Perl is free. You can get it at the CPAN (Comprehensive Perl Archive Network) site *http://www.perl.com/CPAN/*. Windows users can also get it at the ActiveState site at *http://www.activestate.com/*.

Perl has a very large and loyal following. Coders are consistently adding to the hundreds, if not thousands, of modules and applications that have been written and that you can easily implement on your web site. The overwhelming majority of this stuff is free. Perl's popularity means that you'll also find tons of documentation, support, and experienced coders all over the planet.

Perl runs on lots of platforms, including Unix, VMS, MS-DOS, Windows NT/98/95, OS/2, and more. Most of the code you write is fairly portable from operating system to operating system.

What's Not So Good About Perl?

The biggest gripe developers have with Perl is performance. Perl is comparatively slower to execute than compiled languages such as C. In the web environment, CGI scripts (the Common Gateway Interface; more on that shortly) written in Perl (and other languages) must be read from the hard drive and loaded as a new process each time they are called. Technologies such as Active Server Pages and Java servlets can run in the same memory space as the web server, which greatly speeds execution. Developments such as Perl for ISAPI and the more recent PerlEx have increased performance significantly.

Another downside is that Perl is not considered an elegant (looking) language. Perl exchanges beauty for utility. It works, but it can be ugly.

Perl and CGI

If you use your browser to request a file with an *.html* extension from a web server, you're getting a static document. That means that file exists in a directory on the computer. You could sit down at the computer containing the file, open it in a text editor, and view the same data that is being sent to your browser.

If you request a *.cgi* file (or *.pl*, *.plx*, or other file extensions), you're not going to get the code written in the file. The web server instead executes the file with whatever engine it is configured to use (in our case, Perl) and returns that output to the browser. What you're viewing in your browser doesn't exist on the web server. The content was created when you requested it.

This entire process of requesting and receiving output happens through CGI, the Common Gateway Interface. CGI is a standard for interfacing with HTTP servers. By the way, the server-side language doesn't have to be Perl. There are plenty of CGI scripts written in C and C++, Python, Fortran, AppleScript, and others. For more details, check out the Perl CGI Programming FAQ at *http://www.cpan.org/doc/FAQs/cgi/perl-cgi-faq.html*.

Why use CGI?

Though CGI scripts in general can be outperformed by ColdFusion, Active Server Pages, and other technologies, the CGI standard is still used all over the Net. There are also plenty of web servers out there running Perl. And it's free. Since this stuff is nearly everywhere, it made sense to write the server-side portion of the Java-Script applications in something that everybody can get their hands on fairly easily. I think you'll find that these scripts are pretty easy to follow, too.

Getting Perl

You'll need to have Perl installed on your web server. Most web server hosts do. If you need to install Perl yourself, you can get the latest Perl distribution free at *ftp://ftp.rge.com/pub/languages/perl/ports/index.html*.

Just click the link associated with your operating system. If you are running WinNT/98/95, you can get the latest Perl binaries and info at *http://www.activestate.com/pw32/*. If you want more power and features, check out Active-Perl, a significant advance in the Win32 distribution of Perl, at *http://www.activestate.com/ActivePerl/*.

Both web sites provide documentation for installing and configuring Perl. If you have Windows, though, it's pretty simple. Whether you install the regular Win32 binaries or the ActivePerl package, the install takes only a few steps and will even configure your web server (such as Microsoft's Internet Information Server, Peer Web Services, or Personal Web Server) to execute Perl scripts. Installing and configuring Perl for Unix and other operating systems is generally more involved. Be sure to check the included documentation.

Once Perl is installed, the web server needs to be configured to execute Perl scripts. If your web server host is running Perl, this is likely taken care of. Contact your web site administrator to find out. If you're doing this yourself, you'll probably have to configure the web server. Popular web servers such as Microsoft's Internet Information Server, Netscape's Enterprise Server, O'Reilly's WebSite Pro, Apache by the Apache Group, and others usually make it a fairly simple operation. Check the online documentation of your web server software for instructions.

The Shopping Bag Script—bag.pl

Example C-1 is the script from Chapter 8. The script is provided mostly so that you can see how Shopping Bag works from end to end. The script works fine, but it is primitive. If you want a powerful shopping program with numerous server-side options, I suggest you seek a more robust solution.

Remember that shoppers provide sensitive credit card information in the order form. If that information isn't properly protected before it is submitted, it can easily get into the wrong hands and be used illegally. To prevent this, your web server host should support some type of protection such as Secure Sockets Layer (SSL), a protocol used for encryption. Most web server hosts support it. You should contact your web site administrator and find more information about SSL at *http://webopedia.internet.com/TERM/S/SSL.html*.

---

bag.pl has three jobs:

1. Get all the product and customer information
2. Save that information in a uniquely named text file on the web server
3. Print a confirmation page to send back to the browser

Some web server hosts require that you run CGI scripts with a *.cgi* extension instead of a *.pl* extension. No biggie—just rename the file to *bag.cgi*. Quick recovery.

Let's see how *bag.pl* takes care of all three jobs. As you look at this code, remember that you don't have to understand the syntax. This book isn't about Perl. Just try to follow what the code is doing from one step to the next.

Example C-1. bag.pl

```
1 #!/usr/bin/perl
2
```

Example C-1. bag.pl (continued)

```
 3 require "cgi-lib.pl";
 4
 5 print "Content-type: text/html\n\n";
 6
 7 &ReadParse(*in);
 8
 9 srand($$ ^ time);
10 $filename = $in{'lname'} . int(rand(999));
11
12 if (-e "$filename.txt") {
13   print "The order for $filename has already been placed.";
14   exit 0;
15   }
16
17 open(FILE,">$filename.txt");
18 select(FILE);
19 printInfo();
20 close(FILE);
21 select(STDOUT);
22 printInfo();
23
24 exit 0;
25
26 sub printInfo() {
27 $clock = localtime();
28
29 print <<CUSTOMER_INFO;
30 <PRE><FONT FACE=Tahoma SIZE=3>
31 <H2>Shopping Bag Order Confirmation Receipt</H2>
32
33 <B>$clock</B>
34 <B>Reference Code: $filename</B>
35
36
37 --------------------
38 Customer Information
39
40 Customer First Name: $in{'fname'}
41 Customer Last Name   $in{'lname'}
42 Company Name:        $in{'cname'}
43 Street Address 1:    $in{'saddress1'}
44 Street Address 2:    $in{'saddress2'}
45 City:                $in{'city'}
46 State/Province:      $in{'stpro'}
47 Country:             $in{'country'}
48 Zip/Mail Code:       $in{'zip'}
49
50 CUSTOMER_INFO
51
52 print <<PAYMENT_INFO;
53
54 Payment Information
```

Example C-1. bag.pl (continued)

```
55
56 Credit Card Type:     $in{'ctype'}
57 Credit Card Number:   $in{'cnumb'}
58 Expiration Date:      $in{'edate'}
59
60 PAYMENT_INFO
61
62 print "Product Information\n\n";
63
64 $idx = 0;
65
66 while ($in{'prod' . $idx}) {
67   @getProdInfo = split("-", $in{'prod' . $idx});
68   print "Product PLU:\t\t$getProdInfo[0]\n";
69   print "\tQuantity:\t$getProdInfo[1]\n\n";
70   $idx++;
71   }
72
73 print <<TOTAL_INFO;
74
75 Total Information (\$US)
76
77 Subtotal:        $in{'subtotal'}
78 Tax Total:       $in{'taxtotal'}
79 Ship Total:      $in{'shiptotal'}
80 Bag Total:       $in{'bagtotal'}
81
82 -------------------
83 </FONT></PRE>
84 TOTAL_INFO
85 }
```

Getting the Product Information

The first step is actually pretty involved. However, the hard work of other coders makes it a breeze. Let's start with lines 1–7:

```
#!/usr/bin/perl

require "cgi-lib.pl";

print "Content-type: text/html\n\n";

&ReadParse(*in);
```

The first line is common to all CGI scripts. Nicknamed the "shebang" line, this tells the server where to find Perl. The path varies from machine to machine, so you might have to ask your web site administrator. If you're running a Windows machine, this line is ignored. The next line instructs Perl to include code from a library file called *cgi-lib.pl* (which comes standard on most Perl installs). This contains the code that will read the information submitted from the HTML form. The only thing we need to do is call the correct Perl subroutine, and the script will read all the information submitted from the form and store in variables we can get our hands on.

The next line prints an HTTP header. This particular header identifies the MIME type (Multipart Internet Mail Extension) to the browser, which states which type of information to expect. It is set to *text/html.* Other MIME types include *image/gif* and *text/plain.*

JavaScript uses functions and methods; Perl uses functions, methods, and subroutines. Subroutine `ReadParse()` from *cgi-lib.pl* reads the HTML form data from the standard input and places the data in an associative array called *%in*. We'll get the form data shortly, but it's nice to know that we've got it. Let's move on.

Saving the Information to a File on the Web Server

Now we have the form data. Let's create a file to put it in. Lines 9–15 create a unique filename:

```
srand($$ ^ time);
$filename = $in{'lname'} . int(rand(999));
if (-e "$filename.txt") {
  print "The order for $filename has already been placed.";
  exit 0;
  }
```

The code `srand($$ ^ time);` initializes Perl's random-number generator. Next, Perl creates a variable called *$filename* that will hold the unique filename. The filename is created by concatenating the shopper's last name with a random integer 0–999:

```
$filename = $in{'lname'} . int(rand(999));
```

The shopper's last name comes from the form data, right? Since the data is stored in the associative array *%in*, all we have to do is access the element containing the last name. Here is the syntax:

```
$in{'lname'}.
```

If you recall, `lname` was one of the form fields on the HTML form submitted. Associative arrays in Perl (JavaScript, too) are referenced by name, so `$in{'lname'}` points to whatever the shopper entered as his or her last name (e.g., "Jones").

Perl's `rand()` function generates a random floating-point number between 0 and the number it is passed, which is 999. To make things cleaner, Perl's `int()` function returns the integer of whatever random number `rand()` chooses. So *$filename* could have values such as `Jones23`, `Jones997`, `Jones102`, etc.

Once the value of *filename* is determined, Perl checks to see if a file with that name already exists. This is a mild validation technique to avoid overwriting orders that already exist on the file. For example, Jones is a pretty common last name. If Ed Jones and Jimmy Jones go shopping on the same day, and by some chance generate the same random integer, their filenames would be exactly the same. Whoever shopped last would overwrite the order information of the first:

```
if (-e "$filename.txt") {
  print "The order for $filename has already been placed.";
  exit 0;
  }
```

If the file already exists, Perl prints the message back to the shopper that an order with that number has been placed, and exits the script. The shopper need only reload the script to generate another random filename and give it another go. If the file doesn't exist, Perl proceeds with lines 17–20:

```
open(FILE,">$filename.txt");
select(FILE);
printInfo();
close(FILE);
```

This code opens (creates) a file using the variable *$filename* and adds an extension of *.txt*. The code `select(FILE)` tells Perl to print output to the newly created file until otherwise told. The only thing to do is pile in the content. That's what subroutine `printInfo()` does. You can see that in lines 26–85:

```
sub printInfo() {
$clock = localtime();

print <<CUSTOMER_INFO;
<PRE><FONT FACE=Tahoma SIZE=3>
<H2>Shopping Bag Order Confirmation Receipt</H2>

<B>$clock</B>
<B>Reference Code: $filename</B>


-------------------
Customer Information

Customer First Name:   $input{'fname'}
Customer Last Name:    $input{'lname'}
Company Name:          $input{'cname'}
Street Address 1:      $input{'saddress1'}
Street Address 2:      $input{'saddress2'}
City:                  $input{'city'}
State/Province:        $input{'stpro'}
Country:               $input{'country'}
Zip/Mail Code:         $input{'zip'}

CUSTOMER_INFO

print <<PAYMENT_INFO;
```

```
Payment Information

Credit Card Type:        $input{'ctype'}
Credit Card Number:      $input{'cnumb'}
Expiration Date:         $input{'edate'}

PAYMENT_INFO

print "Product Information\n\n";

$idx = 0;

while ($input{'prod' . $idx}) {
  @getProdInfo = split("-", $input{'prod' . $idx});
  print "Product PLU:\t\t$getProdInfo[0]\n";
  print "\tQuantity:\t$getProdInfo[1]\n\n";
  $idx++;
  }

print <<TOTAL_INFO;

Total Information (\$US)

Subtotal:          $input{'subtotal'}
Tax Total:         $input{'taxtotal'}
Ship Total:        $input{'shiptotal'}
Bag Total:         $input{'bagtotal'}


--------------------
</FONT></PRE>
TOTAL_INFO
  }
```

As the name implies, `printInfo()` prints the form data. The first thing it does is to create a time-date stamp by setting variable *$clock* to the output of function `localtime()`. This will be used shortly. Line 29 is where the printing begins. The code <<CUSTOMER_INFO identifies something called a *here string*, which is basically a multiline string located between two identifiers. CUSTOMER_INFO is the identifier. *Here strings* are handy because you don't have to worry about carriage returns or single and double quotes. You use them as if you were typing a letter. That way, Perl prints whatever is between CUSTOMER_INFO and CUSTOMER_INFO, which is this:

```
<PRE><FONT FACE=Tahoma SIZE=3>
<H2>Shopping Bag Order Confirmation Receipt</H2>

<B>$clock</B>
<B>Reference Code: $filename</B>


--------------------
Customer Information
```

```
Customer First Name:   $input{'fname'}
Customer Last Name:    $input{'lname'}
Company Name:          $input{'cname'}
Street Address 1:      $input{'saddress1'}
Street Address 2:      $input{'saddress2'}
City:                  $input{'city'}
State/Province:        $input{'stpro'}
Country:               $input{'country'}
Zip/Mail Code:         $input{'zip'}
```

Notice you don't have to concatenate strings that span multiple lines. You just type and go. Notice also that variables are interpreted. In other words, `$input {'lname'}` doesn't print `$input{'lname'}`; it prints something such as "Jones".

If you study the code carefully, you'll see that the first information printed is the shopper's mailing information. Then comes the payment information. All this information comes from known form fields, such as fields named *fname, lname,* and *city.* These are fields that the shopper filled out, so we know they will be there.

What about the product information, though? There could be any number of products. How will Perl know how many products there are? It doesn't. Lines 62–71 explain why that's OK:

```
print "Product Information\n\n";

$idx = 0;

while ($in{'prod' . $idx}) {
  @getProdInfo = split("-", $in{'prod' . $idx});
  print "Product PLU:\t\t$getProdInfo[0]\n";
  print "\tQuantity:\t$getProdInfo[1]\n\n";
  $idx++;
  }
```

Remember that Shopping Bag generated a hidden form field for every product that the shopper ordered. Each of these hidden fields was named according to a "prod" + integer naming convention (e.g., *prod0, prod1, prod2,* etc.). Perl simply declares a variable *$idx* and sets it equal to 0. Using a familiar **while** loop in line 66, Perl uses `$in{'prod' . $idx}` to see if *prod0* exists. If so, the variable must contain product information.

Perl then uses its **split()** function to create an array called *@getProdInfo* with two elements. The first element contains the product PLU number; the second element contains the quantity ordered. This information is printed, then *$idx* is incremented. Perl runs through *prod1, prod2,* etc. until `$in{'prod' . $idx}` doesn't exist.

Once this process is over, Perl prints the subtotal, applicable taxes, and grand total in lines 73–84. Notice that the dollar sign is escaped with a backslash (\$). Since we actually want to print the string *$US*, we have to tell Perl there is no variable named *$US*:

```
print <<TOTAL_INFO;

Total Information (\$US)

Subtotal:         $input{'subtotal'}
Tax Total:        $input{'taxtotal'}
Ship Total:       $input{'shiptotal'}
Bag Total:        $input{'bagtotal'}


--------------------
</FONT></PRE>
TOTAL_INFO
```

Returning a Confirmation Page to the Shopper

That brings us to the end of the subroutine, so Perl continues executing lines 20–24 below the call to `printInfo()`:

```
close(FILE);
select(STDOUT);
printInfo();

exit 0;
```

Since the file has all the information, we might has well close it. `close(FILE)` takes care of that. What about the shopper? It would be nice to let him or her know that the order has been received. Why not print out the same info back to the shopper as we did in the file? The call to `select(STDOUT)` tells Perl to print once again to the standard output, which means back to the browser (remember that we switched the output destination to *$filename.txt* in line 17). Now we just have to call `printInfo()` again, and this transaction is complete. The shopper gets a printout.

Setting Up the Script

As it stands, this script creates all the text files for the product orders in the same directory where the script is located. In other words, wherever you put the *bag.pl*, that's where your product order files will be. There is no directory structure you have to set up or adhere to. Any directory with execute privileges (so that the web server can call the script) *and* write privileges (so that the script can create and write to files) will do.

If you're new to the concept of privileges, note that they control the type of access users have to directories and files. To retrieve basic HTML files, for example, the directory containing the HTML files needs read privileges assigned to it. To execute CGI and other scripts, the directory must have execute privileges assigned to it. To create and modify files in a directory, that directory needs write privileges. The directory that contains *bag.pl* needs write and execute privileges. That sounds easy enough, but there is a catch.

Granting a directory both execute and write privileges opens at least a couple of security risks. If you have a web server host, the people there know this and so may require you to put the script in a directory with executing privileges only, such as *cgi-bin/* or *Scripts/*, and write your files to another directory with write privileges only. If this is the case, you need to make a simple change in the script to reflect the new directory of the product order files. Just include the directory name when setting the value of variable *$filename*. Suppose you are going to write your files in a directory named *orders/*, which is located one level "above" the directory where your script resides. Just change line 10 from this:

```
$filename = $in{'lname'} . int(rand(999));
```

to this:

```
$filename = "../orders/" . $in{'lname'} . int(rand(999));
```

If *orders/* is off the root directory, the line would look like this:

```
$filename = "/orders/" . $in{'lname'} . int(rand(999));
```

Now your script is in one directory, and your product order files are in another.

You're ready to go. Make sure the **ACTION** attribute in line 276 of *ch08**manager. html* contains the correct URL of *bag.pl*.

The CyberGreeting Script—greet.pl

Example C-2 is the script from Chapter 10. This script will read the information the user submitted, then create a unique file and write the greeting code inside it. Afterwards, the script will return to the sender a confirmation page containing an HTML form. By submitting the form, the sender sends email to the recipient. This email message contains a link to the file *greet.pl* just created. The file will be ready and waiting when the recipient follows the link in his or her email message.

Setting Up the Script

Unlike the script for Chapter 8, you need to conform to a directory structure in order to use *greet.pl*. In whatever directory you place *greet.pl*, the directory must have both read and execution privileges assigned to it. You must also have a directory inside it called *greetings/* that has write privileges.

As I mentioned earlier in this chapter, if you're new to the concept of privileges, note that they control the type of access users have to directories and files. To retrieve basic HTML files, for example, the directory containing the HTML files needs read privileges assigned to it. To execute CGI and other scripts, the directory must have execute privileges assigned to it. To create and modify files in a directory, that directory needs write privileges.

In fact, now might be a good time to consider how your directory structure should look. Let's assume that you are going to place all the files for this application in your web server's *cgi-bin/* directory. This is what your directory structure should look like:

```
cgi-bin/
    greet.pl
    index.html
    back.html
    front.html
    greetings/
    images/
```

cgi-bin/ contains *greet.pl* and the three HTML files of the client-side application. The *images/* directory contains all of the icons and background images that the user chooses to customize the greetings. Keep in mind, though, that this is where the code generated from the client side will point to in order to access those graphics and download them for each greeting.

The *greetings/* directory is initially empty. This is where each uniquely named greeting file is created and stored for the recipient to download. Since the greetings are created here, this directory must have write privileges assigned to it. With this structure in place and all the files where they should be, you're ready to go. Make sure the ACTION attribute in line 186 of \ch10*front.html* contains the correct URL of *greet.pl*.

You might not like the directory structure above. You might want those HTML files somewhere outside the *cgi-bin*. No problem. Just make sure your form points to the correct script path.

 Some web server hosts require that you run CGI scripts with a *.cgi* extension instead of a *.pl* extension. No biggie—just rename the file *greet.cgi*. Quick recovery.

Let's look at the script in terms of three jobs:

1. Get the custom greeting from the submitted form

2. Save that information in a uniquely named text file on the web server

3. Print a confirmation page to send back to the browser, complete with email form

As you look at this code, remember that you don't have to understand the syntax. This book isn't about Perl. Just try to follow what the code is doing from one step to the next.

Example C-2. greet.pl

```
 1 #!/usr/bin/perl
 2
 3 require 'cgi-lib.pl';
 4
 5 &ReadParse(*in);
 6 $msg     = $in{'EntireMessage'};
 7 $fileID  = $in{'UniqueID'};
 8 $recip   = $in{'Recipient'};
 9 $baseURL = $in{'BaseURL'};
10
11 open(FILE, ">greetings/greet$fileID.html") || die "No can do: $!";
12 select(FILE);
13 print <<GREETING;
14 <HTML>
15 <HEAD>
16   <TITLE>Your Personal Cyber Greeting</TITLE>
17 </HEAD>
18 <BODY>
19   $msg
20 </BODY>
21 </HTML>
22 GREETING
23 close(FILE);
24 select(STDOUT);
25
26 print "Content-type: text/html\n\n";
27
28 print <<RESPONSE;
29
30 <HTML>
31 <HEAD>
32   <TITLE>Cyber Greeting Response</TITLE>
33 </HEAD>
34 <BODY>
35 <TABLE WIDTH="500">
36   <TR>
37     <TD>
38     <H2>Congratulations!</H2>
39     You have successsfully created a Cyber Greeting for
40          <B>$recip</B>. All you have to do is send him or her an
41          e-mail to announce the greeting. Just push the button below,
42          and the e-mail will be on the way.
43     <CENTER>
44     <FORM NAME="SendEmail" ENCTYPE="text/plain"
45          ACTION="mailto:$recip?Subject=You Have A Cyber Greeting!">
46    <INPUT TYPE=HIDDEN NAME="Message"
47          VALUE="You have a Cyber Greeting. You can pick it up at
48          $baseURLgreet$fileID.html">
```

Example C-2. greet.pl (continued)

```
49    <INPUT TYPE=SUBMIT VALUE="Send CyberGreeting">
50    </FORM>
51    </CENTER>
52    <BR>
53    You might experience a delay while your e-mail software
54    contacts your mail server.
55    <BR><BR>
56    <A HREF="index.html">Return To Cyber Greeting</A>
57    </TD>
58   </TR>
59 </TABLE>
60 </BODY>
61 </HTML>
62
63 RESPONSE
64
65 exit 0;
```

Getting the Greeting Info

The first thing we need to do is get all the data that the user submitted and put it accessible form. Let's start with lines 1–5, which are almost identical to the previous PERL script:

```
#!/usr/bin/perl

require 'cgi-lib.pl';

&ReadParse(*in);
```

As noted in the "Shopping Bag" section, the first line is the "shebang" line, and tells the server where to find Perl. Line 3 instructs Perl to include code from a library file called *cgi-lib.pl*. This contains the Perl subroutine `ReadParse()` that will read the information submitted from the HTML form.

`ReadParse()` reads the HTML form data from the standard input and places the data in an associative array called *%in,* and then creates an array element with the name of each form element submitted. Each element is assigned a value that corresponds to the value of a submitted form element. Looking at all the elements in the HTML form in *\ch10\front.html, %in* has the following elements:

`$in{'EntireMessage'}`–

This is the formatted message the user typed.

`$in{'UniqueID'}`–

This contains a random number used to create a unique file.

`$in{'BaseURL'}`–

This holds the base directory path.

`$in{'Recipient'}-`

This is the recipient's email address.

`$in{'Message'}-`

This is the original unformatted message the user entered. We don't need this because we already have the formatted version in `$in{'EntireMessage'}`.

`$in{'Greetings'}-`

This contains the name of the greeting the sender chose from the select list in *\ch10\front.html*.

To make references to these elements easier, the script assigns their values to shorter variable names. We need only four of them, though. Here they are in lines 6–9:

```
$msg     = $in{'EntireMessage'};
$fileID  = $in{'UniqueID'};
$recip   = $in{'Recipient'};
$baseURL = $in{'BaseURL'};
```

Saving the Greeting to a Uniquely Named File

We have all the information necessary to print the greeting to a file. We just have to create a unique text file and output the appropriate HTML to it. Check out lines 11–22:

```
open(FILE, ">greet$fileID.html") || die "No can do: $!";
select(FILE);
print <<GREETING;
<HTML>
<HEAD>
  <TITLE>Your Personal Cyber Greeting</TITLE>
</HEAD>
<BODY>
  $msg
</BODY>
</HTML>
GREETING
```

These few lines of code create a new file using that random number JavaScript created in the browser as part of the file name. If the number was 25000, the file would be named *greet25000.html* and would be located in the *greetings/* directory. After creating the unique file, Perl writes some HTML to it, including the DHTML from the *EntireMessage* form field from *front.html*, now stored in the *$msg* variable.

The code `<<GREETING` identifies something called a *here string*, essentially a multi-line string located between two identifiers. `GREETING` is the identifier. *Here strings* are handy because you don't have to worry about carriage returns or single and double quotes. You use them as if you were typing a letter. That way, Perl prints

whatever is between GREETING and GREETING. You just type and go. Notice also that variables are interpreted. In other words, *$msg* doesn't print "$msg"; it prints the formatted greeting.

That's all there is to it. The script closes the file in line 23, and it's ready for the recipient to view.

Printing a Confirmation Page

The only thing left is to send a confirmation page back to the sender. This page will contain an HTML form that, upon submission, sends the recipient the greeting announcement and the URL to retrieve it. Lines 26–63 take care of that.

Line 26, `print "Content-type: text/html\n\n"` prints an HTTP header. This particular header identifies the MIME type to the browser, which states what type of information to expect.

You can see in lines 28 and 63 that RESPONSE identifies another *here string*. Notice the variables in bold:

```
print "Content-type: text/html\n\n";

print <<RESPONSE;

<HTML>
<HEAD>
  <TITLE>Cyber Greeting Response</TITLE>
</HEAD>
<BODY>
<TABLE WIDTH="500">
  <TR>
    <TD>
    <H2>Congratulations!</H2>
    You have successsfully created a Cyber Greeting for <B>$recip</B>
    All you have to do is send him or her an e-mail to announce the
    greeting. Just push the button below, and the e-mail will be on the
    way.
    <CENTER>
    <FORM NAME="SendEmail" ENCTYPE="text/plain"
      ACTION="mailto:$recip?Subject=You Have A Cyber Greeting!">
    <INPUT TYPE=HIDDEN NAME="Message"
      VALUE="You have a Cyber Greeting. You can pick it up at
      $baseURL/greet$fileID.html">
    <INPUT TYPE=SUBMIT VALUE="Send CyberGreeting">
    </FORM>
    </CENTER>
    <BR>
    You might experience a delay while your e-mail software
    contacts your mail server.
    <BR><BR>
    <A HREF="index.html">Return To Cyber Greeting</A>
```

```
     </TD>
   </TR>
 </TABLE>
 </BODY>
 </HTML>
```

RESPONSE

The majority of the code is HTML, which confirms to the sender a successful greeting and also provides instructions for sending the email. Have a closer look at lines 44–50. This is the form responsible for sending email to the recipient:

```
<FORM NAME="SendEmail" ENCTYPE="text/plain"
  ACTION="mailto:$recip?Subject=You Have A Cyber Greeting!">
<INPUT TYPE=HIDDEN NAME="Message"
  VALUE="You have a Cyber Greeting. You can pick it up at
  $baseURL/greet$fileID.html">
<INPUT TYPE=SUBMIT VALUE="Send CyberGreeting">
</FORM>
```

The script outputs a form with a `mailto:` protocol in the `ACTION` attribute and the `ENCTYPE` set to `text/plain`. This form has one hidden field named *Message*, it contains the greeting announcement and the URL where the recipient can access it. The URL is made with the *$baseURL* variable and the *$fileID* variable.

The form also has a button to submit, and hence, send the email. As long as the sender's browser email client is correctly set up (though he or she will be prompted for approval), the mail message will be on its way.

Index

About the Author

Jerry Bradenbaugh is a senior web application developer and technical lead in Los Angeles, California. His web site, HotSyte—The JavaScript Resource, has been around since the early days of JavaScript, making it one of the oldest JavaScript resources on the Internet. He has contributed in developing enterprise applications for Netscape and First Union National Bank.

Colophon

Our look is the result of reader comments, our own experimentation, and feedback from distribution channels. Distinctive covers complement our distinctive approach to technical topics, breathing personality and life into potentially dry subjects.

The animal on the cover of *JavaScript Application Cookbook* is a hippopotamus. A native of several regions in Africa, the hippo makes its home in rivers and their bordering grasslands. Hippopotamus is Greek for "river horse," and these large, cumbersome-looking animals move gracefully through the water for much of the day. Hippos leave the water to eat at night. Their vegetarian diet consists mostly of grass, up to 150 pounds a day, as well as some water plants and fallen fruit. Full-grown hippos have no natural predators other than humans, who have hunted them for their ivory tusk-like teeth, for their hide, and for food. Hippos can live to be forty years old.

A hippopotamus grows to be five feet tall, twelve feet long, and weighs 6,000–8,000 pounds. Its body is covered in a relatively hairless, gray-brown skin that secretes a reddish oil, often mistaken for blood, to keep the skin moist. A hippo's nostrils, ears, and eyes are situated close to the top of its head so that it can breathe, hear, and see, yet be almost fully submerged when it's swimming or walking on the riverbed. Several native marsh animals frequently rest on the backs of hippos in the water, including crocodiles, turtles, and birds.

Nicole Arigo was the production editor for *JavaScript Application Cookbook*. Claire-marie Fisher O'Leary, Jeffrey Liggett, and Jane Ellin provided quality control. Bruce Tracy wrote the index.

Edie Freedman designed the cover of this book, using a 19th-century engraving from the Dover Pictorial Archive. The cover layout was produced by Kathleen Wilson, using QuarkXPress 3.32 and the ITC Garamond font.

Alicia Cech designed the interior layout based on a series design by Nancy Priest. The book was implemented in FrameMaker by Mike Sierra. The text and heading fonts are ITC Garamond Light and Garamond Book. The illustrations that appear in the book were produced by Robert Romano and Rhon Porter using Macromedia FreeHand 8 and Adobe Photoshop 5. This colophon was written by Nicole Arigo.

Whenever possible, our books use RepKover™, a durable and flexible lay-flat binding. If the page count exceeds RepKover's limit, perfect binding is used.

How to stay in touch with O'Reilly

1. Visit Our Award-Winning Web Site

http://www.oreilly.com/

★"Top 100 Sites on the Web" —*PC Magazine*
★"Top 5% Web sites" —*Point Communications*
★"3-Star site" —*The McKinley Group*

Our web site contains a library of comprehensive product information (including book excerpts and tables of contents), downloadable software, background articles, interviews with technology leaders, links to relevant sites, book cover art, and more. File us in your Bookmarks or Hotlist!

2. Join Our Email Mailing Lists

New Product Releases

To receive automatic email with brief descriptions of all new O'Reilly products as they are released, send email to:
listproc@online.oreilly.com
Put the following information in the first line of your message (*not* in the Subject field):
subscribe oreilly-news

O'Reilly Events

If you'd also like us to send information about trade show events, special promotions, and other O'Reilly events, send email to:
listproc@online.oreilly.com
Put the following information in the first line of your message (*not* in the Subject field):
subscribe oreilly-events

3. Get Examples from Our Books via FTP

There are two ways to access an archive of example files from our books:

Regular FTP

- ftp to:
  ftp.oreilly.com
  (login: anonymous
  password: your email address)
- Point your web browser to:
  ftp://ftp.oreilly.com/

FTPMAIL

- Send an email message to:
  ftpmail@online.oreilly.com
  (Write "help" in the message body)

4. Contact Us via Email

order@oreilly.com
To place a book or software order online. Good for North American and international customers.

subscriptions@oreilly.com
To place an order for any of our newsletters or periodicals.

books@oreilly.com
General questions about any of our books.

software@oreilly.com
For general questions and product information about our software. Check out O'Reilly Software Online at **http://software.oreilly.com/** for software and technical support information. Registered O'Reilly software users send your questions to: **website-support@oreilly.com**

cs@oreilly.com
For answers to problems regarding your order or our products.

booktech@oreilly.com
For book content technical questions or corrections.

proposals@oreilly.com
To submit new book or software proposals to our editors and product managers.

international@oreilly.com
For information about our international distributors or translation queries. For a list of our distributors outside of North America check out:
http://www.oreilly.com/www/order/country.html

O'Reilly & Associates, Inc.
101 Morris Street, Sebastopol, CA 95472 USA
TEL 707-829-0515 or 800-998-9938
(6am to 5pm PST)
FAX 707-829-0104

O'REILLY®

International Distributors

UK, EUROPE, MIDDLE EAST AND AFRICA (EXCEPT FRANCE, GERMANY, AUSTRIA, SWITZERLAND, LUXEMBOURG, LIECHTENSTEIN, AND EASTERN EUROPE)

INQUIRIES
O'Reilly UK Limited
4 Castle Street
Farnham
Surrey, GU9 7HS
United Kingdom
Telephone: 44-1252-711776
Fax: 44-1252-734211
Email: josette@oreilly.com

ORDERS
Wiley Distribution Services Ltd.
1 Oldlands Way
Bognor Regis
West Sussex PO22 9SA
United Kingdom
Telephone: 44-1243-779777
Fax: 44-1243-820250
Email: cs-books@wiley.co.uk

FRANCE

ORDERS
GEODIF
61, Bd Saint-Germain
75240 Paris Cedex 05, France
Tel: 33-1-44-41-46-16 (French books)
Tel: 33-1-44-41-11-87 (English books)
Fax: 33-1-44-41-11-44
Email: distribution@eyrolles.com

INQUIRIES
Éditions O'Reilly
18 rue Séguier
75006 Paris, France
Tel: 33-1-40-51-52-30
Fax: 33-1-40-51-52-31
Email: france@editions-oreilly.fr

GERMANY, SWITZERLAND, AUSTRIA, EASTERN EUROPE, LUXEMBOURG, AND LIECHTENSTEIN

INQUIRIES & ORDERS
O'Reilly Verlag
Balthasarstr. 81
D-50670 Köln
Germany
Telephone: 49-221-973160-91
Fax: 49-221-973160-8
Email: anfragen@oreilly.de (inquiries)
Email: order@oreilly.de (orders)

CANADA (FRENCH LANGUAGE BOOKS)
Les Éditions Flammarion ltée
375, Avenue Laurier Ouest
Montréal (Québec) H2V 2K3
Tel: 00-1-514-277-8807
Fax: 00-1-514-278-2085
Email: info@flammarion.qc.ca

HONG KONG
City Discount Subscription Service, Ltd.
Unit D, 3rd Floor, Yan's Tower
27 Wong Chuk Hang Road
Aberdeen, Hong Kong
Tel: 852-2580-3539
Fax: 852-2580-6463
Email: citydis@ppn.com.hk

KOREA
Hanbit Media, Inc.
Sonyoung Bldg. 202
Yeksam-dong 736-36
Kangnam-ku
Seoul, Korea
Tel: 822-554-9610
Fax: 822-556-0363
Email: hant93@chollian.dacom.co.kr

PHILIPPINES
Mutual Books, Inc.
429-D Shaw Boulevard
Mandaluyong City, Metro
Manila, Philippines
Tel: 632-725-7538
Fax: 632-721-3056
Email: mbikikog@mnl.sequel.net

TAIWAN
O'Reilly Taiwan
No. 3, Lane 131
Hang-Chow South Road
Section 1, Taipei, Taiwan
Tel: 886-2-23968990
Fax: 886-2-23968916
Email: taiwan@oreilly.com

CHINA
O'Reilly Beijing
Room 2410
160, FuXingMenNeiDaJie
XiCheng District
Beijing, China PR 100031
Tel: 86-10-86631006
Fax: 86-10-86631007
Email: beijing@oreilly.com

INDIA
Computer Bookshop (India) Pvt. Ltd.
190 Dr. D.N. Road, Fort
Bombay 400 001 India
Tel: 91-22-207-0989
Fax: 91-22-262-3551
Email: cbsbom@giasbm01.vsnl.net.in

JAPAN
O'Reilly Japan, Inc.
Kiyoshige Building 2F
12-Bancho, Sanei-cho
Shinjuku-ku
Tokyo 160-0008 Japan
Tel: 81-3-3356-5227
Fax: 81-3-3356-5261
Email: japan@oreilly.com

ALL OTHER ASIAN COUNTRIES
O'Reilly & Associates, Inc.
101 Morris Street
Sebastopol, CA 95472 USA
Tel: 707-829-0515
Fax: 707-829-0104
Email: order@oreilly.com

AUSTRALIA
WoodsLane Pty., Ltd.
7/5 Vuko Place
Warriewood NSW 2102
Australia
Tel: 61-2-9970-5111
Fax: 61-2-9970-5002
Email: info@woodslane.com.au

NEW ZEALAND
Woodslane New Zealand, Ltd.
21 Cooks Street (P.O. Box 575)
Waganui, New Zealand
Tel: 64-6-347-6543
Fax: 64-6-345-4840
Email: info@woodslane.com.au

LATIN AMERICA
McGraw-Hill Interamericana
Editores, S.A. de C.V.
Cedro No. 512
Col. Atlampa
06450, Mexico, D.F.
Tel: 52-5-547-6777
Fax: 52-5-547-3336
Email: mcgraw-hill@infosel.net.mx

O'REILLY®

TO ORDER: **800-998-9938** • **order@oreilly.com** • **http://www.oreilly.com/**
OUR PRODUCTS ARE AVAILABLE AT A BOOKSTORE OR SOFTWARE STORE NEAR YOU.
FOR INFORMATION: **800-998-9938** • **707-829-0515** • **info@oreilly.com**

O'REILLY WOULD LIKE TO HEAR FROM YOU

Nineteenth century wood engraving
of a bear from the O'Reilly &
Associates Nutshell Handbook®
Using & Managing UUCP.

POST CARD

BUSINESS REPLY MAIL

FIRST CLASS MAIL   PERMIT NO. 80   SEBASTOPOL, CA

Postage will be paid by addressee

O'Reilly & Associates, Inc.
101 Morris Street
Sebastopol, CA 95472-9902